CYPRESS HILLS
Interboro Parkway
Bridgewood Reservoir
Highland Park
Atlantic Avenue
Conduit Blvd.
Linden Boulevard
Pushcart Market
Bushford Street
Christian Duryea Houses
NEW LOTS
New Lots Reformed Dutch Church
A.S.P.C.A.
EAST NEW YORK
BROOKDALE HOSPITAL
Starrett City
Linden
Livonia Ave.
BAPTIST MEDICAL CENTER
Spring Creek Park
CANARSIE
Rockaway Parkway
Brooklyn Terminal Market
Glenwood Ave.
Flatlands Ave.
Bergen Ave.
Canarsie Pier
Canarsie Beach Park
Gateway National Recreation Area
Canarsie Pol
Duck Point Marshes
Jamaica Bay
BERGEN BEACH
Bergen Beach Basin
Ruffle Bar
Big Fishkill Channel
Big Channel
Kings Plaza Shopping Center
MILL BASIN
Mill Avenue
Floyd Bennett Field
Shore Parkway
Marine Park
GERRITSEN BEACH
Plum Beach
Dead Horse Inlet
Gil Hodges Memorial Bridge
(Marine Parkway Bridge)
Sheepshead Bay
Kingsborough Community College
MANHATTAN BEACH
Atlantic Ocean

THE BROOOKLYN
C O OK B O OK

Alfred A. Knopf   New York · 1991

The Brooklyn Cookbook

LYN STALLWORTH AND ROD KENNEDY, JR.

THIS IS A BORZOI BOOK
PUBLISHED BY
ALFRED A. KNOPF, INC.

Copyright © 1991 by Lyn Stallworth and
Rod Kennedy, Jr.

*Grateful acknowledgment is made for
permission to reprint the following material:*

Tamara Engel: "Tamara Engel's Testimony"
about Lundy's restaurant. Reprinted by
permission of the author.

HarperCollins, Publishers, Inc.: "Lundy's
Manhattan Clam Chowder," recipe from *From My
Mother's Kitchen,* Revised Edition, by Mimi
Sheraton. Copyright © 1980, 1991 by Mimi
Sheraton. Excerpt from *A Tree Grows in
Brooklyn* by Betty Smith. Copyright 1943, 1947
by Betty Smith. Reprinted by permission of
HarperCollins, Publishers, Inc.

Sylvia Fine Kaye: "Sylvia Fine Kaye's Stuffed
Eggplant" recipe, "Danny Kaye's Szechwan Beef
or Pork in Bau Bien" recipe, and excerpt on their
Brooklyn neighborhood from *Fine and Danny*
by Sylvia Fine Kaye. Reprinted by permission of
the author.

New Directions Publishing Corporation:
Excerpt from *The Henry Miller Reader* by
Henry Miller. Copyright © 1959 by Henry Miller.
Reprinted by permission of New Directions
Publishing Corporation.

*Marianne Craig Moore, Literary Executor
for the Estate of Marianne Moore, and The
Rosenbach Museum & Library:* "Oatmeal
Cookies" recipe from Marianne Moore's *Reading
Diary 1250/6, 1930–1943.* The Papers of
Marianne Moore, The Rosenbach Museum &
Library, Philadelphia. Reprinted by permission of
Marianne Craig Moore, Literary Executor for the
Estate of Marianne Moore, and The Rosenbach
Museum & Library.

Library of Congress Cataloging-in-Publication
Data
Stallworth, Lyn.
   The Brooklyn cookbook / Lyn Stallworth, Rod
Kennedy, Jr. — 1st ed.
   p.   cm. — (Knopf cooks American ; 7)
Includes index.
ISBN 0–394–58417–1
1. Cookery, American.   2. Cookery—New York
(N.Y.)   3. Brooklyn (New York, N.Y.)—Social life
and customs.   I. Kennedy, Rod, [date].
II. Title.   III. Series.
TX715.S77535   1991
641.5973—dc20   90–52907   CIP

Manufactured in the United States of America

First Edition

To Valerie Moolman
Best pal, best palate. Good advice, too. Thanks.
—Lyn Stallworth

To Aunt Kit
Who gave so much and asked for little in return.
—Rod Kennedy, Jr.

CONTENTS

PRESIDENT OF THE BOROUGH OF BROOKLYN

BOROUGH HALL · 209 JORALEMON STREET · BROOKLYN, N.Y. 11201

HOWARD GOLDEN
PRESIDENT

Dear Friends:

I am proud of Brooklyn, the most famous and influential seventy-three square miles in the world! Legend has it that one out of every seven Americans has roots in Brooklyn. And, throughout our history, we have contributed record numbers of writers, entertainers, inventors, artists and Nobel Prize winners to the world community.

Brooklyn has made another important contribution--its cuisine. Where would we be without such Brooklyn originals as the hot dog, egg creams or that epitome of desserts-- Junior's cheesecake? I am pleased and proud that The Brooklyn Cookbook documents and preserves this unique culinary experience.

Brooklyn, with its ninety-three ethnic groups is truly a world community--a fact well-illustrated in The Brooklyn Cookbook. Recipes like Irish soda bread, pasta y fagioli, curried goat, kugel, cous-cous and Swedish meatballs all mark the passage of peoples and cultures through our Borough and highlight our distinctly international flavor.

The Brooklyn Cookbook tells our story --the tragedies, triumphs, holidays and holy days-- through the foods that have nourished countless generations. Enjoy this unique and colorful "taste" of Brooklyn!

Sincerely,

Howard Golden
Howard Golden

ACKNOWLEDGMENTS

Putting together The Brooklyn Cookbook was much like putting together a giant jigsaw puzzle, with all of the pieces hidden in different places. Further complicating the task was the fact that Brooklyn is one of the most diverse communities in the world, with neighborhoods within neighborhoods within neighborhoods. Happily, hundreds of people helped us fit the jigsaw pieces together, offering support and help that often surpassed generosity. To these people we extend our heartfelt thanks and appreciation. Many appear in the pages of this book. Our thanks to them, and to all those who shared their recipes and reminiscences. Following are those to whom we extend an extra thank you.

Howard Golden, Brooklyn Borough President, gave us his blessings and the services of his staff—in particular, Nanette Rainone, who set us on the true course, and Diane Moogan, who introduced us to invaluable sources. Special thanks to Joan Bartolomeo, at the Brooklyn Economic Development Corporation; Jane Emmett McDonough and Clara Lamers, at the Brooklyn Historical Society; Marguerite Lavin, at the Brooklyn Museum; Holly Redell and Mary Yrizarry, at Prospect Park; Joanne Woodfin, at the Brooklyn Botanic Garden; Elizabeth White, at the Brooklyn Public Library; Al Jennings and Lillian Beckford, at Brooklyn Union Gas; Debra Rice and Mila Santos, at CAMBA; and Ann Coyle and Ruby Istead, at the Reformed Protestant Dutch Church of Flatbush. For spreading the word: Ken Brown, Courier Life Publications; Carla Busardo, The Tablet; Dorothy Rabinoff, Midwood High Alumni Association; Terry Frank, Erasmus Hall High School Alumni Association; Betty Landy, Bensonhurst Redevelopment Corporation; Michael Horowitz, Spring Creek Sun; Merle English, Newsday. The Folklorists, for their expertise, time, and extraordinary resources: Kathy Condon, Diane Esses, Sean Galvin, Dr. Morton Marks, Barbara Kirshenblatt-Gimblett, Joe Sciorra, and Steve Zeitlin. To all the others: Marty

Adler, the Brooklyn Dodgers Hall of Fame; Irving Choban, the Flatbush Historical Society; Dolly De Simone; Tamara Engel; Sharyn Felder; Bruce Paul Friedman, Save the Kings; Mike Gaimaro; Mary Hirschel, at New York State Senator Martin M. Solomon's office; Julia V. Jordan, New York City Technical College; Matt Kennedy, Coney Island Chamber of Commerce; Amy Krakow, board member of City Lore, Coney Island USA, Inc.; Gary Krakow, WNBC-TV, News 4 New York; Tom Lenihan, Erasmus Hall Hospitality Program; Eunice Lewis, Bridge Street AWME Church; John Manbeck, Kingsborough Historical Society; Joan Maynard, Society for the Preservation of Weeksville; Stuart and Annette Mont; Al Mottola, the Coney Island Polar Bear Club; Carolyn Odell, Flatbush Development Corporation; Anita O'Malley, Harry M. Stevens, Inc.; Consuelo de Passos; Tricia Reinus; Mimi Sheraton; Lou Singer; Pat Singer, the Brighton Neighborhood Association; John Sineno, firefighter and author; Roz Starr, of Roz Starr, Inc.; Les Szymanski, Krakus Luncheon Club; Dr. John Tsouris.

Lyn Stallworth's personal thanks to the food professionals who helped so much: Ceri E. Hadda, Linda Romanelli Leahy, Rona Moulu, Yvonne Ortiz, Peter G. Rose, Alice Ross, Michele Scicolone, and Barbara Somers. And to Henry Wiencek, computer doctor and hand-holder.

Rod Kennedy's personal thanks to Steve Barrison, Sigmund Halpern, Beverly Hegmann, Vicki Levi, Evan Marshall, Bob Ohlerking, Chris Pearce, and the Universal Spiritual Church of All Souls, for their support and guidance.

INTRODUCTION

Brooklyn has been called the fourth largest city in America, and it is the Borough's claim that one out of every seven United States citizens has roots here. Brooklyn is also America's most celebrated hometown. Everybody knows where it is (across that bridge), and almost everybody has an opinion about it: don't the people say "boid" and "toity-toid," and act argumentative, brassy, and sassy? Sure they do—at least some of them. They also say what they mean in other tongues, for groups from all over the world call Brooklyn home.

Brooklynites are fiercely loyal to neighborhood, family, and the food that nourishes them, body and soul. That is what this book celebrates. One of the nicest aspects of writing the book was getting to know the various Brooklyn neighborhoods, and the good cooks in them. Sticking to your own neighborhood is a Brooklyn thing to do—a mentality that keeps communities distinct from one another. Although I've been a Brooklyn brownstone-dweller for more than a decade, only with this enterprise did I venture much outside my own neighborhood and range over the Borough. My partner, indefatigable researcher and legman Rod Kennedy, Jr., got to know Brooklyn even more intimately. Interviews in such widely separated communities as Russian Brighton Beach and Polish Greenpoint gave him a lesson in the Borough's diversity. (It also gave him an expert's knowledge of our excellent subway system.) Rod's vision shaped <u>The Brooklyn Cookbook</u>, and his dogged pursuit of every promising lead (hanging on until he got the story, history, or recipe) gave us our material. Rod's roots go deep into Brooklyn, and his family tree even includes a martyr to civic progress: his great-great-grandfather was trampled to death in the stampede that followed the opening of the Brooklyn Bridge.

I can hear you asking, What is <u>Brooklyn</u> food? What makes it special? No one claims that we have the kind of food that characterizes a region, such as Boston baked beans, Maryland crab cakes, or Philadelphia cheese steak. What defines our food is, in short, attitude and memory. The Brooklyn attitude is, "You respect me, I'll respect you; but believe me—my neighborhood, and my food, is best." Memory ensures that the stories of good times, and the food that made them so, are passed along to younger family members.

The neighborhoods are distinct, but they are ever changing. Where most immigrants once came largely from Europe, they now arrive from the Caribbean and Asia. Formerly Scandinavian Bay Ridge is now home to Greeks, Chinese, and the fastest-growing group of Middle Easterners anywhere. Brooklyn is by no means all blue collar (it never was); Wall Streeters and other executive types appreciate the wonderful houses and tree-lined streets. They have their foodways, too.

Thomas Wolfe, a writer who once lived in Brooklyn, was wrong: you <u>can</u> go home again, home to the Brooklyn that lives in the rich memories and cherished recipes of the sons and daughters of the Borough. As we who live on the eastern side of the Brooklyn Bridge say, come on over!

Lyn Stallworth
Park Slope, Brooklyn
October 1990

Early Brooklyn

1

DRINK
MAYIM CHAIM
KOSHER

STAUCH BATHS

STEEPLECHASE FUNNY PLACE

THE EARLY DAYS: The Canarsee Indians to the Great Bridge, including Weeksville, Henry Ward Beecher, the Daily Eagle, Betty Smith, the Roeblings, and Clarence Birdseye ...

THE EARLY DAYS: The Canarsee Indians to the Great Bridge

". . . the best clymate in the whole world where seed may be thrown on the ground except six weekes the yere long; . . . marvelous plenty in all kinds of food . . . ; the sea and rivers abounding with the excellent fat and wholesome fish wch are heere in great plenty."
—Advertisement from the Dutch West India Company, land promoters, early 1600s

This ad may spell the first of myriad Brooklyn hustles. But allowing for hyperbole, it wasn't too far off the mark: soil and climate were good, and this western end of Long Island was a fine place to farm and raise a family.

What we know today as Brooklyn took a while to grow. Kings County, a name given by the English when New Amsterdam became New York, had a number of towns. The major one, Brooklyn, was incorporated in 1834. The other towns of Kings County—Flatlands, Flatbush, Bushwick, New Utrecht, and Gravesend—were the centers of farming communities that grew food for the city of New York. The completion of the Brooklyn Bridge—the Great Bridge—in 1883 stimulated moves into the interior of Kings County, and in 1896, all original six towns became part of Brooklyn. Greater Brooklyn would have only two

The six towns of Kings County—five Dutch towns and English Gravesend.

years as an independent city. New York City, in what local patriots still call "the Mistake of 1898," annexed it. Henceforth, Brooklyn would be a borough.

THE CANARSEE
AND THE DUTCH

Brooklyn's original inhabitants, the Canarsee Indians, dwelt in a number of settlements—in what is now the Navy Yard, in Flatlands, and in Gravesend. They lived in semipermanent villages, planted corn, beans, pumpkin, and squash, gathered fruits and nuts, hunted deer and bear, and dried fish for the winter. Eating rabbit and groundhog was culturally taboo.

These were the people the Dutch found in 1624, when they established their first settlement. They called them the "Canarsies," after the Indians' largest village, and the place name remains. Trading, real estate transactions, internecine warfare with other tribes, conversion to Christianity, fair and foul dealing with the Dutch, and the usual dubious benefits of cultural exchange ensued.

Perhaps the first group to utter the classic Brooklyn cry, "There goes the neighborhood!," the Canarsees began a westward trek that would take them as far as the Illinois country in about 1745. It is highly likely, however, that people of Canarsee descent still live in Brooklyn.

Although the Dutch rule in Nieuw Amsterdam was short—only fifty-five years—Dutch influence in Brooklyn was pervasive and

Dutch settlers trading with Canarsee Indians.

long-lived. To this day Brooklynites sit on the stoops in front of their houses (from the Dutch <u>stoep</u>), and they live and work on streets with names such as Van Brunt, Remsen, and Lefferts. At Erasmus Hall High School (founded as Erasmus Hall Academy in the 1780s and named for the great Dutch thinker), student servers in the food-service program wear an adaptation of Dutch costume. Schoolchildren regularly tour surviving Dutch houses; the colonial past is a heritage for all of Brooklyn.

The Pieter Claesen Wyckoff House

The oldest building standing in New York City (and perhaps in the United States) is the Pieter Claesen Wyckoff House, built around 1652, and later added to. Eight generations of Wyckoffs lived here, working the large farm, until 1902.

Pieter Wyckoff arrived in America in 1637, an illiterate indentured servant. He became the wealthiest man in New Amersfoort, which would become Flatlands. He fathered ten children, and his descendants married into all the old Dutch families.

Now operated as a museum, the Wyckoff House presents programs that depict "domestic life in Colonial Brooklyn," such as butter churning and food preservation. Mint, flax, and parsley are among the plants in the kitchen garden.

In 1959, a Greek family occupied the house. The householder reported that some years earlier a tiny old lady had appeared at the door. "She told me that she'd been born here," he said. "'Be good to this old house,' she cried. 'It has seen much history.'"

That old woman was Helen Anna Wyckoff, born in 1849. A collection of cooking notes in her hand (they can hardly be called recipes; no directions are given, and the jottings for corn bread neglect to mention cornmeal) has recently been unearthed. She did clip and paste a few newspaper recipes into

The Pieter Claesen Wyckoff House, begun in 1652.

her book, however, such as this one for Indian pudding.

Baked Indian Pudding

One cupful "granulated" yellow corn meal, one half cupful wheat flour; mix with these enough cold water to thoroughly moisten; stir into one pint boiling milk; put into a pudding dish, add a small piece of butter, one beaten egg, one small teacupful molasses, one tablespoon sugar, one pint cold milk, salt and ginger to taste; bake three hours.

Note: "Granulated corn meal" is the coarse meal readily available. Pour the mixture into a buttered 1½-quart baking dish and bake at 325 degrees F. Check the pudding after 2 hours; it will probably be cooked. If not, pour on ½ cup additional milk and bake longer.

Living in a Landmark

Pieter Wyckoff's great-great-grandson, Hendrick, built his house (now the Wyckoff-Bennett Homestead) sometime before 1766. The house was sold to Cornelius Bennett in 1835. Four generations later, Gertrude Ryder Bennett Williams (1900–1982), in her book *Living in a Landmark*, recalled the peddlers of her childhood:

"Our community, in transition from farmland to suburbs, depended upon peddlers. A butcher wagon dispatched from a far away store would drive into our yard. The back opened into a counter with scales hanging overhead. Along the inside walls the various meats hung behind cheesecloth designed to keep off flies. The butcher would stand in the barnyard in his large white apron and write in a small book, under the customer's name, the order to be delivered next week.

"Mr. Van Houghton brought pots and pans, crockery, tin ware, medicines and kerosene . . . and if the farmer's children needed a haircut, he turned barber."

Gertrude was the sort who kept *everything*, including an extensive collection of iron cookware and glazed pots, and—happily—a hodgepodge of recipes. Her grandmother's Aunt Addie wrote this "receipt" before the turn of the century:

Yellow Tomatoe Preserves

¾ pound of sugar to 1 pound of fruit—do not skin the tomatoes. Put about ½ a teacup of ginger root in a cloth and fill (a large pot) with the fruits and sugar, boil slowly about 2 hours. About 1 hour before taking from the fire add 2 sliced lemons—I had one of those grape boxes full of tomatoes 4½ pounds—we are all so fond of this I thought perhaps you would like to try it—its good—

With the amount of ginger and lemon specified and the lengthy cooking, it is likely that Aunt Addie would have used much more than four and one-half pounds of tomatoes.

Gertrude's own Aunt Phebe Kouwenhoven sent her a recipe, probably in the 1920s, for Coffee Cream, a candy:

Coffee Cream

½ cup coffee
1 pound light brown sugar
Boil together until it spins a thread, then pour into a bowl containing the white of 2 eggs beaten stiff. Beat, and when ready form into balls and drop on waxed paper.

The Lefferts Homestead

The Lefferts Homestead was built by Peter Lefferts between 1777 and 1783. Peter was a rich and important man, and John, his young son, inherited the 240-acre homestead. John married Maria Lott in 1823, and it is probably she who wrote the manuscript in which the recipe for Oly Cooks appears.

Such manuscripts were not original cookbooks in the modern sense; Maria would have copied the recipes of relatives and friends that appealed to her. These "oil cakes" are forerunners of the doughnut, but without the hole.

Oly Cooks (Maria Lott Lefferts's Recipe)

1 quart milk 1¼ lb sugar ¾ lb butter 8 eggs flour enough to make them soft, a tea cup of yeast and 1 nutmeg

The Lefferts Homestead, circa 1783 (restored).

Mrs. Lefferts's recipe book.

Peter G. Rose's Modern Version

The reconstruction of oil cakes was made by Peter G. Rose, a Dutch-born food historian. It is taken from The Sensible Cook, *the most favored Dutch cookbook of the seventeenth century, which influenced the cooking of New World settlers. It is much more elaborate (and delicious) than Maria's simple version. Alice Ross, an expert in hearth cooking, chose this recipe to use for her demonstrations of oly cooks at the Lefferts Homestead.*

½ cup warm water (105 to 115 degrees F)
Pinch sugar
3 packages active dry yeast
8 tablespoons butter
1¾ cups raisins
4 cups all-purpose flour
¼ teaspoon salt
1 tablespoon cinnamon
½ teaspoon ground cloves
½ teaspoon ground ginger
1½ cups milk, at room temperature
3 medium tart apples, peeled and cut into small slivers
1 cup whole almonds
Vegetable oil or lard, for deep frying
Confectioners' sugar (optional)

❶ Mix the water and sugar and stir in the yeast. Set aside in a warm place.

❷ In the meantime, melt the butter and let cool. Place the raisins in a saucepan, cover with water, and bring to the boil. Boil for 1 minute and remove from the heat. Let stand for 5 minutes, then drain them and pat them dry with paper towels. Mix them with 1 tablespoon of the flour.

❸ In a large bowl mix the remaining flour, salt, cinnamon, cloves, and ginger. Make a hole in the middle. Stirring all the while, pour in the yeast mixture, the melted butter, and the milk. The dough should be very thick. Add the raisins, apples, and almonds and combine thoroughly. Cover and set in a warm place to rise for 1 hour, or until doubled.

❹ Heat at least 3 inches of oil to 350 degrees F. Stir down the dough. Using 2 large spoons, make dough balls at least 2 inches in diameter. Drop dough balls into hot oil and fry about 5 minutes on each side. Drain on paper towels.

❺ Serve warm, dusted with powdered sugar if desired.

≫→ *Makes about 30*

Maria Lefferts's Crullers

4 pounds flour 1 1/4 pounds butter 1 1/2 pounds butter 16 eggs leaving out half the white add some more

Peter G. Rose's
Modern Version of Crullers

5 tablespoons butter
1/4 cup sugar
2 eggs
2 cups all-purpose flour
1/8 teaspoon freshly grated nutmeg

At least 3 inches of vegetable oil or lard,
   for deep frying
Confectioners' or cinnamon sugar
   (optional)

❶ Cream the butter and sugar and add the eggs, one at a time.

❷ Add the flour and nutmeg and stir to make a smooth dough. Turn dough out on a board and cut it into 20 even pieces.

❸ Roll each piece into a 6-inch rope. Fold the rope in half and twist the ends around each other, leaving an opening in the middle. Heat the oil to 350 degrees F.

❹ Deep-fry the crullers until golden. Remove and immediately sprinkle with confectioners' or cinnamon sugar, if desired. ≫→ *Makes 20 crullers*

▲▲▲▲▲▲▲▲▲▲▲▲▲▲▲▲▲▲▲▲▲▲▲▲▲▲▲▲▲▲

The "Old First" Church

In 1654, the Reverend Theodorus Polhemus came to minister to the people of Flatlands, Flatbush, and Breukelen. Breukelen's first church was built in 1666, in the middle of a highway that is now downtown Fulton Street. (Churches had been erected earlier in Flatlands, New Utrecht, and Flatbush.) A growing congregation caused several moves, and in 1889 the present church, known as the "Old First" Reformed Church, was erected in the new and fashionable district of Park Slope.

The minister, the Reverend James Farrar, was zealous in the support of foreign missions preaching the Word. To raise funds, ladies of the congregation in 1910 put together a cookbook, *Tried and Tested Recipes*. It does, of course, reflect the tastes of the congregation, which by 1910 was thoroughly English-speaking and upper-middle-class American in its approach to food. As was the custom with church-guild and other society cookbooks, the majority of the recipes are for sweets. But this was a Reformed church of the Dutch tradition, and there are two recipes for crullers, somewhat sketchy in their instruction. Here is one:

Crullers

Two large-sized cups of sugar, two cups of milk, one-quarter pound of butter, one grated nutmeg, three eggs, three-quarters of a small bottle of Rumford's yeast powder, enough flour to stiffen. Roll out and fry in hot lard.

The "Old First" Church.

Weeksville

Weeksville, named for stevedore James Weeks, throve as an African-American community from about 1820 to 1890. By the 1920s, residents had drifted away to other neighborhoods, and the little settlement was largely forgotten. But in 1968, learning that what was left of Weeksville would be razed for renewal, urban historian James Hurley and two students from the Neighborhood College Workshop at Brooklyn's Pratt Institute began an archeological dig. Their aim was to discover the roots of Weeksville before all traces disappeared between the jaws of bulldozers. They were aided by Boy Scout Troop #342.

The work led to the discovery—and ultimate restoration—of the four remaining wood-frame houses. Schoolchildren helped in the digging. The enthusiasm sparked by the excavation led to the establishment of the Society for the Preservation of Weeksville and Bedford-Stuyve-sant History, tours of the houses, and an educational program involving the local public school.

Public School 243, the successor to Colored School Number 2, stands in the heart of what was Weeksville. The school is a national model for the Follow Through Program, an extension of Head Start. A basic premise of Follow Through is the belief that young children expand their worlds and learn best by doing. Schoolchildren are very much involved in the restoration project. Weekly cooking lessons teach them not only numbers and dexterity, but also the manner of daily life in old Weeksville. "In the old days," says Dr. Marguerite C. Thompson, Staff Developer of the program, "learning was passed on by word of mouth. And a good way to remember is by memorizing a

Restored houses on Hunterfly Road, dating from 1840 through 1883.

ditty. So the children sing the Tea Cake Ditty when they make the cakes."

"Goody, goody, goody,
Tea Cakes, Tea Cakes,
Goody, goody, goody,
Ma Ma Douglas Tea Cakes
Melts in your mouth!"

The Weeksville Lady: tintype of unidentified woman found during the 1968–1969 dig.

Much of what Weeksville produced and ate is known because of Mrs. Elment Blunt Meggs, whose great-great-grandparents lived in Weeksville. According to her, "There was no cooking on the Lord's Day. All food for Sunday was cooked on Saturday, during the day and night."

"Knowing how our forebears lived and what they ate makes them very real to us," says Joan Maynard, Executive Director of the Society for the Preservation of Weeksville and Bedford-Stuyvesant History. "They left a legacy of pride."

Weeksville Tea Cakes

3½ cups sifted all-purpose flour
1 teaspoon baking soda
½ teaspoon salt
½ cup (1 stick) butter
1 cup sugar

2 eggs, beaten
1 teaspoon vanilla
½ teaspoon freshly grated nutmeg
½ cup thick sour cream

Preheat the oven to 450 degrees F.

❶ Sift together the flour, baking soda, and salt. Set aside.

❷ In a large bowl cream the butter and sugar until light and fluffy. Add the eggs, vanilla, and nutmeg and mix well.

❸ Alternately add some of the flour mixture and some of the sour cream, beating after each addition with a wooden spoon until smooth.

❹ Have ready two baking sheets. Gather the dough into a ball and pat it flat on a floured work surface. Roll it out to a ½-inch thickness. Use a 2-inch cookie cutter to cut circles of the dough. Place them 2 inches apart on the baking sheets. Gather odd pieces of dough into a ball, roll out, and cut more tea cakes.

❺ Bake the tea cakes for about 12 minutes, until lightly browned. Transfer them to racks to cool. ≫→ *Makes about 40 tea cakes*

Fried Apples and Bacon

A recipe from old Weeksville that makes a fine supper or brunch dish. It serves two, but it can be doubled or tripled. Choose any apples—Delicious remain firm, but mealier apples such as Rome become soft and sweet.

2 apples   Sugar
¼ pound slab bacon, sliced

❶ Cut the unpeeled apples into ½-inch rings and remove the cores with a melon baller. Set aside.

❷ In a large skillet, cook the bacon until almost done. Drain on paper towels. Pour off all but 1 tablespoon of bacon grease.

❸ Over moderate heat, cook the apple rings in the bacon grease for about 8 minutes on one side. Turn, sprinkle each ring with about ¼ teaspoon of sugar, and return the bacon to the pan. Cook about 5 minutes. Remove the bacon and drain it again. Place the bacon and apple rings on heated plates. ⤖ *Serves 2*

▲▲▲▲▲▲▲▲▲▲▲▲▲▲▲▲▲▲▲▲▲▲▲▲▲▲▲▲▲▲▲▲▲

Henry Ward Beecher and Apple Pie

Henry Ward Beecher (1813–1887) was a spellbinding speaker, lecturer, and editor, as well as minister of the Congregational Plymouth Church on Orange and Cranberry streets in Brooklyn Heights. He took up the post in 1847, championing abolition (Harriet Beecher Stowe, author of *Uncle Tom's Cabin*, was his sister) and advocating women's suffrage and Darwinism. Beecher's wide-ranging interests extended even to apple pie, of which he wrote so enticingly:

"Some people think anything will do for pies. But the best for eating are the best for cooking . . . and who would put into a pie any apple but *Spitzenberg*, that had *that?* Off with their jackets! And now, O cook! which shall it be? For at this point the roads diverge, and though they all come back at length to apple-pie, it is not a matter of indifference which you choose. There is, for example, one made without under-crust, in a deep plate, and the apples laid in, in full quarters; or the apples being stewed are beaten to a mush, and seasoned, and put between the double paste; or they are sliced thin and cooked entirely within the covers; or they are put without any seasoning into their bed, and when baked, the upper lid is raised, and the butter, nutmeg, cinnamon, and sugar are added; the whole well mixed, and the crust returned.

"But, O be careful of the paste! Let it not be like putty, nor rush to the other extreme, and make it so flaky that one holds his breath while eating for fear of blowing it all away. Let it not be plain as bread, nor yet rich like cake. Aim at that glorious medium, in which it is tender, without being fugaciously flaky; short, without being too short; a mild, sapid, brittle thing, that lies upon the tongue, so as to let the apple strike through and touch the *papellae* with a mere effluent flavor.

". . . [The apple-pie] will accept almost every flavor of every spice. And yet nothing is so fatal to the rare and higher graces of apple-pie as inconsiderate, vulgar spicing. . . . It is a glorious unity in which sugar gives up its nature as sugar, and butter ceases to be butter, and each flavorsome spice gladly evanishes from its own full nature, that all of them, by a common death, may rise into the new life of apple-pie! Not that apple is no longer apple! *It,* too, is transformed. And the final pie, though born of apple, sugar, butter, nutmeg, cinnamon, lemon, is like none of these, but the compound ideal of them all, refined, purified, and by fire fixed in blissful perfection.

"But all exquisite creations are short-lived. The natural term of an apple-pie is but twelve hours. It reaches its highest state about one hour after it comes from the oven, and just before its natural heat has quite departed. And after it is one day old, it is thenceforward but the ghastly corpse of apple-pie."

Henry Ward Beecher enthralls the congregation.

Beecher Apple Pie

Pie appreciation ran in the family. In the 1887 Plymouth Fair Cook Book, selected and arranged by Mrs. Henry Ward Beecher, *two recipes for Apple Custard Pie appear. Below is the more interesting one, written in the maddeningly imprecise manner of the time:*
Grate twelve large sour apples. Sprinkle in an even teaspoonful of salt, half a nutmeg, a very little cinnamon, and sugar enough to sweeten to your taste. Add three well beaten eggs, one tablespoonful of butter, the grated rind of half a lemon, if that flavor is relished, the juice of one orange, and a pint of rich cream. Line the plates with rich paste, which should be all ready before the cream is put to the apple. Pour in the custard, and put strips of crust across the top. Bake a light brown, and sift sugar over when done, if liked. If only one pie is wanted, take fewer apples and less cream.
The recipe has been freely adapted to make one nine-inch pie. A different and delicious pie it is, enlivened with crunchy shreds of apple.

··

Pastry

2 cups all-purpose flour
½ teaspoon salt
1 tablespoon sugar
½ cup vegetable shortening
2 tablespoons unsalted butter, cut into bits
3 to 4 tablespoons ice water

Filling

3 cups grated apples (Ida Red, Northern Spy, Winesap, Jonathan, Rome, or Granny Smith), about 4 large apples

2 tablespoons lemon juice
¾ to 1 cup or more sugar, depending on tartness of apples
¼ teaspoon salt
¼ teaspoon nutmeg
¼ teaspoon cinnamon
1 teaspoon grated lemon peel
¼ cup orange juice
2 teaspoons butter, cut into bits
2 eggs
½ cup heavy cream

❶ Make the pastry. Mix the flour, salt, and sugar. Cut in the shortening and butter bits until the mixture resembles coarse meal. Sprinkle on the ice water and mix with a fork until the dough just comes together, using as little water as possible. Press the dough into a flat disk, cover with plastic wrap, and refrigerate for 30 minutes.

❷ Roll out about two-thirds of the pastry and fit it into a 9-inch pie plate. Crimp the edges. Refrigerate along with the wrapped remaining dough while you make the filling.

Preheat the oven to 425 degrees F.

❸ Peel, quarter, and core the apples, and place them in a bowl of water to which you have added the lemon juice. Grate them on the large holes of a grater. When all the apples have been grated, squeeze the shreds to press out most of the water and place them in a bowl. Add the sugar, salt, nutmeg, cinnamon, lemon peel, orange juice, and butter bits.

❹ Beat the eggs and cream together. Combine with the apple mixture and place in the pie shell. Roll out the remaining dough, cut in strips, and make a lattice top.

❺ Bake the pie in the center of the oven for 5 minutes, then lower the heat to 350 degrees F. Bake for 40 to 45 minutes, until the pastry is lightly browned and the custard set. ⟫→ *Makes 1 9-inch pie*

▲▲▲▲▲▲▲▲▲▲▲▲▲▲▲▲▲▲▲▲▲▲▲▲▲▲▲

The Voice of Brooklyn

The Brooklyn *Daily Eagle*, the hometown newspaper founded in 1841 as a temporary broadsheet of the Democratic party, grew into a paper of international reputation, albeit the *Eagle* was ever known, to its editors' chagrin, as the paper that fired Walt Whitman. A number of causes, including changing demographics and rising costs, forced the closing of the newspaper in 1955. A cruel blow to civic solidarity, the loss of the *Eagle* was soon followed by an even more dire event: the defection of the Dodgers to California, in 1957.

Around the turn of the century, the *Eagle* began to run recipes. The following two, for salsify, ran on Saturday, December 6, 1902, under the heading "Table and Kitchen.

Practical Suggestions About What to Eat and How to Prepare Food." The writer promised that "This matter will be found to be entirely different from and superior to the usual run of food articles, in that every item is a nugget of culinary wisdom and eminently practical."

Salsify, or oyster plant, is a root vegetable prized in France and Italy, and was much used in 19th-century American cooking. It is now reappearing, and is worth a try. Called oyster plant because of its supposed oyster flavor, it really tastes more like artichoke hearts with a touch of coconut. Its cousin, *scorzonera*, looks and cooks much the same, and the two are interchangeable.

Salsify must be peeled and,

once peeled, should be placed at once in water to which lemon juice has been added, or it will darken.

Salsify Scallop

This is a nice way to cook salsify. Cook the vegetable in salted water until tender, then drain and put it into a baking dish with alternate layers of bread crumbs seasoned with salt and pepper, and dot with bits of butter. Moisten with cream or milk and a little melted butter; cover the top with bread crumbs and bake in the oven until a light brown.

Note: Peel the salsify and cut it into 2-inch pieces. Boil the pieces for about 7 minutes, until barely tender. Bake the scallop in a preheated 375 degree F oven for about 20 minutes.

Salsify Fritters

This is also a good way to use salsify. Scrape the oyster plant and drop it quickly into cold water to which you have added a few drops of onion juice to prevent its turning dark. Then boil soft in salted water and then mash fine. To every cup of the pulp add a beaten egg, a teaspoonful of cream or rich milk, and a heaping tablespoon of flour, salt and pepper to taste. Drop by spoonfuls into very hot fat and fry a nice brown. Or you can keep the vegetable whole and, after cooking, dip in butter and fry.

Note: Season with salt and pepper after frying.

Front page, November 1, 1914.

A Tree Grows in Brooklyn

A book celebrating the food memories of a Brooklyn childhood must of course include Francie Nolan, the girl Betty Smith wrote so touchingly of in her novel *A Tree Grows in Brooklyn*. Money was very short for the Nolan family in the Williamsburg of 1912. Francie's father, Johnny, was a singing waiter who drank up most of what he earned and her mother, Katie, scrubbed floors to pay the rent. Fiercely proud Katie swore she'd seal the windows and gas them all before she would take a penny of charity. So on Saturday Francie was sent to the bakery with twenty cents to buy six loaves of stale bread and a crushed pie.

"Mama made a very fine bread pudding from slices of stale bread, sugar, cinnamon and a penny apple sliced thin. When this was baked brown, sugar was melted and poured over the top. . . . Bits of bread were dipped into a batter made from flour, water, salt and an egg and then fried in deep hot fat. While they were frying, Francie ran down to the candy store and bought a penny's worth of brown rock candy. This was crushed with a rolling pin and sprinkled on top of the fried bits just before eating. The crystals didn't quite melt and that made it wonderful.

"Saturday supper was a red letter meal. The Nolans had fried meat! A loaf of stale bread was made into pulp with hot water and mixed with a dime's worth of chopped meat into which an onion had been cleavered. Salt and a penny's worth of minced parsley were added for flavor. This was made up into little balls, fried and served with hot ketchup . . .

"Sometimes when she had a spare penny, she bought broken crackers. The groceryman would make a toot, which was a poke made of a bit of twisted paper, and fill it with bits of sweet crackers that had been broken in the box and could no longer be sold as whole crackers. Mama's rule was: don't buy candy or cake if you have a penny. Buy an apple. But what was an apple? Francie found that a raw potato tasted just as good and this she could have for free."

The Great Bridge

The Great East River Bridge, known as the Brooklyn Bridge, was completed in 1883. The first steel-wire suspension bridge in the world, it was also the longest bridge of its time.

Shortly after construction began, John Augustus Roebling, the designer, died of an infection incurred on the job. His son, Washington Augustus Roebling, completed his father's work, but descending deep into the pilings he acquired caisson disease, "the bends," and was confined to his bed throughout the project. His wife, Emily, was liaison between her husband and the foreman; many historians believe that Emily was really the one responsible for the span that linked the cities of New York and Brooklyn.

The Roebling Family's Creamed Parsnips

Mary Roebling, who is a member of the family, contributes an old family recipe.

2 pounds young parsnips, peeled
3 tablespoons unsalted butter
1 cup heavy cream

Salt and pepper to taste
Freshly grated nutmeg

❶ Boil the parsnips in a large pot of lightly salted water until tender. Drain and transfer them to a bowl of cold water.

❷ Slice the parsnips or dice them. Melt the butter in a skillet. Add the parsnips and the cream, and salt and pepper. Stir gently until the cream is hot. Add a light dusting of nutmeg, turn again and serve. ⟫→ *Serves 4 to 6*

The Man with an Imperishable Idea

Brooklyn-born Clarence Frank Birdseye (1886–1956) did not invent the freezing process, nor was he the first to freeze food commercially. As he said, "My contribution was to take Eskimo knowledge and the scientists' theories and adapt them to quantity production."

Trapping furs in Labrador in 1912, he froze duck and caribou out of doors. He noticed that meat frozen in winter was excellent, and meat frozen in the spring and fall was granular.

Humble heads of cabbage led to the method that has revolutionized the way we eat today. When the temperature outside his Labrador cabin reached ten degrees below zero, he layered cabbage heads in barrels and froze them in sea water. The thawed cabbages were perfect. Quick freezing was the answer; large ice crystals do not have the time to form and cause cellular walls to collapse when the food is thawed.

Back in the States, Birdseye began the experiments that led to a practical quick freezer with a capital of seven dollars. In 1924 he and three friends set up the General Seafoods Company, which eventually became the giant Kraft General Foods.

Birdseye was something of a gourmet, though his choice of viands meant that he often dined alone. Later in life he entertained with lavish clam bakes, but in his younger days in the West, he prepared fried rattlesnake and a delicate mouse broth for himself as his companions chewed on spoiled sowbelly. When a smart-aleck asked him, "How would you eat an old shoe in the wilds?" he quickly replied, "I'd cut it in pieces, feed them to an Eskimo dog, and then eat the dog."

Clarence Frank Birdseye, dictating.

Resorts and Neighborhoods

CONEY ISLAND: The Subway Riviera **BRIGHTON BEACH:** Little Odessa by the Sea **SHEEPSHEAD BAY:** Seaside Suburb. Including Polar Bears, the Aquarium, and Lundy's . . .

THE ISLAND, THE BEACH, AND THE BAY:
Coney Island, Brighton Beach, and Sheepshead Bay

Folks first came to play at the southern tip of Brooklyn, but many found that it could be a bracing spot to live year-round. These seaside communities have a colorful past and a promising future.

CONEY ISLAND
THE SUBWAY RIVIERA

Democracy—in the form of thousands of working people in search of a day's sun and fun—didn't come to Coney Island until 1920, when the subways pushed through to Stillwell Avenue. And it took only a nickel to transport you from the sultry city to the cooling beach. **C**oney had had its flashy, even seamy side before that—a hotel in the shape of an elephant, con games and prostitutes—but from the 1870s through the early years of the twentieth century, a posher crowd had come to Coney Island. According to the late Elliot Willensky, the author of <u>When Brooklyn Was the World</u>, Brooklyn was the racetrack capital of America. Swells could catch the Suburban Stakes at the Sheepshead Bay Racetrack, and the Preakness at the Gravesend Course. Elaborate hotels and restaurants catered to these well-heeled crowds. Huge frame hotels had gone up along the shore in the 1870s: the Oriental, the Manhattan Beach, and the Brighton Beach. Charles Feltman's Ocean Pavilion Hotel, opened in 1874, had at its peak two bars and nine restaurants. (Feltman often gets credit for inventing the hot dog judged too humble to be served at his grand establishment.)

The big money evaporated from Brooklyn's southern shoreline in 1910, when the state legislature banned gambling at the track. No more quail under glass; restaurants would serve shore dinners to a plainer crowd.

In 1897, George Tilyou had opened Steeplechase Park (inspired by all those racetracks and named for a mechanical ride where boys sat behind girls on "horses" mounted on tracks; the ride was not thrillingly fast, but the fellas did get to squeeze their cuties). Luna Park, a wonderland of incandescent faery towers, the "Electric Eden," opened in 1903. The stately Dreamland amusement complex opened in 1904. Back then, Coney Island could handle 300,000 people on a summer Sunday, stuffing them with hot dogs, grilled corn, clams, and lobsters. And on one day of the Fourth of July weekend in 1947, over a million souls came to Coney.

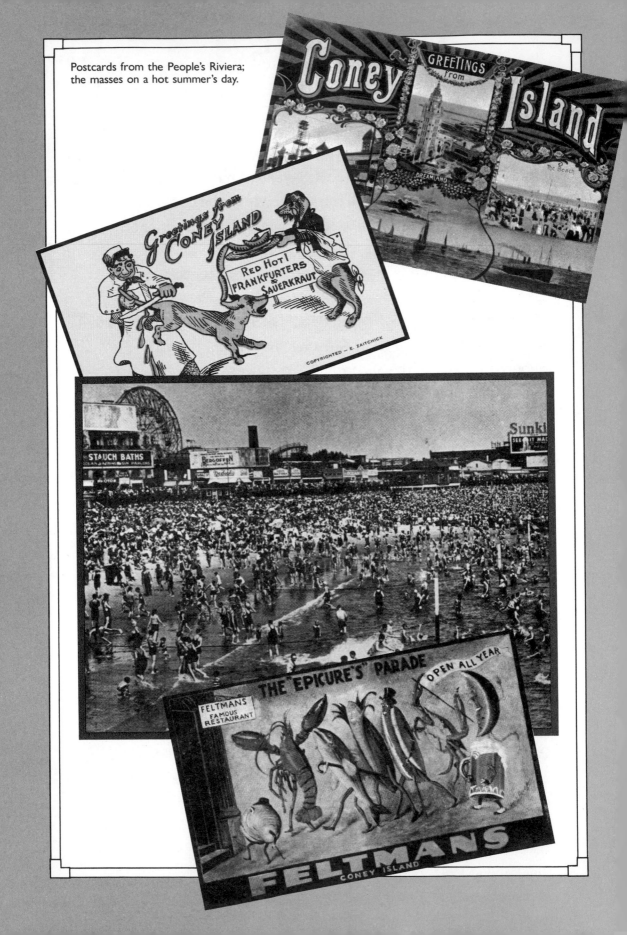

Postcards from the People's Riviera;
the masses on a hot summer's day.

Coney Island, USA

"I've got sand in my shoes, salt water in my veins," says Dick Zigun, self-proclaimed Mayor of Coney Island and founder of Coney Island, USA, Inc., a nonprofit organization dedicated to bringing back the glories of Coney, the Poor Man's Riviera. (Zigun really loves the boardwalk razzmatazz. After moving to Coney he was curator of the World in Wax Musee until its demise in 1984; the last exhibit was Beatle John Lennon. When Lennon's wax hands and head arrived by mail from a sculptor in Pennsylvania, champagne was poured as the box was opened.)

Steeplechase Park, the Parachute Jump, and Luna Park may be memories, but impresario Zigun is dedicated to reviving the traditions of those sun-drenched days of yesteryear. He directs Sideshows by the Seashore ("See the Human Blockhead drive spikes into his cranium! See Satina the Snake Charmer and her Serpents from the Green Hells of the Amazon Jungles!") and sponsors the annual Mermaid Parade held in June, with trophies for best King Neptune and best Mermaid and dancing by the Coney Island Hysterical Society.

Beach-Barnum Zigun and Valerie Haller, Designer in Residence at Coney Island, USA, offer authentic thirst quenchers of Coney's great days: "I saw so much junk food sold around here when I first came," says Valerie. "I thought selling fresh lemonade would be upscale for Coney Island, but it's actually just reviving a tradition. We found from old postcards that fresh juices used to be sold at lots of places, including Nathan's. We also have a popcorn and old-fashioned root beer concession." She is branching out into egg creams and lime rickeys, too.

King Neptune at the Mermaid Parade (Dick Zigun at far right).

"I guess fate drew me to Coney," says Valerie happily. "My paternal grandparents met here; she was a maid on her day off. When I was a little girl, we lived in Yonkers at the end of the subway line, and we'd come to Coney—changing at Times Square—at the other end of the subway line, riding on those scratchy wicker seats. My father always said, 'The best place, and only a subway ride away!'

"Now I live here, putting in my time and effort to make it a memory for other little kids. I see them come in here for the sideshow, and you can see by the faces this is something they'll really remember. When they see the lemonade stand on the boardwalk, they come up and exclaim, 'Wow!' They see us hanging out, doing fun things, and it's not TV, not video games. I grew up in Westchester, but for me Brooklyn is the residential borough, a place where you can have a home and a family, with other families around you. And with the subway it's accessible."

Valerie Haller's Lemonade for the Masses

The easiest way to make lemonade is in two batches. Or you can make a tall glass by adding 2 ounces of concentrate to 10 ounces of cold water: add ice and float lemon slices on top. For "an average day in Coney Island," says Valerie, "multiply this recipe by ten."

Valerie Haller on the boardwalk.

Concentrate

8 cups sugar
4 cups water
Cut-up rinds of 4 lemons

4 cups freshly squeezed lemon juice
3 or 4 lemons for slices

❶ Make a simple syrup by combining the sugar, water, and lemon rinds. Stir over low heat just until the sugar dissolves. Bring to the boil and cook at a low boil for exactly 5 minutes. Let cool and remove rinds. Makes 5 cups of syrup.

❷ To make a batch of concentrate, stir 2¼ to 2½ cups of syrup into 2 cups of lemon juice (use more syrup if the lemons are very tart). The concentrate keeps well in the refrigerator for 1 week, but after 3 days the freshness is gone and the flavor is like that of bottled concentrate.

❸ To make a batch of lemonade, combine the concentrate with 5 times the amount of cold water. For example, to 4½ cups (36 ounces) of concentrate, add 180 ounces of water. Float lemon slices on top. ⫸→ *Each batch makes "A gallon and a half plus change"— 1 gallon 88 ounces per batch*

▲▲▲▲▲▲▲▲▲▲▲▲▲▲▲▲▲▲▲▲▲▲▲▲▲▲▲▲▲▲▲▲▲▲▲

Philip's Candy Store

Since 1930, Philip's candy store on Surf Avenue, Coney Island, has turned out chocolate fudge, large lollipops, Ka-ra-me-la popcorn, and dozens more delicious confections. All are made on the premises of this small shop nestled into the Stillwell Avenue Station, last stop on the subway that leads to the sea. "We mix the butter cream today, we sell it today," says owner John Dorman.

Dorman came here as a young summer worker in 1947; in 1953 he bought the business. He's seen it prosper through the best of times ("This place was paradise . . . every day was like the Fourth of July") and also through the darkest of times after the 21-acre Steeplechase Park closed in 1965. He continues to crank out tooth-jerking Salt Water Taffee and the rest of the candy line as he awaits the Coney Island renaissance: "We've turned the corner," he says confidently.

The only shadow on a future for Philip's even brighter than the past is the threat coming from the local transit authority, which wants to renovate the subway station. In classic bureaucratic fashion, it proposed evicting all tenants from the station, pondering over the project for a while, hiring planners and designers, *then* rebuilding. Understandably John Dorman balked: "We know everyone in Coney Island. To leave here, we'd lose all our friends." But powerful allies rallied round, including the Strap-hangers Campaign, an advocacy group, and the Coney Island Chamber of Commerce. They raised voices loud and clear, and Philip's is preserved, at least for a while, as the Sweet Heart of Coney Island.

Candied Apples

John Dorman, candymaker.

On a summer's day, Philip's sells hundreds of candied apples. They aren't difficult to make at home, as long as you move fast. As the recipe is for only six apples, you should have sufficient time to dip them before the syrup hardens. If it does, reheat it over hot water. You get but one chance—heated more than once, the syrup burns.

6 small apples
1 cup sugar
½ cup boiling water

Pinch cream of tartar
6 drops red food coloring

❶ Have the apples ready, pierced at the stem end with Popsicle sticks or small wooden sticks from an art-supply store. Butter a rack large enough to hold the apples and place it over wax paper.

❷ Put the sugar in a small heavy saucepan and add the boiling water and cream of tartar. Stir just until the sugar dissolves. Cover and boil for 3 minutes over moderate heat; add the food coloring. Insert a candy thermometer, adjust the lid as best you can, and let the temperature reach 290 degrees F. This may take 10 minutes; watch carefully, as the temperature can rise very quickly.

❸ Remove the lid, grasp the pan and tilt it. Working quickly, dip in an apple and twirl it to cover it with syrup. Place it on the rack and dip the remaining apples. ⫸→ *Makes 6 candied apples*

Philip's facade.

Nathan's Famous

Ask for a "Coney Island," and you've got a Nathan's Famous hot dog, from the world's largest producer of the succulent wiener. The flagship store of the frankfurter fleet stands proudly near the boardwalk, at the corner of Surf and Stillwell, on the spot where Nathan Handwerker opened his small stand in 1916.

No one is exactly sure who coined the term "hot dog," referring to the sausages (probably first devised in Frankfurt, Germany) that German-Americans had relished since the middle of the 19th century. At any rate, the term was not always laudatory. "Hot dog" had been around since the turn of the century, and by 1906 Hearst sports cartoonist Tad Dorgan was drawing talking dachshund dogs, giving credence to the rumor that the cheap sausage rolls sold in ballparks and at Coney Island actually contained dog meat. So incensed and alarmed was the Coney Island Chamber of Commerce that in 1913 they banned the use of the term "hot dog." But the catchy phrase won out, and soon public fears faded. Hot dogs just tasted too good to be bad.

Handwerker began before World War I as a roll slicer and part-time delivery boy for Charles Feltman, an immigrant from Frankfurt, who has been credited as the first to place a frankfurter sausage in a *heated* roll. Feltman hawked them from a wagon in Coney Island as early as 1869; success led to the establishment of the large Feltman's Restaurant, in what was then a tony beach resort.

Nathan Handwerker's partner and bride, Ida, devised the secret spice formula for the all-beef hot dogs, which sold for five cents. According to Handwerker family legend, a song of the time, "Nathan, Nathan, Why You Waitin?," sung by a saloon songstress named Sophie Tucker, inspired the owner to name his business Nathan's Famous, instead of his first choice, Handwerker's Hot Dogs.

Note little boy Murray Handwerker, sixth from left.

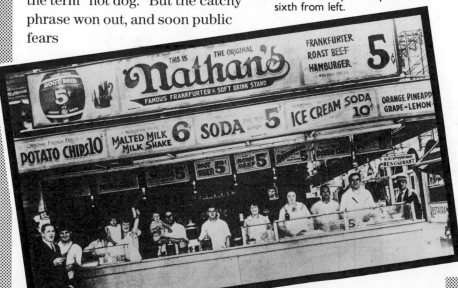

The Coney Island Polar Bear Club

Under the boardwalk, just down the block from Nathan's Famous hot dog stand, is the four-room clubhouse of the Coney Island Polar Bear Club. It's actually a lifeguard station that club members use by permission of the City Parks Commission. Lounging on beach chairs, club members dig into coffee, cake, and soup after their weekly dip in the Atlantic. "That's because when you come out of the water it's phenomenal how hungry you are," says Al Mottola, president of the club since 1970. The clubhouse is unheated, not that the Polar Bears mind. "See that refrigerator over there?" asks Mottola. "On really cold days, we open it up to let some warm air into the room."

Not even severe snowstorms prevent the Bears from honoring a rite that began in 1903: taking an icy plunge of 15 invigorating (they claim) minutes. This crowd, average age 60, declares their ritual keeps them free of colds, viruses, and arthritis. Mottola himself turned 76 in 1990. The group includes a sushi chef, a rabbi, several priests, Russian émigrés, and assorted body builders. Polar Bearing is a way of life, with potluck suppers and music from Mottola's electronic organ.

Ah, those Polar Bears! Nothing invigorates them like a plunge into the frigid waters off Coney Island on a blowy winter's day. Take John Sineno, who's lived here for thirty years: "I prefer to swim in winter," he says firmly. "It gives me zip. I go in even if I'm running a temperature. I swim at night, and in the morning I'm better. The practice is contrary

Polar Bears before the annual New Year's Day plunge, 1989.

to common belief—it must be done to be understood. Attitude is everything."

Over a decade ago, Sineno decided that the unencumbered life is the free life. He got rid of his big apartment, his animals (a cage of squirrel monkeys, a boa constrictor, a tank of piranhas, and roosters), and moved to a simple one-room storefront near the beach. At night friends drop by, and he serves them anisette and coffee. People bring him stale bread so that he can feed the birds, an aggressive lot. "I swear that when I don't feed them, they dive-bomb me," he says.

He also feeds a band of stray dogs with scraps he buys from the

Hoisting the banner before the annual New Year's Day plunge, 1989.

butcher for 24 cents a pound. In the morning, when he's in the water by first light, the dogs form a ring around his clothes to guard them. "That's reciprocity," says Sineno.

"I've been a cook, I've worked for the city, and I've written poems in the Amazon," he says. "What I do now is write. I write about love, flowers and food."

Polar Bear Club Coffee Cake

Do *bears eat cake? They do when Irene Mottola, wife of the club's president, makes it.*

....

2 cups flour, sifted
1 teaspoon baking soda
1 teaspoon baking powder
½ teaspoon salt
1 teaspoon cinnamon
¾ cup light brown sugar
½ cup chopped pecans or walnuts

¼ pound (1 stick) unsalted butter,
    at room temperature
1 cup sugar
2 eggs, at room temperature
1 teaspoon vanilla
1 cup sour cream, at room temperature
2 tablespoons melted unsalted butter

Preheat the oven to 350 degrees F.

❶ Butter and flour a 9-inch tube pan. Sift the flour, baking soda, baking powder, and salt together and set aside. In a small bowl mix the cinnamon, brown sugar, and nuts. Set aside.

❷ Cream the butter and sugar together until light and fluffy. Beat in the eggs, 1 at a time, and add the vanilla. Fold in the flour mixture and sour cream alternately, ending with the flour. The batter will be thick.

❸ Spread half of the batter in the prepared pan. Sprinkle on half the cinnamon-sugar mixture. Pour on the remaining batter and smooth it with a rubber spatula. Cover with the remaining cinnamon mixture and dribble on the melted butter.

❹ Bake for 55 to 60 minutes, or until a tester inserted in the cake comes out clean. Cool the cake on a rack for 30 minutes. Run a knife around the edges to free the cake, invert it on a plate, then turn it right side up.

≫→ *Makes one 9-inch cake*

Olive and Pine Nut Linguine

John Sineno doesn't believe in cooking food for a long time. "You take all the starch out of your ingredients," he says.

½ to ¾ pound linguine or spaghetti
3 tablespoons olive oil
½ cup pine nuts
1 cup chopped pitted Greek or other
    Mediterranean black olives

3 cloves garlic, minced
½ cup or more freshly grated
    Parmesan cheese

❶ Put the pasta to boil in a large pot of lightly salted water and cook according to package directions. In the meantime, heat the oil to sizzling in a medium skillet. Add the pine nuts, olives, and garlic to the oil. Cook the mixture, stirring, for about 8 minutes, mashing some of the pine nuts and olives with a wooden spoon.

❷ Drain the pasta, saving ½ cup of the water to add to the dish in case you find the sauce too dry. Toss the pasta with the olive mixture, and add the water if needed. Serve with grated cheese to pass at table. ≫→ *Serves 3 or 4*

Main Dish Sweet Potato Apple Casserole

Ann Friedman is a vegetarian Polar Bear who swims year-round with the club. She lives in the private seashore community of Sea Gate, adjacent to Coney Island, *which has a working lighthouse. "Polar Bearing and good food make for a positive outlook," says Ann, who is a professional nutritionist.*

6 large sweet potatoes
3 pounds McIntosh apples
½ cup light brown sugar
1 teaspoon cinnamon

3 tablespoons margarine or unsalted butter
3 tablespoons honey

Preheat the oven to 350 degrees F.

❶ Boil the sweet potatoes until cooked but still somewhat firm. When they are cool enough to handle, peel them and cut them in ¼-inch slices. Peel the apples, core them, and cut them into ¼-inch slices. Mix the sugar and cinnamon together.

❷ Grease a two-quart casserole. Put in a layer of sweet potatoes and dot them with margarine. Sprinkle with some of the sugar-cinnamon mixture.

❸ Arrange a layer of sliced apples on the potatoes, and drizzle on about 2 teaspoons of the honey.

❹ Continue making layers of potatoes with sugar and apples with honey, making about five layers in all. Finish with apples and dot with margarine. Bake for 1 hour, until the top is brown. ⟫→ *Serves 6 to 8*

▲▲▲▲▲▲▲▲▲▲▲▲

The New York Aquarium

Coney Island's sea air stimulates the appetite. Look at Nuka; in 1983, when she was found by the U.S. Fish and Wildlife Service on a floating iceberg in Alaska, abandoned by her mother, she weighed a mere 160 pounds. Now this Pacific walrus flips the scale at 1,160 pounds.

The New York Aquarium, just off the boardwalk, is home to over ten thousand aquatic animals, including Nuka. This splendid 14-acre facility moved to Brooklyn in 1957, and is still expanding.

The Aquarium's education department conducts classes in the harvesting and preparation of edible sea vegetables. One imported sea product much used in Japanese cooking is agar-agar, or kanten. It is obtained by boiling down a number of seaweeds, then filtering and

Greetings from Nuka, the Pacific walrus.

drying the jelly. Health food stores sell it in the form of powder, shreds, or sticks. Agar sets, and keeps, at room temperature. Jellies made with agar have a slightly bouncy quality that is appealing. Unlike desserts made with gelatin, these jellies will not melt on the tongue.

Shimmering Apple Cider Jelly

(Based on a recipe from the Aquarium education department)

2 cups apple cider
2 tablespoons agar powder or flakes

Dash of cinnamon
Whipped cream, for garnish (optional)

❶ Bring the cider to the boil. Stir in the agar and cook for 30 seconds longer, stirring to dissolve. Remove the pan from the heat. Add the cinnamon. Let mixture cool for 5 minutes.

❷ Pour mixture into a low flat dish that has been rinsed with cold water. The jelly will set in less than an hour. Refrigerate it before serving.

❸ Cut the jelly into small cubes and serve in dessert glasses. Garnish with whipped cream, if desired. ⟫→ *Serves 4*

Totonno's Pizza (or, as They Say in Brooklyn, Ah-Beetz)

A lot of New Yorkers agree that the finest pizza in the world—that's right, the *world*—is at Totonno's on Neptune Avenue in Coney Island. This place is open only on Friday, Saturday, and Sunday. When the day's batch of dough runs out, that's it. No more pizza until tomorrow. You can get white pizza (made with ricotta, no sauce), regular pizza with sausage, pepperoni, or mushrooms, and sausage and peppers. You also get abrupt service, lengthy waits (each pizza goes into the oven alone), and seats of amazing discomfort. As you wait, divert yourself by reading the wall decorations, yellowing headlines behind cracked glass proclaiming "War Over" and "MacArthur to rule Japs." But the pizza crust is light and crisp, the mozzarella on the pizza is hand-made and hand-cut, and the sauce is delicate.

Brick-lined ovens and coal fires, like those at Totonno's, really do make a difference in taste. Nevertheless, you can make excellent pizza at home, easily and quickly.

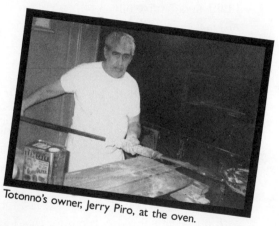

Totonno's owner, Jerry Piro, at the oven.

Totonno's interior.

37

Pizza

The dough makes enough for two 12-inch pizzas, so you can eat one and freeze one. The food processor makes superb dough in no time at all. To make the dough by hand, *stir the yeast mixture into the dry ingredients, add the oil, and knead until the dough is elastic— "smooth and soft as a baby's bottom."*

Dough

⅞ cup warm water

1 package dry yeast

½ teaspoon sugar

2¼ cups all-purpose or bread flour

1 teaspoon salt

1 tablespoon olive oil

Topping

1 cup Quick Marinara (see page 137) or bottled sauce

¼ teaspoon crumbled dried oregano

1 cup shredded mozzarella cheese

2 hot or sweet Italian sausages, cut in rounds

½ cup chopped green pepper

½ cup thinly sliced red onions

½ cup thinly sliced mushrooms

Olive oil

Hot pepper flakes, to pass at table

❶ Put the water in a 2-cup measure. Add the yeast and sugar and stir. Let sit for 3 minutes, until foamy.

❷ Put the metal blade in the bowl of a food processor, add the flour and salt, and pulse to mix. Stir the yeast mixture, turn on the machine, and slowly pour the mixture into the feed tube while the machine is running. Process until a ball of dough forms. Add the oil, then process for 40 seconds to knead the dough.

❸ Put the dough in a large plastic bag and force out the air. Fasten the top with a twist tie, leaving room for the dough to expand. Put the dough in a warm place and leave it until it doubles in bulk, about 45 minutes.

❹ Punch the dough down, flatten it out, and cut it in half. Place one of the halves in the plastic bag, secure it, and freeze it. (It will keep well for several months and will defrost, in its bag, in about 20 minutes.)

Preheat the oven to 425 degrees F.

❺ Roll out the remaining dough and place it on a 12-inch nonstick pizza pan. Slather on half of the sauce, spreading it to the edges. Sprinkle on oregano. Top with the mozzarella. Use a spoon to dot on the rest of the sauce.

❻ Bake in the lower third of the oven for 15 minutes. Meanwhile, brown the sausage rounds in a skillet and place on paper to drain. Cook the peppers, onion, and mushrooms in a little olive oil for about 3 minutes, stirring.

❼ After 15 minutes, arrange the peppers, onion, mushrooms, and sausage on the pizza. Sprinkle on a few drops of olive oil and return pizza to oven. Bake for 10 minutes more, or until the edges are browned and the cheese is lightly browned and bubbling. Serve with the hot pepper flakes. ⟫→ *Serves 2 or 3*

▲▲▲▲▲▲▲▲▲▲▲▲▲▲▲▲▲▲▲▲▲▲▲▲▲▲▲

BRIGHTON BEACH
LITTLE ODESSA BY THE SEA

Although it was named for the English seaside resort, Brighton Beach has been a mainly Russian-Jewish community since the 1920s. Over one hundred years ago, a real-estate speculator who had made his pile selling supplies to <u>both</u> sides in the Civil War built the Brighton Beach Hotel. John Philip Sousa and Victor Herbert played at the Brighton Music Hall, and racegoers could have a flutter at the track, or wager bets at Reisenweber's Casino. Later, middle- and working-class folk in search of summer pleasure built or rented little bungalows off Coney Island Avenue, the main thoroughfare. (These were winterized in the late 1940s.) Fine Art Deco apartment buildings were built to house the more affluent. Brighton had become a year-round place to live.

Changes, both good and bad, happen to all communities. The Brighton Beach Bath and Racquet Club, built in 1907, will be razed for upscale condominiums with a view of the splendid beach and boardwalk. But the club will be missed for many reasons, including the fact that players in what is purported to be the world's longest continual mah-jongg game must cast their final tiles. The game was organized in 1916.

By the 1960s, Brighton Beach had begun to decline. The culprit? Age. Shopkeepers in what had been one of Brooklyn's bigger commercial centers grew old, and retired. Their children had moved away, and no one was left to take over. But before the neighborhood could slide too far, the Russians came! In the 1970s, Soviet Jews gained permission to emigrate, and they came in the thousands. About 30,000 of them settled in Brighton Beach, making it the largest Russian community in the United States.

Eighty percent of the new immigrants are from Odessa, the major port on the Black Sea. The beach, the water, and the bracing air of Brighton Beach remind them of home. But better than home is the abundance of the foods they love; sausages festoon the numerous

Signs and storefronts in Russianized Brighton Beach.

delicatessen windows, and the two floors of M & I International Foods (known as "the Zabar's of Brighton Beach" after the famed Manhattan gourmet specialty market) are crammed with appetizing take-out delicacies, both Russian and American style. There are baked ribs, roast chicken, meatballs, piroshki, and tiny pork cutlets called bitki. There are the marinated vegetables Russians love, including the "vinaigrette" of beets, potatoes, onions, and cucumber known as Russian Salad. And caviar, of course. Gefilte fish, shaped like a large sausage, shares a display case with smoked bacon, baked homestyle pork called vareskha, beef cured with spices, and Italian-style suckling pig, porchetta.

Upstairs, stacked boxes of chocolate jostle cherry cakes and honey cakes, towers of jams wobble precariously in the middle of aisles, counters are piled with candied fruit slices and cartons of sweet biscuits.

The Rakhman family arrived from Odessa in 1976, and started M & I International two years later. They also own the restaurant-nightclub next door, The National. If the smoked fish display at M & I is particularly lavish—there are sable, herring, trout, shad, anchovies, sprats, salmon, and mackerel—it is because Mark Rakhman's daughter Stella is married to Bob Furleiter, owner of the Royal Baltic fish-smoking company on Ditmas Avenue.

Clubs like the National, the Zodiak, and Primorski demand fortitude. First, you must be prepared to eat a gargantuan amount of food: a cold assortment of maybe twenty dishes, followed by a hot meat selection, with shasklik, chicken, chops, and dumplings; served with a liter bottle of vodka for each foursome. You must be prepared for endless, superamplified music, sad and lively Russian airs, jazzy renderings of "Tico Tico," and, at least twice every half hour, "Happy Birthday to You," an all-purpose anthem honoring bar mitzvahs, anniversaries, graduations, and birthdays, too. You should get up and dance, to jiggle around some of that food. Patrons have a wonderful time at these Russian restaurants, and the price for a night out in Odessa by the Sea is ludicrously low.

Not all of Brighton is Russianized; Mrs. Stahl's Knishes still stands at the corner of Brighton Beach Avenue, and the Zei-Mar Kosher Deli serves the same franks and meats it did in the 1940s, when Jerry Sternstein (see page 50) was growing up. But the Russians have surely given this pleasant beachfront neighborhood an economic and gastronomic boost.

Brighton Beach's Russian restaurateurs by no means stick to the food of Odessa—you can order the Siberian dumplings called pelmeni, borscht from the Ukraine, and chicken Kiev. You can have lobster from Maine, too.

These dishes are typical of all the restaurants: Primorski, the National, the Zodiak, and Odessa.

Primorski's
Chicken Kiev

Chef-owner Ruben "Bubba" Khotoveli suggests serving this *dish with fresh tomatoes and pickled cabbage.*

....

4 chicken breasts, halved
Salt and freshly ground pepper to taste
¼ pound (1 stick) unsalted butter, cut
   into finger-sized pieces

1 cup flour
2 eggs, lightly beaten
2 cups fresh bread crumbs
2 cups vegetable oil, for frying

❶ Skin and bone the chicken breasts but leave the shoulder bone attached. Flatten each boned breast to a thickness of ¼ inch by pounding it lightly with a kitchen mallet or rolling pin.

❷ Lay out the flattened breasts, boned side up. Sprinkle with salt and pepper. Place a finger of butter on each breast half. Roll up the butter in the breast as you would a package, tucking in the ends of the meat at the beginning of the roll. Leave the shoulder bone sticking halfway out on one end.

❸ Dip the rolled breasts in the flour, then in the beaten egg, and finally in the bread crumbs. Place them on a tray and freeze them for 1 hour.

❹ In a deep pot or wok, heat the oil to 380 degrees F. There should be enough oil to cover the rolled breasts. Deep-fry the breasts, in batches, for 5 to 7 minutes, until golden brown. Drain them on paper towels and serve immediately.

⋙→ *Serves 4*

Russianized Brighton Beach.

Pelmeni
(Meat-filled Siberian Dumplings)

Dough
4 cups all-purpose flour
3 eggs, lightly beaten
1 cup warm water
1 teaspoon salt

Filling
½ pound ground beef
½ pound ground pork
1 medium onion, grated
2 garlic cloves, minced

2 tablespoons finely chopped fresh dill
1 teaspoon salt
Several grindings black pepper
2 tablespoons water
7 to 8 quarts salted water

For Serving
¼ pound (1 stick) melted butter
Lemon wedges
Sour cream (optional)

❶ Mix together the flour, eggs, water, and salt to make a firm dough. Knead on a floured work surface until the dough is smooth and elastic, about 10 minutes. Form into a ball, cover, and let rest for 30 minutes.

❷ Meanwhile, mix together the beef, pork, onion, garlic, dill, salt, pepper, and the 2 tablespoons of water. Refrigerate until ready to use.

❸ Divide the dough in half. Cover one half and roll out the other until it is ⅛ inch thick. Cut rounds from the dough with a 2½-inch cookie cutter.

❹ Place about 1 teaspoon of filling below the center of each round. Fold each round in half to seal in the filling. Crimp edges with a fork. Dip your fingers in water and bring the 2 corners together, pinching so the edges are well sealed. The finished pelmeni look a little like fortune cookies. (Pelmeni may be frozen at this point.)

❺ Bring the salted water to the boil. Drop in about 10 pelmeni and cook them until they float, about 8 minutes. Repeat, cooking as many as you wish. Remove cooked pelmeni with a slotted spoon to a buttered baking dish, and keep warm in a 250 degree F oven until all are cooked.

❻ Serve with melted butter and lemon wedges or sour cream.

⫸ *Makes about 70 to 80 pelmeni*

Red Cabbage Salad

This is a Georgian dish. Don't use red cabbage—the flavor will not be the same.

A 2-pound white cabbage
2 pounds beets, peeled and cut into
   1-inch dice
8 sprigs parsley, stems removed

1 cup celery leaves
2 cups red-wine vinegar
2 teaspoons imported paprika

❶ Remove the core from the cabbage and chop the cabbage coarsely. Cover it with cold water and bring to the boil. Reduce the heat and simmer, partially covered, for about 25 minutes.

❷ Drain the cabbage well. Put it in a large nonreactive bowl and add the beets, parsley, celery leaves, vinegar, and paprika. Pour in enough boiling water to cover the cabbage by 2 inches. Place a dinner plate on the cabbage to keep it submerged. Pickle the cabbage at room temperature for 5 days. It will turn deep red from the beets. Refrigerate the cabbage in its marinade for 4 hours to 4 days.

❸ To serve, drain thoroughly. ➤ *Makes 8 servings as part of an hors d'oeuvre tray*

Brighton Beach Avenue.

Mrs. Stahl's Knishes

There really was a Mrs. Stahl, who made knishes in her home in the early 1930s and sold them on the boardwalk. "They were Depression food," says Les Green, who now owns the store. "They were cheap, filling, and delicious. I can't tell you how many people come in here and tell me it was their relatives who convinced her to open the store, which she did, in 1935."

A knish (you pronounce the "k") is dough wrapped around a tasty filling and baked. Mrs. Stahl started with the basic filling, mashed potatoes seasoned with onion. She also made fillings from kasha (buckwheat groats), and from apples and cabbage. The Weingast brothers, who bought the store from her some thirty years ago, pepped up the menu, offering fillings such as cherry cheese. "I've added my own specialties in the five years since I bought the store," says Les. "We developed mushroom barley, roast chicken, chili, and, with health in mind, salt-free knishes."

No one is really sure who invented the knish, though it most likely had its origins in Russia or Poland. A knish must be served hot, and the dough should be thin and somewhat crisp. A knish is heavy, weighing between a quarter and a half pound. A serious nosh. On the lighter side are cocktail knishes, 2 inches square, which Mrs. Stahl's makes to order. Among the flavors are cheese, sweet potato, and Spanish rice.

"Mrs. Stahl was a charitable woman," says Les. "She donated knishes to good causes, and she gave leftovers to the poor."

Home of Mrs. Stahl's famous knishes.

Potato Cocktail Knishes

Dough
2 cups all-purpose flour
1 teaspoon baking powder
½ teaspoon salt
1 to 2 tablespoons vegetable oil
2 eggs, lightly beaten
4 tablespoons water

Filling
3 tablespoons rendered chicken fat or
    vegetable oil
2 cups finely chopped onions
2 cups freshly made mashed potatoes
Salt and freshly ground black pepper to
    taste

❶ Put the flour, baking powder, and salt in the bowl of a heavy-duty mixer equipped with a dough hook. Add 1 tablespoon of the oil, the eggs, and 2 tablespoons of water. Knead for 3 to 4 minutes, add the remaining oil and as much water as needed to make a smooth dough. Or mix the ingredients in a bowl with a wooden spoon and knead the dough on a floured surface for 6 minutes.

❷ Put the dough in an oiled bowl, turn it to oil it all over, and cover it with plastic wrap. Let it stand for 1 hour.

Preheat the oven to 350 degrees F.

❸ Heat the fat or oil in a medium skillet and sauté the onions until they are just tender. Mix them thoroughly into the mashed potatoes and add salt and pepper to taste.

❹ Divide the dough in thirds. On a floured surface, roll one piece into a thin rectangle about 10 inches long. Place about ⅔ cup of the potato filling along the long end, about 1 inch from the edge. Roll up dough like a jelly roll and pinch the edges closed. Repeat twice, with the remaining dough and filling.

❺ Arrange the long rolls on a baking sheet, and bake them for about 40 minutes, until browned. Slice and serve.

(Unbaked or baked knishes can be frozen, and baked or reheated. Do not defrost. Unbaked knishes take about 45 minutes, baked 15 to 20 minutes.)

➤ *Makes about 2 dozen 1¼-inch slices*

▲▲▲▲▲▲▲▲▲▲▲▲▲▲▲▲▲▲▲▲▲▲▲▲▲▲▲▲▲

The White Acacia

Simon and Emma Feldman came to the United States from the Ukraine in 1973. "The country was good, but not the management," says Simon. When he was eight, he lost his parents in the Holocaust, and later spent seven years in a prison camp. When he and Emma applied for exit visas, they lost their jobs. "I had a chance to experience the whole beauty of the system," says Simon.

Emma and Simon Feldman of The White Acacia.

The Feldmans brew and sell the lightly fermented drink called *kvass* from a window at the front of their store, The White Acacia. "The store is named for a pretty tree, with lovely blossoms, and smelling them makes you feel younger," he says. Kvass is made from raisins, wheat, sugar, yeast, and water. He says the drink has "a nice prune flavor." They also sell a full range of Russian delicatessen food, including tart pickled watermelon, or Arbos, which is excellent with meats.

Arbos
(Pickled Watermelon)

1½ pounds watermelon with rind, cut into 3-inch chunks
2 stalks celery, sliced
1 bunch fresh dill
5 sprigs parsley
4 to 6 cloves garlic, peeled and lightly crushed

2 small hot peppers
1 tablespoon horseradish, squeezed dry
1 tablespoon salt
1 tablespoon sugar

Place the ingredients in a large jar or bowl with a lid, and cover with water. Let stand on the counter for 2 to 6 days, until the contents just begin to ferment. Refrigerate for a day or two. The pickle will become increasingly pungent; eat within 2 weeks. ➤ *Makes 4 cups of pickles*

Mixed Marriage Mix-up

As executive director of the Brighton Beach Neighborhood Association, Patricia Murphy-Singer fights for the rights of tenants and property owners, not only to maintain the community but to upgrade it to "the jewel of East Coast beach areas."

Brighton is home to more than the older Jewish community and the new Russian emigrants; the population also includes Koreans, Pakistanis, Afghans, Hispanics, and Filipinos. When it comes to dealing sensitively with the needs of these varying cultures, Pat Singer is eminently qualified; her own family life prepared her well.

Pat tells her story:

"In 1933, Sara Koza was a lovely young woman living in Brighton Beach, the daughter of Russian-Jewish immigrants. Longing for a wider world than her old country community, she anglicized her name to Sally, and often took the train to New York City, where her aunt kept a boarding house. There she met a handsome Australian sea captain with wavy red-brown hair. His name was John Patrick Murphy. In 1935, at the age of twenty, she married him in City Hall. These were my parents. Her father disowned her, but when a son was born a year later, he relented. My parents vowed that if their love would last to their fiftieth anniversary, they would be married by a rabbi. And they were, too!

"Sally made it plain to all six of

Pat Singer, neighborhood booster.

her children, of which I was the eldest daughter, that we were Jewish. The aromas in the Murphy household were Jewish ones, of potato latkes, blintzes and kugels, but we did not keep kosher.

"Then I met Mr. Right, a Conservative Jewish fellow whose family was observant. One evening I invited my mother-in-law over to eat with us. We were having meat, but she wanted dairy. Being a good daughter-in-law, I offered to bake her a potato to go along with her dairy meal, and we would have them too. When my husband turned to me and said, 'Are the potatoes ready yet?' I grabbed my meat fork and stabbed all the potatoes. 'You know nothing! Nothing!' screamed my mother-in-law. Silence filled the kitchen. Abashed, I took a dairy knife and cut away the part of her potato touched by the fork. That salvaged the day."

Pat doesn't spend much time in the kitchen.

Life Was a Beach
Growing Up in Brighton

Jerome Sternstein, Professor of History at Brooklyn College, recalls the neighborhood of his youth:

"We moved to Brighton Beach in 1939, when I was six. It was one of the loveliest places you could imagine to grow up in. We lived just behind the beach, and my friends and I spent our lives there. Our parents never seemed to worry about our safety, which was just as well, because nothing bad ever happened.

"My mother was a widow, a corsetiere for ladies from the neighborhood and Kings Highway. She took her profession very seriously; once she mentioned that she'd seen a friend of mine's girlfriend in the store. 'What size bra does she take?' I asked eagerly. My mother drew herself up and snapped, 'How dare you ask that! That is privileged information!'

"I recall that she kept kosher until Chinese restaurants began to infiltrate Jewish neighborhoods, I think in the '40s. The big one in Brighton, near the Oceana movie theater, was called the Kwai Fong. The usual stuff—sub gum, shrimp with lobster sauce—but that was the thin edge of the wedge. I began to cook too, and that further undermined it. But for Passover she changed the dishes and got rid of the leavening. And she was always opposed to milk with meat.

"However, the real change in her cooking came about from the influence of a radio personality, Carlton Fredericks, who convinced her that the road to health lay in putting wheat germ in everything. Formerly good cookies became horrible! But she still made a wonderful borscht, and the best matzo brei anywhere."

1938   Jerome   5 yrs.

1938

Jerry Sternstein's fifth birthday, on the beach.

Anna Sternstein's Borscht

The borscht should have mellow sweet and sour undertones. Like most hearty soups, this one improves when aged for a day or two.

2 pounds flanken, or substitute short ribs of beef
3 tablespoons vegetable oil
3 medium beets, peeled and shredded
2 tablespoons red-wine vinegar
2 teaspoons sugar
8 medium onions, coarsely chopped
2 medium carrots, peeled and coarsely chopped
A 3-pound green cabbage, cored and shredded

6 cups canned tomatoes, puréed (preferably Hunt's or Redpack)
6 allspice berries, crushed
1 tablespoon salt, or to taste
3 bay leaves
2 tablespoons finely chopped parsley
3½ quarts water
1 tablespoon minced garlic
3 tablespoons snipped dill

❶ Cover the flanken with water and bring to the boil. Lower the heat and simmer for 20 minutes. (This parboiling releases the scum.) Rinse the flanken and set it aside.

❷ In a large stockpot, heat the oil and add the beets, vinegar, and sugar. Cook over moderate heat for 10 minutes, stirring occasionally. Add the onions and carrots and cook, stirring, for 3 minutes. Put in the cabbage, tomatoes, allspice, salt, bay leaves, parsley, and water. Bring the soup to the boil, add the flanken, and reduce the heat. Cover and simmer gently for 1 hour.

❸ After 1 hour, stir in the garlic. Cook 30 minutes more, adding a little water if the soup has cooked down.

❹ Remove the flanken and, when it is cool enough to handle, cut it into 1-inch pieces. Return the meat to the stockpot. Correct the seasonings, adding salt, pepper, or a little sugar as necessary. Serve sprinkled with fresh dill.

≫→ *Makes about 4½ quarts*

Anna Sternstein's Matzo Brei

If you like your matzo brei browned and a little dry, cook it longer. It is eaten for Passover, and all year round. Perhaps the dish started as a way to use up stale matzos?

3 sheets matzo
2 tablespoons cream
4 eggs, lightly beaten

3 tablespoons unsalted butter
Salt and freshly ground pepper to taste

❶ Break the matzos into pieces and soak them in warm water for a minute or two. Squeeze out as much water as possible with your hands.

❷ Put the squeezed matzos in a bowl and pour the cream over them. When it is absorbed, pour on the eggs and mix.

❸ Heat the butter in a heavy skillet. As it begins to brown, add the matzo mixture. Cook over moderately low heat. Let the bottom set for 1 minute, then begin to turn the mass with a wooden spoon, as you would for scrambled eggs. Fairly light and fluffy matzo brei is done in about 5 minutes. Taste and season with salt, if needed, and liberal grindings of pepper. ≫→ *Serves 2 or 3*

Trolley to the Beach

"When I was a kid, we lived in Brownsville," says Lou Singer, who knows the neighborhoods of Brooklyn as well as anyone alive. "In its heyday in the '30s, Brownsville had a bigger Jewish population than the Lower East Side. My mother often took us to Brighton Beach, but to go direct, that was two fares on the trolley. In those days my dad earned $20 a week, and we couldn't waste money. So she worked out a one-fare route. It took three hours, but it was one fare. She brought along *hockfleisch*—that's Yiddish for chopped meat—sandwiches to eat on the trolley. She put them on big kaiser rolls, and I mean *big*. Back then, each stretch of beach was the domain of a certain community. Brownsvillers went to the stretch at Brighton 7th Street.

"As a young man, I'd look for girls at the beach or at the Hi Ho Casino. I had poor geographic luck. It never seemed to fail; I'd meet a nice girl, dance with her all evening, and being a gentleman, ask to take her home. 'I live in the Bronx,' she'd say sweetly. The Bronx! Over an hour on the subway to take her home, a chaste little kiss at the door, and then all the way back to Brownsville, alone on the subway."

Hockfleisch Sandwiches

"Here is my reconstruction of the sandwiches Lou's mother made back in the 1930s," says Lou Singer's wife, Lee. "My mother made something similar, but without the hard-boiled eggs. You could say that these patties are made from a sort of meatloaf mixture.

They're plump; none of that fast-food thin burger. When I was a kid, our mothers sent us off to the Saturday-afternoon movies with these sandwiches, to sustain us through the double feature and the cartoons."

....

1½ pounds chopped beef
1 large onion, grated
2 hard-boiled eggs, chopped
1 cup bread crumbs, preferably made
  from day-old challah

1 egg
Salt and pepper to taste
Vegetable oil for frying
. . . .
4 kaiser rolls

    Mix all ingredients (except the rolls) well in a large bowl, using a wooden spoon or your hands. Form 4 plump patties. Fry them in a little oil (very little if you use a nonstick pan) until done to your liking, turning them once. Serve hot or cold on kaiser rolls or other bread. ⟫→ *Serves 4*

▲ ▲

(From the top) Emmons Avenue, view of piers, 1925; the Villepigue Inn, 1913;
The Old Tappen House, 1914.

SHEEPSHEAD BAY
SEASIDE SUBURB

Sharing the southern coastline of Brooklyn with Coney Island and Brighton Beach, Sheepshead Bay was once part of Gravesend, one of the six original towns in Kings County and the only one that was English. The founder of Gravesend, Deborah Lady Moody, was an extraordinary woman who harbored radical ideas for 1643: a town meeting form of government, planned arrangement of town and agricultural land, decent treatment of the Indians, and freedom of religion, to an extent most liberal for her time. The surrounding Dutch were said to be somewhat envious (or disapproving) of "licentious" Gravesend.

After Lady Moody's death around 1660, the area settled into the seasonal ho-hum round of rural life, and Sheepshead Bay itself (named for a local fish called the Sheepshead) was a simple fishing village until the last quarter of the 19th century. But in the mid-1880s, the Sheepshead Bay Racetrack opened, with all the occasions for high living and good eating that follow the sporting set. The Villepigue Inn, Tappen's, and the Sheepshead Bay Club catered to the demanding appetites of Whitneys, Vanderbilts, and Leonard Jerome, a founder of the track and the grandfather of Winston Churchill.

This glittering era ended with the same puritanical thud heard in neighboring Brighton Beach and Coney Island: racetrack gambling was outlawed in 1910. It matters not how fast the horses run; if no one can bet on them, no one cares. The racetrack disappeared under pleasant family housing, while fishing boats and seafood restaurants flourished along the waterfront of Emmons Avenue.

From the Track to the Church

A remnant of the racetrack days remains—the descendants of employees who had come to the track as grooms and jockeys. Don Brown, who describes himself as "retired and carefree," talks about the community:

"My family came north from Tennessee to work at the track. My great-grandmother worked in the kitchen that fed the track help; my grandfather, William Forehand, was a groom. In fact, he was the groom for the great racehorse Man O' War.

"Being a very religious woman, my grandmother, Catherine Forehand, was concerned that there was no house of worship for the people, nor Christian education for the children. Then Mother Maria Fisher came up from Virginia and organized the First Baptist Church of Sheepshead Bay. She supported herself and her children by selling pies and snacks at the racetrack. The first services were held outdoors, with an old icebox for a podium. In 1901, the church building was begun with a donation of used bricks. It is a beautiful church, and it held the community together. Besides the track families, there were a lot of people who kept coming up to work in the restaurants like Lundy's.

"The church was built so the people didn't have to go far to worship; now many have left for places like Bedford-Stuyvesant; parishioners have to commute back to church! To make a day of it, the church organized a program of dinners after services: baked and fried chicken, fresh pork, and

Sheepshead Bay Racetrack, 1925.

always food for the cholesterol watchers. The fee is nominal.

"I can't say my mother, Florence Brown, was a cook; her whole life was the church, and she was Sunday-school superintendent for twenty-five years. My grand-mother, the matriarch, was the cook; I wish I had her recipe for scrapple. But you know, somehow these things just didn't get written down."

Don's grandfather, William Forehand.

Don's Carrot Cake

Don Brown is a good baker. This cake is in demand for parties and fundraisers. Don says, "Use California carrots — they're sweeter."

Batter
2 cups sifted all-purpose flour
2 teaspoons baking soda
2 teaspoons baking powder
2 teaspoons cinnamon
4 large eggs
2 cups sugar
1⅓ cups vegetable oil

4 cups freshly grated carrots
¾ cup broken walnuts
Frosting
8 ounces cream cheese
½ cup butter or margarine
1 teaspoon vanilla
1 pound confectioners' sugar, sifted
1 cup freshly grated carrots

Preheat the oven to 350 degrees F.

❶ Sift together the flour, baking soda, baking powder, and cinnamon. Set aside.

❷ Beat the eggs well and add the sugar and oil. Combine with the dry mixture. Fold in the grated carrots and nuts.

❸ Spoon the batter into a buttered and floured 10 × 3½-inch tube pan. Bake in the center of the oven for 50 to 60 minutes, until a toothpick inserted in the center of the cake comes out clean. Let the cake cool on a rack.

❹ Work the cream cheese and butter together until soft and fluffy. Beat in the vanilla. Combine with the confectioners' sugar. Ice the cooled cake with this mixture, and sprinkle it evenly with the shredded carrots. Refrigerate until ready to serve. ➤ *Makes 1 10-inch tube cake*

▲▲▲▲▲▲▲▲▲▲▲▲▲▲▲▲▲▲▲▲▲▲▲▲▲▲▲

Want a Day's Fun? Go Fish!

Captain Anne O'Driscoll represents the Sheepshead Bay Fishing Fleet Association, a group working to preserve the only private fishing fleet in New York City. She's also an excellent and enthusiastic cook of fish. According to Anne, a day's fishing gives you a lot of fun and food for little money:

"Here in Sheepshead Bay is one of the last remaining party fishing ports in a city. In Boston the yuppies came, the condos went up, and out went the fishing boats. Fisherman's Wharf in San Francisco is great, except that it has no fishing boats. Baltimore has no more boats.

"We've got around thirty boats going out for fish. For a whole day's fishing on a party boat, you'll pay $27.00. You get a pole and bait and some instruction, and after a day's entertainment you wind up with supper to boot. Most customers catch so many fish they leave some for the crew. The crew sells the fish, and that's the major part of their income. People who've been coming here for years buy the fish (it's a lot cheaper than the fish store) and the new Asian community has caught on to it. On a Saturday afternoon, it looks like a carnival with wall-to-wall people.

"I've had my U.S. Coast Guard captain's license since 1987, and there has been a captain in my family as far back as we can trace. My father was a captain and my uncles are captains—it's what the family does. But my mother gets seasick if she looks at a boat.

"My father invented a cod-fishing tournament back in the '50s, with a pool of over a thousand dollars for the winner. That was a big deal then. The guy with the heaviest fish got the prize and his picture in the newspaper. My father insisted that the fish be gutted before it was weighed. That was because people stuffed the fish with lead sinkers to make them heavier.

"When I was about five, my father—who fished all year and could eat codfish every night of his life—brought home an ungutted cod that weighed more than I did, sixty-five pounds. The fish was on the kitchen floor and our old tomcat went up to it to check it out. The codfish suddenly clamped down on his tail! So we had a screaming cat and a codfish with a cat's tail firmly between his teeth. The cod was speedily dispatched with a knife and was served up for dinner. The cat got his piece too, to get even.

"The boats go out from two miles to a hundred miles, depending on the season and the fish you're after. Sometimes they have to chase the mackerel all the way up into Long Island Sound. For the tuna they'll go one hundred miles off-shore to the Hudson and Baltimore Canyon. It's magnificent out there; you see dolphins and porpoises, and the water is crystal-blue.

"People go to Florida to fish

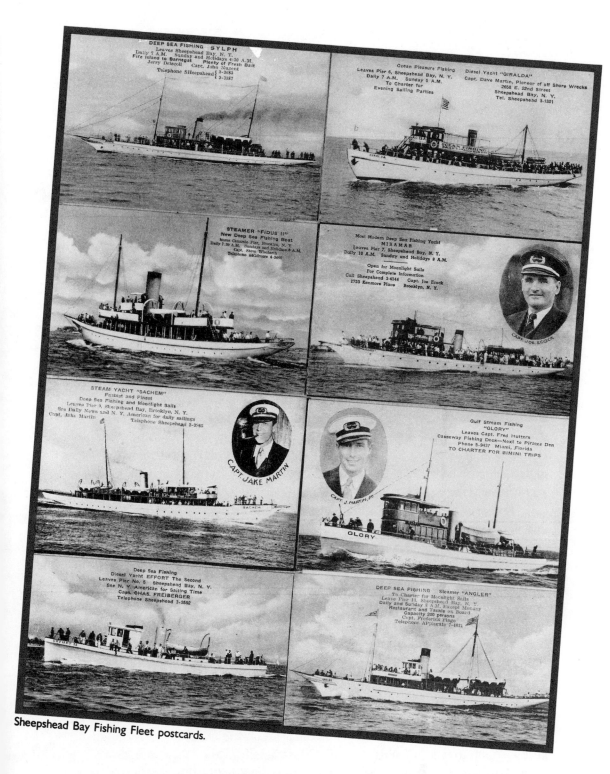

Sheepshead Bay Fishing Fleet postcards.

when they have the best fishing in
the country right here. This isn't a
Tom Sawyer operation—out for the
day and back with two little fish.
This is meat fishing—lots of it."

Flounder or Fluke in Cream Sauce

Captain Anne O'Driscoll reports that flounder are caught in the spring off Sheepshead Bay, and fluke in the summer and early fall.

She says that the fillets can measure from "see-through to three-quarters of an inch. If they are very thin, fold them in half."

....

8 flounder or fluke fillets (1 to 1½ pounds)

Water to cover

1 fish frame, if available*

1 cup dry white wine or dry vermouth

¼ cup chopped celery

¼ cup chopped onion

1 small carrot, chopped

Sprigs of fresh summer savory or chervil, if available

5 tablespoons unsalted butter

5 tablespoons flour

1 cup milk

1 cup heavy cream

Salt and white pepper to taste

1 cup grated Swiss cheese

❶ Arrange the fillets in a large skillet and cover with water. (This is the way to measure the amount of water needed for the poaching liquid.) Remove the fillets and refrigerate them until the poaching liquid is ready.

❷ Put the fish frame, if you have one, in the water; it enriches the broth, but you can do without it. Add the wine, celery, onion, carrot, and a few sprigs of savory or chervil. Bring the liquid to the boil, lower the heat, and simmer for 20 minutes. Strain the liquid and return it to the skillet over medium heat.

❸ As the poaching liquid simmers, make the sauce. Combine the butter and flour in a medium saucepan and cook, stirring, for 3 minutes. Use a whisk to stir in the milk slowly. When the mixture is smooth, add the cream, salt, and pepper. Whisk until smooth, cover with plastic wrap, placing it on the surface of the sauce to prevent a skin from forming, and set aside.

Preheat the oven to 400 degrees F or heat the broiler.

❹ Place the fillets in the poaching liquid. They should be covered by liquid. If necessary, add a little more water. If you have the fish frame, lay it over the fillets to keep them from bobbing up, or use 2 layers of wax paper. Poach the fish over moderate heat; the liquid should just simmer. The fish is cooked when it is milky white. Remove it from the liquid.

❺ Add about 1 cup of the poaching liquid to the sauce, or enough to make it the consistency of cream. Pour a cup of sauce on the bottom of a baking dish large enough to hold the fillets. Arrange the fillets over the sauce, and cover them with a thin layer of sauce and the grated cheese. Put the dish in the oven or under the boiler until browned and bubbling. Garnish with herb sprigs, if you have them, and serve the fish on a platter, surrounded with parslied new potatoes. Put any extra sauce in a warmed gravy boat. ≫→ *Serves 4 to 6*

*A fish frame is the head and bone structure of a fish after it has been filleted. It includes the head, but not the skin, gills, or guts.

Thai-Style Topping for Pan-Fried Fish

Anne O'Driscoll's topping is marvelous with black bass, blackfish, or any other firm fillets dipped into seasoned flour and pan-fried.

....

4 servings of fried fish fillets, prepared
   according to your favorite recipe
4 to 5 Oriental mushrooms, or enough
   to make ½ cup of julienne strips
2 tablespoons Oriental fish sauce
   (*nuoc mam*)
1 to 2 teaspoons sugar
½ cup water

1 teaspoon freshly ground white
   pepper
2 teaspoons vegetable oil
2 teaspoons minced garlic
2 teaspoons minced fresh ginger
¼ pound ground pork
Fresh coriander sprigs for garnish

❶ Soak the mushrooms in warm water for about 30 minutes, until they are soft. Discard the stems and cut them into julienne strips.

❷ Mix the mushrooms with the fish sauce, sugar, water, and pepper.

❸ Heat the oil in a medium skillet and add the garlic and ginger. Cook, stirring, until lightly browned. Add the pork and cook, mashing and turning, until no pink remains. Add the mushroom mixture and heat through. Pour sauce over the fried fish and garnish with coriander sprigs. ➳ *Serves 4*

▲▲▲▲▲▲▲▲▲▲▲▲▲▲▲▲▲▲▲▲▲▲▲▲▲▲▲▲▲▲▲▲▲▲

Plumb Beach Activist

Margaret McCord, who was born in Scotland in 1903, has lived in Sheepshead Bay since 1931. "My husband and I came visiting, and we liked the fishing boats and the village atmosphere," she says. "My husband was a chief electrician on ocean liners, and he was away a lot, so I had to keep busy. I don't drink, I don't smoke, and I like my neighbors. We were strong for starting a civic association, which we formed in 1962. The Plumb Beach Civic Association (Plumb Beach is a part of Sheepshead Bay) helped get us sewers, and kept public housing off Emmons Avenue. We work for the betterment of the community."

The very active Mrs. McCord is

a good cook as well as a civic leader. She tells how she came to invent this very good cake:

"It was a rainy day, and I didn't know what to do with myself. I didn't want to read or to sew, so I thought I'd bake an applesauce cake. I beat up my butter, and my eggs and sugar, and went to get the applesauce. Instead of a cup, I had only half that. The batter was much too thick, so I added orange juice and raisins. It came out beautifully, so I called it by a different name. I call it my Rainy Day Cake."

Rainy Day Cake

½ cup butter or margarine
¾ cup sugar
1 egg
½ cup cold applesauce
1 teaspoon cinnamon
½ teaspoon ground cloves

1½ cups all-purpose flour
1 teaspoon baking soda
3 to 5 tablespoons orange or cranberry
  juice
1 cup raisins
⅓ cup finely chopped nuts

Preheat the oven to 350 degrees F.

❶ Butter a 9- × 5- × 2-inch loaf pan.

❷ Cream the butter, sugar, and egg together well. With a rubber spatula blend in the applesauce, cinnamon, cloves, and flour.

❸ Mix the baking soda with 3 tablespoons of the juice and stir it into the mixture. If the mixture seems dry, add more of the juice. Fold in the raisins and nuts.

❹ Pour the mixture into the prepared pan. Bake in the center of the oven for 1 hour, until the top is browned and a toothpick inserted into the cake comes out clean. Place the cake on a rack and let it cool for at least 1 hour before removing it from the pan. ➤ *Makes 1 loaf cake*

The Plumb Beach activist Margaret McCord.

▲▲▲▲▲▲▲▲▲▲▲▲

F.W.I.L. Lundy Brothers

Frederick William Irving Lundy was born in Sheepshead Bay in 1895. His family was prosperous, but Lundy was ambitious; at the age of nine he opened a dockside stand supplying chowder and coffee to fishermen. By the time he was sixteen, several grown men were working for him.

In 1918, he established Lundy Brothers Co., selling oysters and clams from a barge moored in the bay. Irving, as he was called, was the boss; his brothers dug the clams.

Personal tragedy was always to hound Lundy. In 1920, two of his brothers perished in a clamming accident. Never again would Lundy set foot in a boat. With his surviving brother and his two sisters, he opened a restaurant on Emmons Avenue, built on pilings jutting out into Sheepshead Bay. From the first, Lundy's was a howling success, no doubt aided by free-flowing liquor. Lundy used his boat *Elaine* to run rum during Prohibition while authorities looked the other way.

The restaurant was immensely prosperous; Lundy bought a 7,000-acre farm in the Catskills, where he thriftily raised chickens for the restaurant.

In 1934, the city decided to widen Emmons Avenue, demolishing all buildings along what was called the "Clam Coast." Smaller establishments were ruined. But Lundy moved across the avenue, building the block-square, stucco, red-roofed mammoth, said to be in the Mission style. The original architects, however, acknowledging that Lundy poked his finger into every element of design during the four years of construction, disparagingly referred to the building as "Lundy style." The cavernous clam bar had crushed shells from the old clam bar embedded in its walls, awnings embellished with a Lundy-fabricated coat of arms, and stained-glass windows.

Lundy was a demon to work for—he actually punched waiters on more than one occasion—and he drove his cooks to keep the food up to his expectations. They did, too.

Darkly improbable misfortunes fell to Lundy's lot: he was kidnapped, robbed, and finally swindled of over eleven million dollars. Even his death in 1977 was deemed suspicious. Two years later the restaurant closed.

Now there are plans to revive the restaurant, reestablishing Brooklyn's foremost fishhouse in stuccoed splendor. May Lundy's rise again!

In its time the vast restaurant—it could seat 2,800 diners—was a focal point of Brooklyn dining. Patrons came from elsewhere, of course ("all the way from Europe," publicists boasted), but it really belonged to the Borough. Swallowing a raw clam became a rite of passage for young men ("Come on, Sam! You can do it!"), and a girl's "Sweet Sixteen" was inaugurated with her first lobster.

. . . .

The Memory Lane that leads to Lundy's seafood restaurant on Ocean and Emmons avenues is wider than an interstate highway. More crowded, too. The biscuits! The clam chowder! The Shore Dinner! Even the butter pats evoke deep sighs of nostalgia. Loyal Lundyites recount the glory days:

OCEAN and EMMONS AVENUES in SHEEPSHEAD BAY, N. Y.

Phones — Nightingale 6-9870

COCKTAIL SPECIAL — VODKA MARTINI .65

A La Carte

	Celery	.40	Tomato Juice	.15

RELISHES COCKTAILS

Celery	.40	
Lobster Cocktail	1.75	Olives	.30
Shrimp Cocktail	1.00	Oyster Cocktail	.60
		Crabmeat Cockt'l	1.00

Tomato Juice ...... .15
Clam Juice Cockt'l .30
Clam Cocktail .... .60

OYSTERS and CLAMS

Clam Chowder	.45
Cup	.25
Clam Bisque	.45
Cup	.25
Clam Broth	.45
Cup	.25
Fish Chowder	.45
Cup	.25

Chicken Soup, Cup .... .25
Oysters on Half Shell .... .60
Oyster Stew 1.00
Oyster Pan Roast 1.50
Clams on Half Shell .... .60
Clam Stew 1.00
Soft Clam Pan Roast 1.50
Steamed Clams 1.50

FRIED SEAFOOD

Oysters	1.50
Soft Clams	1.50
Hard Clams	1.50
Bluefish	1.50
Filet of Cod	1.50
Filet of Sole	1.50

Mackerel 1.50
Sea Bass 1.50
Sea Scallops 1.50
Shrimps 1.50
Smelts 1.50
2 Soft Shell Crabs on Toast,
Tartar Sauce 1.75

SALADS

Lobster	2.25
Shrimp	1.75
Crabmeat	1.75
Cold Boiled Lobster	2.25

Sliced Tomatoes .... .50
Hearts of Lettuce .... .50
Lettuce and Tomatoes .... .80

BROILED SEAFOOD

Lundy's Special Hot BOILED Lobster, Butter Sauce	3.00
Broiled Live Lobster	3.25
Bluefish	1.50
Filet of Cod	1.50
Scallops	1.50

Filet of Sole 1.50
Mackerel 1.50
Oysters 1.50
Sea Bass 1.50
Smelts 1.50
Shrimp 1.60

NEWBURGHS or AU GRATIN

Lobster ....2.50 Crabmeat ....2.00 Shrimp 2.00

STEAKS, CHOPS, etc.

Club Steak	4.50
Lundy's Special Steak Dinner	5.00
Lamb Chop Dinner	3.75
Chopped Steak Dinner	3.25
Chopped Steak	2.00

Half Broiled Chicken............1.75
Lamb Chops (2) 2.50
Ham or Bacon and Eggs 1.00
Fresh Long Island Eggs
(any style) .... .50

VEGETABLES and POTATOES

Corn on Cob	.50
Cauliflower	.40
String Beans	.40
Peas	.40
Fried Onions	.50
French Fried Onions	.50

Potatoes —
Julienne .... .45
French Fried .... .40
Lyonnaise .... .45
Hashed Brown .... .45
Baked .... .40
Boiled .... .40

SANDWICHES

Oyster	.60
Clam	.60
Scallop	.60
Shrimp	.60

Filet of Sole .... .60
Cheese .... .60
Ham .... .60
Egg .... .50

.40 Watermelon ...... .40 Ice Cream......... .40
............1.75

Tamara Engel's Testimony

"The biscuit pyramids at Lundy's were as much an architectural symbol of our Borough as the Brooklyn Bridge. The butter pats came on white squares of paper, gently folded up on all four sides, and the biscuits were warm enough for the butter to melt on contact. The thick, golden-brown Manhattan clam chowder—with plenty of clams, potatoes that were not too soft, and more than a hint of thyme—was delicious. This was the way to begin every dinner, especially the Shore Dinner.

"Now, Lundy's was not a perfect place. We had our complaints. It was the best fish restaurant, but we didn't like the catch-as-catch-can way of lassoing a table. There was no hostess, maître d', or numbering system for seating. If we saw a free table, it was a running dash to claim it. If no table was available, more often than not we found one where the people were eating dessert and hovered over them to claim it next.

"My father had a system of his own. We'd send him in first to scan the room for a familiar face. Nine out of ten times he'd spot one, and that secured the table. I have vivid memories of him pulling a chair up to a table and schmoozing with an old crony from Williamsburg, while we waited on the sidelines. As teenagers, my sister, brother, and I hated being introduced to strangers, but it was a price we were willing to pay for a fried-shrimp dinner.

"Service at Lundy's was hit or miss, and we often needed seconds of biscuits and the oysterette crackers already on the table before our clam chowder arrived.

"When I was sixteen, my steady boyfriend had something to give me for my birthday—a lobster. My first. We walked in through one of Lundy's many side entrances and found ourselves in the cavernous salmon-and-turquoise-colored dining room. The waiter helped me tie my little bib. I followed my boyfriend's lead and began with the claws. Ecstasy! Over the years I think we two held the record for taking the longest time to eat lobsters. Then came the finger bowl—elegant and needed.

"I've heard the rumors that Lundy's will be revived. Please tell me that will be possible! My parents left Brooklyn for Florida many years ago. I can accept never going home again, but not going back to Lundy's is even harder."

F.W.I.L. Lundy Brothers.

Mimi Sheraton

"The first restaurant I went to was Lundy's—I was small, and everything looked very big. That was sometime before 1930. This Lundy's was out on a pier, before they built the big place. I see in my mind's eye the windows overlooking the water, room after room of white wood, and the luminous reflection on the ceiling of the moving water. It was like being on a ship. I was in awe of the waiters; they were friendly, but they had a lot of style and dignity. I didn't want to do anything that would make them look askance at me. My parents usually had the Shore Dinner, but occasionally my mother would order something fancier, like lobster Newburg. I remember the restaurant on Sundays as a place teeming with people who knew each other—my parents had a lot of friends, and there was much table hopping.

"When the larger place opened, you could go there at 5:00 or 6:00 in the evening and find a long, long line—you might wait 25 minutes. Not longer, because the turnover was fast. There was a huge parking lot, and the restaurant was said to be the largest in the world."

Lundy's Manhattan Clam Chowder
Mimi Sheraton

This recipe appeared in From My Mother's Kitchen, by Mimi Sheraton (Harper & Row, 1979; revised edition published spring 1991). Says Ms. Sheraton: "After some trial and error, my mother devised the recipe below—as close to Lundy's famed chowder as she could get."

About 1 quart large chowder clams, with their liquor (18 to 20 large quahogs, or 3 dozen medium chowder clams, or 4 dozen cherrystones)
2 medium carrots, diced
1 large onion, finely chopped
1 stalk celery without leaves, diced
2 to 3 tablespoons unsalted butter
1 20-ounce can whole tomatoes, coarsely chopped, with their liquid
2 to 3 cups boiling water, as needed
Salt to taste
1 medium potato, diced
1 teaspoon dried crumbled thyme, or to taste
Black pepper to taste

❶ Trim the hard portions of the clams from the soft. Reserve both, as well as their liquor. In a 2½-quart stainless-steel or enameled saucepan, sauté the carrots, onion, and celery in 2 or 3 tablespoons hot butter, as needed. Sauté for about 5 minutes, or until the vegetables just begin to soften and become bright; do not brown.

❷ Add the tomatoes and their liquid. If there are 2 cups of tomato liquid, add only 2 cups boiling water; if there is less tomato liquid, add enough boiling water to measure 4 cups of liquid. Add the hard portion of the clams and a pinch of salt. Simmer gently about 20 minutes.

❸ Add the diced potato, the soft part of the clams, with their liquor, and the thyme; simmer for 30 minutes, or until all the ingredients are tender. Adjust the seasoning with salt and a pinch of pepper. ≫→ *Makes about 1½ quarts*

Note: This soup has more flavor if cooked the day before it is to be served.

Baking Powder Biscuits

No, this is not the authentic Lundy's recipe. But these little biscuits are light and delicious.

Until the real thing returns, they should keep you happy.

....

1½ cups plus 3 tablespoons all-purpose flour
1 tablespoon baking powder
½ teaspoon salt

4 tablespoons unsalted butter
4 tablespoons vegetable shortening
½ cup milk

Preheat the oven to 400 degrees F.

❶ Sift 1½ cups of the flour, baking powder, and salt together into a large bowl. Add the butter and shortening and, using your fingertips, rub the flour and fat together until the mixture resembles coarse meal.

❷ Make a well in the center of the mixture and pour in the milk. Mix together lightly with a rubber spatula, just long enough to form a dough. If it seems too moist, add some or all of the remaining flour.

❸ Knead the dough for about 30 seconds on a lightly floured work surface. Roll or pat it into a circle about ½ inch thick. Use a 1½-inch cookie cutter to cut rounds of dough. Gather the scraps together, roll out again, and cut more rounds of dough.

❹ Arrange the rounds of dough on a cookie sheet. Bake for 15 minutes, or until golden brown. Serve hot. ≫→ *Makes about 28 1½-inch biscuits*

▲ ▲

A Landmark Goes

Steve Barrison, an attorney active in Sheepshead Bay preservation, has always lived here. Steve remembers:

"When I was a kid in the mid-'60s, Sheepshead Bay was clear enough to swim in; kids used to dive for pennies. I would ride my bike down to the docks and watch the party boats come in. My friends and I never fished, but we hung around the boats in warm weather. The fishermen would lay their catch out on the docks, and people walking up and down would buy fish.

"We're bringing back Lundy's, but we've lost Captain Walter's Bar and Grill. The building was put up in the early '30s—it's had other names—the Lewis House, Popeye's, and Davy Jones. That gathering place was the center of this community. Everyone who grew up in Sheepshead Bay hung out there at one time. Working-class Scottish, Irish, and Jewish—middle-class kids and bikers. During the day, fishermen came in off their boats for a beer. The site is slated for condominium development. But as one of the bartenders said the night it closed, 'It's like a piece of your heart has been taken away.'"

Ethel Brody's Coleslaw

"My grandmother's coleslaw is sharp, and because it contains no mayonnaise it's never gooey. We like it as a side dish with meat," says Steve Barrison. Ethel Brody was born in Russia and lived in Sheepshead Bay from 1925 until her death in 1982, at the age of 89. "She was the quintessential grandma of all time," Steve says. "She'd watch us all, and she shoveled snow and swept leaves well into her eighties."

A medium green cabbage
2 teaspoons salt
2 carrots, coarsely shredded

½ cup white vinegar
¼ cup sugar
¼ cup vegetable oil

❶ Cut the cabbage into wedges, cut out the core, and make coarse shreds of the cabbage, sprinkling on the salt as you shred. Place cabbage in a large bowl and mix in the shredded carrots with your hands.

❷ Combine the vinegar and sugar in a small bowl and stir until the sugar dissolves. Toss with the cabbage, add the oil, and toss again. Chill and serve within one day. ⮞ *Makes about 7 cups*

3

Nationalities

The Italians,
Jews, Scandi-
navians, Irish,
Middle Easterners,
African-Americans,
Caribbeans, His-
panics, Polish,
Germans, Greeks,
and newcomers—
including their
family out-
ings, weddings,
delis, street fairs,
and so on . . .

Brooklyn is the greatest collection of neighborhoods in the country. Not just neighborhoods of place, but of community. People band together for all sorts of reasons: nationality, religion, language, cultural heritage. Of course enclaves change and evolve, and people move. But they know who they are and where they are going, and they take their foodways with them.

Of all the many groups that have lived in the Borough, its Italians and Jews have, perhaps, given the most flavor to what the popular imagination perceives as "Brooklyn"—colorful if fractured language, sassiness, and attitude. And food. All moviegoers know the little Brooklyn restaurant with red-checked tablecloths, straw-covered Chianti bottles, and beaming, plump proprietor. Jewish comedians, Brooklyn boys almost all, have brought the folks in Iowa and Tennessee their heavy-as-lead matzo-ball jokes, and Mama urging her son to "eat, eat!"

Some populations wax, some wane. There are fewer Scandinavians, Irish, and Germans now, more Poles, Russians, Greeks, and Middle Easterners. Large groups from the Caribbean and Latin America call Brooklyn home, as do arrivals from Pakistan and Southeast Asia.

Many different and delicious cuisines appear on the tables of Brooklyn. That's because people tend to stick with the cooking they know best, that comforts them and makes them happy.

MEDITERRANEAN PEOPLES
THE BROOKLYN ITALIANS

The Italians of Brooklyn have always been southerners, from Sicily, Calabria, and Naples. As with every other immigrant group, hard times and political unrest caused them to seek a home in the New World.

Many of those who arrived in the 1800s and later had been farmers, and even though most found jobs in the factories, a love of the land, of growing food, suffused their souls. In the gardens hidden behind the rowhouses in the communities of Bensonhurst, South Brooklyn, and Williamsburg are plum, fig, and cherry trees. In the evenings, men still till their plots, growing cabbages, zucchini, tomatoes, and grapes for homemade wine.

And those with no garden improvised. Celia Cacace's mother grew herbs and tomatoes on the fire escape. Dolly De Simone's mother placed orange peels on the lid of the coal stove, permeating the house with a warm citrus scent.

The food of Italian Brooklyn is robust, abundant, and varied. It is richer than in the old country. Embellishing spaghetti with meatballs is an American—maybe even a Brooklyn—invention. A groaning table signifies the good life.

Squash Blossoms and Johnny Pumps
Gowanus in the 1930s

Dolly De Simone and her friends grew up on President Street, between Nevins and 3rd Avenue. It was the Depression, nobody had spare money, but that never stopped the fun. Dolly, Catherine Del Pezzo, Jeanie Totillo, and Jennie Russo remember summers long past:

"In summer when it was hot we'd sleep on roofs and fire escapes. It wasn't scary, it was exciting. And the johnny pump—the fire hydrant —was on from morning to night with kids jumping in the spray. We'd

Happy times on President Street.

pick zucchini flowers early in the morning when the flower was open. We'd wash them, dip them in pancake batter, and fry them."

Squash Blossoms with Anchovy

*Y*ou can dip the blossoms in pan- cake batter as Dolly does, or use this recipe based on a beer batter.

Follow the cook into the kitchen and eat them as they come from the fryer, with a dash of salt.

3 tablespoons vegetable oil
½ cup all-purpose flour
Pinch salt
⅔ cup tepid beer, preferably flat
1 egg white

1 to 1½ pounds zucchini squash blos- soms, gently washed and patted dry
Anchovy paste
Vegetable oil for deep frying

❶ Stir the 3 tablespoons of oil into the flour. Add the salt and beer and stir until the batter is the consistency of smooth cream. Let the mixture stand for 2 to 3 hours at room temperature.

❷ Just before you fry the blossoms, beat the egg white until stiff and fold it into the batter.

❸ Place a dab of anchovy paste inside each squash blossom and gently press the petals together.

❹ Heat 3 inches of oil in a deep fryer, wok, or heavy pot until sizzling. Dip a blossom in the batter and let the excess drip off, then fry it until golden brown. Fry several blossoms at once, turning them with a slotted spoon. Drain on paper towels and eat them quickly. ⟫→ *Serves 6 to 8 as an appetizer*

▲▲▲▲▲▲▲▲▲▲▲▲▲▲▲▲▲▲▲▲▲▲▲▲▲▲▲▲▲▲

Coconut Grove
The Block Party

"**P**resident Street was really a party place," says Dolly De Simone. "What excuses we had for parties! Every saint!" Those block parties were celebrations of solidarity and a chance to let off steam; they were important social events in Italian neighborhoods. Dolly De Simone describes these great events on her block, President Street in what was then Gowanus:

"We started our block parties when the war ended, in '45. Each house put up a table in front of the door and set out the food. It was cooked food, too—no cold cuts. We had eggplant parmigiana, tripe, sausage and peppers, chicken cacciatore, stuffed peppers—you name it, we had it on the tables. Plus we had big kegs of beer, and sodas for the children. The parties became a tradition.

"At the first block party we fenced off this section with coconuts from Florida placed around the top of the fence. We called it 'Coconut Grove.' My friends and I love to get together and look at the pictures. We reminisce!

"We'd have a block party in July, and on Labor Day. The party started in the morning, and ended the next day. I used to go get the police permit, and they'd put up wooden horses and close off the street. After breakfast, we'd come out and set up the streamers and lights that went from building to building. We took up a collection for cases of soda and for the band. It played in the middle of the block, and the music never ended. Those were the days, believe me. Everyone was an intimate friend, or friends of the family. When the band rested, my brother, who had a candy store, brought out his juke box and all the records. Once we borrowed the piano from Our Lady of Peace School. We danced in the street, and it was standing room only! Some would get up on the stand and sing, if they had the nerve. A few drinks, clean fun, nothing dirty. If a person got overdrunk we gave him to the ones he belonged to, and they took him home. And all the kids were very good.

"The second day of the block party we made breakfast outside—nobody wanted to be in the house! We took our bacon and eggs and ham and cooked them on the charcoal barbecue. We put a piece of tin over the coals and set the skillet right on it. We made our coffee there too—it took a while, but you were afraid if you went inside your mother'd make you stay there.

"That first party, in 1945, started on Saturday morning and didn't end till Sunday night. And after eating for two days solid, the men had the nerve on Sunday night, when the food gave out, to order pies! Pizza pies! And no one went to work Monday morning—the bosses knew they wouldn't show up after that end-of-the-war celebration. The block parties only ended a few years ago. Times change."

V-J Day, 1945: Coconut Grove at the block party (Dolly is wearing glasses).

Mama's Steak Pizzaiola

This is based on a recipe of Dolly De Simone's mother, who cooked the sauce for 1 hour and finished the steak in a 350 degree F oven. Pan broiling on top of the stove is easier to control.

4 tablespoons olive oil
1½ teaspoons minced garlic
2½ cups crushed canned imported
   tomatoes
4 parsley stems
1 teaspoon crumbled dried oregano
Salt and freshly ground black pepper to
   taste
Water as needed
A 1½- to 2-pound chuck or top sirloin
   steak, 1 inch thick, at room
   temperature
Cooked rice
Grated Romano cheese to pass at table

❶ In a heavy saucepan, heat 2 tablespoons of the oil. Off the heat add 1¼ teaspoons of the garlic, reserving the rest for the steak. Stir in the tomatoes, parsley, oregano, and salt and pepper. Return the pan to moderate heat, cover, and bring to the simmer. Lower the heat and simmer, partially covered, for 20 to 25 minutes. If needed, add water by the quarter cup to keep the sauce flowable. Set the pan aside in a warm place.

❷ Pat the steak dry and season it lightly with salt and pepper. Heat a dry heavy skillet, preferably cast iron, large enough to hold the steak comfortably. Add the remaining oil and garlic, and heat until sizzling. Immediately add the steak, and over high heat brown it for 2 minutes on each side, turning it with tongs. Pour the sauce over the steak, cover it, and cook over moderate heat for 10 to 20 minutes, depending on how rare or well done you like it.

❸ Scrape off the sauce and transfer the steak to a cutting board. Slice it thin, transfer the slices to a heated platter, and pour a little of the sauce over them. Serve the rest of the sauce in a heated gravy boat, along with the rice and grated cheese. ⇛ *Serves 4*

Josie's Pork Chops
(Costolette de Maiali alla Pizzaiola)

Josie De Simone, Dolly's sister-in-law, makes these delicious pork chops.

6 green or red bell peppers, or a
    combination
5 tablespoons olive oil
8 center-cut pork chops, ½ inch thick
3 medium onions, thinly sliced
½ teaspoon dried oregano, crumbled

½ bay leaf
½ cup red or white wine, or water
2 8-ounce cans Del Monte or another
    seasoned tomato sauce
3 sprigs Italian parsley, including stems
Salt and pepper to taste

Preheat the oven to 375 degrees F.

❶ Core and seed the peppers, and cut each into 4 to 8 strips.

❷ In a large heavy skillet, heat the oil until sizzling. Pat the chops dry and brown on both sides for 2 minutes; do this in batches. Place the chops in a single layer in a large, low baking dish.

❸ Add the onions to the skillet and cook, stirring often, for 5 minutes, or until soft. Use a slotted spoon to lift the onions, leaving as much oil as possible in the skillet. Cover the chops with the onions. In the remaining oil cook the pepper strips for several minutes until they begin to soften. Transfer them to the pan with the chops.

❹ Pour off most of the oil in the pan. Add the oregano, bay leaf, and wine and boil briskly, scraping up any bits of meat. Reduce the liquid to ¼ cup.

❺ Stir in the tomato sauce and parsley sprigs and season to taste with salt and pepper. Bring the sauce to the boil and pour it over the chops.

❻ Cover the pan tightly with aluminum foil. Bake in the center of the oven for 1 hour, or until tender. After ½ hour, remove the foil and turn the chops. If the sauce is too thick, add a little water. Replace the foil and reduce the heat to 350 degrees F for the last ½ hour of cooking. Serve the chops accompanied by rice. ➺ *Serves 4 to 6*

Tripe President Street Style

Based on a recipe by Jeanie Totillo, a friend of Dolly De Simone. Dolly says that tripe sandwiches are popular. At Football Weddings, they were reserved for the family.

2 pounds ready-to-cook honeycomb tripe
¼ cup olive oil
1 cup chopped onion
½ cup finely chopped celery
4 medium garlic cloves, peeled and crushed
2 teaspoons tomato paste
1 28-ounce can peeled Italian tomatoes
1 teaspoon salt
½ teaspoon crushed dried marjoram or oregano
1 small dried red pepper (*peperoncino*), or ¼ teaspoon red pepper flakes
½ cup water
1 cup or more freshly grated cheese, preferably a mixture of Parmesan and Romano, to pass at table

Preheat the oven to 350 degrees F.

❶ Cut the tripe into 2 × ½-inch strips. In a large pot, boil 4 quarts water and immerse the tripe strips. Cover and let return to the boil. Then lower the heat and boil, uncovered, for 15 minutes. Drain the tripe strips.

❷ Meanwhile, heat the oil in a heavy casserole until it barely sizzles. Add the onion and celery, and cook until soft and golden, stirring often, about 8 minutes. Add the garlic cloves and cook, stirring, for 2 minutes longer.

❸ Add the tripe strips and the remaining ingredients, except the cheese, to the casserole. Mix well, crushing the tomatoes with a wooden spoon. Bring to the boil on the top of the stove. Cover the casserole and place it in the center of the oven.

❹ Bake for 3 hours, stirring every hour. Add a little water if the mixture seems dry. The dish is cooked when the tripe is very tender when pierced with a knife point, and the sauce is thickened. Serve in deep soup plates, and pass the grated cheese. ⫸ *Serves 6*

The Football Wedding

At the end of World War II and into the 1950s, many of Brooklyn's young Italian couples chose to have what came to be known as the Football Wedding. It was simple, it was inexpensive, all the relatives and friends could pile into the hall, and everybody had a wonderful time. Sometimes the hall was hired, sometimes it was the basement of the church, or the meeting place of the Catholic Youth Organization. Why the name, Football Wedding? To be blunt, the name arose from the custom of pitching sandwiches from one side of the hall to the other. "Hey, Tony, send me a capocol'!" came a cry, and Tony obligingly snapped a neatly packed cold-cut sandwich on a roll to the hungry guy across the room. These receptions may not have been grand, but they are fondly remembered:

Joe Laurice met his wife Theresa in 1947, at a Football Wedding at the Tropic Isle, a hall across the street from the Brooklyn Paramount: "I asked her for a dance, and I said, 'I'm going to dance at your wedding.' She was only seventeen, and her mother made us wait three years before we got married. The night I met her, two guys got into a fight and the cops came and threw us all out.

"We were married on November 12, 1950, at Our Lady of Guadalupe in Bensonhurst. The reception began about five o'clock and went on till eleven. You could buy 100 sandwiches for $25. You got capocol', salami, ham and cheese, provolone on rolls. A big wedding cake, trays of Italian pastries, and pitchers of beer. Sodas, too.

"I think there's nothing like a Football Wedding. Today's weddings are a waste of food and money. In the old days, you ate all the sandwiches you wanted, and then

Guests at a Football Wedding, Our Lady of Peace Youth Center, 1958.

you put some in bags to take to work the next day."

"My wedding was in June of 1945," recalls Edith Romanelli. "It was in Our Lady of Grace in Gravesend. After the wedding, we went to a photographic studio, then back to the church to our reception in the basement. There were no tables, but chairs were placed around the edge of the room. We had pitchers of beer, soft drinks, and of course the sandwiches I and my bridesmaids had put together the night before. We had little dishes of olives, mustard, and mayonnaise. Joe, my husband, and I can't agree if there was a cake or not. He says yes, but I just recall trays of cookies. We had a small band, and before ending with a wedding march around the hall we formed a conga line."

"I got St. Vincent de Paul's CYO hall for my reception," says Lena Gaimaro. "That was in 1946. My father brought the tablecloths and glasses because he was a waiter. We bought the sandwiches from the corner grocery store. When the windows were opened, the kids

Joe and Edith Romanelli, 1946.

threw sandwiches down to their friends on the street below. We gave out little heart-shaped boxes of sugar-coated almonds, which were called confetti. My brother had the big catered affair, but I was satisfied with this kind of wedding."

"The night before the wedding, the bridesmaids and ushers—and there could be as many as twelve of each—came to the bride's house and made sandwiches," remembers Dolly De Simone. "The mother would stand over them and say, 'Put on a little more salami!' My mother made tripe sandwiches too, but these were special for the family. And you could bring all the kids, no limitation. People brought shopping bags to take home extra sandwiches."

Recipe for a Football Wedding

1,000 assorted sandwiches: capocollo, salami, provolone, ham and cheese
Limitless sodas and pitchers of beer

1 band
Wedding cake or trays of pastries
Hundreds of relatives and friends

▲▲▲▲▲▲▲▲▲▲▲▲▲▲▲▲▲▲▲▲▲▲▲▲▲▲▲▲

Marvels with a Nickel
Red Hook in the 1940s

Celia Cacace, a community volunteer, grew up on Rapelye Street in South Brooklyn. ("Don't call it Carroll Gardens!" she says fiercely. "That's a made-up gentrified name.") When she was thirteen, the family moved to Van Brunt Street in Red Hook. Money was very tight, but her mother could do marvels with a nickel.

"In tomato season in September, my mother organized us nine kids into an assembly line making sauce. We had to wash and boil bottles, cut the tomatoes, take out the seeds, grind the pulp. We must have done twenty, thirty bushels every fall. She made her own tomato paste, too. She grew basil and parsley on the fire escape, and pickled mushrooms, eggplants, and peppers. My mother was a very dignified woman, but she'd do unusual things if she thought they were appropriate. For example, she'd go to the Army and Navy store and buy bib-front dungarees, to wear picking mushrooms in the countryside. And no one ever got sick from her mushrooms, either. She'd buy fresh pine cones on Union Street and put them on top of the coal stove. As they heated they opened, and we'd take out the pignoli nuts.

" 'The only things you ever show in public is the wash you hang on the line,' my mother said. 'Family business stays inside the house.' She did that wash in an old-fashioned Maytag, with a wringer. The washer was in the kitchen, along with a china closet, a small sink, the stove, and a slop sink. The icebox was in the dining room. There was a meter in the bathroom, and on Saturday night you put in a quarter for hot water. Besides eleven of us fitting into five rooms, when relatives came we got out folding daybeds. My sisters and I slept on the floor then, and we thought that was an adventure. The rest of the time we slept head to foot. The first time I had a bed to myself, I was seventeen. I got my brother Tony's room when he went into the service.

"To us kids, the stoop and the streets were life. In summer we didn't always have pennies for the Red Hook pool, so we opened the johnny pump—the hydrant. The parents would come down with food. It was like going to the beach! Summer was the time for making skate wagons out of wooden fruit boxes. We took the metal wheels off worn-out roller skates, nailed them to two-by-fours scrounged from the lumberyard, using nails pulled from the fruit boxes and straightened with a rock. Later on, my mother saved to buy me a hammer and a penknife. I still have them. To buy Red Devil paint for our wagons, we'd sneak up to our kitchens and take the empty milk bottles and return them for the three-cent deposit.

"We made googies in the street for marbles. A googie is a tiny pothole; the object of the game was to hit your opponent's marble into the googie. To make them we'd put paper into a tin can, light it, and hold it upside down to soften the asphalt. If a grown-up looked out the window and noticed the smoke, we'd run. Then we poked a hole in the soft asphalt. The biggest and best marbles were called jollabinos. If you had one of those, you were king of the block! You had a chance to knock more than one marble into the googie. The game was sort of like pool, without a cue stick. We played it kneeling.

"The docks were our resource. From there we'd get boxes, flatten them, and use them as slides on the stoops. We'd find balsa wood and make boats to float in the gutter after the rain or when the johnny pump was on. And when I was a teenager, we'd go to the docks and smoke! When my kids asked me, 'What was the worst thing you ever did?' 'Smoked without permission,' I said, and they got hysterical.

"At Mary Scollara's ice cream parlor, we'd take the juke box out on the sidewalk and dance. A soda was fifteen cents, and you could stay there all evening. It was the doo-wop era, and the guys harmonized under the street lights. I recall twin brothers, we called them Ham and Eggs. A cop used to come and disperse us; he didn't permit hanging out. We called him Snotty.

"You ate what was set before

Celia rides the South Brooklyn range, 1952.

you, always macaroni, meat, and salad. We did our homework around the table, listening to programs like 'Inner Sanctum' on the radio. On Thanksgiving, and from Christmas Eve through New Year's Day, there was a clean tablecloth throughout the day for when guests came. People were always welcome. If my mother was cooking for thirty, she'd make enough for thirty-five, just in case. To my mother, everything was a challenge. What a nice gift to have!"

Philomena's Calamari
(Celia's Mother's Calamari)

"All of us are proud to cook like our mother," says Celia Cacace. "My sister Linda put this recipe together from the way we cook: all by eye and hand, a little of this, a pinch of that. We recommend that you buy whole calamari, clean it yourself, and let it 'relax' overnight in the refrigerator to make it more tender. And don't buy large calamari—they're tough. We usually make stuffed calamari for the whole family, so it's hard to cut the recipe down. But if you want to do it the way we do, here it is."

If you're not in an Italian neighborhood, ask for squid (English for calamari).

6 medium calamari, bodies about 4 inches long, not including the tentacles

Stuffing

2 tablespoons olive oil

3 cloves garlic, minced

¼ to ½ cup minced parsley

Salt and pepper to taste

½ teaspoon McCormick's Italian Seasoning, or to taste*

¼ cup pignoli nuts

¼ cup raisins

1½ cups of soft bread pulled from an Italian loaf

2 eggs

½ cup Romano or Parmesan cheese

For cooking

3 tablespoons olive oil

2 cloves garlic, minced

½ cup red or white wine

1 tablespoon tomato paste

A 28-ounce can crushed tomatoes

1 bottle clam juice

½ teaspoon McCormick's Italian Seasoning, or to taste*

2 teaspoons sugar

½ cup of fresh whole basil leaves

1½ pounds linguine

❶ Put the calamari in a basin of cold water. Work near the sink; you will need running water. Lay each calamaro on a work surface and cut or pull off the tentacles. Cut away the hard little button in the center. Reserve the tentacles. Pull out and discard the innards, including the quill bone. Rinse the tentacles and bodies very well under cold running water. With your hands or a paper towel, rub off the pale lavender skin on the bodies. Rinse again and place in a colander to drain. (At this point either refrigerate the calamari or cook them right away.)

❷ Cut the tentacles into ¼-inch rings.

❸ Heat the oil in a large skillet. Cook the garlic, stirring, just until it begins to turn golden. Then stir in the tentacle pieces, parsley, salt and pepper to taste, Italian seasoning, pignoli nuts, and raisins. Cook over moderate heat, stirring often, until the raisins are plump, about 10 minutes.

❹ Put the stuffing mixture in a large bowl. Moisten the bread with water, pull it apart with your fingers, and add it to the bowl. Beat the eggs, and add them with the grated cheese. Mix well.

❺ Stuff the calamari lightly; if you use too much filling, they will burst. Sew the openings closed with needle and thread.

❻ Heat the oil in a medium-sized heavy pot and cook the garlic until almost golden, stirring. Add the stuffed calamari and brown them over moderate heat, turning them gently with a wooden spoon. When the calamari are browned, add the wine to the pot. Cook until the wine has evaporated, then remove the calamari. Set them aside.

❼ Add the tomato paste to the pot. Cook, stirring, for 2 minutes. Add the crushed tomatoes (breaking them up with a wooden spoon), the clam juice, Italian Seasoning, sugar, and basil leaves. Cover and bring to the boil. Reduce the heat and simmer for 2 hours. Stir occasionally.

❽ Add the stuffed calamari and cook for 1 hour more.

❾ As the dish ends its cooking time, bring a large pot of lightly salted water to the boil and cook the linguine. Drain it, mix with the calamari and sauce, and place in a large serving bowl. ⟫→ *Serves 6*

*If you cannot find McCormick's Italian Seasoning, substitute pinches of thyme, rosemary, savory, and sage.

▲▲▲▲▲▲▲▲▲▲▲▲▲▲▲▲▲▲▲▲▲▲▲▲▲▲▲▲

▲▲▲▲▲▲▲▲▲▲▲▲▲▲▲▲▲▲▲▲▲▲▲▲

Carol Alvino's S & M

"**M**y grandma Angelina Balsamo came to Red Hook in 1903 from the village of Terrazina in Sicily," says Carol Alvino, a baker born and raised in Carroll Gardens (formerly Red Hook). "And this is the S and M, as I call it, that she taught me, my mom, my Aunt Violet, and my brother Mike. We all make it just a little differently—this is my mom's version." Carol's mother, Prudence Alvino, serves this dish every Thursday evening.

Spaghetti and Meatballs

There is nothing typically Sicilian about these exceptionally tender, fluffy meatballs in a light and savory sauce. (It is the addition of water that makes the meatballs *so tender.) However, Sicilians appreciate sweetness; the carrots in both sauce and meatballs temper the acidity of the tomatoes.*

....

Meatballs

1½ pounds chopped beef chuck or
   round
3 medium garlic cloves, finely chopped
Dash hot red pepper flakes
¼ to ½ teaspoon crushed fennel seeds
½ cup grated carrot
⅓ cup finely chopped parsley
2 eggs
1¼ cups bread crumbs
1 teaspoon salt
1 cup water
Corn oil for frying

Sauce

2 tablespoons olive oil
2 medium garlic cloves, finely chopped
2 tablespoons finely chopped parsley
¼ cup finely chopped onion
2 tablespoons grated carrot
1 6-ounce can tomato paste
1 28-ounce can Italian crushed
   tomatoes
28 ounces water
Dash hot red pepper flakes
1 teaspoon salt
1 to 1½ pounds thin spaghetti,
   rigatoni, or any other dry pasta

❶ Mix all of the meatball ingredients together very well, using your hands or a wooden spoon. Form the mixture into sixteen 2½-inch balls. Chill until ready to use.

❷ In a skillet, heat a small amount of corn oil. Fry the meatballs until well browned, turning them gently with a wooden spoon. Reserve.

❸ Make the sauce. Heat the oil in a saucepot. Add the garlic, parsley, onion, and carrot and let them simmer over medium heat for 3 minutes, stirring constantly. Stir in the tomato paste.

❹ Cook the mixture for 6 minutes, stirring occasionally. Stir in the tomatoes and fill the can with water. Add the water, pepper flakes, and salt. Bring to the boil, reduce the heat, and let the sauce simmer, uncovered, for 1 hour and 15 minutes. Stir occasionally. Add the meatballs, partially cover the pot, and cook for 30 minutes more. Turn the meatballs from time to time.

❺ In a large pot of lightly salted water, cook the pasta. Drain the pasta when it is cooked *al dente* (just firm to the bite), put it in a warmed serving dish or platter and pour some of the sauce over it. Add the meatballs. Serve the rest of the sauce in a warmed gravy boat. ⮞ *Serves 6 to 8*

The Venerable Monte's Venetian Room

❶wner Nick Montemarano is proud of his establishment, and of the fact that it is the oldest family-owned restaurant in New York City. Nick's father and mother, Angelo and Filomena, opened their no-frills, home-style Angelo's Tavern in 1906. Nick was born in 1916, in the family apartment upstairs. Nick and his brothers, Rocco, Vincent, Michael, Peter, Angelo, and Joseph, worked in the tavern as they were growing up.

When the boys came back from the service after the war, Angelo's Tavern got a massive facelift and became Monte's Venetian Room, the landmark of South Brooklyn. Despite the name, most of the cooking is solidly Neapolitan. "Great food, great people, and a wonderful place to work," says waitress Marie

Mother Philomena and brother Joe in uniform.

Sessa. "I've been here thirty years, and so have most of the other waitresses."

Sole with Artichoke Hearts from Monte's Venetian Room
(Filletti di Sogliola con Cuori di Carciofi)

1½ pounds fresh sole fillets
1½ cups all-purpose flour
Salt and freshly ground white pepper
1 teaspoon paprika
2 tablespoons minced parsley
1 egg, well beaten with 2 tablespoons
    of water

2 tablespoons unsalted butter
1 tablespoon vegetable oil
1 package frozen artichoke hearts,
    defrosted and drained

❶ Rinse the fillets and pat them dry. Have ready a shallow bowl of seasoned flour, made by thoroughly combining the flour, salt and pepper to taste, paprika, and parsley. Have ready another shallow bowl with the beaten egg.

❷ Heat the butter and oil in a 10-inch skillet. (Add more butter and oil as needed while cooking the fillets in batches, as described below.)

❸ Dip each fillet in the seasoned flour. Shake off the excess flour and dip the fillet in the egg mixture. Let the excess egg drip back into the bowl, then dip the fillet into the flour again.

❹ Cook the fillets in the sizzling oil, adding at one time only as many as fit comfortably in the pan. Turn them once. Depending on their thickness, the fillets will cook in 2 to 3 minutes per side.

❺ Remove the fillets to a warm platter. After all the fish is cooked, add the artichokes to the pan and heat them through. Serve each portion garnished with artichoke hearts. ⫸→ *Serves 4*

▲▲▲▲▲▲▲▲▲▲▲▲▲▲▲▲▲▲▲▲▲▲▲▲▲▲▲

The Moonstruck Bakery

When the moon hits your eye like a big pizza pie, you're in Cammareri's, the Carroll Gardens establishment featured in the movie *Moonstruck*. Gilberto Godoy is now the owner, having bought the bakery from the Cammareri family in 1985. The Cammareri family had owned the bakery for three generations, and they still live over the store.

The film company found the unrenovated bakery perfect for their script about a young Italian-American baker in love with Cher. They even rewrote part of the script to include it. It was also a natural to include Godoy, a native of Argentina who came to Brooklyn in 1970 and has been a baker since the age of nine.

The smell of bread from the coal-fired ovens drove the cast past temptation. They gorged on lard bread (which contains cold cuts) for breakfast, cheesecake and cookies the rest of the day. Godoy played a baker called Ronnie Cammareri. He juggled his acting duties (he had one line) with regular business, which includes five thousand loaves of bread each day. Much of it goes to important New York and Brooklyn restaurants, such as the River Cafe. Not too hard a task for Godoy, who customarily works fourteen hours a day, seven days a week. Work begins at 10 p.m. In the afternoon, he sleeps, except for Tuesdays and Thursdays, when he coaches soccer for the Brooklyn-Italian Club. Godoy played professional soccer back in Argentina, but the bakery now comes first. "I was born in a bakery," he says. "I was born in bread."

Nelida Godoy selling at the Cammareri Bakery.

Michele Scicolone's Prosciutto Bread

Even Hollywood stars couldn't coax Gilberto Godoy to divulge his recipe for lard bread. Our recipe, suitable for the home baker, makes bread that is equally good, and contains no lard.

2 envelopes active dry yeast
1½ cups warm water
⅓ cup olive oil
3½ to 4 cups all-purpose or bread flour
1 teaspoon salt
1 teaspoon coarsely ground black pepper
1 teaspoon minced fresh garlic

8 ounces prosciutto sliced ¼ inch thick and diced (or a combination of prosciutto and salami)
1 cup chopped provolone cheese (about 4 ounces)
1 egg yolk beaten with 1 tablespoon water

❶ Dissolve the yeast in ½ cup of the warm water in the large bowl of a heavy-duty mixer equipped with a dough hook. Stir in the remaining water, oil, 3 cups of the flour, the salt, pepper, and garlic. Blend well. Stir in the prosciutto, cheese, and enough additional flour to make a soft dough. Knead the dough with the dough hook until soft and elastic. Turn it out onto a lightly floured surface and knead it by hand for 1 minute more.

❷ Oil a large bowl and place the dough in it, turning the dough to coat it with oil. Cover it with plastic wrap and let it rise in a warm, draft-free place until it is doubled in bulk, about 2 hours.

❸ Oil a large baking sheet. Punch the dough down and divide it into 4 pieces. Roll each piece into a 24-inch rope. Twist two ropes together, then form them into a circle. Pinch the ends together to seal them. Repeat with the remaining ropes of dough.

❹ Place the circles on the baking sheet, 2 inches apart. Cover with oiled plastic wrap and let rise until doubled, about 1 hour.

Preheat the oven to 400 degrees F.

❺ Brush the egg-yolk mixture over the loaves. Bake for 30 minutes, or until golden brown. Cool on wire racks. ⟫→ *Makes 2 loaves*

The Fifth Avenue Fish Market

The new truck, 1928. The little boy is John Savarese.

"There's been a fish market here for about one hundred years," says John Savarese. "The first owner was an Irishman named Murray. Then a relative of ours named Appecella came in. He sold it to Antonio Savarese just after the First World War."

The third and fourth generations of Savareses work in the store, the oldest surviving fish store in Brooklyn and one of the largest. Ferdinando, Anthony, John, George, and Andre all like fish, as did founder Antonio. "He lived a long time, and he said eels and porgies kept him healthy," says Andre. The fifth generation is growing up, and "We hope they work here too," says Anthony.

Jackie Savarese's Scallops

"We eat fish three or four times a week," says Jackie Savarese, who is married to Anthony. "I'm glad I married a man in the fish business."

....

2 pounds large scallops
1 cup fine dry breadcrumbs

1 cup freshly grated Parmesan cheese
4 tablespoons butter

Preheat the oven to 350 degrees F.

❶ Rinse the scallops and pat them dry. Dip each one first in breadcrumbs and then in the cheese.

❷ Arrange the scallops in a buttered 8-inch square baking dish. Dot them with butter and bake until they are browned and bubbling, about 25 minutes. Serve with white rice and a tossed salad. ⟫→ *Serves 4 to 6*

The New Little Italy

"**T**his neighborhood of Bensonhurst is now the real Little Italy of New York," says Father Ronald Marino, assistant director of the Immigration Office of the Diocese of Brooklyn. "The historic one in Manhattan is now only a row of restaurants; the Italians have moved out. Some six thousand Italian families arrive and settle right here in Bensonhurst each year.

"I go to Italy a lot in my work, and I love to visit the supermarkets. I notice that when I come home and shop in Bensonhurst, I see imported Italian products. If you were to go down to 18th Avenue and walk the ten blocks from 65th to 75th Street, you'd find everything you'd see in Italy, including baby food. Most of the imported things have American equivalents, but people want familiar brands.

"The Korean greengrocers, who are all over New York now, carry broccoli rabe and the green stalks called cardoons that the immigrants like. And these Korean merchants speak to the newcomers! I was standing in the fish store, waiting to be served, and a little old lady rattled off in Sicilian dialect just how she wanted the fish cleaned and prepared, and the Korean fishmonger understood *everything*. I was stupefied. I asked him how he'd learned. He said, 'How can you not learn Italian here? Nobody speaks English.'

"We have wonderful Italian delicatessens, called *salumerias*.

They all make their own sausages, and each store's is different. Same for the bread bakeries; each one mixes the dough in a special way.

"In this neighborhood we have a great feast, the Feast of Santa Rosalia, who is the patron saint of Sicily. The parish is called Santa Rosalia Regina Pacis. Santa Rosalia is a church, but Regina Pacis is a *shrine*. This magnificent votive shrine was built in 1950, as a vow for peace. 'Regina Pacis' means Queen of Peace in Latin. The plan was to close the smaller Santa Rosalia, but the Sicilians wouldn't have it. So we service both. Regina Pacis is still considered the mother church of Bensonhurst, and when the Italians have their local feast days, they come here from all the parishes of Bensonhurst. It's pretty much the

Regina Pacis votive shrine, Bensonhurst.

wedding capital of the diocese here, too. The shrine is very beautiful. What I'm proudest of is our little chapel of Mary, Mother of the Unborn. It is a great comfort to pregnant women of the community.

"My hobby is cooking. I've studied cooking in New York, and when I'm in Italy I'll go to a class, a seminar, or workshop. I don't aspire to be a chef—it's just for pleasure."

Pasta with Breadcrumbs, Catania Style
(Pasta con la Mollica Catanese)

Father Marino says to use the largest skillet you have; you'll put all the spaghetti in it at the end.

10 tablespoons olive oil
1 garlic clove, sliced
A 1-inch peperoncino (dried hot red pepper)
6 tablespoons anchovy paste
1 16-ounce can Italian plum tomatoes, drained and cut up

1½ tablespoons chopped parsley
⅓ cup coarse breadcrumbs, made from stale bread
1 pound spaghetti

❶ Heat 6 tablespoons of the oil in a large skillet with the garlic and hot pepper. Cook until the garlic is golden brown, then discard the garlic.

❷ Off the heat, add the anchovy paste, tomatoes, and parsley to the skillet. Return to the heat and bring to the simmer. Let mixture simmer for 10 minutes, mashing the tomatoes well with a wooden fork or spatula.

❸ Put the 4 remaining tablespoons of oil and the breadcrumbs in a smaller skillet. Cook over moderate heat, stirring constantly, until the crumbs are golden brown. (This color is known as "monk's habit.")

❹ Meanwhile, bring a large pot of lightly salted water to the boil and cook the pasta until it is *al dente*, just firm to the bite. Drain the pasta and put it in the skillet with the sauce. Mix well and cook over moderate heat for several minutes. Place the pasta on a serving platter and sprinkle with a spoonful of the breadcrumbs. Serve the remaining crumbs at the table. ⟫+ *Serves 4*

▲▲▲▲▲▲▲▲▲▲▲▲▲▲▲▲▲▲▲▲▲▲▲▲▲▲▲▲▲

Louise Tumminia and Family

"I was born in Brooklyn, and lived a good deal of my life in Benson-hurst," says Louise Tumminia. "During the war, when my husband was in the service, I and my babies lived with my mother-in-law, Antoinetta Scotto. She came from a tiny island called Procida, off the coast of Naples. She taught me a lot of my cooking skills, and a lot of recipes. The Genoese Sauce with Pot Roast [below] and the Panzarotti [page 94] are hers."

July 3/1948

Louise Scotto Tumminia and daughter Michele, 1948.

Genoese Sauce with Pot Roast

Although the sauce, or "gravy," is named for the city of Genoa, it is really Neapolitan in origin. And very rich! Traditionally pasta, either fusilli or mafalde *(a large noodle with curly edges), is served first with some of the sauce, followed by the sliced meat. Salad with oil-and-vinegar dressing is served next, on the same plate; the remaining gravy mingles with the dressing, and is delicious. As with other Sunday "gravies," the practice is to save some of the sauce for Wednesday night's pasta.*

A 4-pound pot roast, bottom round or rump
Salt to taste
1 tablespoon olive oil
1 cup water
3 pounds onions, sliced very thin
4 large carrots, cut in rounds

2 ounces Genoa salami, sliced into ribbons
2 ounces prosciutto, sliced into ribbons
Pepper to taste
Pasta of choice, 2 pounds or more
Grated Parmesan cheese, to pass at table

Preheat the oven to 325 degrees F.

❶ Choose a heavy pot with a lid that will hold the roast and vegetables comfortably. Salt the roast lightly—the sauce itself will be somewhat salty—and brown the roast in the oil, turning it often.

❷ Remove the roast, pour off most of the fat, and deglaze the pot with ½ cup of the water, scraping up any bits of meat. When the liquid has boiled down to a few spoonfuls, add the onions, carrots, salami, and prosciutto. Place the roast on top of the vegetables, pepper it, and add the remaining ½ cup of water. Cover the pot and bring to the boil.

❸ Place the roast in the center of the oven. Check often to see that the sauce is just bubbling; lower or raise the heat if necessary. Baste the roast often with some of the juices. Cook until the meat is tender and the vegetables have cooked down, about 3½ hours.

❹ Arrange to cook the pasta in time for the first course. Transfer the meat to a warm place. Put the contents of the pot into a blender or food processor and purée them. Pour some of the sauce over the cooked pasta, and serve it with Parmesan cheese. Follow this with the meat course. ≫→ *Serves 8 to 10*

Stuffed Artichokes

Mediterranean people—and Neapolitans and Sicilians are Mediterranean—like the combination of parsley and mint. These *artichokes are a mess to eat, but very good. Paper napkins are needed here. The recipe is Louise Tumminia's.*

4 small (but not extra-small) artichokes
Salt to taste
1 tablespoon red-wine vinegar
¾ cup fresh breadcrumbs

¼ cup Romano cheese
⅓ cup chopped parsley
¼ cup chopped fresh mint
Olive oil

❶ Slice off one-third of each artichoke top and discard it. Trim the stems so the artichokes sit firmly on their bottoms without toppling. Pull off any small leaves at the base. Use scissors to trim off the sharp points of the leaves. Wash the artichokes under cool running water.

❷ Have ready a large pot of boiling salted water to which you've added the vinegar. (Never use aluminum; it will discolor the artichokes.) Add the artichokes to the boiling water. When the water boils again, lower the heat and let the artichokes simmer until a leaf at the base pulls off easily. This will take about 20 minutes. Drain artichokes, stem side up, in a colander. When they are cool, gently spread the artichokes open and use a teaspoon to remove from their centers the tough tiny leaves and fuzzy chokes.

Preheat the oven to 350 degrees F.

❸ Mix together the breadcrumbs, cheese, parsley, and mint. Stuff each artichoke with ¼ of the mixture, beginning at the center and working toward the outside, pushing the stuffing down between the leaves as it is added. Press the artichoke leaves closed with your fingers. If they seem too floppy, tie them around the center with kitchen string.

❹ Place the artichokes in an ovenproof dish at least 2 inches high that is just large enough to hold them. Pour in ½ cup of hot water and 1 tablespoon of olive oil. Wrap the dish in foil; the wrapping should be sealed, but leave enough headroom for the artichokes to steam. Bake them for 45 minutes, uncover, and bake for 10 minutes longer. Drizzle with a little olive oil. ⫸ *Serves 4*

Louise Tumminia's Panzarotti

These Neapolitan potato croquettes are served at important occasions. They are a bit of trouble, but you can prepare them up to a day ahead and fry them when you like. *(Just cover them with plastic wrap and put them in a cool place; don't refrigerate them.) They also reheat very well: 10 minutes in a 350 degree F oven should do it.*

2 pounds boiling potatoes (about 4 large)
3 eggs, separated
½ cup freshly grated Parmesan cheese
Salt and pepper to taste

3 ounces mozzarella cheese, cut into ¼-inch bits
1½ cups fine breadcrumbs
Vegetable oil for frying

❶ Peel the potatoes and boil them until soft; drain them and mash until smooth.

❷ Stir in the egg yolks, cheese, salt, and pepper. Mix well, and let the mixture sit for a few minutes until it is cool enough to handle.

❸ Put a small amount of potato mixture in the palm of your hand—about 5 teaspoonfuls. (You can make the panzarotti larger or smaller, as you wish.) Pat the mixture to firm it, then make an indentation in the center with one finger. Poke a few bits of mozzarella into the indentation, then fold the mixture around it. Gently roll the ball on a surface into a sausage shape, taking care that the mozzarella bits are well enclosed; otherwise they will ooze into the frying oil. Continue forming the little sausages.

❹ Spread the breadcrumbs out on a work surface or tray.

❺ Beat the egg whites with a fork. Dip each panzarotti into the egg whites, then roll it in breadcrumbs. Set aside.

❻ In a heavy frying pan, deep fryer, or wok, pour oil to a depth of 1½ inches. Heat it until it sizzles when you flick in a drop of water. Fry the panzarotti in the oil, a few at a time, until golden brown, turning them once. Set aside to drain on paper towels. ➠ *Makes 30 medium or 40 small panzarotti*

Aunt Katie's Crescent Cookies

"My Aunt Katie was a fine baker," says Michele Scicolone. "She's gone now, but we think of her every *Christmas when we make these cookies."*

....

8 ounces (2 sticks) unsalted butter, at
    room temperature
⅓ cup sugar
2 teaspoons vanilla extract
1 tablespoon water

2¼ cups flour
½ teaspoon salt
2 cups finely chopped walnuts
Confectioners' sugar, for dusting

Preheat the oven to 350 degrees F.

❶ Cream the butter with the sugar, vanilla, and water.

❷ Sift the flour and salt together and stir it into the butter mixture. Add the nuts and mix thoroughly.

❸ Form the mixture into 2-inch balls, and roll each into a small rope. Place on cookie sheets, 1½ inches apart, bending them into crescents.

❹ Bake for 25 to 28 minutes, reversing the cookie sheets after 15 minutes. Let cool on racks and dust with confectioners' sugar. ➠ *Makes 36 cookies*

Linguine with Mussels and Anchovies

*"**B**oth my parents were wonderful cooks," says Michele Scicolone, a cookbook author and cooking teacher who lives in Park Slope, "and they passed their enthusiasm down to me." Michele's mother is Louise Tumminia.*

Use farmed mussels in this recipe, if possible. They are much cleaner than wild ones. Most fishmongers now carry them.

3 tablespoons olive oil

3 cloves garlic, finely sliced

¼ cup chopped fresh parsley

¼ teaspoon crushed red pepper flakes

2 28-ounce cans Italian peeled tomatoes, chopped in a blender or food processor

3 pounds mussels, debearded and scrubbed

4 flat anchovy fillets, rinsed and chopped

6 or more small Sicilian olives, rinsed and pitted

1 tablespoon capers, rinsed and drained

1 pound linguine

1 tablespoon chopped parsley

❶ Heat the oil in a large pot over moderate heat. Add the garlic and cook for 30 seconds, stirring. Stir in the parsley, pepper flakes, and chopped tomatoes. Add the mussels and cover the pot. Cook for 5 minutes, or until the mussels open. Use a slotted spoon to transfer the mussels to a bowl.

❷ Simmer the sauce, uncovered, stirring it from time to time, for about 20 minutes, or until it is thickened. Remove the mussels from their shells and discard the shells. When the sauce is ready, stir in the anchovies, olives, capers, and mussels.

❸ Meanwhile, bring a large pot of salted water to the boil. Add the linguine. Cook until *al dente,* or still slightly firm to the bite.

❹ Combine the drained pasta and the mussel sauce in a large heated tureen. Sprinkle with parsley. ≫→ *Serves 4*

Two Memories and a Frittata

A lack of ready money was never an excuse not to eat well. Brooklyn is part of New York City, but those with a will can find edible plants in unlikely places, grow vegetables in scraps of back yards, and make a feast with stale bread. Two friends talk about a father and a mother, and of a time when nothing went to waste:

Mary Hirschel's father, John Inella, was a conductor on the F train in the late 1940s and early '50s. "He brought his lunch to work every day," she recalls. "Last evening's leftovers. Veal cutlet or sausage if he was lucky, and sometimes it would be spaghetti, or peas or spinach. He'd put everything together in an omelet—add what would make it taste good, like onions. He'd buy a fresh loaf of Italian bread, make a hero sandwich, and heat it up on the radiator.

"Early on a Saturday or Sunday morning in the spring, when he wanted greens for salad, he'd ride the train out to Sheepshead Bay. He'd take his penknife and cut the dandelions along the waterfront where the fishing boats docked. Dad ate them raw with vinegar and oil, or cooked; he called them his dandelion catch. And he liked to pick green plum tomatoes from my grandfather's garden in Bensonhurst, and put them in an Italian omelet."

"That's a terrific taste!" says Alex Mastrocola. "Slice the tomatoes very thin, beat up eggs with a touch of water, add locatelli cheese, breadcrumbs, and sliced squash flowers if you have them. With salad and Italian bread, you can't beat it.

"I was born in 1910," says Alex, "and the family was very poor. When I was eight years old, I had two jobs. The first was helping deliver milk. I'd get up at 4 a.m. and come down with a lump of sugar for the horse. He'd put up his leg and we'd 'shake.' That horse knew the route—he had more brains than a human being. I got home at 8 a.m., had breakfast, and went to school. After school I shined shoes and sold newspapers.

"My mother made a terrific dish with stale bread. She made her own bread. When it got stale, she cut it in slices with a sharp knife. The bread was really hard, at least a week and a half old. She'd put the slices into

Conductor John Inella on the F train.

enough water to soften them; they had to be moist, but not soggy. She'd add salt, pepper, garlic, oregano, and put it in the oven—we had a coal stove—till it got brown. Then we squeezed on garlic juice, added olive oil, and sprinkled on red paprika. That and half a glass of wine was better than any steak you could eat."

Mastrocola's Frittata

This is a flat omelet that sets in the pan without being stirred. Using a nonstick pan makes it very simple to do.

2 eggs
¼ cup freshly grated locatelli cheese
2 tablespoons finely chopped parsley
Salt and pepper to taste
¼ cup grated zucchini, squeezed dry, or 1 sliced zucchini blossom

1 to 2 tablespoons olive oil
1 garlic clove, minced
2 tablespoons coarse dried breadcrumbs
2 green plum tomatoes, very thinly sliced from top to bottom

❶ Beat the eggs in a bowl and add the cheese, parsley, salt and pepper. Add the squeezed zucchini shreds, if you are using them.

❷ Have a plate ready to receive the frittata when you flip it. Heat the oil in an 8-inch nonstick skillet. Add the garlic and let it sizzle for a few seconds. Lower the heat, sprinkle on the breadcrumbs, and lay on the sliced tomatoes and the squash blossom, if you are using it. Let them cook for about 2 minutes, until they begin to soften. Stir the egg mixture and pour it over the tomatoes.

❸ Let the mixture set over low heat. Shake the pan gently from time to time. In 4 minutes or so the frittata should be fairly firm, though wet on the top. Shake the pan again and ease the frittata on to the waiting plate with its wet side up. Turn the skillet upside down over the plate, and quickly flip the two over. The bottom is now facing up. Return the pan to the heat and cook for an additional minute. Slide the frittata onto a warmed serving plate.

➤➤ *Serves 1 or 2*

▲▲▲▲▲▲▲▲▲▲▲▲▲▲▲▲▲▲▲▲▲▲▲▲▲▲▲▲▲▲▲

The Prince of Firehouse Cooks

There are some 3,400 uniformed firefighters in the Borough of Brooklyn. Danny Prince, of Ladder Company 156 in Midwood, is one of them. He's also an experienced firehouse cook, and a contributor to *The Firefighter's Cookbook* (Vintage Books, 1986). All proceeds from the book—over $65,000—have been donated to the Burn Center at New York Hospital–Cornell Medical Center, which serves all of New York.

"You work two day tours, then you're off a day. You work two night tours and you're off for three days," says Danny. Night tours run from 6 p.m. until 9 a.m., with dinner scheduled for 8:30. Scheduled, that is, subject to alarms. "That's the part that really hurts," he says, "when you're just sitting down to something great and a call comes in."

Because they're never sure when they will eat, firehouse cooks pretty much forgo most seafood, except for salads, and hot pasta dishes too. "I've sat down to too much ruined lobster and linguine with clam sauce to take chances," Danny says philosophically. He prepares a lot of chicken, soups, and stews, and "anything that can be zapped back to life in the microwave." It's a stressful life, and crews are now paying a good deal of attention to their health. "We use corn oil and 1 percent milk, and everybody drinks a lot of juices and bottled water now instead of sodas," he says.

This man is happy in his work. "Being with the Fire Department is the greatest job I can think of; no two days are ever the same— whether you're saving someone in a fire, a car accident, or with a heart attack, it's a good feeling to be helping—just a great feeling."

Danny Prince in full regalia.

Danny Prince's Blizzard Stew

"During a whiteout blizzard we were held over at the firehouse," Danny Prince recalls, "and we had thirteen for dinner. A few cops came over, then more, and the count was up to twenty-one. I was making stew and it was clear that I'd have to stretch it. No one could get out to buy any more provisions, and I didn't want to add more water. I put in a couple cans of V-8 juice, and the results were delicious. Ever since, the guys say, 'When are you going to make more Blizzard Stew?'"

Add the chili paste if you want a pleasant touch of heat. Quantities have been reduced from Danny's original stew. However, if you find yourself with a full firehouse, double the recipe.

2½ pounds chuck, shoulder, or other stew meat, cut into 2½-inch chunks
½ cup flour, seasoned with salt and pepper
4 tablespoons vegetable oil
3 pounds onions, cut into chunks
4 cups V-8 juice
1 cup canned beef broth
1½ cups water

½ teaspoon dried thyme
1 teaspoon Oriental chili paste with soybean, or ¼ teaspoon red pepper flakes (optional)
6 medium carrots, peeled and cut into 2-inch lengths
1 pound green beans
2 pounds new potatoes, peeled

❶ Dredge the meat chunks in the seasoned flour. Heat 2 tablespoons of the oil in a large skillet and brown as many cubes as will fit without crowding. When they are brown on all sides, remove them to a heavy Dutch oven or stewpot. Brown the rest of the meat, adding oil as needed.

❷ Add the onions, V-8 juice, beef broth, water, and thyme. Bring to the boil, lower the heat and simmer, partially covered, until the meat is tender, about 2½ hours. If the liquid reduces too much, mix water with beef stock half and half and add by the ½ cup. Add the optional hot seasoning.

❸ Cook the carrots, beans, and potatoes separately until they are tender but a little firm. Add them to stew and simmer for 5 minutes. ⮞ *Serves 6 to 8*

▲▲▲▲▲▲▲▲▲▲▲▲▲▲▲▲▲▲▲▲▲▲▲▲▲▲▲▲

A Wonderful Daughter-in-Law

Debbie Chechilo grew up in Bensonhurst, went to New Utrecht High, and loves the Borough. Her cooking gets the highest praise possible—from her mother-in-law. Says Louise Bove: "Debbie's hands are golden. My son is blessed."

Chicken Francese

Debbie finds this is a good company dish—you can sauté the cutlets ahead of time and heat them in the oven when you choose.

Debbie serves this dish with rice and mushrooms, and a green vegetable.

2 pounds chicken cutlets
2 eggs
½ cup milk
3 tablespoons minced parsley
3 tablespoons pecorino cheese, grated
¼ teaspoon garlic powder
1 cup flour

Vegetable oil, for sautéing
2 small beef bouillon cubes
1 cup water
½ cup (1 stick) butter, melted
3 tablespoons freshly squeezed lemon
   juice

Preheat the oven to 350 degrees F.

❶ Have the butcher pound the chicken cutlets as thin as possible, or do it yourself. Pat them dry with paper towels.

❷ In a shallow bowl beat together the eggs, milk, parsley, cheese, and garlic powder. Spread out the flour on a sheet of wax paper. Roll each cutlet in flour, shake off the excess, then dip it into the egg mixture. Let the excess egg mixture drip off, then roll the cutlet lightly in more flour.

❸ Heat a thin layer of oil in a large sauté pan. When the oil is sizzling, sauté the cutlets, a few at a time, until browned and crisp, turning once. Use more oil as needed. Place the cutlets in a single layer, or overlap them slightly, in a large ovenproof baking dish.

❹ Dissolve the beef bouillon cubes in 1 cup of water in a small saucepan. Add the butter and lemon juice and bring to the boil. Pour the mixture over the cutlets and place the dish in the oven until the cutlets are heated through and the sauce is bubbling, about 10 minutes.

❺ If the sauce is too thin, remove the cutlets to a heated platter and reduce the sauce over high heat to half its volume. Spoon over the cutlets and serve, or serve the cutlets separately with the sauce in a heated sauceboat.

≫→ *Serves 4 or 5*

Debbie Chechilo's Baked Sausage and Cabbage

1 medium head green cabbage
1 pound Italian rope sausage, flavored
   with cheese and parsley
2 tablespoons olive oil
2 cups finely chopped onion
1½ teaspoons minced garlic
1 6-ounce can Hunt's Italian-style

tomato paste, or any other tomato
   paste plus 2 teaspoons crumbled
   dried thyme
6 ounces water
8 ounces whole-milk mozzarella, cut
   into small cubes
½ cup grated Romano cheese

❶ Quarter the cabbage, core it, and chop it into small pieces, ½ inch to 1 inch. Don't shred it; you want the cabbage to have some body. (You should have approximately 12 cups.)

❷ Cut the sausage into bite-sized pieces. Heat the oil in a 5-quart heavy saucepot. Add the sausage pieces, onion, and garlic. Cook over moderately high heat, stirring often, until the sausage is browned.

❸ Add the cabbage and cover the pot. Lower the heat and cook until the cabbage has cooked through but still retains a little crispness, about 30 minutes. Add the can of tomato paste, fill the can with water, and add the water to the pot. Stir well and simmer, uncovered, for 10 minutes.

❹ Stir in the mozzarella and Romano cheeses. Cover the pot and let the cheese melt. Stir it occasionally. Serve directly from the pot, accompanied by warm Italian bread. ⫸ *Serves 4 to 6*

▲▲▲▲▲▲▲▲▲▲▲▲▲▲▲▲▲▲▲▲▲▲▲▲▲▲▲▲▲▲▲▲

"The Lily of Paradise"

When the Brooklyn–Queens Expressway slashed through the Williamsburg section of Brooklyn in the late '40s, it all but destroyed the Italian community there. The center of the community was, and is, the parish of Our Lady of Mount Carmel. The church, the second on the site, was demolished for the roadway, and the neighborhood was effectively sliced in half. The third home of Our Lady of Mount Carmel was built in 1950, on Havemeyer Street.

"I'm only the seventh pastor here," says Msgr. David Cassato, pastor of the present Church of Our Lady of Mount Carmel, "and the church was founded in 1887. In those days, the boats from Ellis Island would bring the immigrants up to the foot of Williamsburg. They'd climb up the hill from the East River and settle in their national groups. You had the Italians here, the Poles over there, the Germans farther along. There are eighteen Catholic churches in this area, and they were built as national parishes. Our Lady of Mount Carmel was founded for Italian-speaking people, and if you did not speak Italian, you weren't welcome. Catholics still identify themselves by parish, more than by neighborhood. If you ask one of my parishioners where he comes from, he'll say 'Mount Carmel,' not 'Williamsburg.'

"The people in this neighborhood are very strong. They are survivors. And they are very proud of their feast. It's a tremendous effort to build the *giglio* for it each year, and to dance it."

Father Cassato refers to the festival that takes place each July, called the Feast of Our Lady of Mount Carmel and Saint Paulinus. To be brief, Saint Paulinus is the patron of the town of Nola, in Italy, ancestral home of many of Williamsburg's residents. Legend tells that around the year A.D. 400, Nola's bishop, Paulinus, offered himself in exchange for children of the town captured by Turks. So impressed was the Turkish sultan that he returned Paulinus to Nola. The people met him with lilies, signifying purity of heart and love for mankind. Centuries later, the structure called the giglio came to be built in his honor, and carried in a procession yearly. In 1903 the custom came to Williamsburg, sponsored by a mutual aid society.

The giglio, which means "lily," is a pale blue, 3,000-pound, eighty-five-foot-high tower of wood and plaster, which is lifted on the shoulders of one hundred and twenty men. Casts of Saint Paulinus and the Virgin adorn it, as do cherubim and lilies. The men bear the tower aloft, with a band riding on it, in three-minute segments called "lifts." The lifts are highly ritualized; a leader, called a *capo*, barks an order. The band plays *O Giglio e Paradiso* (The Lily of

Paradise) and the men lift the structure, sometimes executing a rotation, a drop and lift, or a back-and-forth jiggle called the "giglio chacha." Elaborate "dancing" takes place in front of the church. The feasts of Mount Carmel and the Giglio have merged, and run from Sunday to Sunday in mid-July.

Clouds of pungent smoke rise from open-air stalls selling sausage and peppers, hot dogs and grilled steak. Other stalls vend hats and buttons ("Kiss Me, I'm Italian"), funnel cakes, Italian ices, and the stuffed turnovers called calzone. The mixture of food, religious devotion, and carnival exuberance is sincere, vigorous, and proud.

Dancing the giglio through the street.

Someone has described the Feast's effect on the community as "recharging its ethnic batteries." Says Msgr. Cassato, "You can close your eyes, stand on the corner, and believe that the 1950s never ended."

Calzone
(Cheese Turnovers)

Always sold at feasts, calzone— literally, "pant legs"—are the Neapolitan version of filled turn- overs that can be easily carried around: Italian knishes, if you will. These are typical street fare at feasts. Make the filling while the dough is rising. Michele Scicolone (see page 96) developed the recipe.

....

Filling
1 pound ripe tomatoes, peeled, seeded, and diced
½ teaspoon salt
8 ounces mozzarella cheese, diced
¼ cup freshly grated Parmesan cheese
2 tablespoons olive oil
2 medium garlic cloves, minced
8 fresh basil leaves, minced

½ teaspoon crumbled oregano
Freshly ground pepper to taste
Dough
1 cup warm water
1 envelope active dry yeast
¼ cup olive oil
2½ to 3 cups flour
1½ teaspoons salt

❶ Make the filling. Place the tomatoes in a colander, sprinkle with salt, and let drain for 30 minutes.

❷ In a medium bowl, combine the cheeses, oil, garlic, basil, oregano, and pepper. Add the drained tomatoes and toss.

❸ Put the warm water in a small bowl and sprinkle the yeast over it. Let it stand until it is foamy, about 5 minutes. Stir in the olive oil

❹ Make the dough. *Hand method:* Combine 2½ cups of flour and the salt in a large bowl. Add the yeast mixture and stir to blend ingredients well. Turn dough out onto a floured surface and knead it until it becomes smooth and elastic, 8 to 10 minutes. Add more flour if needed; the dough should remain slightly soft.

Processor method: Combine the flour and salt in a food processor equipped with the metal blade. With the motor running, add the yeast mixture through the feed tube; process until the dough is smooth and cleans the side of the bowl. Turn the dough out onto a lightly floured surface and knead briefly, adding more flour if needed. The dough should remain slightly soft.

❺ Place the dough in a lightly oiled bowl; turn it to coat it evenly with oil. Cover it with plastic wrap and let it rise in a warm place until it is doubled in size, about 1 hour.

❻ Punch the dough down and turn it out onto a lightly floured surface. Divide it into 4 equal pieces. One at a time, roll out each piece into a 10-inch circle. (For a very tender dough, wrap the circles in plastic wrap and let them rest for 30 minutes.)

Preheat the oven to 450 degrees F.

❼ Arrange the circles of dough on a large greased baking sheet, with half of each circle off the edge of the sheet. Place about ½ cup of the filling on the half of each circle that is on the sheet, leaving a ½-inch border of dough. Fold the dough over, forming a semicircle. Press the edges to seal them, then crimp them by folding the bottom edge over the top edge and pinching the edges at ¾-inch intervals.

❽ Bake the calzone in the lowest part of the oven for 20 to 25 minutes, until brown and puffed. Transfer to a rack and let cool for 10 minutes before serving. ➤➤ *Makes 4 servings*

▲▲▲▲▲▲▲▲▲▲▲▲▲▲▲▲▲▲▲▲▲▲▲▲▲▲▲▲▲

Jimmy Venezia

In a borough teeming with characters, Jimmy Venezia probably takes the cake. Which is only fitting, because this strongman/ballroom dancer/retired sandhog/boxer/professional cook makes one terrific cheesecake. Jimmy tells how he changed himself, by willpower and exercise, from a sickly weakling to a spike-bending powerhouse:

"I inherited the rheumatics. I used to be in bed thirty to forty days every fall until I was sixteen years of age.

"During that time, I started learning about the body, about food and exercise, and I started training. I built my own exercise contraptions because I couldn't buy what I needed at the store. I started running and jogging and doing pushups and chinning the bar. Then I went to strongmanism. As my joints became stronger, I started bending spikes, first with my hands and then with my teeth and my jaws.

I'd put a handkerchief around the head of an 8-inch spike to protect the roof of my mouth, and I'd bend that spike over. I've bent maybe ten thousand spikes in my lifetime. And I started picking up weights with my hair until gradually I was able to pull cars and trucks with my hair. I could swing a person around with my hair.

"I worked with the Ripley show for about five months: seven shows a day, six days a week. In the act I'd let somebody jump off a ladder—six, eight, ten feet high, depending on the weight of the person—and land on my stomach. If the guy was a well-trained athlete, it was okay, but with the volunteers, one foot landing on my chest and the other . . . I eliminated the stunt, too dangerous.

"Once a year Williamsburg has the Giglio Festival, and all our friends and relatives who moved away come back for that occasion. I

Jimmy expands his chest to break a chain, 1939.

cook for fifty or sixty people; I do a fresh fruit gelatin in a huge bowl shaped like a wine goblet, or I do my cheesecake. And I spike watermelons with rum. I use a hypodermic needle for that.

"I'm seventy-five years old. I boxed until I was fifty, but now dancing is my life. I'm into English ballroom-dancing, it's the highest dance. I do almost all the dances, rumbas, chachas, even disco now. But when you're solo, freestyle, it doesn't appeal to me. When you dance with a partner, it's beautiful. It lets me be free."

Jimmy Venezia's Cheesecake

Jimmy says, "Have all ingredients at room temperature and don't waste any time as you prepare the cake." Let the cake cool in a turned-off oven. "I usually make it before I go to bed and leave it in overnight."

Crushed graham cracker crumbs
3 pounds ricotta cheese
2 cups sugar
6 egg yolks
1½ teaspoons vanilla
½ cup sifted all-purpose flour
¾ cup heavy cream
6 egg whites
½ cup sour cream

Preheat the oven to 425 degrees F.

❶ Butter a 12-inch springform pan and sprinkle the bottom and side with graham cracker crumbs.

❷ Beat the ricotta cheese until smooth. Gradually add 1½ cups of the sugar, beating as you add it. Beat in the egg yolks, one at a time. Add the vanilla and flour, beating after each addition.

❸ Whip the cream until soft peaks form. Beat the egg whites with the remaining ½ cup of sugar until stiff.

❹ Fold the whipped cream and the sour cream into the ricotta mixture, then fold in the egg whites.

❺ Pour the batter slowly into the springform pan so as not to disturb the graham cracker crumbs.

❻ Bake the cake in the center of the oven for 10 minutes, then lower the heat to 325 degrees F. Bake for 1 hour and 15 minutes longer. Turn off the oven and let the cake cool in the oven for 2 hours. It will crack on the top and gradually settle. Remove from the oven and set the cake on a rack.

⫸ *Makes 1 12-inch cake*

▲▲▲▲▲▲▲▲▲▲▲▲▲▲▲▲▲▲▲▲▲▲▲▲

The Gaimaros

Lena and Lou Gaimaro have lived in Williamsburg all their lives. Lena says, "My father never let us put a pot on the table, and we always had a tablecloth. When I saw that scene in *The Godfather* when they ate in a sloppy fashion, I was offended by that."

Escarole Soup with Tiny Meatballs

Lena Gaimaro prefers to use spinach leaves in place of the traditional escarole. The recipe can easily be doubled.

6 cups Rich Chicken Broth (see page 178) or canned broth
1 small boned chicken breast, 4 to 6 ounces (optional)
3 eggs
½ cup grated cheese, a combination of Parmesan and Romano
⅓ to ½ pound ground chuck or top round

1 tablespoon dried bread crumbs
2 teaspoons minced parsley
1 teaspoon minced garlic
1 large head escarole (to make about 5 firmly packed cups), or equivalent in fresh spinach leaves
Salt and freshly ground pepper to taste

❶ If you plan to use the chicken breast, poach it in the broth for 4 to 5 minutes, or until cooked through but firm. Set it aside to cool, then cut it into strips.

❷ Beat the eggs and cheese together and set aside.

❸ Make the meatballs. Use your hands or a wooden spoon to mix together the meat, bread crumbs, parsley, garlic, and 1 tablespoon of the egg-cheese mixture. Roll the mixture into marble-sized balls and place them on a plate.

❹ Wash the escarole and slice the leaves crosswise into 1-inch pieces; slice the stems very fine. Add the escarole to the simmering broth and cook it for 5 minutes.

❺ Add the meatballs and cook for 5 minutes. Add the chicken, if you are using it, and stir in the remaining egg-cheese mixture. Bring to the boil, correct the seasoning, and serve in deep soup plates, accompanied by Italian bread.

⟫→ *Serves 4*

Lena Gaimaro's Linguine with Zucchini Sauce

Most probably this was a dish for Friday in summer or autumn, in the days when Catholics forbore to eat meat on that day. Actually, it is a light and pleasant dish for any time. The recipe can be doubled.

3 medium zucchini
3 tablespoons mixed vegetable and olive oil
1 large garlic clove, peeled and crushed

Salt and freshly ground pepper to taste
¼ pound linguine, or more
2 tablespoons chopped parsley
⅓ cup freshly grated Romano cheese

❶ Scrub the zucchini and cut them into quarters lengthwise. Cut each piece again, and chop into ¼ pieces.

❷ Heat the oil in a heavy saucepan until it sizzles. Add the garlic and cook it for 1 minute, turning it often. Add the zucchini bits and turn them to coat them with oil. Cover the pan and lower the heat. Cook for 20 to 25 minutes, stirring often, until the zucchini is completely soft. Mash it with the back of a wooden spoon and season it with salt and pepper.

❸ Meanwhile, bring a large pot of salted water to the boil and cook the linguine according to package directions. Drain the linguine, place it in a heated bowl, and pour the zucchini sauce over it. Sprinkle it with the parsley and half of the cheese. Toss and serve. Pass the rest of the cheese at table.

≫→ *Serves 2 as an appetizer or light luncheon dish*

▲▲▲▲▲▲▲▲▲▲▲▲▲▲▲▲▲▲▲▲▲▲▲▲▲▲▲

▲▲▲▲▲▲▲▲▲▲▲▲▲▲▲▲▲▲▲▲▲▲▲▲▲▲▲▲▲▲▲

Eels and Urchins in Bensonhurst

Joanne Alicia's recipe is very like the preceding one of Lena Gaimaro, but she uses even more garlic and onion. Joanne, who works in the office of State Senator Martin M. Solomon, remembers — with a shudder — the writhings that went on in her grandmother's house at holiday time: "She brought live sea urchins with spines home from the fish store, and eels, too. These creatures were swimming in the sink, and the urchins crawling on the table.

Those are things I'll never cook! I'll make a separate meal for my kids if they don't like what I'm eating, but if you didn't eat what Grandma made, all you got was a piece of bread.

"But I loved being at my grandmother's. She set out bowls of jujubes and little chocolates, and I'd sit there for hours watching her cook. That extended family is so important. It gives you a foundation that lasts your whole lifetime."

Pasta with Vegetables

1 pound thin spaghetti, or any short
    tubular pasta
4 cups mixed peas, and zucchini,
    cauliflower, or broccoli cut into small
    chunks (use any combination of the
    vegetables)

¼ cup olive oil
3 to 4 cloves garlic, minced
1 large onion, chopped
¼ cup water
Salt and red or black pepper to taste

❶ Bring a large pot of lightly salted water to the boil. Add the pasta and cook it according to directions on the package. At the same time, cook the vegetables. They should finish cooking at about the same time.

❷ Heat the oil in a large skillet. Cook the garlic and onions, stirring, just until they begin to brown. Add the 4 cups of vegetables and ¼ cup of water. Simmer, stirring often, until the vegetables are cooked through but not soft. Add the salt and pepper.

❸ Drain the pasta, reserving a little of the cooking water to add to the dish if it seems dry. Toss the pasta with the vegetables. ≫→ *Serves 4 to 6*

▲▲▲▲▲▲▲▲▲▲▲▲▲▲▲▲▲▲▲▲▲▲▲▲▲▲▲▲▲▲▲

Bamonte's Restaurant

If a place is really great, why move? Peter Luger's under the Williamsburg Bridge is all that's left of a once-thriving German community, yet it never lacks for patrons. Same with Bamonte's, tucked under the Brooklyn–Queens Expressway, which sliced through neighborhoods in the late 1940s. The restaurant was founded in 1900. "When my grandfather opened the place, it was called Liberty Hall," says Anthony Bamonte, the present owner. "Politicians and businessmen bought beer and wine, and my grandfather gave the food away."

Word spread, and by the time of World War I, Bamonte's drew crowds from Manhattan and Queens as well as from Brooklyn. The name was changed, but the club-like atmosphere remained. There is a red-painted pressed tin ceiling, a long bar, walls filled with photographs, and an open kitchen. The food is Neapolitan style, carefully cooked. Bamonte's is a place that understands garlic wonderfully well.

Celebrating the season: Christmas, 1946.

Bamonte's
Grilled Scampi

*S*campi *is the Italian word for shrimp, but in Italian-American restaurants and homes, "scampi" means broiled shrimp with garlic butter. This dish needs a lot of good Italian bread to sop up the sauce.*

1 pound large or jumbo shrimp

4 tablespoons unsalted butter

1 teaspoon freshly squeezed lemon juice

1 tablespoon dry white wine

Salt and freshly ground pepper to taste

2 teaspoons minced garlic

2 teaspoons olive oil

2 tablespoons minced parsley

Lemon wedges

❶ Shell the shrimp, leaving the shell on the tail and last small segment next to it. With a pair of scissors or a small sharp knife, slit each shrimp down the back and remove the dark intestinal vein. Rinse the shrimp under cool running water and pat them dry. Preheat the broiler to its highest temperature.

❷ Melt the butter in a shallow flameproof dish just large enough to hold the shrimp in one layer. Stir in the lemon juice and wine, and season with a little salt and a few grindings of black pepper. Turn the shrimp in the mixture, coating them evenly. Mix the garlic with the oil and spoon it on the shrimp.

❸ Broil the shrimp 3 to 4 inches from the heat for about 5 minutes, then turn them and broil the other side for 5 minutes. The shrimp should be lightly browned and firm and bouncy to the touch. They may need to broil a few minutes more. Transfer the shrimp to a heated platter with tongs, pour the sauce over them, and garnish with parsley and lemon wedges. ⟫→ *Serves 2 to 4*

▲▲▲▲▲▲▲▲▲▲▲▲▲▲▲▲▲▲▲▲▲▲▲▲▲▲▲▲▲▲

An Italian-American Sunday Dinner in 1960

Linda Romanelli Leahy recalls a typical Sunday meal at her parents' home in Gravesend: "This was the way Italian-Americans ate when I was a kid," she says, "and the meal originated with their parents. They didn't have meat every day—meat was rich man's food. So Sunday, the only day of rest, became party day. But it was balanced out; on Monday they'd have beans and escarole, and not much meat all week. It was changing in my time, and we did eat meat in the week. As people got more affluent this meal became almost archaic. My mother only cooks this way now for Christmas or Easter.

"My parents began cooking at nine in the morning. They were not big churchgoers. They'd send us four kids off—we'd get killed if we didn't go—but they cooked. My dad usually made the meatballs. They were always different; sometimes I'd love them, sometimes I hated them. No recipe—he'd just throw in chopped garlic and parsley, grated Romano cheese, egg and bread crumbs. Sometimes there'd be too much of one ingredient, too little of another. They were a little bigger than a golf ball. I used to be shocked at other people's houses when they seemed the size of cannon balls.

"The meal started about two o'clock. First we had antipasto, with

Linda Romanelli's First Communion, 1952.

olives, roasted red peppers, mozzarella, and pepperoni. My mother bought all that, and doctored up the peppers with olive oil, garlic, and parsley. We had the antipasto with Italian bread.

"Then we had the meat course, with all of the meats in the 'gravy,' as we called the sauce. The fried meatballs, spareribs, once in a while braciol', sometimes a big hunk of beef or pork which had cooked so long it was almost shredded. Then came the pasta, which went by the name of 'macaroni,' no matter what the shape. We'd mix it with ricotta and the gravy and grated Romano, never Parmesan. We always had two kinds of pasta, because all of us liked short things like ziti or rotelle except my father, who liked linguine or spaghetti. So every Sunday there was a battle over the pasta, and my mother wound up cooking two kinds.

"Then after the pasta we'd have salad, always lettuce, tomato, and onion, with vinegar and oil, never measured, and lots of salt. We ate it on the same plate and the little bit of meat sauce with salad was delicious.

"We'd clean up a little, wait about half an hour, and then we'd have the American meal. Roast beef, some kind of potatoes, broccoli or another fresh vegetable. Sometimes the broccoli showed up the next day cold, with garlic, oil, and lemon juice.

"After the American meal, I'd get sent to Cuccio's bakery for whatever pastry we were craving at the moment, or to Carvel's for ice cream. At Easter, though, my mother would make a Pizza Gran. Then people might drop in. As I said, we sat down at two, and the last coffee was probably served about seven."

Pizza Gran
(Traditional Sweet Easter Pastry)

"It makes me laugh to think that wheat berries are a newly discovered 'health' food," says Linda Romanelli Leahy, a cookbook author and consultant. "Neapolitan-Americans have always known how good they are. Italian stores always sold the berries, called 'gran,' before Easter but now health-food stores carry them year-round. I have heard that some Italian stores sell them already soaked, but I've never seen it. You can't keep soaked wheat berries too long; they ferment."

½ cup raw wheat berries, or
    2 cups cooked

Pasta Frolla (Pastry Dough)

1¾ cups all-purpose flour

¾ cup sugar

½ teaspoon grated lemon peel

Pinch salt

6 tablespoons unsalted butter, cut in
    small pieces

2 tablespoons vegetable shortening

1 large egg, lightly beaten

2 to 4 tablespoons ice water

Filling

¾ cup sugar

3 tablespoons all-purpose flour

⅛ teaspoon salt

2 cups (about 1 pound) drained ricotta
    cheese

5 large eggs plus 3 yolks

1½ tablespoons orange-flower water

1½ tablespoons rose water

½ teaspoon vanilla

½ teaspoon grated lemon peel

2 tablespoons finely chopped glacé
    fruit

❶ Soak the wheat berries overnight in water to cover.

❷ Drain the wheat berries and put them in a large saucepan with 2 quarts of water. Bring them to the boil over high heat, stirring. Reduce the heat and simmer about 45 minutes until the wheat is puffed and tender. Drain thoroughly. You will use 2 cups of the cooked wheat berries.

❸ Prepare the pastry dough. In a large bowl combine the flour, sugar, lemon peel, and salt. Cut in the butter and shortening until the mixture is crumbly. Beat in the egg and ice water, 1 tablespoon at a time, until a ball forms. Wrap the dough in plastic wrap and refrigerate it for 1 hour.

Preheat the oven to 375 degrees F.

❹ Prepare the filling. In a small bowl combine the sugar, flour, and salt. In a large bowl, whisk together the ricotta, eggs and yolks, orange-flower and rose waters, vanilla, lemon peel, and glacé fruit. Add the sugar mixture and drained wheat berries; set aside.

❺ On a lightly floured work surface, shape the dough into a round. Roll it into a circle ¼ inch thick. Fold the circle in half and gently lift it into an 8-inch springform pan. Unfold it and with your fingers gently press it to fit the pan. Cut away the excess dough and set it aside.

❻ Pour the filling into the pan. Roll out the remaining dough and cut it into four ½-inch-wide strips; place them over the filling in a lattice pattern.

❼ Bake the pastry for 1 hour and 15 minutes, or until the center is puffed and the crust is browned. Place on a rack to cool for 2 hours. Refrigerate the Pizza Gran for at least 3 hours before serving. When ready to serve it, run a knife around the rim of the pan before releasing the spring.

⏵ *One Pizza Gran*

Pizza Rustica

Not the conventional pizza, but a savory cheese pie, Pizza Rustica heralds the Easter celebration in Italian households. Linda Romanelli Leahy speaks: "While Mama was making the pie, Papa and his brothers would sit around drinking homebrew and playing pinochle. They were waiting for 12:01 a.m., the end of Lent, when they could break their Easter fast. (A tough group, they bowed to the church on this one.)

"Years later, my dad took over making the pie, and he'd 'hide' it under a towel on top of Grandma's chifforobe (she lived downstairs). The pie was never refrigerated, and he served it only to his friends; we kids got very little of it."

This is Linda's version of the pie.

Dough

3 cups all-purpose flour

2 teaspoons baking powder

½ teaspoon salt

½ cup vegetable shortening, or lard

3 large eggs at room temperature, lightly beaten

3 to 4 tablespoons ice water

Filling

2 pounds ricotta cheese

1 pound *toma* cheese cut in cubes, or 1 pound shredded mozzarella

7 large eggs, lightly beaten

¼ pound Sicilian salami, with peppercorns

¼ pound diced pepperoni or dried sausage

⅓ cup coarsely chopped fresh flatleaf parsley

2 ounces prosciutto in one piece, trimmed of fat and diced

¼ cup grated Romano cheese

Salt and freshly ground pepper to taste

Glaze

1 large egg, lightly beaten with a pinch of salt

❶ To prepare the dough, combine the dry ingredients in a large bowl. Cut in the shortening until the mixture is crumbly.

❷ Beat in the eggs and ice water alternately, 1 tablespoon at a time, until a ball forms. Wrap the dough in plastic wrap and refrigerate it. (The dough can be made up to 1 day ahead and kept refrigerated.)

❸ To prepare the filling, combine all the ingredients in a large bowl. Set it aside.

Preheat the oven to 375 degrees F.

❹ Remove the dough from the refrigerator and divide it into thirds. Combine 2 of the pieces and roll them out on a lightly floured surface to a rectangle about ⅛ inch thick. The rectangle should measure approximately 11 × 16 inches.

❺ Fold the dough in half. Carefully lift it and place it in a 7-inch × 12-inch × ½-inch baking dish. Press the dough onto the sides and bottom of the dish, leaving a 1-inch overhang. Spread the filling evenly over the dough.

❻ On a lightly floured surface, roll out the remaining piece of dough to a rectangle about ⅛ inch thick. Place the dough over the filling and pinch the overhanging edges together with your thumb and forefinger. Brush the top with the egg glaze and prick it all over with a fork, about 20 times.

❼ Bake for 1 hour and 30 minutes, or until golden brown. (The top crust will puff up, but it will settle in cooling.) Place the Pizza Rustica on a rack and let it cool for 3 hours. If it is to be eaten within 36 hours, you need not refrigerate it. Just cover it with a towel. ⫸ *One Pizza Rustica*

▲▲▲▲▲▲▲▲▲▲▲▲▲▲▲▲▲▲▲▲▲▲▲▲▲▲▲▲▲

Baked Ham

"I've been cooking since I was eight years old, and I've been making this ham since I was fourteen," says Anne Amendolara Nurse of Kensington, who teaches Italian-American cooking to professionals and home cooks, and works to make the James Beard House in Greenwich Village a center of American gastronomy. "My family is from Grumo, near Bari, on Italy's Adriatic coast, so naturally most of my cooking is Italian. The ham is not Italian, but I learned the dish as a young teenager from two big girls I admired. I cook the ham often for parties at the James Beard House."

A 14- to 18-pound smoked ham, presoaked if necessary
Whole cloves
3 cups pineapple juice
1 pound dark brown sugar
1 bottle dark corn syrup

Preheat the oven to 325 degrees F.

❶ Peel off any skin on the ham and score the fat in diamond shapes. Stud each diamond with a clove. Put the ham in a shallow baking dish and pour the pineapple juice over it. Bake 12 minutes to the pound.

❷ After 1 hour and 30 minutes, remove the ham and carefully pat on the brown sugar, covering the top of the ham. Slowly pour on the corn syrup, being careful not to disturb the sugar coating.

❸ Return the ham to the oven and baste it every 15 minutes with the juices. When the ham has cooked its allotted time, remove it from the oven. Continue basting it frequently until the ham is cool; this gives a beautiful glaze. The remaining syrup can be used again over yams, butternut squash, or sweet potatoes. ⫸ *Serves 18 or more*

Edie Romanelli's Struffoli

A *Neapolitan Christmas treat made by Linda Romanelli Leahy's mother, Edie. To avoid tedium, making* struffoli *should be a two-person operation: one to cut and one to deep fry. Otherwise, as the cook tires, the struffoli balls get bigger. With two at work, this takes about one hour to do.*

As with matzo balls, size and weight is a matter of fierce opinion. Do you like them big and cakey, or small and slightly chewy? Do you like them with or without chopped fruit? These are about the size of a very large pea, and somewhere between substantial and ethereal.

2 cups all-purpose flour
3 tablespoons sugar
2 teaspoons baking powder
¼ cup vegetable oil
5 eggs, lightly beaten
1½ teaspoons vanilla

¼ cup candied fruits, chopped
  (optional)
Oil for deep frying
1 cup honey
⅓ cup nonpareil colored sprinkles

❶ Add the flour, sugar, and baking powder to the bowl of a food processor equipped with a dough blade. Pulse 10 times to mix the ingredients.

❷ Pour the oil, eggs, and vanilla into a 2-cup measure. With the processor running, slowly pour the liquid through the feed tube. (Add the chopped fruits if you are using them.) Process, stopping occasionally to scrape the side of the bowl with a spatula, until the dough forms a ball.

To make struffoli by hand, combine the ingredients and knead for 5 to 10 minutes, or until the dough forms a ball.

❸ Put the ball of dough on a lightly floured work surface. Knead it gently with floured hands and divide it into 10 equal pieces.

❹ Using the palms of the hands, roll out each ball on a work surface into a rope about 18 inches long and ½ inch thick. Cover the ropes with a damp cloth while you heat the oil.

❺ Pour 2 inches of oil into a wok, deep fryer, or deep saucepan. Heat slowly until a drop of water flicked on the surface sizzles.

❻ Cut each rope into ¼-inch pieces, then cut the pieces in half.

❼ Tip about half the pieces into the hot oil, and turn with a slotted metal spoon until golden brown, a matter of seconds. Place on paper towels or paper bags to drain. Transfer to a large bowl.

❽ Keep slicing and frying struffoli until all are cooked. Mix in the honey. Sprinkle with the nonpareils. Keep at room temperature, covered with plastic wrap. Serve throughout Christmas week mounded in glass bowls, with or without spoons; from time to time add more nonpareils for a fresh appearance.

≫→ *Makes 8 cups*

Panelle

Panelle, "little breads" made of chick-pea flour, are a standard at street fairs and the old-time Sicilian snack shops called focaccerie. At Joe's of Avenue U, the ladies who lunch are partial to Panelle Rolls. They are the snack of choice at Ferdinando's in Carroll Gardens, too. A one-inch stack of panelle is topped with a scoop of ricotta cheese (Ferdinando's adds cacciocavallo cheese) and piled on a sesame-seed bun. No special sauce.

Buy chick-pea flour at a store specializing in Italian goods.

3 cups water
1¾ cups chick-pea flour (½ pound)
½ teaspoon salt
Pepper to taste

2 tablespoons chopped parsley
¼ cup grated pecorino or Parmesan cheese
Vegetable oil for deep frying

❶ Pour the water into a blender or the bowl of a food processor equipped with a metal blade. Stir in the chick-pea flour and whirl to blend. Transfer the mixture to a heavy saucepan. Stir in the salt, pepper, parsley, and cheese.

❷ Cook the mixture for 15 minutes, stirring constantly, until the dough is thick and easily comes away from the side of the pan.

❸ Pack the dough into a 3-cup loaf mold (or use smaller, individual molds). Chill thoroughly.

❹ Using a sharp knife, cheese wire, or tautly held length of dental floss, cut the loaf into pieces about 3 inches by 2 inches. (If the dough is too soft to cut, measure it out by teaspoon.)

❺ Pour oil to a depth of ¾ inch into a heavy frying pan, deep fryer, or wok. Heat the oil until it sizzles when you flick in a drop of water. Fry the panelle, a few at a time, turning them once. They will turn golden brown in 3 to 5 minutes and will puff slightly. Set them to drain on paper towels. Serve them hot or at room temperature; don't refrigerate them. Panelle stay crisp for some time. They are excellent with drinks. ⇒➔ *Makes about 50 panelle*

Sorting Lentils in Gravesend

Gioia Timpanelli, a poet who is also a professional storyteller, recalls a precious moment of her childhood:

"Sometimes, on a late afternoon in March, I would come home from school to find the special Brooklyn end-of-winter ocean light streaming through the kitchen window, falling on my grandmother and the mound of lentils on the table before her. She had taken them from jars stored in the pantry and was about to spend a bit of time sorting through them to make a good thick lentil and pasta *minestra*.

"Now, I would hate to think I have given an inaccurate picture of my grandmother: Giuseppina Milano Timpanelli did exquisite embroidery, was known for her equanimity and good nature, loved music and reading. And yet my memory holds this luminous picture of her, sorting the lentils in the way, I suppose, generations had done before her. She would pull a few lentils from the heap with a bent index finger and draw them to her, discarding any bits of dirt, tiny stones or chaff, and then with an unbroken motion push the clean lentils into the waiting pot on her lap. She never asked for help, but I always got a bowl, sat down beside her and began sorting in the same manner. How wonderful it was to be so busy for a time, to patiently touch each small lentil so carefully, to work quietly and steadily at a useful activity that brought peace and a feeling of community through this shared gesture. I am sure that the serene and natural way my grandmother always worked had much to do with how good the lentil minestra tasted on those last days of winter."

Giuseppina and Vincenzo Timpanelli taking coffee in their Gravesend garden, 1936.

Lentil and Pasta Minestra

A minestra is a thick soup, the main dish of a meal. This one frugally uses up broken strands of pasta, which are then further broken into a size that just fits a soup spoon. Pecorino Romano cheese, *black pepper, and a cruet of olive oil accompany the minestra to the table. Those who choose to may pour a thin X of olive oil over the minestra.*

1 cup brown lentils
1 tablespoon olive oil
1 cup finely chopped onions
½ cup finely chopped celery
1 bay leaf
5 cups water
½ teaspoon salt

1 large Knorr or Maggi chicken bouillon cube (optional)
1 cup broken pasta: spaghetti or linguine
Extra-virgin olive oil
Grated pecorino Romano cheese

❶ Sort the lentils, and rinse them in a sieve. Set aside. Heat the oil in a large saucepan and add the onions and celery. Cook them, stirring, for about 5 minutes, until they are limp and fragrant. Add the lentils, bay leaf, water, and salt. Bring to the boil, lower the heat, cover the pot, and simmer for 20 minutes. Add the bouillon cube, if you are using it, and cook the soup 5 minutes longer. If you do not use the bouillon cube, add an additional teaspoon of salt. Set the pot aside, covered.

❷ As the lentils are cooking, bring a pot of lightly salted water to the boil. Add the pasta and cook it until it is fairly soft. Drain the pasta and add it to the soup. Serve accompanied by a cruet of olive oil, grated cheese, and a pepper mill. ➛ *Serves 4, heartily*

Pork or Beef?
Only Nana Knew

Marie Simmons, a culinary professional who lives in Clinton Hill, tells the story of her grandmother's Christmas soup: "My grandmother Antoinette Abbruzzese, whom we called Nana, died recently at the age of 98, but she left us the tradition of her Christmas soup. It's a rich chicken broth, thickened with farina and threads of beaten egg, and embellished with the most endearing little meatballs. During Nana's last years, her daughter, my Aunt Tess, took over the soup-making under Nana's eye. Retired after 40 years of school-teaching, Aunt Tess knows just how to recruit 'volunteers' for her Christmas Eve meatball assembly line from among her 30 nieces, nephews, grandnieces, and grandnephews. Aunt Tess insists that the meatballs are made of lean ground beef, but I, who constantly quizzed Nana about her wonderful recipes, am certain she said they were made of pork. So, pork or beef—it's up to you!"

Nana's Christmas Soup

A 4-pound chicken
12 cups water
2 medium carrots, pared
1 large onion, skin on, halved
1 bay leaf
Sprig of parsley
¼ cup fine dry breadcrumbs
¼ cup plus 2 tablespoons cold water
8 ounces moderately lean ground pork
   or beef

2 extra large eggs
2 tablespoons grated Parmesan cheese
½ clove garlic, crushed
Salt
Freshly ground black pepper
⅓ cup farina
Grated Parmesan cheese, to pass at
   table

❶ *One or two days before serving:* Rinse the chicken well under running water; pull off any clumps of fat and discard them. Place the chicken in a large soup pot and add 12 cups of water, the carrots, onion, bay leaf, and parsley. Bring to a slow simmer over moderate heat; skim foam from surface as necessary. Let the chicken simmer for 2 hours; do not let it boil. Remove the chicken from the heat and let it cool in the broth for 1 hour. Remove it to a platter. Discard all vegetables except the carrots. Remove them, wrap them in plastic wrap, and refrigerate them.

❷ Pull the meat from the bones and shred it into bite-sized pieces. Discard the bones, gristle, and skin. Put the chicken meat in a bowl, add a ladleful of broth, cover, and refrigerate. Refrigerate the remaining broth, covered, until the following day.

❸ Next day, lift off and discard the solid fat covering the chilled broth. Pour about ½ cup of broth into a measuring cup and reserve for later. Pour the remaining broth into a large soup pot; cover and heat to a gentle boil. Remove the carrots and chicken pieces from the refrigerator and let stand at room temperature until ready to use.

❹ Meanwhile, combine the breadcrumbs with the ¼ cup plus 2 tablespoons of cold water in a bowl. Let them stand until the crumbs have absorbed all the water, about 10 minutes. Add the ground meat, 1 of the eggs, the cheese, garlic, ½ teaspoon of salt, and a few grindings of black pepper to the moistened crumbs. Mix the ingredients until they are thoroughly blended. Rinsing your hands frequently with cold water to prevent sticking, shape the meat mixture into tiny meatballs, ½ inch in diameter. Fill a large broad saucepan halfway with water, and heat it to simmering. With a slotted spoon gently add the meatballs to the simmering water. Partially cover and cook, taking care that the water does not boil, for 15 minutes, or until the meatballs are cooked through. Drain the meatballs and set them aside until ready to use.

❺ Beat together the reserved half cup of broth and the remaining egg. While stirring the gently boiling chicken broth constantly, slowly pour in the egg mixture; it will form long threads. Cut the carrots into thin slices and add them to the broth with the shredded chicken and the meatballs. Sprinkle the farina over the broth and stir gently to blend. Cover and cook for 10 minutes, over low heat, to soften the farina and heat all the ingredients through. Season with salt to taste.

❻ Ladle soup into soup plates and pass a bowl of grated Parmesan cheese.

➤ *Makes 12 servings*

▲▲▲▲▲▲▲▲▲▲▲▲▲▲▲▲▲▲▲▲▲▲▲▲▲▲▲▲▲▲

Broccoli Rabe
with Spaghettini

Broccoli rabe, or broccoli raab, is a member of the turnip family and is slightly bitter, a taste long appreciated by Italians and increasingly sought by discerning eaters. Thanks for this recipe go to Biagio Strongi, parrucchiere superiori (first-rate hair stylist), who learned the recipe from Sal Leone of Laura's Restaurant on Prospect Avenue.

....

1½ pounds broccoli rabe
1 teaspoon salt, or to taste
¼ cup olive oil
2 or 3 garlic cloves, crushed

¼ teaspoon red pepper flakes
1 teaspoon anchovy paste (optional)
½ pound spaghettini

❶ Rinse the broccoli in a colander. Peel the larger stalks, those that are about the size of your finger. Use a vegetable peeler or, better, a small knife, stripping the peel towards the leaves. Cut off the larger stalks and chop them into pieces about 3 inches long.

❷ Bring a large pot of salted water to the boil. Ideally, the water is heavily salted. This dish needs salt for flavor.

❸ Meanwhile, put the oil in a saucepan, heat it, and sauté the garlic cloves over moderately high heat until they are nicely browned. Watch carefully; they burn easily. As you brown them, add the pepper flakes. When the garlic is brown, add the anchovy paste if you are using it and mix well. Set aside.

❹ Put the stalks into the boiling water, and boil them for 1 minute. Add the rest of the broccoli rabe and the spaghettini at the same time. Cook until both the broccoli and spaghettini are tender, about 4 minutes. Drain, pour on the garlic oil, and serve. ➤ *Serves 2 as a lunch or light supper, or 4 as a first course*

Sausages and
Peppers

Carla Busardo is the food columnist for The Tablet, *the weekly newspaper for Brooklyn's Catholics. "We have a circulation of 100,000 and a mixed readership, older people and younger, too,"* says Carla. *"Our emphasis is on family values. I try to keep my recipes low in fat and cholesterol, and when I do a traditional Italian dish like this one for a party, I bake rather than fry, using less oil."*

....

2 to 3 pounds sweet Italian sausages
5 pounds large red and green bell
    peppers (about 8 to 10)
2 large onions, sliced

3 garlic cloves, minced
Salt and pepper to taste
3 tablespoons olive oil

❶ Broil the sausages until brown but not cooked through, turning them often. Drain them and cut into 2-inch chunks.

Preheat the oven to 350 degrees F.

❷ Core and seed the peppers and slice them into strips about 1½ inches wide. Put the sausage chunks, the sliced onion, the peppers, and garlic in a 13- × 11-inch baking dish and toss them together. Add salt and pepper to taste, and drizzle on the oil. Bake for about 45 minutes, tossing the ingredients from time to time. ≫→ *Serves 6 to 8 as part of a buffet*

Pepper-Flecked Cheese Bread

Jack Clemente shows his form.

Jack Clemente, a Williamsburg baker who is a champion bowler, tells you what to do with bread past its prime: "If your Italian bread is stale, you make breadcrumbs. If it's a day old and only a little past its prime, you make cheese bread."

1 loaf day-old Italian bread
⅓ cup olive oil
⅔ cup freshly grated Romano cheese

Freshly ground black pepper, to taste
Pinch dried red pepper flakes
    (optional)

Preheat the oven to 400 degrees F.

❶ Split the loaf in half lengthwise. Brush the halves evenly with the oil, and cover with the cheese and as much black and red pepper as wanted.

❷ Cover a baking sheet with foil; that way the baking sheet stays clean. Bake the loaf until the cheese is toasted, 8 to 10 minutes. Cut into wedges and serve hot. ≫→ *Serves 4*

The Vendange in Bay Ridge

"When I was a kid in Bay Ridge," says Sal Sciallo, "every year at wine-making season you could smell the grapes for blocks. One year—now we're talking maybe forty years ago—my grandfather's wine press broke. We had a washing machine with a wringer attachment; you'd run the clothes through it and squeeze water out. Grandpa looked at it and realized all was not lost. In a matter of seconds, he had the wringer off the machine. My cousin and me went to the coal bin, got the long coal chute, and Grandpa poked the chute through the basement window, over the wine barrel. He put the wringer over the barrel, too. My cousin slid the grapes down the chute and I cranked them through the wringer. Boy, was Grandpa proud! Until Grandma found out. It cost my cousin and me red behinds, and Grandpa a new washing machine. Funny part is, that was the best wine I ever remember tasting."

Sal also labored in the vineyard, or he did if his grandfather could catch him. Gathering, um, fertilizer was a kid's duty: "I'd be playing ball or something, and my grandfather used to run out and cry, 'Toto, get the shovel, the horse is here!' and I'd start crying. It was time to follow the vegetable-man's horse. All the kids on the block had the same job to do. I was a little skinny kid, and I knew I was going to get beat up, because everyone fought over the horse manure. And if I didn't run and get the shovel, Grandpa hit me on the side of the head. So one way or another I'd get hit, which was why I cried.

"You had to run after the horse, sometimes for two or three blocks. When the horse stopped, we'd feed him carrots from home. That was to make the horse grow more of what we were after.

"The horse manure was important for the gardens. It was mixed with the crushed grapes after the wine was made, and dug into the soil. In our neighborhood, certain families were known for growing the best grapes, tomatoes, squash, whatever. My grandfather was famous for the grapes and tomatoes. If he had an abundance, he'd trade off with somebody who had too much lettuce or carrots. For a whole season, you didn't have to go to the vegetable market. What made everything grow so good was the organic stuff—the crushed grapes, the horse droppings, all natural, all going back to the earth. That was back in the '40s. In the '50s, everybody got trucks. And the horse was gone."

Chicken Cacciatore

Thanks *to Rosalie Sciallo of Bay Ridge, Sal's mother.*

My mom Rosalie Sciallo, "Miss Rheingold," 1950.

A 3½-pound chicken
Salt to taste
1 tablespoon butter
2 tablespoons olive oil
1 medium onion, sliced
2 cloves garlic, crushed
½ cup red wine
Pepper to taste

1 sprig marjoram, finely chopped, or
   ¼ teaspoon dried, crumbled
2 tablespoons finely chopped parsley
1 cup drained imported tomatoes,
   chopped

❶ Cut the chicken into serving pieces and lightly salt it. In a heavy skillet with a lid, melt the butter and oil. Brown the chicken, in 2 batches if necessary; don't crowd the pan.

❷ Transfer the chicken pieces to a plate. Brown the onion and garlic, stirring frequently, about 10 minutes. Drain off the drippings but reserve them.

❸ Put the chicken back in the skillet and add the wine. Let the chicken cook over moderate heat for about 3 minutes, then add a few grindings of pepper, the marjoram, parsley, tomatoes, and 2 tablespoons of the reserved drippings.

❹ Cover the skillet. Cook the chicken over low heat for 20 minutes or until tender, turning the pieces once. Uncover the skillet, raise the heat and cook for 5 more minutes to allow the sauce to thicken slightly. ⫸ *Serves 4*

▲▲▲▲▲▲▲▲▲▲▲▲▲▲▲▲▲▲▲▲▲▲▲▲▲▲

Fried Potatoes, Italian Style

Originally Italian-style potatoes were fried in a good deal of oil, but that does not suit today's taste.

These are crisp and very light. This is Mario Nucci's recipe.

1 pound new potatoes, scrubbed but not peeled

½ to 1 teaspoon salt
4 tablespoons olive oil

❶ Slice the potatoes very thin, and put them in a large shallow bowl. Sprinkle them with the salt and turn them with your hands so that they are evenly coated. Let them stand for an hour, as the salt draws out water. Tip the bowl from time to time to pour off the liquid.

❷ Pour 2 tablespoons of the oil into a large heavy skillet. Squeeze the potato slices and pat them dry. Heat the oil to sizzling and add the potatoes. Cook, turning constantly, until they are brown and crisp, about 10 to 12 minutes. Add the remaining oil, as necessary. Drain on paper towels if you like.

≫→ *Serves 2 or 3*

Citrus Granita

This snowy-textured Italian ice is most refreshing after a heavy meal like Genoese pot roast (see page 92).

The color is a beautiful pale coral. The recipe is from Millie Torrono.

2 cups water
¾ cup sugar
½ cup fresh lemon juice

½ cup fresh orange juice
1 tablespoon grenadine syrup

❶ In a heavy saucepan bring the water and sugar to the boil over moderate heat. Stir only until the sugar dissolves. Boil the syrup for exactly 5 minutes, then let it cool to room temperature.

❷ Stir in the lemon and orange juices, and the grenadine syrup. Pour mixture into a cake pan or metal ice-cube tray without dividers.

❸ Put pan in the freezer for 3 to 4 hours. Stir mixture every half hour and scrape around the edge of the pan. Serve in parfait glasses.

≫→ *Makes 1½ pints*

L. & B. Spumoni Gardens

Since 1939, the Barbati family has run this quintessential Bensonhurst joint, serving "number one pizza" and fresh spumoni. "Spumoni is an American version of Italian gelati," says Lou Barbati, a fourth-generation worker at the place. "It's rich in butterfat, and it's flavored with cinnamon and almonds. Spumoni comes in vanilla, chocolate, and pistachio, or you can ask for rainbow—a mix of all three." The Barbatis make spumoni in the small factory in the back, and sell it wholesale to mom-and-pop stores as well as retail.

In summer, especially, the Gardens is packed with young and old, spilling out onto the sidewalk. Sandy Koufax of the Dodgers used to go there, and now Johnny Franco, the Mets' All Star relief pitcher, stops by from time to time.

L. & B. Spumoni Gardens, old photo. Founder Ludovico Barbati, Sr., in 1938 (left).

Hometown Cooking in the Governors' Mansions

No matter how high they fly, Brooklynites tend to remain hometown people, and the following home-style food appears in both Trenton and Albany.

Florio's First-Love Chili

Jim Florio, born in Red Hook and raised in Flatbush, is now Governor of New Jersey. Is his favorite food pheasant under glass? Heck no, it's his wife Lucinda's chili. Very satisfying.

1 tablespoon lard or vegetable shortening
1 large onion, finely chopped
2 medium garlic cloves, finely chopped
1 pound lean beef, coarse chili grind
2 tablespoons ground pure chili pepper, hot or mild, or a combination of the two
1 teaspoon celery salt
1 teaspoon ground cumin

½ teaspoon crumbled dried basil
1 teaspoon salt
1 16-ounce can plum tomatoes
1 small bay leaf
3 cups water
1 small cinnamon stick
2 whole cloves
1 green bell pepper, cored, seeded, and coarsely chopped
1 16-ounce can kidney beans, drained

❶ Melt the lard in a large heavy pot over moderately high heat. Add the onion and garlic and cook, stirring, until the onion is translucent.

❷ Add the meat to the pot, breaking it up with a wooden spoon or fork. Cook, stirring occasionally, until the meat is evenly browned.

❸ Stir in the rest of the ingredients, except for the bell pepper and beans. Stir well, breaking up the tomatoes. Bring to the boil, lower the heat, and simmer, uncovered, for 2½ hours. Stir occasionally. If it is too dry, add a little water.

❹ Stir in the green pepper and beans and simmer, uncovered, for 30 minutes more.

❺ Remove the bay leaf, cinnamon stick, and, if possible, the cloves. Taste and adjust seasoning. ≫→ *Serves 4*

Matilda Cuomo's Crumbed Baked Bluefish

Matilda Raffa Cuomo, First Lady of the State of New York, graduated from Midwood High School in 1949. A former elementary school teacher, she married Governor Mario Cuomo in 1954. Baked bluefish suits him fine.

You won't need all the crumb mixture for this amount of blue-fish, but the topping keeps well for weeks in the refrigerator and can be used with any kind of fish.

Crumb Topping

1 pound plain (approximately 4 cups well packed) breadcrumbs
3 tablespoons paprika
1 teaspoon ground white pepper
1 teaspoon onion powder
1 teaspoon garlic powder
1 teaspoon crumbled dried thyme

½ teaspoon salt
½ cup sherry
½ cup melted butter, plus more for drizzling

. . . .

3 to 3½ pounds boned bluefish fillets, about ¾ inch thick

Preheat the oven to 350 degrees F.

❶ Place all the dry ingredients in the bowl of a stationary mixer equipped with a paddle. Mix on low speed. Add the sherry and ½ cup of the melted butter and mix until well combined.

❷ Oil a sizzle platter or heavy oven pan and heat it on top of the stove until moderately hot. Add enough water just to cover the bottom of the platter.

❸ Place the bluefish fillets, skin side down, on the platter. Cover each fillet with a coating of the crumb mixture, and drizzle a little melted butter over them.

❹ Bake the fillets for 25 minutes, or until the flesh is milky white and the topping is browned and bubbling. (Timing will differ for thinner or thicker fillets.) ⋙ *Serves 4 to 6*

The Crabbing Expedition

Philip E. Juliano recalls the great crab feasts of his childhood: "In the late 1930s and early '40s, usually on the hottest days of July and August, the family went crabbing. Aunt Jean, Uncle Ed, Mom, Dad, my older brother Juny and me, Bubby, would go to a calm little Brooklyn bay. Mom and Aunt Jean packed sandwiches—pepper and egg, salami and provolone, meatball and sausage. They brought soda, beer, and wine.

"Uncle Ed would rent two rowboats, hook his trusty Evinrude outboard motor on one, and pull the second boat holding Mom, Dad, and Juny. I'd be in the lead boat with Aunt Jean and Uncle Ed. He first let me steer the outboard when I was six; I felt like the captain of a great liner.

"We'd anchor not far from shore and drop our lines and baskets, baited with junk fish. When we felt a tug we'd pull in the line, hand over hand, till we saw the crab below the water line. Then slowly, slowly we'd net the crab. It had to be done ever so gently or the crab would jump for freedom. Avoiding the claws, we picked up the crab by the back and dropped it into a burlap bag on the bottom of the boat.

"On one of our crabbing trips, the bottom of Uncle Ed's boat was covered with crabs. As Aunt Jean was attempting to put one in the bag, it grabbed her finger. It held firmly. Yelling and screaming, Aunt Jean stood up, swinging her arm, trying to shake the crab free. Escaping crabs ran out of the bag, all over the bottom of the boat. Laughing hard at Aunt Jean's swinging and yelling, we had to hold our bare feet high to avoid getting pinched ourselves. She finally shook the crab free—it flew across the boat and caught Uncle Ed on the nose. We laughed for ten minutes. Even Uncle Ed laughed after he got the crab loose. We must have caught two hundred crabs that day.

"That evening everyone met at Aunt Jean's for a feast of crabs and mac, with all the cousins. She and Uncle Ed had a typewriter and vacuum-cleaner store on Nostrand Avenue. Their apartment in the back was very small, so to accommodate

132 The whole gang, ready for crabbing.

everyone we had to set up trestle tables in the store: plywood laid over wooden horses. The front of the store was about twenty feet wide, and all glass. People walked by and saw all us Italians eating, drinking, and having a grand time. Uncle Ed loved to eat, he was the life of the party. I can still see him sitting there with sauce running down his chin, his shirt spattered with bits of crab. The wine flowed freely, and we ate until eleven at night. One of the great times of my life!"

Aunt Jean's Crabs and Mac

To old-fashioned Italian-Americans, "mac," or macaroni, used to mean every kind of dried noodle from spaghetti to fusilli.

Now, of course, we all say pasta.

Be prepared for a gloriously messy feast. Wear old clothes and bibs.

2 dozen live blue crabs (hard-shelled crabs)
1 teaspoon salt
¼ cup olive oil
6 cloves garlic, peeled and sliced
A 32-ounce can crushed Italian plum tomatoes

1 teaspoon crumbled dried oregano
1 cup red wine
2 teaspoons sugar
1 teaspoon crushed red pepper flakes (optional)
1½ pounds vermicelli or linguine

❶ Fill a tub or sink with very hot water and dump the crabs in. The water will anesthetize them enough so that you can scrub them quickly without fear of being nipped by claws. (If they drop claws, no matter; steam them also.)

❷ Place a rack on the bottom of a large pot that has a tight lid. Pour in enough water to come just below the rack. Transfer the crabs to the rack with tongs and sprinkle them with the salt. Cover the pot, and steam the crabs over moderate heat for 20 to 25 minutes. They should be red. Transfer them to a platter. When they are sufficiently cool to handle, chop them in half. At this point you can pull out the spongy gills and intestines. Set the crabs aside.

❸ Wipe out the same large pot and put in the oil and sliced garlic. Over moderate heat cook the garlic until it is soft but not brown. Add the tomatoes, oregano, wine, sugar, and pepper flakes, if you are using them. Bring the mixture to the boil, lower the heat, and cook, uncovered, stirring from time to time, for 1 hour. If the sauce is too thick, thin it with water. Add salt to taste. Put in the crab pieces and simmer for 10 minutes or until the meat is tender.

❹ Meanwhile, bring a large pot of salted water to the boil. Add the pasta and cook it according to package directions. Drain it and put it on a heated platter. Toss with some of the crab sauce. Put the crab pieces on another platter and the rest of the sauce in a gravy boat. Accompany the crabs and mac with crusty bread, green salad, and lots of red wine. ⋙→ *Serves 6*

▲▲▲▲▲▲▲▲▲▲▲▲▲▲▲▲▲▲▲▲▲▲▲▲▲▲▲▲

Cavolfiore Fritto
(Fried Cauliflower)

You can do this in stages; boil the cauliflower one day, and bread it several hours before you fry it. The recipe is from Luisa Nucci.

1 head cauliflower, about 2 pounds
1 cup or more fine dry unflavored
    breadcrumbs

1 egg, beaten with 2 teaspoons water
    and ½ teaspoon salt
Vegetable oil for frying

❶ Remove all the leaves from the cauliflower, cut the stem level with the bottom, and cut a deep cross in the stem end. Boil it in lightly salted water to cover until it is tender. Let it cool.

❷ Spread the breadcrumbs out on wax paper. Cut the cauliflower into wedges about 1 inch thick at the widest part. Dip wedges in egg, then in breadcrumbs.

❸ Pour oil in a large heavy skillet to a depth of ½ inch and heat until it sizzles. Fry the wedges, a few at a time, until golden all over. Drain on paper towels and serve on a heated platter. ⋙→ *Serves 4 to 6*

Grandma Meets a Cake Mix

"**A**t home we spoke Sicilian dialect, which I thought was Italian," says Father Ronald Marino. "My grandmother, Rosalia Lillina Caruso, lived with us. When I was about ten, my sister and I wanted to make a cake as a surprise for our mother's birthday. We went to the store and bought a cake mix, with a beautiful picture on the package.

Father Marino blesses his grandmother Rosalia Caruso.

"Grandma spoke almost no English. Now, baking cakes is not done at home in Sicily. She looked at the recipe, with its measurements, and tried to figure out what to do. She never measured anything!

"We wanted to whip cream for the frosting. We had never had whipped cream—cream was too expensive. We had no beater, or even a whisk. So Grandma got a wooden spoon and tried really hard to whip the cream—you can imagine how poorly that worked—so she turned it over to us. A big mistake. We splattered and splashed, and she decided to mix in the can of chocolate frosting. That was new to her too; Sicilian cakes are not frosted. She made a mixture of liquid cream and chocolate that wouldn't work as frosting. 'Let us lick the spoon!' we pestered. She knew little English, but she did recognize the word 'lick.' All patience gone, she flung the spoon across the room, splattering chocolate cream all over the kitchen. She flung the bowl across the room, too, threw up her hands, and yelled,

in dialect, something very rude indeed.

"The kitchen was covered with chocolate and cream. She opened the oven door, and the cake wasn't moving. She decided that it needed something. Olive oil! She got the gallon can of oil and poured some into the batter, where it sat in a glob on top. We thought that was fine; everything we ate had olive oil. She closed the oven. Soon the oil heated up and bubbled in the middle of the batter. The cake wasn't rising, it was frying! After an hour and a half, we took out the fried cake. We didn't know there was anything wrong, except that we couldn't frost it. We put candles on it. Our mother was pleased. And you know, that cake was absolutely *delicious!*"

Life Al Fresco

Picnics and outings were highlights of the Brooklyn summer. People ventured near and far; to the park—Prospect, Leif Ericson, Brower—to Staten Island on the ferry from Bay Ridge, and on church outings that transported the congregation on a Hudson River Dayliner up to Bear Mountain or Indian Point. Some folks went to Westchester, or to Long Island.

Carol Mazzola has vivid memories of the enormously elaborate picnics her grandmother, Mama, prepared in the 1950s for family excursions to a park in Tarrytown:

"Mama lived for her Sunday picnics. Saturday morning she'd take out her blue spackleware pot and start on Sunday's food. Meatballs with plenty of garlic and pignoli nuts for my dad, sautéed mushrooms for Cousin Connie—at least one favorite food for everyone, and there were a dozen of us. By 8 p.m. on Saturday, everything was cooked and packed, including a huge box of 'love knots'—sections of newspaper rolled lengthwise and tied in knots.

"My family were the scouts. We'd be on the road by 6 a.m, to claim our spot between two oak trees. My parents would move three picnic tables together and fire up two barbecues, using charcoal and the love knots. On one grill they cooked coffee, bacon and eggs. By 10 a.m., a 10-quart pot was set on the second grill, with a rolling boil expected at exactly 1 p.m. And at 1 the blue pot, filled with Mama's meatballs, sausages, braciole, and spareribs, was set down on the grill next to the boiling pot. When Mama gave the signal, salt and three pounds of ziti went into the boiling water. Of course we had salad and chicken too, vegetables and pastry, and cling peaches soaked in Papa's homemade wine. The tables were set with cloths, matching napkins, crystal glasses, and the china service.

"After the meal, the children played ball or swam in the lake, the men and Mama played penny poker, and my mom, my aunts, and my older cousin took the dinnerware and pots to a nearby spigot and spent two hours on their hands and knees washing everything, and working on the pots, especially the blue pot, with scouring pads. In those days the women didn't seem to mind cleaning up. After all, Mama did the shopping, cooking, and packing, and the men 'worked' all week long.

"As the day drew on, we had supper too. Then we packed up the three cars, and we were back in Brooklyn by about 7:30 p.m."

Pasta e Fagioli
(Pasta Fazool)

"This is Italian-American comfort food," says Carol Mazzola. "It's really winter food, but sometimes we'd have it for a picnic too. Add cooked sausage rounds, if you like."

1½ cups dried pasta (tubetti, ditalini, etc.), to make 2½ cups cooked pasta
1 can cannellini beans, or 1½ cups cooked white beans (the beans should be soft)
2 tablespoons olive oil
3 garlic cloves, finely chopped

½ cup chopped onion (optional)
¼ to ½ cup Very Quick Marinara Sauce (recipe follows), or prepared tomato sauce of any sort
½ teaspoon crumbled dried oregano
Salt and pepper to taste

❶ Cook the pasta and heat the beans separately.

❷ Heat the oil in a skillet; cook the garlic and the optional onion over moderate heat until soft. Stir in the tomato sauce and oregano and heat through.

❸ Drain the pasta and beans and place them in a large heated bowl. Toss with the sauce. ⋙→ *Serves 4*

Very Quick Marinara Sauce

Not all tomato sauces have to be simmered a long time. This one is ready in less than ten minutes. For pasta, dress it up with sautéed sausage rounds and bell pepper strips; for pizza, add crumbled dried oregano. The recipe is Lyn Stallworth's.

1 tablespoon olive oil
3 garlic cloves, peeled and lightly crushed
1½ cups canned imported crushed tomatoes

½ teaspoon salt
½ teaspoon sugar

❶ Heat the oil in a 10-inch skillet and brown the garlic cloves, turning them frequently. They should be well browned but not burnt.

❷ Stir in the tomatoes, salt, and sugar. Cook over medium heat, stirring constantly, for 5 minutes. (The wider surface of the skillet allows some of the liquid to evaporate so the sauce thickens slightly.) ⋙→ *Makes a scant 1½ cups*

A FINE FAMILY LIFE
THE JEWS OF BROOKLYN

Was Brooklyn a great place to grow up? I ask you. A lot of high achievers along with ordinary folks may not live here <u>now</u>, but they look back on their Brooklyn years through a rosy haze of nostalgia that time does not dim.

Families maybe weren't rich, but neither were the neighbors. Every kid seemed to come home from school to the smell of wonderful baking; it's unlikely that Mama or Bubba baked every afternoon, but in retrospect they did.

Some families kept kosher, some not. The style of food for both, however, was "Jewish": roast chicken, matzo-ball soup, kugels, and brisket. A brown cuisine, it's been called, but it was a sustaining one.

Then an intruder took this bagel-and-blintz society by culinary storm; Chinese food arrived. Soon every Jewish neighborhood sported its Hanging Garden or New China. The food was Cantonese, and bland. No one had heard of Szechwan or Hunan. People loved it. Loved it! And they still do. Sophisticated Jewish palates are the mainstay of upscale Chinese restaurants. What caused this instant affinity for such different food? "Perhaps," muses Jerry Sternstein, "they're the lost tribe."

Aromas in the Old Neighborhood

A holiday meal at his grandmother's in East New York, 1951. Four-and-a-half-year-old Arthur is in the foreground; his mother, Sydell, is in the doorway.

Arthur Schwartz is a restaurant critic for New York's *Daily News* and a cookbook author. He says: "My bed is in Manhattan, but my heart is still riding a bicycle along the Belt Parkway in Gerritsen Beach.

"Whenever I go back to Brooklyn, which is frequently, my friends say, 'Oh, Arthur is making a pilgrimage to the Holy Land.' It is true that my spirits soar when I see the open skies, clear light, tree-lined streets, and lush little gardens of my old stomping grounds—the central- and southern-tier communities of the borough, including Flatbush, Midwood, East Flatbush, Flatlands, Canarsie, Marine Park, Mill Basin, Sheepshead Bay, Gravesend, Borough Park, Bay Ridge, and my family's old neighborhood, East New York. I grew up, in the 1950s, thinking I was lucky to have been born and raised in such a wonderful place. And I still do.

"I remember when whole blocks of Flatbush, Borough Park, and Bensonhurst smelled of pot roast and kasha on Friday after-noons, though Friday night was actually chicken night in most Jewish households. You had chicken soup and roast chicken.

"There are good reasons for pot roast being the Saturday, end-of-Sabbath meal. First, it is festive. In the old days, when a Jew thought of a festive meal, he thought of pot roast, a big brisket. It was succulent and expensive, a hunk of meat you never would have gotten in the old country. Second, if you are a Sabbath observer, you can't cook after sundown on Friday until after sundown on Saturday. But pot roast and the accompanying kasha not only can be reheated the next day, they taste better reheated.

"That's why on Friday certain Brooklyn streets smell of Saturday's dinner."

My Mother's Pot Roast

*"**M**y mother went through various stages with her pot roast," says Arthur Schwartz. "This recipe is the one she started with—because her mother, and her mother's Rus-* *sian immigrant mother, made it this way—and the one she ended with. In between, we suffered through pot roast made with Sauce Arturo, pot roast made with ketch-*

up, with Lipton's onion soup mix, and the worst, pot roast made with Harvey's Bristol Cream. (I have no idea where she came up with that one.) During diet-conscious times, we also suffered through 'first cut' brisket only, the leanest part of the meat.

"Near the end of her life, my mother finally realized that the essentials for great pot roast number only two: the whole brisket, fat and all, and a lot, a lot of onions; about half the meat's weight is a good rule of thumb.

"Don't worry about the enormous amount of fat between the layers of meat in a whole brisket. Much of it will cook off and can be skimmed from the juices. The rest can be trimmed off after the meat is cooked. But if you don't leave all the fat on, the meat will be stringy, dry, and/or mealy."

- -

2 cloves garlic
A 7- to 8-pound brisket
Salt and freshly ground black pepper
3 to 4 pounds onions, sliced

4 to 5 carrots, sliced into ¼-inch rounds
2 or 3 bay leaves
½ cup beef broth, red wine, or water

Preheat the oven to 350 degrees F.

❶ Split the cloves of garlic and rub the meat well with them. Slice or dice what is left of the garlic and put it in a roasting pan large enough to hold the piece of meat.

❷ Salt and pepper the meat well on both sides.

❸ Spread the onions and carrots on the bottom of the pan. Put the meat on the vegetables. Tuck 1 or 2 of the bay leaves under the meat, and put 1 on top. Pour in the broth, wine, or water.

❹ Cover the pan tightly with foil and cook for 2½ to 3 hours, until the meat is just tender. Let the meat cool slightly, then refrigerate it until the following day.

❺ Skim the fat off the surface of the liquid that has collected around the meat, and off the surface of the meat. Allow it to come to room temperature before the final heating.

Preheat the oven to 350 degrees F.

❻ About an hour before serving it, slice the meat ¼ to ½ inch thick. Do not disturb the conformation of the brisket. Return it to the roasting pan as though it were still a whole brisket.

❼ Return it to the oven. Baste it with pan juices and heat it uncovered for 45 minutes to 1 hour, basting it a few times. The surface of the meat will have browned nicely and the slices should be heated through and fork tender. Trim excess fat off the meat, as it is eaten.

❽ Serve the meat with kasha, kasha varnishkas (recipe follows), mashed potatoes flavored with schmaltz (chicken fat) and *gribenes,* the cracklings and blackened onions left from rendering chicken fat. Top them all with pan juices and onions. A green vegetable is up to you. ⟫→ *Serves 8*

▲▲▲▲▲▲▲▲▲▲▲▲▲▲▲▲▲▲▲▲▲▲▲▲▲▲▲▲▲▲▲

Kasha Varnishkas

Rona Moulu, whose recipe this is, is a professional chef with roots in Eastern Europe—and Brooklyn, of course.

2 cups beef broth
1 egg
1 cup kasha
2 cups Jewish-style bow-shaped egg
    noodles
2 teaspoons butter
2 teaspoons olive oil
1 cup minced onion
1 teaspoon salt
¼ teaspoon pepper

❶ In a small pan, warm the beef broth and set it aside.

❷ In a small bowl, beat the egg slightly. Add the kasha and mix well.

❸ Heat a dry skillet that has a lid. Spoon in the kasha. Stir it, mashing, so as to toast and dry out the groats without burning them. Slowly add the warmed broth, stirring. Cover and cook for 10 minutes, or until the kasha is tender. Set it aside in a warm place.

❹ In a large pot of boiling water, cook the noodles according to package directions. Drain them and keep them warm.

❺ Heat the butter and oil in a skillet. Cook the onion until soft and slightly brown.

❻ Combine the onion, kasha, and noodles in a large bowl and season with salt and pepper. ⟫→ *Serves 6*

Grandma Edie's Brooklyn Brisket

This authentic period piece comes from actress Ilene Kristen, best known as Delia on the soap opera "Ryan's Hope." She grew up in Flatbush: "My first memory of my Grandma Edie Levin's brisket was on Passover when I was very young. Since it was so easy to make, we usually had it once a week. I recently went down to Palm Beach to visit Myrna and Arthur Schatz, my parents, and we ate this served over Uncle Ben's white rice."

Edie Levin in the 1940s.

The Brisket

1 5- to 8-pound piece of brisket
Ground pepper to taste
Garlic powder to taste

1 package Knorr Onion Soup
Accent to taste
1 12-ounce bottle Pepsi-Cola

Preheat the oven to 325 degrees F.

❶ Put the brisket in an ovenproof pot with a cover. Pierce the brisket all over with a skewer and rub in the pepper, garlic powder, onion soup, and Accent. Pour on the Pepsi-Cola, making sure it gets under the brisket.

❷ Cover the pot and roast the brisket for 3 to 4 hours, depending on how well done you like your meat. Baste often.

❸ If made the day before, cut off any fat and defat the gravy. Cut the meat in very thin slices and reheat it in the gravy. ⟫⟶ *Serves 8*

The Boys from Manhattan Avenue

In the great world of Manhattan, the names of Raoul Lionel Felder and Doc Pomus are not unknown. Felder is one of the country's leading matrimonial lawyers, and his brother Doc (Doc Pomus is a theatrical name) is a lyricist. Among his hits are "Save the Last Dance for Me," "This Magic Moment," and "Teenager in Love"; Elvis sang his "Surrender, Little Sister," and "Viva Las Vegas." He's also done songs for the movie *Dick Tracy*.

Another Manhattan, though—Manhattan Avenue in Williamsburg—is just a memory's spin away. There the Felder boys grew up over half a century ago in the contained and lively world of a six-story apartment house with four families on each floor. But the Felders' building was torn down for a housing project; Zuckerman's appetizing store moved across the

river; the Lyric, a Jewish repertory theatre whose troupe included Joseph Schildkraut and Paul Muni, is gone; and the Rainbow Theatre is now a Pentecostal church. But it was a swell place to grow up! The Felder brothers speak:

"What happened in our household, no matter what kind of financial shape the family was in, there was always enough food to feed at least 14 people for two weeks. And when I say feed, I mean *stuff*. Our mother really catered to everybody. She made noodles by hand, and she'd cut a different size for each kid. She did well-done rib steaks, kasha varnishkas, and Jell-O every night. My mother kept kosher, so she wouldn't have bacon in the house, but she had this idea it was good for us. She'd take us to Rudy's

Raoul's bar mitzvah: left to right, Doc, Mrs. Felder, Raoul, and his proud father.

luncheonette for bacon and tomato sandwiches.

"I remember the icebox with the drip pan underneath, just like the one in 'The Honeymooners.' The iceman delivered ice from a wagon pulled by a horse. Once my brother reached under to pull out the drip pan, and pulled out a drowned mouse instead! Later we had a refrigerator, with the motor on top.

"Near us was the live chicken market, where they slit the throat of the chickens while you watched. Our mother liked to get a hen with unborn eggs; very tasty in soup.

"You could take the trolley to Ebbets Field, and you could stay in the park all night, or sit on the step in front of the house, no problem. Joe Papp, the producer, lived around the corner—he was the neighborhood shoeshine boy. José Greco was from the neighborhood

too. Bickford's cafeteria was near the Folly Theatre. Bickford's was a 24-hour hangout, famous for the best coffee in town. We used to swipe their napkins to use as handkerchiefs. It was also the meeting place for deaf people. Passersby could observe the dance of silent fingers as they made conversation. The Folly had top vaudeville headliners: Jackie Gleason, Abbott and Costello, and Edgar Bergen and Charlie McCarthy all played the Folly. Once a year, they used to have a show about Hawaii, when they'd drop a girl down a volcano.

"Manhattan Avenue was a center for bridal wear—brides came from all over the city. Tailors were there too; Big Hearted Herbert had a clothing store. He'd stick you in a suit two sizes too big, march you to a mirror, grab the suit by the back, and say, 'See, a perfect fit!'"

The Felder Family Meatloaf

Each slice should show a nice round bull's-eye of hard-boiled egg. The onion and garlic flavors inten- *sify as the loaf (or what remains of it) sits overnight, and the firm slices make excellent sandwiches.*

2 pounds ground chuck or top round
2 tablespoons matzo meal
¼ cup grated onion
1 teaspoon finely chopped garlic
1 teaspoon salt

Freshly ground pepper to taste
1 raw egg
4 hard-boiled eggs, peeled
4 tablespoons coarse breadcrumbs

Preheat the oven to 375 degrees F.

❶ With your hands or a wooden spoon, mix together the beef, matzo meal, onion, garlic, salt, pepper, and raw egg.

❷ Pack half the mixture along the bottom of a 5-inch × 9-inch loaf pan. Arrange the eggs down the center, end to end, pushing them gently into the meat. Pack the remaining meat mixture into the pan, over the eggs. Sprinkle on the breadcrumbs evenly.

❸ Bake the loaf until cooked through, about 1 hour. After 30 minutes, tilt the pan and spoon off the fat. Pour a little of the clear juices over the top of the loaf. Near the end of the cooking time, spoon off fat again. If you choose, briefly place the loaf under the broiler to further brown the breadcrumbs.

❹ Let the loaf rest in its pan for about 20 minutes to settle. ⯈⯈ *Serves 6*

▲▲▲▲▲▲▲▲▲▲▲▲▲▲▲▲▲▲▲▲▲▲▲▲▲▲▲▲▲▲▲▲▲▲▲▲

Lou Singer, Man with Van

Lou Singer.

This man has a driving (pun intended) ambition to share his encyclopedic, geographic, architectural, and culinary knowledge of Brooklyn. "I spent twenty-seven years watching Brooklyn change—neighborhoods that were crumbling coming back to family life," he says. "In 1969 I began giving tours; I used to do over three hundred a year, but I cut back and now I do about two hundred." For a modest fee, Lou will take you on a trip tailored to your interests. Are you fascinated by the works of Louis Comfort Tiffany? Lou says: "Unlike Manhattan, Brooklyn was not beset by tearing-down fads. We have the finest Tiffany works in existence here, including a private house decorated by the firm, and a church with twenty-one pristine Tiffany windows."

Lou's Brooklyn Noshing Tour takes you on a gastronomic spin around the borough that will leave eyes and taste buds popping. From kielbasa and cold cuts in Polish Greenpoint, you go to Italian Williamsburg's Galleria for cappuccino and chocolate pudding with pignoli nuts. Then on to Bedford-Stuyvesant, for ribs and peach cobbler at McDonald's Dining Room (a nice restaurant not to be confused with the fast-food outlets). Next is Atlantic Avenue, with half a dozen of the Middle Eastern appetizers called *mezze*.

Then it's across Brooklyn to Brighton Beach, for two or three Russian dishes. Courage! Next stop is Bay Ridge, for coffee and pastry at a French place, then on to Leske's bakery for a Scandinavian treat. "We shift around," says Lou. "Sometimes we'll get a knish at Mrs. Stahl's in Brighton Beach, or the best fresh mozzarella in Williamsburg."

Lou thinks his interest in food was fated; he arrived in this world on the kitchen table. That was not an unusual place to give birth in the old days. At any rate, his mother always said, "The sweetest thing I ever put on that table was you."

Singer's Luckchen Kugel
(Sweet Noodle Pudding)

"Here is my wife's, originally my mother's, recipe for noodle pudding," says Lou Singer. "My mother was from Lithuania, and she taught my wife this classic Eastern European dish. This is the sweet version, which you can eat as dessert. You can add thinly sliced apples or substitute other fruit. You can enrich it by adding sour cream and cottage cheese. And so on."

½ pound medium or broad noodles
3 eggs
3 tablespoons vegetable oil
1 teaspoon ground cinnamon
¼ teaspoon freshly ground nutmeg

½ cup sugar
Pinch salt
½ to 1 cup raisins (depends on how much you like raisins)

Preheat the oven to 350 degrees F.

❶ Cook the noodles according to package directions. Drain and rinse under cold water.

❷ While the noodles are cooking, separate the eggs. To the yolks, add the oil, cinnamon, nutmeg, sugar, and salt. Mix well. Combine with the noodles.

❸ Beat the whites until stiff, and fold them into the noodle mixture. Fold in the raisins. Tip: Bury the raisins under the noodles so they don't burn. Bake the kugel for 45 minutes, or until the top is nicely browned. ➤ *Serves 4*

▲▲▲▲▲▲▲▲▲▲▲▲▲▲▲▲▲▲▲▲▲▲▲▲▲▲▲▲▲▲▲▲

The Yiddish Shirley Temple

"I sang on the BBC when I was three years old," says Roz Starr, who, as the founder of the Starr Information Service, eases the lot of celebrities and those who seek their services. She's been asked the weight and dress size of Marlene Dietrich (she knew them) and if a Very Famous Producer needs the private phone number—now!—of an up-and-coming Face, Roz has it.

But back to the BBC. "That was the *Brooklyn* Broadcasting Company," she says with a laugh. "I sang on the 'Jewish Hour,' in Yiddish. I could also play the xylophone. I was 'discovered' as the winner of a kiddie contest in Betsy Head Park, where the contestants were aged two to five. These contests went on all through Brooklyn. I recall that I was Little Red Riding Hood."

Speaking of hoods, Louis "Lepke" Buchalter, a racketeer, rub-out artist, and one of the founders of the infamous gang known as Murder, Inc., thought little Rosalyn was adorable. "My mother was very careful," says Roz. "She'd take me to a social club to perform, and Lepke loved Yiddish songs. I sat on his lap, and he'd give me a quarter. That's all. In those days you could buy out the candy store for a quarter! And my mother was standing by."

Matzo Lasagna

"Our family was kosher," says Roz, "and we ate in a lot of delis. The good cook is my sister Anita. This is her recipe."

....

6 sheets matzo
2 pounds cottage cheese
1 can mushrooms, drained
1 green pepper, slivered

1 32-ounce jar spaghetti sauce
1 6-ounce package of sweet Muenster
  cheese

Preheat the oven to 375 degrees F.

❶ Liberally oil a 9- × 13-inch lasagna pan. Crumble two sheets of matzo over the bottom.

❷ Spread the cottage cheese over the matzo. Sprinkle on the mushrooms and green pepper. Cover evenly with one-third of the sauce.

❸ Break up the Muenster cheese, and sprinkle on one-third of it. Crumble on two more sheets of matzo and cover with one-third of the spaghetti sauce and one third of the Muenster. Crumble and scatter on the last two sheets of matzo.

❹ For the third layer, sprinkle on the rest of the Muenster and spread on the remaining spaghetti sauce. Bake for 40 minutes. ⇒ *Serves 6*

▲▲▲▲▲▲▲▲▲▲▲▲▲▲▲▲▲▲▲▲▲▲▲▲▲▲▲▲▲▲▲▲

▲▲▲▲▲▲▲▲▲▲▲▲▲▲▲▲▲▲▲▲▲▲▲▲▲▲▲

Sylvia Fine Kaye and Danny Kaye

"Both Danny and I came originally from East New York, the home of Murder, Inc. It was a true melting-pot neighborhood. It was alive, vibrant, and intense.

"My family then moved to Flatbush on East 18th Street between Avenues N and O. [It was] a neighborhood of mostly detached clapboard houses with big front porches, front yards, and back yards. Each family, of course, had a dog, and on East 18th they would all assemble every afternoon at the corner of Avenue O at 5 just when everyone was beginning to prepare dinner. They'd then proceed down the block in solemn single file."

Sylvia Fine Kaye's Stuffed Eggplant

"I *consider this a one-dish meal to be followed by salad."*

· ·

1 medium to large eggplant
1 chicken breast, boned and skinned
8 fresh tomatoes
1 small onion
2 small garlic cloves
1 green pepper
4 chopped mushrooms
1 tablespoon tomato paste
¼ cup chicken broth
Salt and pepper
Basil
Oregano
Rosemary
Thyme
Grated Parmesan cheese

❶ Bake the eggplant in a 350 degree F oven until it is soft when pierced with a skewer, about 25 minutes. Set it aside to cool and leave the oven on.

❷ Cut the chicken breast into bite-sized pieces. Peel, seed, and cut up 6 of the tomatoes. Cut the remaining 2 into slices and reserve them. Chop the onion and garlic cloves. Chop the green pepper coarse.

❸ Put the chicken pieces, onion, garlic, green pepper, mushrooms, tomato paste, chicken broth, salt and pepper to taste, pinches of basil, oregano, and rosemary and a good pinch of thyme into a large nonstick skillet. Cook over moderate heat until the onion is softened and the chicken pieces just cooked.

❹ Cut the baked eggplant in half and scoop out the flesh. Combine the flesh with the chicken mixture. Stuff the eggplant halves with the mixture and cover with the sliced tomatoes and a healthy sprinkling of Parmesan cheese over all. Bake for 25 minutes. ⇒ *Serves 2 or 3*

Danny Kaye's Szechwan Beef or Pork in Bau Bien

Chinese chefs of the first rank considered Danny Kaye to be their equal. When he remodeled his California kitchen, he installed a professional Chinese range.

"The following recipe has been approved by the Master," says Sylvia Fine Kaye, "with the dire warning that unless cooked on a proper Chinese stove, it won't be the same. Get hoisin sauce, Lau Ju wine, and Szechwan peppers at a Chinese grocery. Cooking sherry as a substitute for the Lau Ju will not do."

....

Bau Bien ("Chinese Tortillas")
2 cups all-purpose flour
½ cup hot water or more
Szechwan Beef or Pork Filling
1 pound sirloin beef or pork, sliced thin
1 green bell pepper
1 carrot
Green Szechwan peppers (or chilis, but taste is different)

3 tablespoons Oriental sesame-seed oil
Salt to taste
Garlic
1 to 2 tablespoons Lau Ju wine
Soy sauce
1 tablespoon cornstarch
2 tablespoons hoisin sauce

❶ Make the Bau Bien. Mix the flour and water and knead until smooth, shiny, and elastic. (Add more water if needed.) Let the dough rest until it wakes up—about 15 minutes. Roll into a sausage shape 1 inch in diameter and slice into 1-inch pieces. Makes 24.

❷ Roll each piece very thin and fry in a hot dry skillet until it blows up and bubbles. Flip, then cook until done on the other side.

❸ Make the filling. Pound the slices of beef or pork very thin and cut into 2-inch strips. Cut the washed green pepper and peeled carrot into matchsticks. Grind the hot peppers into a paste.

❹ Put 2 tablespoons of the oil in a wok or skillet; add salt and a pinch of finely chopped garlic. Get the oil very hot and cook the meat until it begins to turn color; remove with a slotted spoon.

❺ Throw the green pepper and carrot sticks into the same oil; toss for 1 minute over high heat. Add the meat, wine, soy sauce, and about 1 tablespoon of hot pepper paste. "Season discreetly, trusting your nose."

❻ Stir in up to 1 tablespoon of cornstarch dissolved in water. Remove the meat and vegetables with a slotted spoon, letting the oil drain off.

Szechwan Beef in Bau Bien (continued)

❼ Mix the hoisin sauce with the remaining tablespoon of oil and spread like jam on the Bau Bien. "Place Szechwan dynamite on Bau Bien; roll like Swedish pancakes or blintzes, depending on your ancestry. Eat like tacos, with pancake in one hand and a glass of ice water or chilled *vin rosé*—or a fire extinguisher—in the other." ⟫→ *Makes 4 servings*

▲▲▲▲▲▲▲▲▲▲▲▲▲▲▲▲▲▲▲▲▲▲▲▲▲▲▲▲▲▲▲

The Cooking Munster

He's been called "the only vampire with a Brooklyn accent," but Al Lewis, who was Grandpa on "The Munsters" television series, is now in the pasta and pizza business. His Belle Gente (that means "beautiful people") restaurant in Greenwich Village serves excellent Italian food. "No one has finer master chefs than I do," says Al.

"I went to Thomas Jefferson High School on Pennsylvania Avenue. I have the fondest memories. I loved school, and as I grew up, I learned to love restaurants. The marvelous Hopkins Cafeteria on Pitkin Avenue stands out, and so does Jack Fisher's Jewish-American place. The Kishka King was originally in Brownsville; it was run by a tall Jewish guy in a pith helmet who called himself Jungle Jim. He sold papaya and coconut drinks. I played cards with Nathan Handwerker, may he rest in peace. I once went out to Nathan's in

Al Lewis stirs it up.

a limo, bought two hot dogs, and jumped back in!"

Al Lewis has been a vegetarian since the 1940s. "I learned to cook by necessity," he says. "I rode a unicycle in the circus (if you like it, you'll become good at it). I lived alone, and I wanted control over what I ate. Later when my kids were growing up in California, I cooked probably ninety percent of what they ate. My former wife hated to cook.

"I knew Danny Kaye back in Brooklyn, but I was older so we didn't socialize then. But in California, we got together over Chinese cooking. Danny was the best Chinese chef in the U.S.A. He was a great entertainer. Somewhere he's making them laugh—and I hope he's holding a spot on the bill for me!"

Grandpa's Spinach Fettuccine with Crabmeat Sauce

1 pound fresh spinach fettuccine
4 tablespoons olive oil
6 medium shallots, chopped
8 ounces crabmeat or sea legs, chopped
4 tablespoons butter, at room temperature
2 fresh tomatoes, peeled, cored, and chopped
1 pint heavy cream
⅓ cup Chablis
Parsley for garnish
Grated cheese for garnish

❶ Cook the pasta in a large pot of lightly salted, rapidly boiling water for 3 to 6 minutes. Drain.

❷ Heat the oil in a saucepan over moderate heat. Add the shallots and cook for 1 to 2 minutes. Add the remaining ingredients and cook, stirring, for about 3 minutes more. Divide the pasta among bowls and pour the sauce over it. Garnish with parsley and cheese. ⮞ *Serves 5*

▲▲▲▲▲▲▲▲▲▲▲▲▲▲▲▲▲▲▲▲▲▲▲▲▲▲▲▲

Play That Pickle Melody

When something catches his fancy, Irving Fields just has to write a song about it. Take pickles: "I love half-sour pickles, and I bought a jar of beautiful bright green ones. The label said 'Ba-Tampte'—after a moment I realized that meant 'tasty' in Yiddish. And they were so delicious! I sat down and wrote 'The Pickle Polka,' and sent it off to them as a fan letter. They kindly sent me a case of pickles."

Mr. Fields has had a thoroughly satisfying career as pianist, composer ("Managua, Nicaragua" and "Miami Beach Rhumba" are two of his hits), recording artist, and "pianist entertainer." He was born in Coney Island, later moved to Bensonhurst, and took his first piano lesson at the age of eight.

As a very young man, he won on a "Fred Allen Amateur Program." In those days, the $50 prize was worth a lot, and winning was about the only way to get a professional break. "The applause meter was for real," he recalls. Before he found his preferred performing home of supper clubs and fine hotels, he played in "boozy, smoky beer joints and gin mills, including those on Coney Island's famous strip called the Bowery, but it was great training. I learned to play every kind of music for every kind of person. You can imagine the kind of bad food young entertainers had to live on. I really appreciate my wife's wonderful cooking."

"I met Irving at a resort in the Catskills when he was playing with his trio," says Ruth Fields. "I lived many years in Coney Island but we never met there. I find something very earthy and heartwarming about people who grew up in Brooklyn; I just had a reunion with friends from Coney Island I've kept in touch with all my life. We reminisced about teenage dances, and sleeping on the beach on very hot nights. One of my friends hadn't seen another one for forty-two years! But those friendships were binding."

The Palm Court at the Plaza Hotel is where Irving Fields currently works, playing "the music of thirty-five countries" for visitors. And he's written what we hope will be a smash hit—"What's Cookin' in Brooklyn"—celebrating this book!

Ruth Fields's Tzimmis

"This is a delicious dish, one we always have on Passover and other holidays," says Ruth Fields.

6 large sweet potatoes, peeled and cut into chunks

8 large carrots, peeled and cut into chunks

1 16-ounce can pineapple chunks, including the juice

4 tablespoons honey

¼ teaspoon cinnamon

4 ounces (1 stick) butter, cut into pieces

8 ounces orange juice

½ cup pitted prunes

❶ Put all the ingredients except the prunes into a heavy pot with a lid. Bring to the boil, lower the heat, and cover. Let the tzimmis barely simmer for 1½ hours, or until tender. Do not stir it for the first 30 minutes. Check from time to time, and if the tzimmis is dry, add a little more orange juice.

❷ Twenty minutes before the tzimmis is done, add the prunes and mix them in. Just before serving, mix gently to combine. ⟫→ *Serves 8 to 10*

▲▲▲▲▲▲▲▲▲▲▲▲▲▲▲▲▲▲▲▲▲▲▲▲▲▲▲▲▲▲

Henny Youngman's Cheese Blintzes

Funnyman Youngman's blintz sauces are pretty elegant fare, intended for a grown-up brunch. For humbler occasions, or for children, serve the blintzes with sour cream and blueberry or strawberry jam. If you use nonstick cookware, you will need very little butter to make the blintzes.

Batter

3 large eggs

1 cup milk

2 tablespoons vegetable oil

½ teaspoon salt

¾ cup all-purpose flour

Unsalted butter, melted

Filling

2 cups (16 ounces) cottage cheese

1 lightly beaten egg

2 tablespoons sugar

1 tablespoon unsalted butter, melted

1 teaspoon vanilla

¾ teaspoon salt

❶ To make the batter, put the eggs, milk, oil, and salt in a blender container. Blend well.

❷ Add the flour and blend until just combined, scraping down the sides once.

❸ Brush an 8-inch frying pan with melted butter. Pour in 2 to 3 tablespoons of batter, tilting the pan so the batter flows to coat the bottom. Use just enough batter to make a very thin pancake. Cook until the edges begin to turn golden. Shake the pan to loosen the pancake. Quickly turn the pancake out onto a paper towel, browned side up. Repeat with the remaining butter and batter, stacking the cooked pancakes between sheets of paper towel.

❹ Combine all the ingredients for the filling in a mixing bowl. Arrange a pancake, browned side up, and place a heaping spoonful of filling just above the center. Fold the sides toward the middle, overlapping the edges. Fold down the top to seal in the filling, then roll the pancake. You want to make a neat little packet.

❺ Arrange the blintzes, seam side down, on a heated griddle or in a large skillet brushed with butter. Cook until browned, turning once.

≫→ *Makes 14 to 18 blintzes*

Cinnamon Hot Apple Sauce for Blintzes

2 tablespoons unsalted butter
½ cup sugar
2 tablespoons grenadine syrup
2 cups sliced tart cooking apples
    (2 medium apples)

2 tablespoons sour cream
2 tablespoons heavy cream
¾ teaspoon cornstarch
1 tablespoon Calvados or apple brandy
    (optional)

❶ Melt the butter in a medium skillet over moderate heat. Add the sugar, syrup, and apple slices. Stir to coat the slices. Cover and cook, stirring once, until the apples are translucent, about 5 minutes.

❷ Stir together the sour cream, heavy cream, and cornstarch. Stir the mixture into the apples. Bring to the boil, cook for 1 minute, and remove from the heat. Stir in the Calvados. ≫→ *Makes 1¼ cups*

Spirited Blueberry Sauce for Blintzes

¾ cup white grape juice
¼ cup sugar
1 3-inch cinnamon stick
1 teaspoon freshly grated orange zest

2 cups blueberries
2 tablespoons sweet vermouth
1½ teaspoons cornstarch

❶ Combine the juice, sugar, cinnamon stick, and orange zest in a medium saucepan. Boil mixture for 5 minutes.

❷ Add the blueberries and cook, stirring occasionally, until the fruit begins to burst, about 3 minutes.

❸ Stir together the vermouth and cornstarch. Add to the saucepan, bring the mixture to the boil, and cook for 1 minute. Let cool, and remove the cinnamon stick. ≫→ *Makes 2 cups*

When Second Base Was a Sewer
Brownsville in the 1930s

Alvin Cooperman, a theatrical producer, director, and writer, was formerly president of Madison Square Garden, and a founder and past president of the New York Television Academy. Much sophisticated cuisine has come his way since boyhood (one of his three daughters, Karen, owned restaurants in New York and Boston, and was head pastry chef at Manhattan's Tavern on the Green), but his favorite food in all the world remains *potlajella*, an eggplant appetizer his mother made (recipe follows).

"I was born in Brownsville, in a two-family house. My father, mother, sister, and I lived downstairs, and upstairs lived my grandparents, my mother's two sisters, and my great-grandmother, who lived to be 106. I was raised with a lot of women, and always the smell of delicious food. I'd come home from school to the aroma of Grandma's *mandelbrot* or spongecake cooling on top of her china closet, in the dining room upstairs. And on Friday afternoons, there would be the smell of her stuffed derma, which we called *kishka*, wafting through the house. She used goose neck, hand-sewn and stuffed with her own special recipe of matzo meal, vegetables, beef fat, and spices. Our house was kosher, so there was no cooking from Friday at sundown until Saturday at sundown. But the house always smelled of wonderful food.

"I was a stickball nut. On Saturdays I'd go with my grandfather to temple, where he was the president. Of course there was no Saturday stickball near my Orthodox house, so I'd sneak over to another street. If my grandfather got wind of it, he'd chase after me with his cane! On other days we'd play in our street, where second base was a sewer. Herby Nathanson's father had the only car on the block, and we'd ask him to move it because it interfered with first base.

"My mother, father, sister, and I ate in the kitchen, on a porcelain table covered with oilcloth. No dining room for us. Our neighborhood was an enclave of working-class Orthodox Jews. We had respect for religion—ours and other people's. It was a time when personal dignity was very important. People had little money, but they knew the care of the family, and we had love and respect for older people. I started working at 15, and I would always give my seat on the subway to an older person.

"Gorelick's deli was at the corner of New Lots and New Jersey avenues. I remember that they laced their hot dogs with homemade potato salad. The candy store on New Jersey was a source of great satisfaction. With no money, you'd go in and smell the wonderful aroma of soda fountain. If you had a penny, you'd buy a chocolate mint with white filling. But if the filling was pink, you got a free piece of candy!

"Life was joyous; I didn't know we were poor until I grew much older."

Potlajella

"**O**ne of my favorite dishes is the Rumanian-Jewish appetizer my mother called* potlajella," *says Alvin Cooperman. "One eggplant will*

Young Alvin Cooperman with grandfather David Steinman.

satisfy two potlajella lovers. The method of chopping is very important. You need a little wooden bowl with a curved-blade rocker, like a half moon. Hand chopping gives a pleasant uneven consistency. We always liked our potlajella chopped fine."

Writer Andrew Ramer remembers that his grandmother added a great deal of garlic and used vinegar, whereas the Coopermans used only a little garlic and preferred lemon juice. In both households, the eggplant was charred on top of the stove until black. Messy, but it gives a characteristic smoky flavor that oven-baking can't accomplish. Serve it with black bread or on challah, adding more salt and olive oil if you like. "It hits the spot, too," says Cooperman, "on a kaiser roll with a slice of beefsteak tomato. Add more salt and olive oil, if you like."

- -

A 1½-pound eggplant
1 medium onion, finely chopped
1½ teaspoons minced garlic (or less, according to taste)

½ teaspoon salt
½ teaspoon lemon juice or vinegar
¼ cup olive oil

Preheat the oven to 400 degrees F.

❶ If you have a gas range, remove the grid of a burner and line the burner with foil, tearing it open to expose the gas element. (The foil will catch drips from the eggplant.) Replace the grid, prick the eggplant all over with a skewer, and place it directly over the gas element. Roast it over a high flame, turning it with tongs, until it is charred all over. Then put it in an ovenproof dish and roast it in the oven for 20 minutes or until tender all the way through.

If you prefer, skip the burner operation and roast the eggplant in the oven for 30 minutes, or until tender. In either case, let the eggplant cool and remove the skin.

❷ Chop the eggplant fairly fine with a chef's knife, and add the remaining ingredients. Or chop it with a curved rocker, along with coarsely chopped onion and garlic. Add the remaining ingredients. Refrigerate for 1 hour or longer to let the flavors blend. ⋙➤ *Makes 2 cups*

▲ ▲

My Grandmothers' Kitchens
Bensonhurst in the 1960s

Andrew Ramer, a writer, remembers the very different cooking in the households of his two grandmothers:

"Both my parents' families lived in Bensonhurst. My mother's mother was a fabulous baker who made all kinds of cookies, both sweet and salty. I don't know if it was just her custom, or had to do with where she came from in Russia, but first you had a sweet cookie, then a sip of very strong tea, then a salty cookie. Then you'd start again. She claimed alternating the cookies and tea refreshed the palate. The tea was always in a glass. The cookie I loved the most was called *tsibele kichel*, a little onion cookie. She was a great baker, but not the greatest cook.

"If we visiting kids were very good, she'd give us what she called 'colored tea.' You took a spoonful of Jell-O—any color you wanted—put it in a glass, and added tea. My grandmother always had three large mayonnaise jars of shimmering Jell-O in her refrigerator, just waiting for me. I thought they were so beautiful!

"My other grandmother was a really good cook. I remember her mushroom-barley soup, the unborn eggs in the chicken soup, and lots of *kreplach*, a sort of Jewish won ton. A great treat at her house was onion rubbed on matzo, with chicken fat and a lot of salt. She rendered her own chicken fat, of course.

"She made my father's favorite

Nan Herman, my grandmother, in her kitchen.

food in the world: eggplant, burned to a cinder on top of the stove, peeled and mixed with salt and pepper, oil and vinegar, and lots of garlic, chopped up in her wonderful wooden bowl with a half-moon chopper. That was a major taste of my childhood" (potlajella, preceding recipe).

Happy Birthday!

Mamaliga
(Cornmeal Cereal)

"Mamaliga is the only dish I recall my father making," says Andrew Ramer. "It's a Rumanian-Jewish *favorite. He ate it for breakfast with milk and sugar, or with sour cream and cottage cheese."*

....

3 cups water
1 teaspoon salt

1 cup yellow cornmeal
Vegetable oil
Sour cream

❶ Put the water and salt in a heavy saucepan. (If you want a very runny mamaliga, add an extra cup of water.) Stir in the cornmeal with a wooden spoon. When the mixture is smooth, cover and bring to the boil.

❷ Cook for 20 minutes, stirring frequently; the more you stir, the smoother the mamaliga.

❸ Serve runny mamaliga as a breakfast cereal, or turn firmer mamaliga out onto a board or marble slab and smooth the top with a spatula to form a rectangle about 1 inch high. When cold, cut into squares. Chill the mamaliga squares for up to 2 days, or freeze them. Fry lightly in vegetable oil and serve with sour cream. ⟫→ *Makes 2½ cups*

Tsibele Kichel
(Onion Rounds)

"These taste just like my grandmother Nan Herman's savory onion cookies. When I tasted my *recipe," Andrew says, "it took me right back to her house in Bensonhurst."*

....

¼ pound (1 stick) unsalted butter
2 teaspoons sugar
1 teaspoon salt
Liberal grindings of black pepper

1 egg yolk
1 tablespoon sour cream
1½ to 1¾ cups all-purpose flour
3 tablespoons finely chopped onion

❶ Cream the butter with the sugar, salt and pepper. Blend in the egg yolk and sour cream. Blend in 1½ cups of flour until the mixture resembles a coarse meal. Knead in the onion. If the dough seems too wet or buttery, add the extra ¼ cup of flour. Chill the dough for at least an hour.

Preheat the oven to 400 degrees F.

❷ On a lightly floured work surface, roll the dough out ¼ inch thick. Cut with a 2½-inch cookie cutter. Transfer them to a baking sheet. Bake for 12 to 15 minutes, or until lightly browned. Cool on a rack. ⟫→ *Makes about 20 rounds*

▲▲▲▲▲▲▲▲▲▲▲▲▲▲▲▲▲▲▲▲▲▲▲▲▲▲▲▲▲▲▲▲▲▲

The Belle of Flatbush

▲▲▲▲▲▲▲▲▲▲▲▲▲▲▲▲▲▲▲▲▲▲▲▲▲▲▲▲▲▲

Belle Silverman, born in Flatbush on May 25, 1929, was radio's "Rinso White" girl. She attended Erasmus Hall High School, as did another songbird, Barbra Streisand. Belle grew up to be the international opera star Beverly Sills. Below is her recipe for cookies ethereal as a floating high C, and appropriately named.

Beverly Sills' Air Cookies

3 large egg whites
¼ teaspoon cream of tartar

¾ cup sugar
3 tablespoons cocoa

Preheat the oven to 275 degrees F and line several baking sheets with aluminum foil.

❶ In a large mixing bowl, beat the egg whites and cream of tartar with an electric beater until foamy. Add sugar, 1 tablespoon at a time, and beat until stiff and glossy; do not underbeat. Put ¾ cup of the meringue in a small mixing bowl and set it aside.

❷ Stir the cocoa into the meringue in the large mixing bowl. Drop level measuring spoonfuls of the mixture 1½ inches apart on the baking sheets. With the top of a teaspoon, make a small indentation in the center of each cookie. Spoon ½ teaspoon of plain meringue into the center.

❸ Bake the cookies for 25 minutes. Turn off the oven and leave the cookies in the oven with the door closed for 1 hour. Remove and cool on racks.

≫⋅ *Makes 3 dozen cookies*

▲▲▲▲▲▲▲▲▲▲▲▲▲▲▲▲▲▲▲▲▲▲▲▲▲▲▲▲▲▲

A Stir-Fry and a Drink

Author Norman Mailer, who has lived for many years in Brooklyn Heights, contributes two recipes:

Stir-Fried Broccoli

"My favorite simple recipe is for stir-fried broccoli. Cut the flowers to the size of small flowers, approximately three-quarters of an inch, trim the stems so they're not much more than an inch long, and stir-fry in a very hot skillet with a minimum amount of oil for about 30 seconds, just long enough to allow the broccoli to turn emerald green. Then sprinkle generously with teriyaki sauce (I confess to liking Kikkoman the best for this) and remove from the fire. If cooked properly, the broccoli has a marvelous flavor. People who detest broccoli are startled by this dish."

Recipe for a Drink

"The recipe for a Gin and Tonic Presbyterian can also be used for a Vodka and Tonic Presbyterian, or Bacardi White Rum and Tonic ditto. Fill a highball glass with ice cubes; pour in an inch of the spirits being used; fill to within an inch of the top with water and add three-quarters of an inch of tonic (preferably Schweppes tonic). Add a thin slice of lemon. Stir well enough for the ingredients to mix. Club soda can be substituted for the water. Made properly, it tastes like a dry lemonade with a kick, and takes away the curse of drinking too many gin and tonics: the sour taste on one's tongue is notably absent. Caution: You can get just as drunk on this as on a number of gin and tonics."

When the Tradesmen Came to You

▲▲▲▲▲▲▲▲▲▲▲▲▲▲▲▲▲▲▲▲▲▲▲▲▲▲▲▲▲▲

Adele Miller Horowitz grew up in Borough Park in the late 1920s and early 1930s, on 47th Street between 15th and 16th avenues. In those pre-supermarket days, when people who had automobiles rarely used them for shopping, itinerant entrepreneurs who came right to the door eased the housewife's lot:

"A horse-drawn wagon with vegetables and fruits came by about every other day. This 'vegetable man' was Italian, and so was the 'fish man.' On Thursday or Friday, the 'fish man' brought two or three different kinds of fish, lying on ice on what could be described as a very large wheelbarrow or pushcart. He'd clean the fish for you. If you wanted live fish, you went to a store on 16th Avenue.

"My mother used to buy eggs from a very tall man, Mr. Kaufman, who delivered them from a farm. I have a special memory of this man. Once around Easter, when I was ill with scarlet fever, my father bought me some chicks to amuse me. (Only the thought amused me, as the chicks weren't allowed to be with me in quarantine.) One of the chicks grew up to become a fierce rooster with a strong territorial sense. He would let no one other than the family on our grounds without jumping at them and pecking at their legs. The only thing he was afraid of was the broom. Most people simply shooed Jack the Rooster away, but Mr. Kaufman was terrified of him.

So, on the day he was due to come, we would leave a broom at the curb so that he could approach the door with 'armor.' I still remember that man—so big and burly—fearfully fighting off the rooster.

"As I recall, my mother probably bought butter from him, too. At Passover she would buy a case of eggs; a dozen dozen. Nobody knew about cholesterol. We ate matzo brei and matzo-meal pancakes and matzo-ball soup, and other things too. But Passover required a lot of eggs!

"Another salesman was Mr. Kaplan, from Ireland, who came around with table linens and dishes. My mother loved fancy linens, and I do too; I still have her Passover dishes and many of her linens.

"The milk, in very cold weather, always had the cream popping out of the top—it wasn't homogenized. Milk from the Sheffield Dairy was delivered in the early hours, and one had to remember to leave a list of what was wanted. I recall the wagons, before the milkmen had trucks. The horse knew the route as well as the driver.

"Dugan's bakery delivered in the daytime. Their whole wheat muffins were wonderful. Only my mother's muffins were better."

Adele Horowitz's Mother's Muffins

"My *mother used to whip these up at a moment's notice," says Adele Horowitz, "or so it seemed to me. But she took the recipe with her up to the kitchen in the sky, and we thought that was the end of it. Then years later, Craig Claiborne published a recipe for a Jamaican 'rub-up' cake. Something made me feel that with adaptations this could duplicate my mother's muffins, and it does."*

2½ cups all-purpose flour
4 teaspoons baking powder
½ teaspoon salt
4 ounces (1 stick) unsalted butter

1 cup sugar
3 eggs
1 whole orange, rind included, washed
½ cup milk

Preheat the oven to 350 degrees F.

❶ Sift together the flour, baking powder, and salt. With a pastry blender, or in the food processor, work the butter into the flour mixture until it resembles coarse meal.

❷ Mix together the sugar and eggs, and the orange, cut into pieces. (Discard the seeds, but use the rind.) In a blender or food processor, whirl the ingredients for a few seconds, until the orange is in tiny bits. Add the milk. Stir this mixture quickly into the flour mixture with a wooden spoon; some lumps will remain.

❸ Fill greased muffin cups two-thirds full with the batter. Bake for about 45 minutes, until the muffins are lightly browned and a toothpick inserted in the center comes out clean. Let them rest in the tin for a few minutes before removing. The muffins are moist, with an open texture. ⟫→ *Makes 12 muffins*

Note: The recipe can also be made as a cake, in a tall heavy greased 10-inch tube pan. Bake for 45 to 60 minutes.

▲▲▲▲▲▲▲▲▲▲▲▲▲▲▲▲▲▲▲▲▲▲▲▲▲▲▲▲▲▲▲

Pan-Fried Sesame Tofu

Cathy Deutsch is a second-generation Brooklynite, born in Brownsville. She now lives in Park Slope, where she runs a neighborhood metaphysical store that specializes in books, crystals, and other New Age materials. "Mostly" a vegetarian, she loves all ethnic food. This tofu dish represents her style of healthful daily cooking.

A 1-pound solid cake firm organic tofu, or the equivalent in smaller tofu cakes
Sesame seeds
3 tablespoons olive oil
3 cloves garlic, pressed or minced
1 tablespoon Oriental sesame oil
3 tablespoons tamari (wheat-free soy sauce)
¼ cup water
1 cup chopped green beans or broccoli

❶ Cut the tofu into 1-inch cubes. Pat dry and set aside.

❷ In a medium cast iron skillet, heat the sesame seeds over moderate heat, turning them constantly until they are brown. Watch carefully; they burn easily. Add the olive oil; when it begins to sizzle, stir in the pressed garlic. Cook, stirring, until the garlic bits are lightly browned.

❸ Immediately add the tofu cubes and cook, turning gently, until they are brown and crispy on all sides. (If necessary, raise the heat a little.) Sprinkle on the sesame oil. Add the tamari, water, and chopped vegetables. Bring to the boil, cover, lower the heat, and steam for 15 minutes until the vegetable is cooked through but somewhat crisp. ≫→ *Serves 4*

Fried Noodle Pie

Jim Kalett lives in Park Slope with his wife, Carolyn, and Portuguese water dog, Chester. He is a photographer whose work includes Brooklyn and How It Got That Way, done in collaboration with writer David W. McCullough.

"This recipe is inspired by one I found in a James Beard book," says Jim. "What you want is a thin pie. If you're serving eight, make two pies."

4½ cups broad egg noodles
3 to 5 tablespoons olive oil
3 garlic cloves, peeled and sliced
1 teaspoon salt
Freshly ground black pepper
2 tablespoons dried basil
1 cup freshly grated Parmesan cheese

❶ Bring a large pot of lightly salted water to the boil. Cook the noodles according to package directions and drain them.

❷ Meanwhile, heat the oil in a 12-inch nonstick skillet and brown the garlic well. Remove and discard it.

❸ Off the heat, put the drained noodles in the pan, sprinkle them with the salt, pepper, and basil and turn them well in the oil. With a spatula or back of a wooden spoon spread them out evenly to cover the pan. Turn on the heat very low. Cook the noodles, uncovered, for 45 minutes. From time to time, shake the pan to see that they are not sticking, and use a spatula to peek underneath to see how they are browning. After 45 minutes the noodles should be dark brown. If a few are black, don't fret. The pie is even better.

❹ Invert a warmed serving plate over the pan and flip the noodle pie onto it. Immediately cover the pie evenly with the cheese, and add lots of freshly ground pepper. Serve at once. ⟫→ *Serves 4*

Jean Fink Hooker's Chocolate Fudge Cake

"I*'ve made this cake so many times I can't count them," says Jean Hooker, the third generation of her family to live in Brooklyn Heights, "and it will not fail. It also freezes well." Jean taught cooking to children at the YWHA in Manhattan,* *and now teaches at nearby Packer Collegiate Institute. Her class put together a cookbook,* Delicious Dinners, *for five- to eight-year-olds. At home, three-year-old Elizabeth helps in the kitchen, where she is a whiz at cracking eggs.*

Cake
1 teaspoon baking soda
1 cup all-purpose flour
1½ teaspoons baking powder
¼ teaspoon salt
5 large eggs, separated
1¾ cups sugar, divided
½ teaspoon lemon juice (optional)
8 ounces (2 sticks) unsalted butter
½ cup plus 2 tablespoons cocoa
    powder

½ cup plus 2 tablespoons sour cream
2 teaspoons vanilla
Glaze
2 tablespoons water
2 tablespoons unsalted butter
½ cup (3 ounces) semi-sweet
    chocolate chips
¼ cup confectioners' sugar
1½ tablespoons finely ground blanched
    almonds

Preheat the oven to 350 degrees F.

❶ Butter and flour a 12-cup Bundt pan or three 9-inch cake pans. Put the baking soda in a small sieve and press it into a mixing bowl with the back of a spoon, to remove any lumps. Add the flour, baking powder, and salt.

❷ In the work bowl of a food processor equipped with the metal blade, put the egg whites and 3 tablespoons of the sugar. Turn the motor on and off, pulsing until the egg whites have mounted and hold their shape. With a rubber spatula, gently transfer the whipped whites to the mixing bowl. It is not necessary to wash the work bowl. (To ensure that the whites rise, you may add ½ teaspoon lemon juice.)

❸ Process the egg yolks and the remaining sugar for 40 seconds, stopping once to scrape down the work bowl. Add the butter and cocoa and process for 40 seconds, stopping once to scrape down the work bowl. Add the sour cream and vanilla and process for 5 seconds.

❹ Spoon the dry ingredients in a ring on the batter, then spoon on the egg whites. Pulse on/off two times. Run a spatula around the inside of the work bowl to loosen the mixture. Pulse twice more, just so the ingredients are combined; do not overprocess. Some streaks of egg white should still be visible. Pour the batter into the prepared pan.

❺ Bake in the center of the oven until a toothpick inserted in the center comes out clean, about 40 minutes. Let the cake cool in the pan on a rack for 10 minutes, then invert it onto the rack.

❻ To make the glaze, place all the ingredients, except the almonds, in a small heavy saucepan. Place over very low heat and stir constantly, until the chocolate is melted. Refrigerate the glaze in its pan until it just begins to thicken. While the cake is still warm, drizzle the glaze around the top, letting it run down the side. Garnish with the ground almonds. ⟫➔ *Makes one 12-cup Bundt cake or one 9-inch 3-layer cake*

Margaret Palca's Chocolate-Filled Rugalach

"I *developed this recipe with my partner, combining recipes from our grandmothers,"* says Margaret Palca. *She is now owner of Margaret Palca Bakes, a wholesale-retail bakery on President Street.*

The Yiddish word is rogele *for a single pastry,* rogelekh *in the plural.*

If you have doubts about your ability to handle a somewhat sticky dough, Margaret suggests that you beat in 2 or 3 extra tablespoons of flour when you make the dough.

Dough

14 ounces (3½ sticks) unsalted butter, at room temperature
8 ounces cream cheese, at room temperature
½ cup confectioners' sugar
2 cups all-purpose flour

Filling

1½ cups chopped pecans
1½ cups mini–chocolate chips
¾ cup sugar
2 teaspoons cinnamon
½ cup apricot preserves

❶ Using a heavy-duty electric mixer, beat the butter and cream cheese together on medium speed until light and fluffy. Reduce the speed to low, add the confectioners' sugar, and continue beating until well blended. Gradually add the flour, a little at a time, until the dough is blended. Scrape down the side of the bowl as needed.

❷ Divide the dough into 4 portions, place each on a sheet of plastic wrap, and enclose the dough with the wrap. Refrigerate the dough overnight; it must be well chilled and firm.

❸ When ready to bake, cut four 12-inch squares of wax paper and set them aside. Grease three large baking sheets. Work with one portion of dough at a time and leave the remaining portions in the refrigerator.

❹ Place a portion of the dough on a floured surface and knead it slightly until it is smooth, about 10 seconds. If it is too firm to knead, let it soften slightly, about 5 minutes.

❺ Flour one square of wax paper. Place the dough in the center and form a 6-inch circle of dough with your fingertips. Sprinkle the dough with flour and roll it into a 12-inch circle. Set aside on a cookie sheet or flat surface. Repeat the process with the 3 remaining portions of dough. Chill the dough for at least 1 hour.

Preheat the oven to 350 degrees F.

Rugalach (continued)

❻ In the meantime, prepare the filling. Combine the chopped nuts, chocolate chips, sugar, and cinnamon; blend well. Remove one circle of dough from the refrigerator at a time and, working quickly, spread 1½ to 2 tablespoons of preserves in the center. Then sprinkle with 1 cup of the filling mixture, spreading it evenly to the edge. Cut the dough into 16 even wedges. Starting from the outside edge, roll each wedge toward the center. Place the rugalach on greased baking sheets ½ inch apart.

❼ Continue the process with the remaining dough rounds. Bake rugalach for 25 to 30 minutes, turning the pans after 15 minutes. Cool on wire racks.

⫸ *Makes 64 portions*

"Bungalow Bar, Tastes Like Tar"

Amy and Gary Krakow recall the goodies that sweetened their Brooklyn youth. Seems like yesterday . . .

Gary. "Dugan's Bakery trucks delivered to your house, just like the milkman. The bran muffins were like lead, but everybody bought the cupcakes."

Amy. "They came six to a package, two white, two red, and two chocolate. Yellow cake below and perfect icing. You lifted off the icing and threw away the cake."

Gary. "The Bungalow Bar man and the Good Humor man went around in trucks, too."

Amy. " 'Bungalow Bar, Tastes Like Tar, The More You Eat, the Sicker You Are.' Actually, we liked them. The Good Humor men wore all-white uniforms. They had trucks, and also carts they pushed. They came out on April 15th, and they went back in on October 15th. That was the only time you got Good Humor."

Gary. "Then there was the Chow Chow cup, sold in the early '60s. The trucks played Oriental music. The stuff was chow mein in a cup formed from noodles. A tiny scoop of rice and then this terrible chow mein on top. But it was so popular and successful they opened stores."

Kamish Bread

Sarah Brash got this recipe from a friend who was not sure of the origin, though it seems pretty certain that it is a cousin of mandelbrot. The word "kamish" shows how language can deform. The friend thought it meant "homey and comforting," mistaking it for the real Yiddish word, hamish or heimish. Kamish or hamish, it's not too sweet and just right with coffee.

1 cup vegetable oil
4 eggs
1 cup sugar
1 teaspoon salt
3 teaspoons baking powder
¼ teaspoon baking soda
1 cup finely chopped walnuts, almonds, or pecans

2 teaspoons vanilla
1 teaspoon lemon extract
4 to 4½ cups flour
1 teaspoon cinnamon
½ cup sugar

❶ Blend the oil, eggs, and sugar together. Stir in the salt, baking powder, soda, nuts, vanilla, and lemon extract; mix well. Stir in 4 cups of the flour, a little at a time. You want a stiff dough; work in some or all of the extra half-cup of flour as necessary.

Preheat the oven to 350 degrees F.

❷ On a lightly floured work surface, form the dough into 6 thin rolls, each about 14 inches long. Arrange the rolls on baking sheets, 3 to a sheet. (You may prefer to make the rolls shorter and plumper; if so, bake them somewhat longer.) Bake the rolls until they are lightly browned, about 30 minutes.

❸ Transfer each baked roll to a board and cut it into 1-inch slices while still warm. Mix the cinnamon and sugar in a small bowl. Coat each slice with cinnamon and sugar mixture and return it to the baking sheet. Return them to the oven and bake until crisp, about 15 minutes. ➤ *Makes 84 slices*

My Bubie's Latkes

Zeide and Bubie—Mr. and Mrs. Morris Miller—holding their twin great-granddaughters.

Barbara Sigety Gregory lives in Dallas now, but she fondly remembers the latke noshes at the Ocean Avenue home of her maternal grandparents, Gussie and Morris Miller:

"Bubie and Zeide, as I and my friends from Erasmus Hall High School called them, made us welcome in their home, and we would drop by often. No matter what time of day or day of the week, Bubie would greet us with bear hugs and kisses, and say, 'You're just in time to eat. I'm making potato latkes. Sit, you'll have some.'

"It seemed a miracle to us that her latkes were *always* ready, even though she had no way of knowing when we would visit. It got to be a challenge to catch Bubie latke-less, but we never did."

Latkes
(Potato Pancakes)

The addition of dill weed to traditional latkes is unusual but pleasant. If you add it, serve the latkes with sour cream only. The recipe may be doubled.

1 small yellow onion, peeled
1 pound Idaho potatoes, peeled
1 lightly beaten egg
1 tablespoon matzo meal
½ teaspoon salt

Freshly ground black or white pepper
   to taste
¼ teaspoon dried dill weed (optional)
3 tablespoons vegetable oil
Applesauce
Sour cream

❶ Grate the onion into a bowl on the medium-coarse holes of a hand grater. Grate the potatoes the same way. Stir now and then to keep the potatoes from discoloring. Lightly squeeze handfuls of the mixture over the sink to get rid of some of the liquid, but keep the white starch that settles in the bottom of the bowl. Stir in the egg, matzo meal, salt, pepper, and optional dill weed.

❷ Heat 1 tablespoon of the oil in a 10- or 12-inch nonstick skillet. When the oil is rippling, spoon in ¼ cup of the mixture for each latke and flatten it out with the back of a spoon; you will be able to make 2 or 3 latkes at one time. Cook over moderately high heat for about 3 minutes. Turn and cook for 3 minutes on the other side. The latkes should be crisp and nicely browned. Add more oil as needed for each batch. Serve immediately, with applesauce and sour cream. ⟫→ *Makes six 5-inch latkes*

▲▲▲▲▲▲▲▲▲▲▲▲▲▲▲▲▲▲▲▲▲▲▲▲▲▲▲▲▲▲

Aunt Bertie's Potato Kugel

Uncle Jimmy and Aunt Bertie Schwartz.

Food *professional Joan Garvin's aunt, Bertha Schwartz, was born in Russia. She came to Flatbush over 40 years ago, via the Lower East Side. Of her kugel she says: "Mama made potato pancakes, and I did too. Then I thought, why stand in a lonely kitchen making batch after batch? This bakes in the oven and everyone enjoys it at once, as an accompaniment to meat. You can serve it with applesauce, too."*

3 pounds potatoes, not Idahos (about 7 medium potatoes)
1 large onion, grated
2 teaspoons salt

2 eggs, beaten
¼ cup peanut oil
5 tablespoons matzo meal

Preheat the oven to 350 degrees F.

❶ Grease a 9-inch × 7-inch × 2-inch pan (or a round or square 8-inch pan).

❷ Grate the potatoes fairly fine, using a processor or hand grater. Squeeze the grated potatoes and discard the excess liquid.

❸ Put the potato and onion shreds in a large bowl. Add the salt, eggs, and oil and mix well. Add the matzo meal to bind; the mixture should not be too runny, nor too dry either. Add a little more meal, if necessary. Pour into the pan and bake for 1 hour. Run the baked kugel under the broiler for 2 minutes or so, to crisp the top. ⟫→ *Serves 4 to 6*

Mother-in-Law's Stuffed Cabbage

"My *mother-in-law, Nan Herman, was controlling, loving, demanding, and tenderly tyrannical," recounts Gerry Shields, "but she thought I was good enough for her son. And what a cook that woman was!*

"She brought this recipe with her from Hungary, and adapted it to American products. I've made her holopches through many migrations, from Brooklyn to Queens to Long Island to California. I've battled my sister-in-law over who is the owner of the true recipe, and I know I'm right. The only modern touch I've added is freezing the cabbage. That makes the leaves soft and pliable, perfect for rolling."

....

Cabbage Rolls
A 3-pound green cabbage, frozen solid
1 pound lean ground round
1¼ cups chopped onion
1¼ cups diced apple, Granny Smith or Rome
½ cup long-grain rice, rinsed
1 tablespoon ketchup (Heinz preferred)

1 tablespoon cider vinegar
3 tablespoons maple syrup
2 teaspoons salt

Sauce
2 cups water
½ cup ketchup
4 tablespoons cider vinegar
½ cup maple syrup

❶ Defrost the cabbage thoroughly. Cut around the base and pull off the outer leaves. Keep making shallow cuts and removing leaves until you get to the inner core.

❷ In a large bowl, combine the meat, onion, apple, and rice. In a small bowl, mix the ketchup, vinegar, maple syrup, and salt. Pour the ketchup mixture over the meat mixture and combine well, using your hands or a wooden spoon.

❸ Spread out a cabbage leaf. Cut out and discard a small "V" from the tough portion at the bottom. Place 1½ to 2 tablespoons of filling (depending on the size of the leaf) in the center of the leaf and use your fingers to form it into a sausage across the width of the leaf. Roll up the leaf from bottom to top, neatly tucking in the sides to make a small package. Place it seam side down. Continue rolling leaves until the filling is used up. (If you run out of big leaves, patch two small ones together.)

❹ Combine all the ingredients for the sauce and mix them well.

❺ A chicken fryer or other straight-sided wide pot that is not too high is ideal for cooking cabbage rolls. Arrange some of the extra or torn leaves on the bottom and place the rolls, seam side down, in the pot. (Use two pots if necessary.) Pour the sauce over the rolls and place a plate on top to keep the rolls from rising and bobbing. Bring the liquid to the boil, partially cover the pot, and braise the rolls until the cabbage is tender, about 1 hour. (Can be done ahead to this point.)

Preheat the oven to 300 degrees F.

6 When the rolls are cool enough to handle, place them fairly tightly side by side in a wide baking dish in a single layer. Pour the sauce over the rolls and bake for 1 hour, or until the cabbage is lightly browned.

➤➤ *Makes approximately 30 rolls*

Mannie's Luncheonette

Marion D. Meyerson lives in San Francisco now, but in the late '40s and early '50s she hung out at Mannie's, on Saratoga Avenue. "Their potato salad was my dietary staple all through high school," she recalls. "Mannie really understood service. Buttered English muffins were provided for the dogs of favorite patrons."

Smiles at the counter: Mannie's, circa 1950.

The Zei-Mar Deli

"**M**y cousins the Schwartzes owned a deli in Brighton Beach, next to the Oceana Theatre," recalls Jerry Sternstein, a professor of history at Brooklyn College. "It was called the Zei-Mar, and it was one of the largest-grossing delis in Brooklyn, because of its proximity to the beach. I worked there after school, in the 1950s. Abe, the father, was in the deli business since he came from Europe early in the century. His sons were Leo and Jack.

"This was a kosher deli and sold strictly meats, no whitefish or other smoked fish. Hours were from 9 a.m. to 2 a.m. They had about 16 tables, but the main business was take-out. People stood three deep at the counter. The sandwiches were huge. They used seeded rye, and also did what was called a club sandwich—not with three slices of bread, as you might think, but on a long roll, called a club roll. It was crusty in the morning, soft in the afternoon. For a meal, you got your sandwich, potato salad or coleslaw, a quarter of a pickled green tomato, half a pickled pepper, and a big slice of pickle. Everything was made in the store—the pickled tomatoes, half-sours, and kraut.

"The major role of the counterman was speed, speed, speed. Get it out. If you were selling sliced meat and let the needle on the scale settle exactly, you wouldn't last long. There were a lot of tricks in the deli trade, such as bouncing an order on the scale. The meat hit with an impact, the needle shot up, you grabbed the package off the scale, and no one noticed that it was short an ounce or two. Except some elderly Jewish women. They were fierce! And you'd pack the sandwich so it looked even bigger—pile all the meat in the center, so it made a sort of dome, but the ends were empty!

"All the meats were excellent. They had roast beef, turkey, baloney, and a variety of pastramis. The Zei-Mar did a lot of catering platters too, for bar mitzvahs and the like. Catering is closely connected to Jewish temples—so much so I'm sure there is some allusion to it in the Talmud. And the drink of choice was Dr. Brown's Cel-Ray tonic, the *vin du pays* of Brighton Beach."

"We smoked all our own meats," says Leo Schwartz, a retired owner of the Zei-Mar, "and we made our own corned beef. It takes three to four weeks to cure good corned beef. Now it's often just pumped with brine and it's ready in two days. One of our best sellers was what we called 'honey beef Israeli style'; it was corned beef boiled but not too soft, then topped with honey, brown sugar, and cloves like a Virginia ham, and baked. And we sold a lot of Rumanian pastrami, for those who demanded very lean meat. You had to cut it very thin or it was too chewy. I like a little fat myself. Rumanian pastrami looked like Canadian bacon. But in a kosher deli you couldn't even *breathe* the words 'ham' and 'bacon.'"

Deli Potato Salad

Kosher deli potato salad never contains milk.

4 large boiling potatoes, or 6 medium new potatoes
2 teaspoons sugar
3 tablespoons white vinegar
3 tablespoons vegetable oil
Salt and pepper to taste

1 cup mayonnaise
1 teaspoon celery salt
¼ cup finely chopped carrot
¼ cup finely chopped drained bottled pimento

❶ Boil the potatoes in lightly salted water until just tender. When they are cool enough to handle, peel and slice them about ¼ inch thick. Put in a bowl.

❷ While the potatoes boil, mix the sugar into the vinegar, stirring to dissolve it. Whisk in the oil, salt and pepper. Pour this mixture over the warm potatoes, and mix gently.

❸ Mix together the mayonnaise, celery salt, chopped carrots, and pimento. When the potatoes have cooled, mix them with the dressing. ⫸ *Serves 4*

Window of the Zei-Mar Deli.

Bagels in Brooklyn

We make no claims that bagels, the round, chewy yeast breads with the hole in the middle, are indigenous to Brooklyn, but as waves of Jewish immigrants moved across the East River to a better life, they brought this vital foodstuff with them.

"I am part of a bagel-baker dynasty," says Lily Lifshutz. "My father, my stepfather, my half brothers, and my uncles all were in the business. And I married Leon, a bagel baker! My father came from Russia and my mother, from Poland in the early 1900s. Like so many others, they went directly from Ellis Island to lower Manhattan. The life of a bagel baker was dismal then—choking, dark, windowless cellars and long, long hours. My father brought his skill with him, and he earned $5 a week. Not much, but a trade gave a man dignity—he wasn't a *luftmensch*, a ne'er-do-well—he had something solid. The Lower East Side was a hellish place to live, old-law dumbbell apartments with toilets in the hall, crowding, and a tremendous amount of ill health. As fortunes improved a little, people were able to move. Whole sections of Brooklyn were opening up. We moved to Williamsburg. My parents divorced, and my mother remarried, a man who owned a bagel bakery in Bensonhurst. The bagels then were superb!"

"Until 1950, bagel bakeries were underground," says Leon Lifshutz: "the earth served as insulation for the coal-fired ovens. Gas and oil came in, and better insulated ovens, but those coal ovens made a beautiful golden brown bagel. I think the hand work affected the quality too; but with progress came the dough mixer. I still think the hand-made ones tasted best.

"My bakery was on Linden Boulevard. It was called the Triple L: two of us partners had wives named Lillian, and the third partner's wife was named Lorraine. The name honored the ladies.

"The man who makes the dough must figure in advance how long rising will take: I had a formula—to bake at 5 p.m., we started at noon. If it was humid, I'd use less yeast; if dry, more. To produce 60 dozen bagels, I'd use 100 pounds of high-gluten flour, 24 quarts of water, 24 ounces of a combination of malt, brown sugar, or honey, or just one of those sweetenings, 24 ounces of salt, and yeast for proofing. I'd mix the dough slowly and let it rest half an hour.

"You put the dough on the bench and cut strips of it. Your left hand is constantly rolling, then you quickly shape the bagel around your hand. There is a definite rhythm. A friend and I had a speed contest one time. He made 112 dozen bagels in an hour. I made 117 dozen in that hour!

"There were 12 bagel bakeries in Brooklyn out of 34 in the New

York area. All staunch union shops. I sold bagels for 4 cents apiece, 48 cents a dozen. Our union has a monopoly, so we were able to raise the price to 5 cents. Bagels were generally eight to the pound, much smaller than those of today. We made big ones only for restaurants; they were called 'bulls.' For grocery stores, we threaded them onto a string, and the grocer hung the string on the door. It's more sanitary now. All in all, bagels afforded us a good life."

Bagels

Very good bagels can be made with a food processor. Note that bagels are briefly boiled before they are baked. They can be topped with coarse salt, poppy seeds, or sesame seeds before baking. The recipe was developed by food processor expert Barbara Somers.

1 package active dry yeast
⅓ cup warm water
1 teaspoon salt
4 cups all-purpose or bread flour
2 tablespoons sugar

1 cup milk
1 egg, beaten with a little water, for glaze
Coarse salt, or poppy or sesame seeds (optional)

❶ Sprinkle the yeast over the warm water, stir, and let dissolve.

❷ Put the salt, flour, and 4 teaspoons of the sugar in the bowl of a food processor equipped with the dough blade. Pulse the mixture several times to mix it well. (This action aerates the ingredients.)

❸ Combine the yeast mixture and milk in a measuring cup. With the motor running, pour the mixture through the feed tube. Knead until the mixture balls together and is no longer sticky, about 60 seconds. Lightly flour a large plastic bag, place the dough in it, squeeze out the air, and close the end of the bag with a twist tie. Let the dough rise until doubled, about 45 minutes. Punch it down. (At this point, the dough can be refrigerated for up to 4 days. Bring it to room temperature before proceeding.)

❹ Let the dough rest for 10 minutes. Pull off pieces of dough to form 12 2-inch balls. Poke a finger through the ball, making a hole the size of a golf ball. With your fingers, shape the bagel evenly. Put the bagels on a tray or cookie sheet, cover them with oiled plastic wrap, and let them rise until puffy, about 30 minutes.

Preheat the oven to 400 degrees F.

❺ Bring 4 quarts of water to the boil in a wide pot. Add the remaining 2 teaspoons of sugar. Poach the bagels, 3 or 4 at a time, for 30 seconds. Turn them and poach for 30 seconds more. Remove them with a slotted spoon, let them drip briefly on a towel held under the spoon, and place them 1 inch apart on baking sheets. Brush each bagel with a little of the egg glaze. (At this point you may sprinkle on coarse salt, or poppy or sesame seeds.) Bake until golden, about 15 minutes. Let cool on racks. ⟫➔ *Makes 1 dozen bagels*

Tip from Leon Lifshutz: To revive a bagel past its prime, preheat the oven to 350 degrees F. Sprinkle the bagel with water and place it in the oven for 1 to 2 minutes. It will taste fresh.

▲▲▲▲▲▲▲▲▲▲▲▲▲▲▲▲▲▲▲▲▲▲▲▲▲▲▲▲▲▲

Chicken Soup, and This Is It

Some of the best and most opinionated minds in Brooklyn have been consulted on this serious subject. Some opine that a chicken (always called a "hen") should be cooked only a short time, removed, and either baked or used in some other dish. These experts insist that this method gives a delicate broth and tender meat to work with.

Others feel just as strongly that when we're talking soup, that is the chicken's destiny, nothing else. Some use the meat in the soup, some discard it altogether.

Below is a succulent broth that you can use for a soup base or for any recipe calling for broth. Following are other recipes and digressions upon the subject.

Rich Chicken Broth

Soup hens used to be easy to find: over-the-hill layers ending their careers in a deeply flavorful broth. If you can't find a hen, use the equivalent weight in chicken parts.

Don't try to save any of the meat for eating; it should give its all to the broth. Leave the skin on the onions to add color to the broth.

A 5- to 5½-pound soup hen, or
   equivalent weight in parts
3½ quarts water
3 medium onions
1 clove
2 carrots scraped but not peeled, cut in
   two

2 celery stalks with leaves, cut in two
1 bay leaf
10 peppercorns
1 teaspoon salt
2 teaspoons any type of vinegar

❶ Put the hen or parts in a tall stockpot. Cover with the water and, over moderate heat, bring slowly to the boil. As scum rises, skim it off and discard. The scum will continue to rise for about 10 minutes.

❷ Meanwhile, top and tail the onions and stick one of them with the clove. When only white froth is rising from the liquid, add the remaining ingredients. (The vinegar is added to leach calcium from the bones; any vinegar flavor will dissipate.)

❸ When the liquid boils again, lower the heat, partially cover, and keep the stock at a simmer until the meat is falling off the bones, about 2½ to 3 hours.

❹ Strain the broth, pressing down on the solids with the back of a wooden spoon. When the stock is tepid, refrigerate it, uncovered, until the fat rises and solidifies. Lift off the fat and discard it. Use or freeze the broth.

➤ *Makes 3¼ quarts*

Phyllis Schweiger's Soup, "Just Like My Grandma's"

"**M**y Grandma Esther Barson, who was a pants finisher and a fine cook, would send me to the store with a verbal list of things to ask for," says Phyllis Schweiger. "The list was in Yiddish, and I'd just parrot what she said. I didn't really pay attention to what I was getting.

"Much later, I wanted to duplicate that great soup, but I didn't know the English for what I needed. I kept trying until I was satisfied the soup tasted like hers. Her vegetables were very chunky, and I remember that she always asked for a 'petrushka.' I recalled that it looked like a parsnip, so that's what I used. Someone recently told me that a petrushka is really a small Italian parsley root, that just looks like a parsnip. But as I put in a lot of parsley anyway, I got the taste I wanted. Serve the soup with matzo balls."

8 chicken legs

1 medium parsnip, cut into rounds

3 or 4 carrots, cut into chunks

3 stalks celery, cut into chunks

2 medium onions, sliced

¼ bunch parsley, chopped

¼ bunch dill weed, chopped

Salt to taste

❶ Put all the ingredients in a stockpot. Add 12 cups of water, bring it to the boil. Lower the heat and let simmer, partially covered, skimming from time to time. Cook for 2 to 2½ hours. Let the soup sit in the uncovered pot for another hour. If you are planning to serve it at once, skim off the fat. Reheat before serving.

❷ If you plan to serve the soup the following day, refrigerate it when cool. Lift off the fat that has risen to the top and discard it. Reheat, serve.

≫→ *Serves 8*

Matzo Balls

"Here is the perfect matzo ball," claims chef Rona Moulu. "Not too dense, not too light, just right! You can also freeze them in broth and they're fine."

2 eggs

8 ounces matzo meal

¾ cup cold water

2 heaping tablespoons chicken fat

Pinch of salt

❶ In a medium bowl, beat the eggs. Alternately add the matzo meal, cold water, and chicken fat. Add the salt and mix well. Cover the dough with plastic wrap and refrigerate for at least 4 hours or overnight.

❷ Have ready a large pot of salted boiling water.

❸ Form walnut-sized balls, about 1½ inches in diameter. Drop them into boiling water, partially cover the pot, and let simmer for 1 hour. Remove the matzo balls and drop them into cold water. Use them at once, reheated in chicken soup, or refrigerate until needed. ≫→ *Makes 12 to 16 matzo balls*

Thoughts on Chicken Soup,
Julia Waldbaum and Randie Malinsky

"When you boil the meat for kreplachs," says Julia Waldbaum, matriarch of a very large family and consumer advocate for the Waldbaum supermarket chain, "you can add a chicken. That's the base for a great soup!" "Around the Jewish holidays we carry what are called 'yearlings' in the stores," says her granddaughter Randie. "Those are extra-fatty fowl that make wonderful soup."

Both agree that perfect chicken soup should have carrots, parsley, dill ("That's the taste," says Randie), and turnips. "Skim the soup well," Randie advises.

Diane Berg Remembers Schmaltz

"My father had a kosher butcher shop on Livonia Avenue, and I used to sit in the window as a little kid, plucking chickens. You cannot put kosher chickens in water to make the feathers come out easily. You have to pluck them carefully. Women would blow on the live chickens' necks to part the feathers and see the color of the skin. They were looking for fat chickens because they all wanted a lot of schmaltz—that's fat. We lived on it! Our mothers used it in herring, in chopped liver, in chopped eggs, and I loved it on matzo. My mother put schmaltz on mashed potatoes. It had crispy bits of onion from the rendering. It gives a flavor that kids today don't know. Now I make soup with fryers. There's less fat."

Mother's Chicken Soup with Dill

"I *was born in Borough Park and grew up in Bensonhurst," says Adele Shrem. "It was a mixed neighborhood, Jewish and Italian. We got along great and we exchanged recipes." This chicken soup recipe was taught Mrs. Shrem by her seventy-nine-year-old mother, Aurelia Caske. "My mother always says there's nothing like fresh dill. And she saw that we ate right; never any white bread in our house."*

A 3½-pound chicken, skin and fat removed, cut into 8 pieces
1 medium onion, peeled
3 ribs celery, sliced

1 bunch carrots, sliced
½ bunch fresh dill, washed and tied in a bundle with white thread
1 teaspoon salt, or to taste

❶ Put the chicken in a 6-quart pot and pour in enough cold water to cover it by 1 inch. Add the onion and celery, cover, and bring to the boil.

❷ Lower the heat and let liquid simmer for 30 minutes, skimming off the scum frequently. Add the carrots and continue cooking and skimming for 20 minutes more, with the pot partially covered.

❸ Add the dill bundle and cook for another 10 minutes. Add the salt and let the soup cool. (One hour of cooking altogether.)

❹ When the soup has cooled, remove the onion and press it lightly to extract any juices. Discard the onion. Remove the dill bundle and press the juices into the soup. Discard the bundle. Remove the chicken, take the meat from the bones, put the meat back in the pot, and adjust the seasonings.

➤ *Makes 8 to 10 cups chicken soup*

▲▲▲▲▲▲▲▲▲▲▲▲▲▲▲▲▲▲▲▲▲▲▲▲▲▲▲▲

Do You Remember Dubrow's?

Arthur Schwartz does. "I remember Dubrow's Cafeteria on Eastern Parkway and Utica, where Mama, my maternal grandmother, always said her sister Irene could spend an entire day gossiping with her cronies over a single cup of coffee. There was also the Dubrow's nearer home, on Kings Highway and East 16th Street, where the cool kids went to hang out after Madison High School events.

"I remember the three Cookie's restaurants, at the Avenue M, J, and K stops on the Brighton Line. I loved the deep-fried French toast made from challah, and the tall 'black and whites.' That's what Brooklynites called a chocolate soda with vanilla ice cream, one scoop in the glass and another hanging lavishly over the side.

"I remember the famous Famous Dairy Restaurant on Eastern Parkway, where my paternal grandfather was a grumpy old waiter. And the Little Oriental, a Rumanian-style steakhouse off Pitkin Avenue, still in the late '50s 'the Fifth Avenue of Brooklyn.' Grandpa was also a grumpy waiter there. Both restaurants were unofficial clubhouses for Brooklyn Democrats, like Borough President Abe Stark and Abe Beame, who later became mayor of the whole city. We got an earful about them when we went to visit my grandparents on Sunday afternoon."

Dubrow's Cafeteria, Kings Highway, 1975.

Garfield's Cafeteria

Garfield's Cafeteria stood on the corner of Church and Flatbush avenues, a hangout for the whole neighborhood, most of whom seemed to regard it as a club without dues—certainly they were tight with a nickel. Bruce Paul Friedman, Erasmus Hall High School class of 1961, recalled Garfield's for his high school reunion:

"The cafeteria was open 24 hours a day, seven days a week. Management couldn't have made much of a profit since most people never seemed to buy food. The place was massive, a miracle of stainless steel. And tile as far as the eye could see. High ceilings were supported by giant columns, all in multicolored mosaic. A huge cavern with no sound cushion, it was a haven for yodelers. There was a magnificent mural, two stories high, showing Indians selling Manhattan Island.

" 'Just spend the minimum,' said Murray the Bouncer. Everyone spent the minimum. Through the turnstile passed Daily News drivers, truckers bound for Bohack's, even Fulton Fish marketeers. Regulars were the senior citizens and the Erasmus crowd. Regulars had their own tables. It was a great place for people-watching. Folks munched Danish and sipped coffee. Sipping turned to nursing, and you spent the day! People read the paper, played checkers, or just socialized. Some brought their own coffee in a thermos. I remember one guy with a cup of hot water, salt and pepper, Tabasco sauce, and Heinz ketchup. He made his own free tomato soup.

"Some had their social security checks sent to them at Garfield's. There was an exodus at 11 a.m. to visit the broker and check the ticker, then back to Garfield's by lunchtime.

"As soon as you sat down to eat, over came the clean-up lady. 'Lift your hands, move that sandwich,' she said, cleaning around the glasses with a dirty rag. Iris Prager gave counsel on how to meet the minimum. She was leader of the brown-bag brigade. French fries and a Coke was the dietary supplement, along with onion rings. A boon for Clearasil. One day Murray the Bouncer caught Harvey Kolonko with a lunch bag. It contained raw onions. Harvey had grabbed the wrong bag! Bringing the bag in was not grounds for eviction. But Harvey *ate* the onions. *That* was grounds!

"The countermen's aprons advertised the daily specials. 'Does the Salisbury steak have onions inside or just on the top?' you'd ask. They answered all questions cheerfully: 'Who do I look like, Betty Crocker?' "

Garfield's Vegetable Cream Cheese,
The Engel Family

Some items at Garfield's were very good. Tamara Engel, a classmate of Bruce Friedman's at Erasmus, has reconstructed their Vegetable Cream Cheese: "As best my family can recall, scallions, radishes, and carrots were always included. Our collective taste buds agree on that. Some remember a fourth ingredient—it may have been celery, cucumber, bell pepper, parsley, or dill. To my memory, parsley and dill were added. However, we all agree that it was a sumptuous mound piled on a large oval platter, and completely covered with chopped scallion greens. It was always placed next to the chopped liver."

8 ounces Philadelphia Brand cream
   cheese
½ cup diced carrot
½ cup diced radishes
½ cup diced scallions
½ cup diced celery, red or green bell
   pepper, or cucumber (optional)

1 tablespoon combined minced dill and
   parsley (optional)
¼ cup chopped scallion greens, for
   garnish

Let the cream cheese come to room temperature. Fold in the vegetables. Arrange on a serving dish and garnish with scallion greens. ⟫→ *Makes 2½ cups*

The Candy Store Reunion

Everyone goes to high school and college reunions. But a *candy store* reunion? Only with guys from Brooklyn. Jonathan Pearlman remembers Flinks, on Newkirk Avenue and Westminster Road: "It was a kind of progression, kids just old enough to hang out at that store, and then growing old enough to leave it. Of course, there were some who stayed forever, growing pot bellies and keeping their '57 Chevies.

"It was a tight group of kids in the '50s. We'd sit around listening to music, bum cigarettes, and brag. There was a pecking order. The older boys had the choicest seats, near the juke box. Actually, the choicest spot was near the *Playboy* magazine, and *then* the juke box. The younger you were, the further back in the crowd.

"After I played ball in the schoolyard across the street, my favorite drink was a cherry lime rickey, cold and full of ice. It was made with a squirt of cherry syrup, a squirt of lime syrup, seltzer, and ice. We all had our favorites. Cherry Cokes were big, cherry lime rickeys and egg creams.

"We all had nicknames, too, nicknames that often cut a bit. Big John was called 'Whale,' and his brother Paul was called 'Little Whale.' 'The Schnoz' needs no explanation. My nickname was 'Mighty Mouse,' because I was small and fast.

"At the far end of the store was the counter. Carl and Benny worked behind it, at the grill. There were four or five tables, racks for school supplies, magazines, and papers. Flinks was pretty small.

"From time to time we've had reunions. The last one was a year and a half ago, at a Chinese restaurant in midtown Manhattan. Maybe thirty to forty people came. Because we all knew where we came from and all knew each other so well, there was an honesty and lack of pretension that you don't get at school reunions.

"As in any group, there are those who've done very well, those who've been moderately successful, and those who haven't done well at all. But the feelings for each other are strong and the lack of pretension sweet to see. The big surprise of that reunion was that Carl, who owned the candy store in our time, came to the reunion and made his famous egg cream. Carl was eighty-two. He got the Fox's U-Bet syrup, seltzer, and milk, whipped them up, and we all got drunk on egg creams.

"There was one girl, at the reunion we talked about her, she was everyone's first soul kiss. She was terrific, we all had fond memories of her. Her name was Marilyn K. I'd still like to see her. I felt as if she did something for me. Many of us remembered Marilyn."

A Date in Flatbush

Bruce Paul Friedman is a successful salesman, but his heart belongs to Save the Kings. This organization, of which he is chairman, is seeking the restoration and reuse of Loews Kings Theatre on Flatbush Avenue as a center for the performing arts. Opened in 1929 and closed in 1978, this exuberant minglement of Italian Renaissance, Louis XIV, Beaux Arts, and Art Deco architectural styles enchanted generations of Flatbush youth and their elders. The Kings was one of the country's greatest flamboyant palaces of the cinema.

. . . .

The year is 1961. Bruce Friedman describes a date—movie, eating, and, uh, making out—when he was a hot-shot senior at Erasmus Hall High School:

"At the Kings Theatre, I bought the tickets for Annie and me at the bronze-domed ticket booth, and we entered the grand lobby. Fluted walnut columns with Corinthian capitals soared ninety feet above us, meeting a gold-leafed ceiling. Ushers in snappy red jackets stood in formation; the head usher gave the signal, the velvet ropes parted, and the crowd surged forward.

"The aroma of freshly made popcorn with real butter perfumed the air. The candy counter offered Goobers, Raisinettes, Chunkys, and Cracker Jack. The strictly kosher franks came sizzling off the roller grill. We got the orange soda mixed with Coke, the Kings' special. Annie asked for Good & Plentys: 'First I eat the pink ones,' she said, 'and then the white.'

"We climbed the grand staircase to the balcony. It always filled before the orchestra. The

The lobby of Loews Kings Theatre.

balcony had wide seats, with extra elbow room for serious dating. The lights dimmed, and it was time for my 'tired' routine. I gave a big yawn, and stretched an arm over the back of her seat. I went for an over-the-shoulder shot, lowering my hand. Her fingers slipped between mine. What I'd started as a caress became a hammerlock. Squeals came from the front row, where two people seemed to be sharing the same seat. Everyone watched, except my date. She was watching the movie. I stroked her back and her nails dug into my wrist. She relented, and rested her head on my shoulder. At last(!) she turned her face to mine. We kissed. And kissed. Up came the credits and the house lights; across the rows the heavy action ended. The make-out artists in the front row stood and lit cigarettes. The rest of the balcony cheered. Now came the eating part of the date.

"At Flatbush and Church was Jahn's Ice Cream Parlor. Entering was a trip back to the Gay Nineties. The chandeliers were salvaged from the Grand Hotel in Saratoga, and the marble soda fountain was encased in elaborately carved woodwork. The soda jerk was a precision artist; he lined up a row of sparkling glass dishes, and with a flipping wrist action, opened little trap doors to various ice cream flavors, spading up slabs to build the various 'Tummy

Tickler' sundaes. A thump of his palm on a pumper squirted a stream of syrup or hot butterscotch. I ordered a Hot Fudge sundae and Annie a Marshmallow one.

"Our sweet teeth satisfied, it was on to the best part of the evening—parking (an activity that teenage radio idol Murray the K called 'let's go submarine-race watching')! I didn't own a car, so I had to borrow one. Once, in desperation, I took a cab to go parking. The tricky part was persuading the driver to go for a cup of coffee. This evening I had Mom's car. 'Annie's a neighborhood girl— why not take the Church Avenue bus?' she'd asked. 'The bus doesn't suit my image,' I'd replied. And besides, the Church Avenue bus didn't go parking. We headed for Plumb Beach, off the Belt Parkway. It was crowded. Just as we were getting comfortable in our parking paradise, up pulled a patrol car, revolving light illuminating the parkers. At least the cops had the decency not to use the siren. In unison, a long line of drivers revved their engines. A procession of headlights followed the police car onto the Belt Parkway. So much for submarine-race watching."

Jahn's "Kitchen Sink"

Bruce and Annie couldn't possibly have downed Jahn's specialty, the super sundae called "The Kitchen Sink." It was billed as a treat for eight, but twelve people might have difficulty putting it away. Bruce remembers:

"Lights dim as two waitresses enter, pushing a stainless-steel cart. In the center is a giant crystal punchbowl, filled with two and one-half gallons of vanilla, chocolate, strawberry, pistachio, cherry vanilla, black raspberry, banana, coffee, mint chip—or any of fourteen flavors. Toppings include nuts in syrup, pineapple chunks, marshmallow fluff, preserved fruits, and chocolate sprinkles. Bananas are impaled with maraschino cherries. The servers dip slices of melba toast in orange extract and set them afire. They deal bowls, spoons, and slabs to the patrons to dig in with. Wonderful! Exhausting!"

"To Jahn's, To Jahn's on Friday"

Amy Ginzig Krakow has a few vivid memories of Jahn's, too:

"I went to Erasmus Hall, class of '67. Every Brooklyn high school had an event called 'Sing,' sort of like a class play, and the kids wrote a story and lyrics set to pop songs or Broadway show tunes.

"When I was a soph, the Sing did a song called 'To Jahn's, To Jahn's on Friday,' set to the tune of 'To Life, To Life, L'chaim,' from *Fiddler on the Roof.* In those years, if you were part of a certain crowd, you'd be at Jahn's every Friday. In winter, you went to the skating rink in Prospect Park, then to Jahn's. In the warmer months, you hung out on the corner of Church and Flatbush, and then to Jahn's. You'd see all your friends there.

"Invariably, every single Friday, some jerk would say, 'I could eat a whole Kitchen Sink.' The deal was that if you did eat one all alone, you got it for free. And each week, halfway through it, the jerk would turn blue and then purple, and of course all of us teenagers thought that the height of hilarity. Actually, there was one guy who did manage a whole Kitchen Sink. He was sick for weeks afterward."

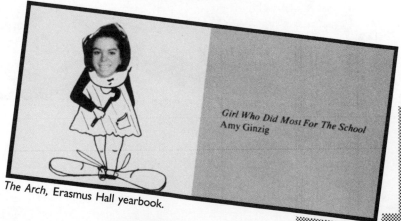

Girl Who Did Most For The School
Amy Ginzig

The Arch, Erasmus Hall yearbook.

(From the top) butcher shop with chicken; guests at a Hasidic wedding; Purim masquerade; kosher beverage truck.

THE OBSERVANT
THE ORTHODOX JEWS
OF BROOKLYN

Good food is a fundamental part of life for all groups, but for Orthodox Jews it is much more than that. The choice, preparation, combination, and eating of kosher food is integral to a moral, spiritual, properly lived existence. Most non-Jews know that meat and milk are never eaten at the same meal, but many, many more rules govern the management of a kosher kitchen and dining table in an Orthodox home. "We don't think of eating or not eating kosher food as an option," says Mayer Brandwein, who owns the Brighton Beach Dairy Restaurant. "We follow the rules because they are the Law."

"Brooklyn probably has the largest concentration of Orthodox Jews in the world," says Rabbi Jacob Goldstein, who is Director of the Manhattan Rent Office for the State Division of Housing, and also a chaplain with the National Guard. "The end of World War II saw the rise of Orthodoxy. We live in settled neighborhoods: Crown Heights, Williamsburg, Flatbush, Midwood, Borough Park, along Ocean Parkway, and in parts of Canarsie and Bensonhurst."

ike Rabbi Goldstein, Margaret Rottenstein is Hasidic, a member of a group that practices the strictest Orthodoxy. "Our traditions may be strange to outsiders," she says, "but we love our way of living. Our fathers came here from Poland and Rumania after the war with only the shirts on their backs. They worked so hard for their children. We have very large families, trying to make up for the people we have lost."

All of the following recipes are kosher. They can be enjoyed by everyone else, as well.

An Orthodox Childhood

Gabrielle Greenstein and her sister Arliene grew up in Borough Park, now a mostly Orthodox Jewish community. "We are Orthodox, but when we were young, the neighborhood was mixed," says Gabrielle. "On our street were an Italian family, an Indian family next door, Irish across the street, and one Chinese family. We all had large gardens, and we used to exchange vegetables. We went to the Catholic families' baptisms, and their children helped us light our menorahs at Hanukkah.

"Our grandparents, Bubba and Zaida, lived downstairs, in the same building. I'd stop by on my way home from school. Bubba would ask, 'Are you checking on what I'm cooking for dinner?' 'Oh, no,' I'd say, 'I just came for my hug.' I'd get a cookie, too.

"I remember the fish swimming in the bathtub. At Passover, to make certain the fish was kosher, they were brought home alive and put in the bathtub. We laughed, thinking we would get away without taking a bath for two days, but instead we were bathed in the kitchen. It was so funny to hear the 'flip, flop' in the tub, and Bubba had to put a cover across so the fish wouldn't jump out.

"My mother was one of nine children, and we had bar mitzvahs for our boy cousins all the time. Relatives came from Washington, Oregon, Ohio, and Illinois for the service in Zaida's *schul*. Everyone slept in the two apartments. All the mothers and children slept in our place upstairs, and the men and boys slept downstairs in the grandparents' place. There were feather mattresses, called *perinas*, all over the floors for the children. We loved these giant slumber parties!

"As we took our Friday evening *spazier*, the walk to the synagogue for prayers, we must have looked like an entire village: at least sixteen children, the aunts and uncles, the older children pushing baby carriages.

"On Saturday, after the bar mitzvah, we had a tradition. We had made up little bags of raisins and almonds. After the bar mitzvah boy had finished his reading, we all looked at Zaida. He nodded, and that

Rope jumping, Lee Avenue, 1963.

was our cue to pelt the celebrant with the bags. The children loved that part of the ceremony, and they liked eating the sweets afterward, too.

"The festival of Purim is masquerade time for Orthodox children. Purim commemorates Queen Esther, who saved the Jews of Persia from massacre by the wicked Haman. A certain sweet called *hamantaschen* is made for this holiday, in the shape of Haman's three-cornered hat. Our mother made enough hamantaschen for the neighbors, and Arliene and I, in costume, delivered boxes of it along with jars of homemade preserves. Mother was showing us that children must share."

Hamantaschen

Gabrielle Greenstein writes for Anglo-Jewish publications in the United States and Canada. Her sister Arliene Stempler is president of Flair, a printing concern that has published over one hundred organizational cookbooks, including two that the sisters wrote. This recipe is from their book We Remember, Bubba!, *with recipes collected by Zippora (Gabrielle) and Chana (Arliene). Those are their Jewish names.*

Dough
⅔ cup vegetable shortening
½ cup sugar
1 egg
3 tablespoons water

½ teaspoon vanilla
2 cups sifted all-purpose flour
Filling
1 cup prepared prune butter (lekvar), apple butter, or your favorite filling

❶ Cream the shortening and sugar together. Add the egg; continue beating until smooth. Add the water and vanilla. Blend in the flour, mixing well until the dough forms a ball. Chill for at least 2 hours.

Preheat the oven to 350 degrees F.

❷ Roll the dough out on a lightly floured work surface to a ⅛-inch thickness. Cut 2-inch circles of dough. Place ½ teaspoon of filling in the center of each circle, and pinch the dough up in three points to make a triangle. Pinch it well to seal.

❸ Arrange on lightly greased baking sheets and bake for 25 to 30 minutes, or until the pastry is golden brown. ≫→ *Makes about 2 dozen hamantaschen*

Gefilte Fish

Of course The Brooklyn Cookbook *must have a recipe for gefilte fish! This one is from* We Remember, Bubba! *"Bubba and Mother's gefilte fish balls were so light and fluffy,"* says Gabrielle Greenstein. *"The first time I made them, they were like rocks. I realized that I was handling them too much. Work quickly, handling the balls just enough to shape."*

We Remember, Bubba!

A COOKBOOK OF JEWISH TRADITIONAL HOLIDAY & SPECIAL OCCASION RECIPES ...
collected by Zippora & Chana

3 pounds whitefish, pike, and carp
4½ cups water
5 onions, sliced
3 carrots, sliced
2 teaspoons sugar
Salt and pepper, to taste

⅓ cup matzo meal
4 eggs, beaten

❶ Bone and skin the fish. Rinse the bones well and place them in a pot with 4 cups of the cold water; bring to the boil. Lower the heat and simmer for 30 minutes. Strain the broth and discard the bones.

❷ Return the broth to the pot. Add 3 of the onions, along with the carrots, sugar, and salt. Cook over low heat.

❸ Rinse the fish fillets well. Grind them with the 2 remaining onions; mix well. Add the matzo meal, eggs, salt and pepper, and the remaining ½ cup of water.

❹ With wet hands, form the fish mixture into 2-inch balls, and place them over the vegetables in the pot. Continue shaping more fish balls, wetting your hands as you do so. Layer fish balls in pot until all of the mixture is used up.

❺ Cover the pot, bring to the boil, then lower the heat and cook for 1 hour. Shake the pot occasionally to prevent the balls from sticking. Remove cover, taste the broth, and correct seasonings if needed. Add more water, if necessary. Replace the cover and cook for 1 hour more. Allow the fish balls to cool before removing them to a bowl. Strain the broth over the fish balls and surround them with sliced carrots. Allow the liquid to jell. ≫→ *Makes 12 to 14 fish balls*

The Lubavitcher Hasidim of Crown Heights

Hasidism, a movement of Orthodoxy that began in Poland in the first half of the seventeenth century, is flourishing in today's Brooklyn. Hasidic life is fervid: to Hasidim prayer, mysticism, dancing, singing, and the sanctification of daily life are as important as Talmudic scholarship. Among the groups are the Satmarers of Williamsburg and the Bobovers and Belzers of Borough Park, as well as the Lubavitchers. The Hasidim dress alike—black hats, long coats, and beards for the men; modest elbow- and knee-covering clothing, often fashionable, for the women.

The Lubavitcher are named for the Byelorussian town of Lubavitch, meaning "city of brotherly love." Unlike other Hasidim, Lubavitchers actively reach out to non-observant Jews, persuading them to return to *Yiddishkeit*, a fully Jewish life, including adherence to all laws of *kashruth* governing food. "We awaken people who are asleep," says Rabbi Jacob Goldstein.

About 25,000 Lubavitchers live in a few blocks of Crown Heights off Eastern Parkway, but their Chabad-Lubavitcher movement ("Chabad" means "wisdom, understanding, and knowledge") has more than one thousand Chabad Houses, or places of worship, in thirty countries, with a following of over half a million people. Crown Heights, home of the charismatic leader Rebbe Menachem Mende Schneerson, is headquarters for the movement.

"It's fair to say that most Hasidic cooking is very traditional, women cooking as their mothers did," says Esther Blau, who is on the editorial board of the Lubavitch Women's Cookbook Publications. "But our cooking also represents what is coming in from other communities—we have people from all over the world visiting us. It's exciting. We not only teach, we learn." For the Lubavitchers, as for all Orthodox, food and spirituality cannot be separated. Adhering to kosher laws is not only a religious duty, it is a source of pride. As their latest cookbook states, "The Jewish home is a miniature sanctuary, and its table is like an altar."

The following recipes are adapted from *Spice and Spirit: The Complete Kosher Jewish Cookbook*, Lubavitch Women's Cookbook Publications, 1990.

Heavy-Duty Mixer Challah

The braided Sabbath loaf called challah is named for the gift of food called challah *that in ancient days was given by the people to the priestly tribe of Israel, the* kohanim. *Since the destruction of the First Temple, the gift has not been made. Instead, whenever she uses more than 2 pounds 11 ounces of flour in making challah, the Jewish woman must perform the* mitzvah, *or ritual good work, of "separating challah." She takes about an ounce from the batch of dough, says a blessing, and burns the small challah in remembrance of the gift, and in anticipation of future redemption.*

In this recipe, less than the required amount of flour is used, so separating challah is not necessary.

....

2 ounces fresh yeast
1¾ cups warm water
½ cup sugar
3 egg yolks
7 cups all-purpose flour

¼ cup vegetable oil
1 tablespoon salt
1 egg, beaten
Poppy seeds

❶ Put the yeast, warm water, and sugar in the bowl of a mixer equipped with a dough hook. Let stand until the yeast bubbles. Add the egg yolks, 5 cups of the flour, the oil, and salt. Mix on low speed until the ingredients are combined. Add 1 more cup of the flour and mix until combined. Add the rest of the flour, mix to combine, and knead on low speed for 10 minutes.

❷ Remove the bowl from the machine. Oil the top of the dough, cover it, and let it rise for 1 hour.

Preheat the oven to 350 degrees F.

❸ Divide the dough into thirds, to make 3 loaves. Keeping two of the portions covered, divide one portion into 3 pieces. Roll each piece into a long uniform strand. The strands should be a bit longer than the pan in which the challah will be baked. Braid the strands together, and tuck the ends under to finish. Repeat with the other two portions of dough. Place the shaped loaves in greased loaf pans or on a baking sheet.

❹ Brush the loaves with beaten egg and sprinkle with poppy seeds. Bake until brown, 45 minutes to 1 hour. Remove from pans, if used, and cool on a rack. ≫→ *Makes 3 loaves*

Ceviche

Only fish that have both fins and scales are kosher. These include cod, flounder, haddock, halibut, herring, mackerel, pickerel, pike, salmon, trout, and whitefish.

The raw fish is "cooked" by the lime juice. It must be marinated from 3 to 24 hours before eating.

1 pound firm white-fleshed fish, such as whitefish, haddock, or red snapper fillets
1 cup freshly squeezed lime juice
1 cup peeled and diced tomatoes
1 medium onion, diced
¼ cup vegetable oil
1 tablespoon white wine

1 teaspoon oregano
½ teaspoon basil
1 teaspoon coriander
Salt and pepper to taste
½ teaspoon hot pepper sauce
1 ripe avocado or 1 red onion or 2 limes, thinly sliced, for garnish

❶ Cut the fish fillets into 1-inch cubes. Place the cubes in a glass bowl and pour the lime juice over them. Allow to marinate at least 3 to 4 hours in the refrigerator, turning occasionally. (The fish can marinate up to 24 hours.)

❷ When the fish has marinated, add the remaining ingredients except the garnish. Mix gently.

❸ Refrigerate the ceviche for several hours before serving. Just before serving, drain off the liquid, if desired. Serve as an appetizer in tall stemmed glasses or on small plates, garnished. ⟫→ *Makes 4 servings*

Beet Waldorf Salad

2 large raw beets, peeled
1 large carrot, peeled
1 medium green apple, peeled
1 stalk celery
½ cup fresh ripe pineapple, cut into bite-sized pieces

¼ cup mayonnaise, mixed with 1 tablespoon pineapple juice
½ cup chopped walnuts
Juice of 1 lemon
2 tablespoons sugar (optional)

❶ Coarsely grate the beets and carrot into a large bowl. Chop the apple and celery. Combine all ingredients and toss well.

❷ Chill the salad for at least 20 minutes before serving.
⟫→ *Makes 4 servings*

▲▲▲▲▲▲▲▲▲▲▲▲▲▲▲▲▲▲▲▲▲▲▲▲▲▲▲

The Satmar Shmura Matzoh Bakery of Williamsburg

The assembly-line pace is unrelenting at the Satmar Shmura Matzoh Bakery in Williamsburg; workers have exactly eighteen minutes to complete the job, from moistening the flour to pulling baked matzos from the oven.

Matzo is unleavened bread like that the Jews, fleeing Egypt, took with them in the Exodus—the bread was baked in haste, with no time for it to rise. In remembrance, all Jews who observe the Passover eat matzo at the two *Seders*, or ritual meals, and Orthodox Jews eat it for the full week of Passover. Jewish law requires that all leavening, called *hametz*, be cleansed from the house before Passover; thus the only baked grain product that can be eaten is matzo.

Matzo is simply flour and water, mixed, rolled flat and baked until golden and crisp. But to the very pious, the danger of fermentation is ever present; airborne yeasts might mix with the flour and water and begin fermentation. The rabbis reason that safety lies within an eighteen-minute margin to mix, roll, and bake the matzo. This scrupulously prepared matzo is called *shmura*, meaning "watched." Members of the Satmar community, the largest Hasidic group in Brooklyn, oversee every aspect of production, from growing the grain on Long Island and in upstate New York, to seeing that the harvested

Baking handmade matzos.

grain does not come in contact with water, to grinding and baking. The matzos are "the best in the world," according to the bakery's manager.

Shmura matzo is round, not square, and must be baked in ovens heated only by coal and hard wood. The water, drawn once a day at 6 p.m. from a well under the bakery, must sit for twenty-four hours before it is used. The bakery produces over 100,000 pounds of shmura matzo a year, two thousand pounds a week in the frantic rush just before Passover. The mixer hands the dough through a window to a woman who divides it and hands it to workers at a long table, holding dowel-like rolling pins at the ready. Matzos are rolled out and pierced with holes, blessings are intoned, a baker gathers the matzos onto a ten-foot-long peel and thrusts them into the oven. Another man turns them and retrieves them. All done in under the prescribed eighteen minutes.

The workers are vigilant. Because tiny particles of left-behind dough could rise, activity periodically ceases. Tables are scraped down, rolling pins scoured, hands washed, and production begins again. The faithful are assured that their matzo is as ritually correct as human hands can make it.

The Surest Way to a Man's Heart

"I'd brought one of my lemon meringue pies to the home of a friend. She had several guests that weekend, one of whom asked to meet the baker of 'this heavenly dessert.' I was introduced to Jacob Goldstein. Well, I married him, as the old story goes. I can't guarantee the same success for every young woman, but the pie is great."

Seema Goldstein.

Seema Goldstein's Lemon Meringue Pie

1 fully baked 9-inch pie crust
1¼ cups sugar
⅓ cup flour
1½ cups water

2 egg yolks
2 tablespoons margarine
⅓ cup strained fresh lemon juice
2 egg whites

❶ Stir 1 cup of the sugar together with the flour in a saucepan. Gradually add the water, stirring with a whisk or wooden spoon to prevent lumps. Place over moderate heat and cook, stirring, until the mixture thickens. Remove it from the heat.

❷ Beat the egg yolks in a bowl and beat in one-third of the hot mixture. Beat it into the contents of the saucepan, and return the pan to very low heat for 2 minutes, stirring the mixture all the while. Stir in the margarine and the lemon juice. Pour the mixture into the pie shell and let it cool for 20 minutes.

Preheat the oven to 375 degrees F.

❸ Beat the egg whites until they begin to stiffen. Gradually beat in the remaining ¼ cup of sugar and beat until stiff and glossy. Spoon over the filling and bake pie for 10 minutes or until golden brown. ≫→ *Makes 1 pie*

Aleppo in Flatbush
The Sephardic Jews of Flatbush

Like the Orthodox Ashkenazim of Eastern European descent, the Syrian Jews adhere to the Mosaic laws of *kashruth*—no mixing of milk and meat, no shellfish or any fish at all without scales, no deviation from the myriad rules that govern every aspect of daily life. And though methods of preparation are much the same in all strictly observant households, the foods that the Syrian Jews of Brooklyn eat are very different from the blintz and brisket cuisine most people think of as "Jewish." Lamb, eggplant, tamarind syrup, chick-peas, and Middle Eastern spice mixtures enliven their strictly kosher food.

Over 35,000 Sephardim live within a five-square-mile area of Flatbush. ("Sephardim" comes from the Hebrew word *Sepharadh*, meaning a region mentioned in the Bible and assumed to be Spain. Many Jews who were expelled from Spain in 1492 settled in the Middle East.) Egyptian, Moroccan, Lebanese, and Iranian Jews are part of the community, but the great majority are Syrian, originally from the trading center of Aleppo—so many, in fact, that this community is called "Aleppo in Flatbush."

Their very difference from other Jews is what has kept the group so tightly knit. When they began arriving early in the century, they found the Jews of the Lower East Side, and their strange food and Yiddish language, almost as alien as the rest of the culture. When a few moved to Williamsburg, many followed, going thence to Bensonhurst and ultimately to Flatbush.

Although an outsider might find little difference between Sephardic food and that of the Arabs who cluster around Atlantic Avenue, the Syrians patronize their own stores along Kings Highway. "People are perhaps more religious now than ever," says Rae Dayan, a teacher of Sephardic cooking who has made a videotape, "Mid-Eastern Cooking with Rae." "And they need to know that whatever they buy is totally kosher."

The anchor of Aleppo in Flatbush is the commanding Sephardic Community Center on Ocean Parkway, part of the YM-YWHA movement. The center, which opened in 1982, supports and perpetuates the community; thousands who had left for the suburbs returned. The Sephardic population intends to remain in Brooklyn.

Staying true to the ways of their forebears is paramount. "The young women must know how to prepare our food," says Rae Dayan. "Our old ways must not be lost."

Sweet and Sour Tongue, Sephardic Style

Rae Dayan.

Rae Dayan says that the Sephardim serve tongue on Rosh Hashanah, the Jewish new year. Tongue symbolizes the hope that in the coming year people will be at the head and not at the tail, meaning that we will go forward, not backward. "I also use this sauce with stuffed cabbage," she says. "Delicious!"

Tongue
A 2½- to 3-pound fresh calf's tongue
2 teaspoons salt
1 medium onion, halved

Sauce
2 tablespoons vegetable oil
2 medium onions, thinly sliced
1 teaspoon minced garlic
2 cups canned whole tomatoes
1 8-ounce can tomato sauce
⅓ cup dark-brown sugar
⅓ cup raisins
Juice of 2 lemons (scant ½ cup)
1 teaspoon kosher salt
⅛ teaspoon freshly ground white
   pepper

❶ Place the tongue in a large saucepan with the salt and onion. Cover with water, bring to the boil, lower the heat to moderate, and simmer the tongue for 1½ hours, or until it is tender when pierced with the point of a sharp knife.

❷ While the tongue cooks, prepare the sauce. In a large heavy skillet, heat the oil until sizzling. Reduce the heat and cook the onions and garlic, stirring often, until soft and lightly browned, about 5 minutes. Stir in the tomatoes, tomato sauce, brown sugar, raisins, lemon juice, salt and pepper. Simmer the sauce, stirring it often, for about 20 minutes. Set aside.

❸ When the tongue is tender, transfer it to a pot of cold water. When it is cool enough to handle, strip off the outer skin and cut away bones and gristle. Slice the tongue on the diagonal and arrange it in a casserole. Pour the sauce over it and bake it for 35 minutes at 350 degrees F. ≫→ *Serves 6 to 8*

Rae Dayan's Sambusak
(Filled Pastries)

Sambusak *are the most popular Syrian-Sephardic pastries, and are eaten throughout the year. Cheese is the traditional filling for Hanukkah, meat for the Sabbath. This recipe makes a lot of pastries, but they freeze perfectly, so you can enjoy sambusak at any time.*

If you are making cheese sambusak, use butter in the filling because these pastries will be eaten at a dairy meal. If you make meat sambusak, you must make the pastry with margarine, according to dietary laws.

Dough

3 cups all-purpose flour

2 teaspoons salt

8 ounces (2 sticks) unsalted butter or margarine, at room temperature

½ cup cold water

½ cup sesame seeds

Cheese Filling

1½ pounds Muenster cheese, grated

3 lightly beaten eggs

1 teaspoon baking powder

1 teaspoon salt

1½ cups sesame seeds

Meat Filling

1 cup finely chopped onion

2 tablespoons olive oil

1 pound chopped kosher shoulder beef

1 teaspoon ground allspice

1 teaspoon salt

½ teaspoon cinnamon

¼ cup pine nuts

❶ To make the pastry, first combine the flour and salt. Using an electric mixer, cream the butter or margarine and gradually blend in the flour mixture. Add the water. Knead until a ball forms. Let the dough rest as you prepare one of the fillings.

❷ To make the cheese filling, mix all ingredients together well.

To make the meat filling, sauté the onion in oil until soft and translucent, about 5 minutes. Add the chopped meat and brown it, breaking it up with a wooden spoon, about 20 minutes. Let meat cool, then add the spices and pine nuts.

Preheat the oven to 400 degrees F.

❸ Spread the ½ cup of sesame seeds on a large plate. Break off walnut-size pieces of dough. Shape each into a ball and dip it lightly on one side into the sesame seeds, then roll it, seed side down, into a 3-inch round. Place a teaspoon of filling in the center of the round. Fold it over to make a half-moon and crimp the edges together tightly so that filling will not burst through. (Sambusak can be frozen at this point. Place them in a single layer on a tray lined with wax paper and freeze them. Place frozen sambusak in double plastic bags and return them to the freezer. To bake frozen pastries, place them on ungreased baking sheets and bake for 20 minutes in a 400 degree F oven, or until golden.)

❹ Place pastries on ungreased baking sheets and bake them for 15 to 20 minutes, or until golden. ≫→ *Makes about 60 pastries*

Sephardic Vegetable Pickles

These are refrigerator pickles, un-cooked and all ready in three to four days. They should also be con-sumed quickly, within a week. They are not to be eaten at Pass-over.

Cauliflower

1 medium cauliflower
3 cloves garlic, peeled and cut in half
1 small beet, peeled

3 cups water
1 cup white vinegar, preferably Heinz
2 tablespoons kosher salt

❶ Cut the cauliflower into florets, discarding most of the stem. Wash the florets, and pack them into a 2-quart jar. As you pack, layer the garlic cloves among the florets. Place the beet on top. (It will color the cauliflower a pretty pink.)

❷ Mix the water, vinegar, and salt together. Pour it over the contents of the jar. Close the jar tightly and refrigerate. Shake the jar occasionally.

Turnips

Peel 2 pounds of turnips and cut them into rounds. Follow the directions for pickled cauliflower, eliminating the beet.

Cabbage

Core a medium head of cabbage and cut it into chunks. Follow the directions for pickled cauliflower, eliminating the beet.

▲▲▲▲▲▲▲▲▲▲▲▲▲▲▲▲▲▲▲▲▲▲▲▲▲▲▲▲

SKOAL! AND KIPPIS!
TO THE SCANDINAVIANS

Scandinavians are by and large calm and measured people, going about their business in a down-to-earth way—until someone throws a party, that is. Then Norwegian, Danish, and Swedish rafters ring with cries of "Skoal," a word that derives from "bowl," harking back to the ancient custom of passing a drinking bowl among friends. There is a ritual to saying skoal. You pick up your glass of wine or schnapps, salute a friend, look him in the eye, say skoal, and take a sip. The word "skoal" should accompany each sip, and an older person says it to a younger one, never the other way around. Finns don't say skoal, they say "kippis"—a toast when the drink is wine or spirits, but not beer. Skoal, kippis, or cheers, Scandinavians understand a party.

Scandinavians are fewer now in the borough than formerly, but the smaller communities are still vigorous. The Swedish and Danish clubs have many members, and open their doors in Nordic solidarity to all revelers on the Seventeenth of May, Norwegian Independence Day, when thousands attend the annual parade. Bands play, people dance, eat, laugh, drink, and—of course—say skoal!

Norwegian Singing Society, 1890.

Norge in Brooklyn

"**B**ay Ridge was a place of million-aires' mansions at the turn of the century," says Alan Thompson, whose Norwegian parents settled in Bay Ridge in the 1930s. "These splendid houses overlooked the Narrows flowing out to the Atlantic. What changed the character of the area was the arrival of the subway in 1915. The Transit Authority let people ride for free for some time, to overcome their fear of going in 'the black hole,' as the Irish called it. Norwegians had been here for a time, but they really came in large numbers after World War I."

"The men were seamen and carpenters," says Norma Andreasen, who was born in Brooklyn but spent some of her childhood in Norway before returning to Bay Ridge. "The women worked as maids and cooks, many for Jewish families.

"We learned English in school, but the language of church and home was Norwegian. The Bible was important. We had no radio and no television, and when I saw my first movie when I was six, I screamed in fear and they had to take me outside. I thought they'd take me behind that big white screen and kill me!

"Papa had a car and when he was free, we'd go to orchards and farms in the country and pick fruits and berries. Mama made jam, preserves, and pickles. We went on picnics with the church, and took the ferry to Staten Island from the 69th Street Pier in Bay Ridge to picnic over there.

"When we moved to a big house from an apartment, we could lay in a supply of potatoes for the winter. That's the main food for Norwegians—potatoes."

"Right away Norwegians build a church, a hospital, a children's home, and an old-age home," says

Celebrating Norwegian Independence Day, 1989.

Bjorn Jacobsen, president of the Norwegian Singing Society and a former cold-table chef and restaurant manager. "The Swedes and Danes do this too. We Scandinavians build institutions."

The Norwegian Singing Society celebrated its hundredth anniversary in 1990. "We sing a lot of Grieg, of course," says Mr. Jacobsen. "Scandinavian folk melodies, and also Finnish, Estonian, and German songs, whatever lends itself to male voices. We've gone a number of times to Norway, and in 1979 I took the group to my little town and saw my old schoolteacher.

"Once or twice a year the Ladies' Auxiliary of the Norwegian Singing Society will arrange a great smorgasbord. We had three hundred and twenty people at the Hundredth Anniversary party. Scandinavians like fancy open-faced sandwiches that you eat with a knife and fork. One popular one is called 'Going Steady.' To make it, you butter a slice of rye bread and trim the crusts. You arrange slices of hard-boiled egg, then anchovies, and a little dill. Another is called 'Veterinarian's Night Snack.' That is bread, lettuce, tongue, scrambled eggs, chopped parsley, and an olive or two. These sandwiches must be appetizing to the eye."

Fiskegrateng
(Fish Pudding)

Norwegian Fiskegrateng lies somewhere between a pudding and a soufflé. This one is the recipe of Solveig Hauge, who attended the Haugesund Cooking and Homemakers School in 1939, and worked as chef in a student home in Sweden. A resident of Bay Ridge for 32 years, she retired and now lives in her ancestral homestead in Haugesund, Norway.

For Norwegians, fish must be absolutely spanking fresh, and Bay Ridge fishmongers know it.

Fiskegrateng is customarily served with boiled potatoes and a pitcher of melted butter.

1 pound fresh codfish fillets,
   or 1½ pounds cod with bones
Salt to taste
3 tablespoons unsalted butter

4 tablespoons flour
1½ cups milk
3 large eggs, separated

❶ Boil the cod in salted water just to cover until it flakes easily. Drain it (save the cooking water for soup) and when the cod is cool enough to handle remove the skin and bones, if any, and discard them. Flake the fish with your fingers.

Preheat the oven to 350 degrees F.

❷ Make a thick white sauce with the butter, flour, and milk.

❸ Stir the egg yolks, one by one, into the tepid sauce. Stir in the flaked fish.

❹ Whip the egg whites until stiff peaks form. Fold half of them into the fish mixture. Spoon the mixture into a 2-quart soufflé dish and cover the top with the remaining egg whites.

❺ Place the dish in a larger ovenproof vessel and pour in enough boiling water to reach halfway up. Cook for 1 hour, or until the fiskegrateng is somewhat firm and the egg white topping is delicately browned. If the top seems to be browning too fast, loosely drape a sheet of foil over it. ⟫⟶ *Serves 3 or 4*

Makrellkaker
(Mackerel Fish Cakes)

If you cook Solveig Hauge's fish cakes in a nonstick skillet, you do not need to add oil for frying. They are traditionally served with sautéed onions.

2 medium mackerels, to make 1¼
    pounds of fillets
¾ teaspoon salt

⅓ cup minced onion
3 tablespoons bread crumbs
2 tablespoons heavy cream

❶ Cut and scrape the meat from the fillets, discarding skin and bones. If you are using a meat grinder, put the fish pieces through the medium disk. Grind again, adding the salt and onion. If you are using a food processor, put the pieces of fish and the salt in the work bowl. Pulse until the fish is uniformly chopped, but not too fine.

❷ Place the fish in a bowl (you should have about 1½ cups). Mix in the onion, if you used the processor, and the bread crumbs. Add the cream. (If the mixture seems too wet, add another tablespoon of bread crumbs.)

❸ Form the mixture into 3-inch patties. Heat a nonstick skillet and fry the cakes in batches, until browned on both sides and cooked through.

⟫⟶ *Makes eight 10-inch patties*

Krumkaker
(Curled Cookies)

Alfhild Kolste lived in Bay Ridge for thirty-nine years, and worked as a chambermaid at the Pierre Hotel in New York. Like Solveig Hauge, she has retired to her birthplace in Norway.

The old-fashioned top-of-the-stove krumkaker iron with its decorative design is rarely used now; Norwegians have electric irons. You can use the pizzelle grid of a waffle iron. Krumkaker are curled around a cone while still warm, or draped in a cup. Either way, they are filled with sweetened whipped cream mixed with cloudberries, or with ice cream.

12 tablespoons (about ⅞ cup) sugar
4 eggs
½ teaspoon vanilla
7 tablespoons butter

1½ teaspoons ground cardamom
1¼ cups all-purpose flour
2½ teaspoons cornstarch
3 to 4 tablespoons cold water

❶ Using a stationary or hand-held mixer, beat together the sugar, eggs, and vanilla until the mixture is light and airy.

❷ Melt the butter and let it cool. Sift the cardamom and flour together. Mix the cornstarch and water until smooth. With the mixer on low speed, alternately add the butter and flour to the sugar-egg mixture. Beat in the cornstarch mixture.

❸ Pour a spoonful of batter on a heated krumkaker iron, press it shut, and bake the cookie until golden on each side. Drape around a cone or in a cup until dry. ⫸→ *Serves 8 to 10*

Får i Kål
(Lamb and Cabbage Casserole)

"The Atlantic is the only authentic Norwegian restaurant in Brooklyn," says Mrs. Ivan Johnson of Bay Ridge. "My late husband and I opened it in 1962. We have had waitresses here since 1964. People tell me that eating here is like eating with family. We have good homestyle cooking, traditional dishes like kjottkaker, Norwegian meatballs. They are like Swedish meatballs, but we use nutmeg in them, not allspice, and we often make them larger, like a patty. We serve krumkaker, the rolled crisp cookies, and får i kål. That's a wonderful winter dish."

Salt

4 to 6 thin round-bone shoulder lamb chops, trimmed but with some fat

½ cup all-purpose flour

1 to 1½ pounds white cabbage, cored and thinly sliced

2 tablespoons butter

½ cup hot water

3 tablespoons whole black peppercorns

❶ Lightly salt the chops, preferably an hour before you plan to cook them. Oil a heavy casserole that can be placed on top of the stove and that is just wide enough to hold two chops.

❷ Put in two chops and sprinkle them with flour. Place a ½- to 1-inch layer of cabbage over them, sprinkle with salt and then flour, and dot with butter. Continue making layers, ending with cabbage and a little butter. Pour on the hot water.

❸ Tie the peppercorns securely in cheesecloth and lightly bruise them with a rolling pin, or bruise them with pestle and mortar and put them in a metal spice-holding ball. Bury the peppercorns in the casserole.

❹ Cover and bring to the boil. Immediately lower the heat and simmer very gently for about 1½ hours, until the meat is very tender and the cabbage almost melted. Remove the peppercorns. Serve with boiled potatoes. ≫→ *Serves 4 to 6*

Finntown

The hilly section of South Brooklyn just north of Bay Ridge has been home to changing populations for over a century. Irish fleeing the Famine began to arrive in the 1840s; Poles came in the 1880s, and so did Scandinavians. Italians would follow, and now this area, called Sunset Park since 1965, is largely Hispanic. The newest arrivals are Asian and Arab.

Most of the Scandinavians have moved on, but the Finns, who were once so populous that a section between Fifth and Eighth avenues was called Finntown, still convene in Imatra Hall, headquarters of the Finnish Aid Society and center for Finnish social and charitable activities.

"Imatra was a workman's society when it was organized in 1890," says Veikko Laiho, president of the society. The building was begun in 1907. The purpose at the outset was to help Finns financially and spiritually. Moral behavior and total abstinence were expected of members, "but around 1940 we got the right to have alcohol," says Mr. Laiho. Hard times at home had driven the Finns to America, and though most pressed on to Minnesota, Michigan, and the Northwest, many seamen settled in Brooklyn, looking for work on the waterfront. The club has always been a place for good times; in former years Club Finlandia, a club within Imatra, put on revues and theatrical events.

Besides the club, the Finns built the first cooperative apartment house in America, in 1916. Families put up $500 each for a place in the building, called Alku I, meaning "the first one." Other co-ops followed, all still standing.

"I was born in 1953," says Anne-Marie Asmann, who is the manager of Imatra, "and when I was growing up this was still a Scandinavian neighborhood. There were stores carrying our foods. There's only one left, but it's now owned by Italians.

"My parents were born in Brooklyn, and my father was a longshoreman. My grandfather was a cook; he cooked on the boat coming over, and then got cooking jobs here.

"I'm trying hard to keep my children and other young people aware of Finnish culture and Finnish food. It's very much like other Scandinavian food, plainly but carefully cooked. When the club has a big event, there is a cold salmon, lots of salads, and fancy open-faced sandwiches. The ladies who cater these events vie to see who can do the most elaborate decorating.

"The old-timers use the club a lot, and on weekends the young adults, like me, practically live here. We have barbecues, a Friday night buffet, and we all bring our kids."

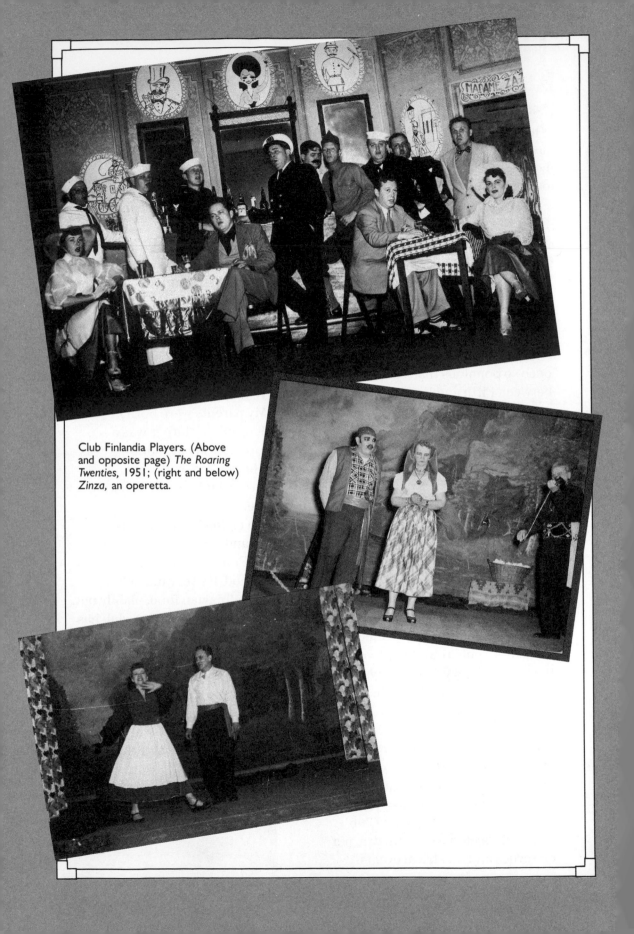

Club Finlandia Players. (Above and opposite page) *The Roaring Twenties*, 1951; (right and below) *Zinza*, an operetta.

Karelian Piirakka
(Savory Pies)

"These little pies are served at buffets, and they are somewhere between a bread and a pastry," says Anne-Marie Asmann, who thinks they are worth every bit of fuss to make. You have a choice of rice or potato filling.

Crust

1 cup water
1 teaspoon salt
2 tablespoons melted butter
1½ cups all-purpose flour plus a little
    for dusting
1½ cups rye flour

Egg Butter

1 cup butter, at room temperature
3 hard-boiled eggs, finely chopped
Salt to taste

Basting Sauce

½ cup hot milk
2 tablespoons melted butter

❶ Mix the water, salt, and butter in a large bowl. Stir in the all-purpose flour and mix until smooth. Add the rye flour and blend. Turn the dough out onto a floured work surface and knead it until smooth, about 10 minutes.

❷ Make one of the fillings (recipes follow).

    Preheat the oven to 450 degrees F.

❸ Shape the dough into a roll 2 inches in diameter. Divide it into 12 portions and dust them with a little flour. Pat each one into a small round cake, then roll it out into a 7-inch circle.

❹ Put 3 to 4 tablespoons of rice or potato filling on each round of dough and spread it to within 1 inch of the edge. Fold 2 sides of the dough over onto the filling, to make an oval shape, leaving an inch-wide strip of filling exposed. Crimp the cut edges of the dough with your fingers to raise them a little, and place the *piirakka* on lightly greased baking sheets. Bake for 15 minutes, or until lightly browned.

❺ Make the egg butter. Mix the butter, chopped eggs, and salt, and pack into an attractive crock or dish. Chill until cool but not cold.

❻ Mix the hot milk and melted butter for the basting sauce. Remove the piirakka from the oven and baste them with the sauce while still hot. Cover the pies with a cloth to soften the crusts, or wrap the whole batch in foil. Serve the egg butter separately with a knife for spreading on the piirakka. Serve hot or cold. ➨ *Makes 12 piirakka*

Rice Filling

1 cup raw long-grain rice
1 teaspoon salt

6 cups milk
2 tablespoons butter

Combine the rice, salt, and milk in the top of a double boiler. Cook over boiling water, stirring occasionally, for 2 hours or until the milk is absorbed and the rice is creamy. Stir in the butter and let the mixture cool.

Potato Filling

2 cups cooked mashed potatoes
¼ cup hot milk

2 tablespoons melted butter
Salt to taste

Whip the potatoes with the milk, butter, and salt until fluffy.

The Swedes in Brooklyn

"**A**tlantic Avenue was known as 'the Swedish Broadway' back in 1874," says Mabelle J. Lundahl, who spent fifty years as Director of Education at the Bethlehem Lutheran Church on Pacific Street. "That was the time of great emigration from Sweden. In fact, one quarter of Sweden's population moved to North America. Of course the farmers and sharecroppers wanted land, and moved to the Midwest, but a great many Swedes came to Brooklyn. They settled downtown, and one of the first things they did was to write home for a pastor.

"Lots of the men were seafarers, and the young girls were employed as cooks and nursemaids by wealthy people in Manhattan. The pastor held services on Thursday nights—maids' night out—for them, because they couldn't come on Sundays. These girls didn't make much money, but the records show they contributed a lot to our beautiful church, which was dedicated in 1895. Our population has changed. Many Swedes moved to Long Island, and some to Bay Ridge. Now our church has a mixture of everyone—blacks, Germans, Italians, and, of course, Scandinavians.

"For Swedes, Christmas is ushered in on St. Lucia's Day, when the eldest daughter serves coffee and buns to her parents in bed. The Christmas season lasts until January 13th, ending with a big smorgasbord celebration. I wrote a pageant for our church youth group about St. Lucia, who is represented

The St. Lucia Festival, 1960s. Mabelle Lundahl is at left.

by a blond girl with long hair who wears a crown with lighted candles and a long white robe. The boys wear bakers' hats and aprons.

"I love to cook, and now I often cook for the Senior Citizens group at our church. They're especially fond of Pea Soup."

Ärter Med Fläsk
(Swedish Pea Soup)

1 pound dried yellow Swedish peas, or substitute domestic yellow peas
5 cups cold water
2 medium onions, finely chopped
1 whole onion, peeled and studded
with 4 cloves
1 pound lean salt pork in one piece, or one pork tenderloin
2 teaspoons salt
½ teaspoon ground ginger

❶ Wash the dried peas under cold running water. Place them in a 2- to 3-quart saucepan and cover them with the cold water. Bring to the boil over high heat. Boil briskly for 2 to 3 minutes, remove from the heat, and let the peas soak for 1 hour.*

❷ Skim off the pea husks that may have risen to the surface. Add the onions, pork, salt, and ginger and again bring to the boil. Immediately lower the heat and simmer, covered, for 1½ hours or until peas are tender. Remove the whole onion and the pork.

❸ Slice the pork. Place a slice in each serving bowl and pour the soup over it, or serve the soup alone with the the sliced pork on the side. ⧫→ *Serves 4 to 6*

*Domestic peas do not need to soak, and will cook faster than the hard Swedish peas.

Kottbullar
(Swedish Meatballs)

Serve as an appetizer or part of a smorgasbord.

....

½ cup finely ground rusk or toasted
   bread crumbs
½ cup cream, heated to a boil
½ pound ground beef
½ pound ground lean pork
2 egg yolks, lightly beaten
2 teaspoons salt

⅓ teaspoon black pepper
¼ teaspoon allspice
1 teaspoon butter
1½ tablespoons minced onion
1 cup all-purpose flour
½ cup or more vegetable oil

Preheat the oven to 350 degrees F.

❶ Soak the crumbs in the hot cream. Mix the crumbs with the meat, egg yolks, salt, pepper, allspice, butter, and onion. Beat vigorously with a wooden spoon or use your hands to combine well. The mixture should be smooth.

❷ Roll into balls the size of a walnut, about 1 inch in diameter. Arrange them on a baking sheet and refrigerate for at least an hour to firm.

❸ Roll the balls in flour. Heat ¼ inch of oil in a large skillet and brown the meatballs in batches over moderate heat, turning them constantly to brown evenly. Add more oil as needed.

❹ Place the meatballs in a casserole with 1 tablespoon of the oil and 1 tablespoon of water. Cover and bake 10 to 15 minutes. To check if the meatballs are cooked, break one open. It should show no trace of pink. You can also simmer the meatballs in an electric skillet on low heat.

≫➔ *Makes about 40 to 50 meatballs*

▲▲▲▲▲▲▲▲▲▲▲   ▲▲▲▲▲▲▲▲▲▲▲

Brooklyn Day Sunday School in Prospect Park. The Bethlehem Lutheran Church, 1952.

THE IRISH
FROM VINEGAR HILL
TO WALL STREET

"**F**latbush had a constable in the 1750s named Murphy," says John T. Ridge, who has been called the unofficial historian of Brooklyn's Irish and is the author of <u>The History of the St. Patrick's Day Parade in New York</u> (Ancient Order of Hibernians, 1988). "The first big wave came around 1803, though, and settled in a place called Vinegar Hill, near the Navy Yard. Many were refugees from the 1798 Uprising. A lot of them were shipwrights or longshoremen.

"**B**y 1830, Vinegar Hill had turned into a full-fledged colony called Irishtown. Later a lot of Irish settled in South Brooklyn, Red Hook, and Gowanus. Bay Ridge and Park Slope, too. At the turn of the century a lot of very rich Irish built mansions—not just big houses, mansions—in Park Slope.

"**T**he Irish will speak of parishes, not neighborhoods; they'll identify themselves as from St. Theresa's—that's north of Prospect Park— or from OLPH—that's Our Lady of Perpetual Help in Bay Ridge— or Holy Cross in Flatbush. Immigrants and their sons tended to be tradesmen, carpenters, cops, and firemen. And you could say the Irish once ran the transit system. A lot of today's young people work for corporations, or on Wall Street.

"**N**owadays I guess you'd say Irish Brooklyn is in Bay Ridge, Marine Park, and Gerritsen Beach, where I live. I'll have to say our food is simple, without a lot of seasonings, but it's kept me happy all my life."

The Great Irish Fair at Coney Island, 1989. Selling soda bread.

Jimmy Gavin

Born in County Mayo in 1903, Jimmy Gavin has called Brooklyn home for many years. However, he doesn't recall how he got here: "I know I sailed out of Oakland, and next thing I knew I was in a Scandinavian dance hall, and they told me I was in Brooklyn. I heard someone addressed as 'bos'n,' and I went up and said, 'You're the bos'n?' He said, 'You should know. You've been with me the last couple of months as an able seaman, and a damn' good one, too.' I relate that memory lapse to a beating I got campaigning for Al Smith in a longshoremen's bar. They were all for Hoover, and I couldn't keep quiet about the issues of the day."

Most of Gavin's life has been spent at sea, or fighting for the rights of merchant seamen. A founder of both the National Maritime Union and its predecessor, the Marine Workers Industrial Union, in 1937 Gavin began to organize merchant seamen in ports from Maine to Florida for the CIO. In his time on the boats, Gavin held a number of jobs, including that of cook, but in the tale told here his job was to provide the center of the feast, not cook it. Let Jimmy tell the story:

"We got a ship out of Bush Terminal, and that ship was starvation. The food was terrible in them days. In Seattle, I went ashore and there was a fella selling turkeys for one dollar each. I bought one, and built a cage for him. Everyone fed the Seattle turkey—he grew terrific! Never stopped eating. Must of weighed fifty pounds. Now the crew was contemplating the great feast of Thanksgiving, and everyone was sitting on the Number 3 hatch, discussing the coming feast. We had a Portuguese cook, a fine cook, though there wasn't much for him to work with. He came up with his cleaver, and I hands him the turkey. Instead of taking him below, he took him by the head, laid it on the hatch, and chopped off the head. Well, the turkey flew up in the air, and dropped in the ocean. Someone ran to the bridge, to the officer on watch, yelling 'Man overboard!' The ship was turned around, and a lifeboat lowered. I was the first man in. We could see the turkey floating. We're rowing, about twenty feet away from him, when the big dorsal fin of a shark, the largest I ever saw, rose up. There was a swirl in the water, and there goes the turkey. Very broken-hearted, we come back on board. Joe Wiener, the chief steward, says, 'Come see what we've got for Thanksgiving dinner.' It was hot dogs, and there must have been a foot of moss on them. So we had hot dogs and beans at the feast, and not a word was said about the turkey."

Jimmy Gavin's
Hot Cakes

To make his hot cakes, it helps to be as dexterous as Jimmy Gavin; the man moves fast. "When I was a ship's cook," says Jimmy, "I'd clean off a section of the cast iron stove top, grease it with a rind of bacon, and make four hot cakes at a time."

In his opinion, "Two hot cakes, two strips of bacon, and two poached eggs make a nice breakfast." If you don't want to grease the pan for each hot cake, add 2 tablespoons of melted butter to the batter and use a nonstick pan.

1½ cups all-purpose flour
1 tablespoon baking powder
¼ teaspoon salt
1 tablespoon brown sugar
½ teaspoon baking soda
½ teaspoon cinnamon

½ teaspoon freshly grated nutmeg
½ teaspoon powdered cloves
   (optional)
2 eggs, lightly beaten with a fork
½ cup raisins or blueberries
2 cups milk

Preheat the oven to 200 degrees F.

❶ Mix the dry ingredients and spices together in a large bowl. Fold in the eggs with a fork, add the raisins or blueberries and the milk. Grease an 8-inch pan, preferably cast iron, with bacon grease or butter; bacon grease is best. Set a warm plate at the side of the stove.

❷ Pour in about ⅓ cup of batter, tilting the pan to let the batter flow to cover the bottom. When bubbles appear, pick up an edge. If the cake looks brown, lift it onto the plate with a spatula.

❸ Put a little more fat in the pan and flip the hot cake in to brown the other side. Move it to a warm platter set in the oven, and top it with a little butter. Continue making hot cakes, greasing the pan for each side.

⇒ *Makes 8 large hot cakes*

▲▲▲▲▲▲▲▲▲▲▲▲▲▲▲▲▲▲▲▲▲▲▲▲▲▲▲▲

All Good Boys Love Pasta

"No one could accuse the Irish of being great culinary artists," says Bob Bailey, president of the Brooklyn Chamber of Commerce. "Poets, soldiers, writers, but not really cooks. My mother-in-law came from Ireland, where she had eaten lamb, but not the tender lamb you get here. She bought the finest lamb chops, and what did she do with them? She boiled them!

"Most of the cooking in our Gravesend neighborhood was multi-ethnic when I was a kid," says Bob. "We discovered other people's cuisines at a young age. When I was about twelve, a friend's mother cooked pasta with shrimp. Another guest was a kid who'd just arrived from Eastern Europe. Now, we were poor, and I'd never seen shrimp.

After lunch Mrs. Messineo said, 'Bob, what happened to the shells?' I didn't know you weren't supposed to eat them.

"The new kid went home and convinced his mother that she should cook pasta too, and she invited all his friends over. She must have boiled that spaghetti for an hour. You can't believe how bad it looked and tasted. He'd told his mother that the sauce was red. So she'd poured two bottles of ketchup on it. We had boiled moosh with ketchup. But he was so proud."

Bob Bailey speaking; New York Mayor David Dinkins is second from the left.

Bob's Pasta

*"**M**y friends call this Bob's Pasta, my kids call it Dad's Pasta. The key to success is using extra-virgin* *olive oil. The green peas make it Irish."*

1 pound rigatoni
½ cup extra-virgin olive oil
¼ pound (1 stick) unsalted butter
2 cloves garlic, finely chopped

4 slices boiled ham, cut into strips
½ tomato, peeled, seeded, and chopped
¼ cup LeSueur tiny canned peas

❶ Bring a large pot of salted water to the boil and add the rigatoni.

❷ Ten minutes or so before the pasta is cooked, heat the oil and butter in a medium skillet. Cook the garlic over moderate heat, stirring, for 5 minutes. Add the ham and tomato and cook for a minute or two.

❸ Drain the pasta and put it into a large bowl. Just before serving, add the peas to the skillet and just heat through. Pour over the rigatoni, toss, and serve. Accompany with salad and crisp Italian bread. ≫→ *Serves 4 to 6*

No Party Without Soda Bread

*"**Y**ou drop a hat around here and there's a party,"* says Nell Moogan, who is a secretary at St. Boniface Church. *"And me, Aunt Nell, I have to make the soda bread. I make it for christenings, birthdays, holidays. My home is the focal point for the family.*

Nell Moogan toasts the season with grandson Thomas, 1976.

"My parents both came from Ireland. We lived in Park Slope, which was very Irish then, and I was married at St. Francis Xavier Church. We moved to Midwood twenty years ago.

"My mother never wrote a recipe down, but I watched her carefully. This is the recipe of Mary Flaherty McDonough of Clifton, County Galway, but it's a Brooklyn recipe now. As my daughter-in-law says, 'As long as there's soda bread with butter, everything's okay.'"*

Nell Moogan's Soda Bread

3 cups all-purpose flour
¼ cup sugar
½ teaspoon salt
1 teaspoon baking soda
½ teaspoon baking powder

¼ teaspoon cream of tartar
6 tablespoons butter
¼ cup caraway seeds
2 cups raisins
1½ cups buttermilk

Preheat the oven to 350 degrees F.

❶ In a large bowl, combine the flour, sugar, salt, baking soda, baking powder, and cream of tartar.

❷ Cut in the butter with two knives or a pastry blender until the mixture resembles coarse meal. Mix in the caraway seeds and raisins. Add the buttermilk, stirring until blended. Knead the dough briefly on a floured work surface. Shape it into a round loaf and place it in a buttered and floured 8-inch cast iron pan, or use a loaf pan. Bake for 45 minutes and cool on a rack.

⫸ *Makes 1 loaf*

Irish Soda Bread

Here is another version of soda bread, somewhat different from Nell Moogan's. Both are excellent.

"My mother was born in Donegal," says Noreen Monaghan Black of Bay Ridge, "and she came to Brooklyn as a teenager. Somewhere along the way, she found out about self-rising flour, and stopped making soda bread in the traditional way. Very easy, very good."

4 cups self-rising flour
⅓ cup sugar
1 cup dark raisins

2 tablespoons caraway seeds
1¾ to 2 cups milk

Preheat the oven to 375 degrees F.

❶ Butter and flour a 9-inch cake pan. In a large bowl, combine the flour, sugar, raisins, and caraway seeds. Slowly stir in enough milk to make a somewhat runny batter.

❷ Bake for 35 to 40 minutes, until a toothpick inserted in the middle of the bread comes out clean. Let the bread cool in the pan for 10 minutes, then remove it to a rack. ⫸ *Makes 1 round loaf*

▲▲▲▲▲▲▲▲▲▲▲▲▲▲▲▲▲▲▲▲▲▲▲▲▲▲▲▲▲

Oatmeal Bread

*"**H**ere is a version of the bread my grandmother, Mary Harrigan, an Irish lass, made as a bride in Brooklyn Heights in 1887," says Mary Harrigan Sheedy. "I like it with meat or fish like salmon, and as toast for breakfast."*

1 cup quick-cooking oatmeal
1 teaspoon salt
2 cups simmering water
1 package active dry yeast

½ cup lukewarm water
½ teaspoon powdered ginger
¼ cup molasses
4½ cups unbleached bread flour

❶ Put the oatmeal and salt in a large bowl and pour the simmering water over it. Stir and let cool to lukewarm.

❷ Meanwhile, sprinkle the yeast over the warm water, stir, and let dissolve. Add the yeast, ginger, molasses, and 4 cups of the flour to the oatmeal. Stir with a wooden spoon but do not attempt to knead; the mixture will be very sticky. Cover with plastic wrap and let rise in a warm place until doubled in bulk, about 45 minutes.

Preheat the oven to 375 degrees F.

❸ Butter two 8-inch loaf pans. Punch the dough down and place it on a floured work surface. Knead it, adding up to ½ cup of the reserved flour. Knead for about 10 minutes to incorporate the flour, but be aware that this dough is sticky. Shape it into loaves, place in the pans, and bake for about 45 minutes. If the loaves seem to be baking too fast, lower the heat to 350 degrees. Cool on wire racks. The loaves will be somewhat soft; they will firm as they cool.

⟫➔ *Makes 2 loaves*

Corned Beef and Cabbage with a Twist

"I always hated corned beef till I tried it this way," says Cornelius Walsh, known as Neil, who has lived all his life in Clinton Hill. "The meat is like butter, but not greasy, and the aroma is fantastic. For our St. Patrick's Day party, we have a ten-pound brisket, which takes longer to cook. We have my wife Kathleen's cabbage, and lots of interesting people. That's a foolproof mix."

Neil and Kathleen Walsh.

Cornelius J. Walsh's Corned Beef

A 5-pound packaged ready-to-cook
   corned beef
1 large onion, sliced
1 large orange, sliced

2 tablespoons pickling spices
2 stalks celery with leaves
¼ cup cold water

Preheat the oven to 300 degrees F.

❶ Line a roasting pan with a double layer of heavy-duty foil, enough to wrap the meat tightly.

❷ Rinse the corned beef and pat it dry. Place it on the foil. Arrange the onion and orange slices over and around the meat. Sprinkle on the pickling spices, lay on the celery stalks, and pour on the water. Wrap very tightly and pinch the edges well to seal.

❸ Bake the corned beef for 4 hours, or until a few bubbles begin to escape.

⋙ *Serves 8*

Kathleen Walsh's
Cabbage Dish

*"**M**y husband Neil cooks his corned beef with orange, so when I made the cabbage to accompany it for our St. Patrick's Day party, I thought of including apples. The outcome depends on the cook's preference: if you like tart cabbage, use Granny Smith apples; if you want it sweeter, use Romes or even Golden Delicious."*

A 2½- to 3-pound cabbage
2 apples (see above)
5 tablespoons butter

3 tablespoons water
Salt (optional)

❶ Cut the cabbage in quarters and discard the outer leaves. Core the cabbage and slice it as for coleslaw; it's best to have some shreds thicker than others for contrast.

❷ Cut the apples into quarters, take out cores, and cut the quarters in half. Don't peel them.

❸ Put 2 tablespoons of the butter and the water on the bottom of a large heavy pot. Mix the cabbage and apples with your hands, put them in the pot, add salt if you like, and cover with a lid. Cook the mixture over low heat, shaking the pot from time to time to prevent sticking and to shake the cabbage down as it wilts. Turn it with a wooden spoon if you like, being careful not to break the apples. Steam 20 minutes for slightly firm cabbage, 30 minutes for softer cabbage. Some of the apples will have melted into the cabbage, some will be more or less intact. Put the cabbage in a warmed serving bowl, and toss gently with the remaining butter at room temperature. ⟫→ *Serves 6 to 8*

▲▲▲▲▲▲▲▲▲▲▲▲▲▲▲▲▲▲▲▲▲▲▲▲▲▲▲▲▲▲

The Fall of the Roman Empire, and Other Great Parties

"**I**'ve been cooking since the Boy Scouts," says Father Walter Mitchell, who is a priest working in the New York City prison system. "In the '60s I was assigned to teach in the seminary, and in my job I was liaison to the kitchen. Every Monday night, I'd cook for the faculty. We started planning parties. Wonderful parties, inviting all sorts of fascinating people. We held the Fifteen Hundredth Anniversary of the Fall of the Roman Empire Party for sixty-five people in a place down on Hicks Street in Brooklyn Heights. We began that dozen-course extravaganza about 7 p.m., and the last person left at 9 the next morning. A delightful dinner. We threw a lot of fruit around; that looks like revelry and decadence. A tremendous party.

"A St. Martin's Day party be-came an annual do; that's November 11th, the same date as the festival of Bacchus. An excellent reason for a party! And St. Martin is the patron of innkeepers and drunkards. Not that we overindulge; the object is to eat, talk, laugh, and have a wonderful time.

"The biggest party I ever did was when I cooked for six hundred. It was for the twenty-fifth anniversary of the ordination of a friend. I made two pastas, and a vegetable dish. I'm Irish, but I love to cook pasta. I used a catering hall, so I had tremendous tubs to cook the pasta in. Trying to make pasta al dente for six hundred is a task.

"As I say, you plan a party, then you work hard at finding the right excuse for it! What's in the works now is Ladies' Day at Ebbets Field. Should be fun!"

Curried Quenelle Muffins

"**H**ere's a recipe from our 1976 Bastille Day dinner. Poaching quenelles is a pain in the neck, and too risky," says Father Mitchell, "so I figured out a way of making them so there's no danger they'll fall apart. I make the basic mixture, then steam them in buttered muffin tins. You need a food processor for these.

"This recipe makes 12 cupcake-size quenelles. You can also cook the mixture in the tiny muffin pans called gem pans for appetizers."

1 pound boneless chicken breasts, cut into pieces	Salt and pepper to taste
2 egg whites	2 teaspoons curry powder
10 ounces (1 cup plus 2 tablespoons) heavy cream	Watercress, for garnish

Preheat the oven to 350 degrees F.

❶ Put the chicken pieces in the bowl of a food processor. Pulse to break the pieces up, then process for several minutes to purée the chicken. Add the egg whites and process 1 to 2 minutes longer. The purée should be smooth. Add 7 ounces of the cream and the seasonings. The mixture should coat a spoon and be heavier than heavy cream. If it seems too thick and not spoonable, add as much of the rest of the cream as you need for the right consistency.

❷ You are going to steam the quenelles. Set a pan that is larger and higher than the muffin tin on a large double thickness of heavy-duty foil large enough to cover the top of the pan. Set the buttered muffin tin in the larger pan and fill the cups almost to the rim; the mixture expands very little. Pour in enough warm water to come halfway up the muffin tin. Wrap tightly in the foil to make an airtight "steambox."

❸ Place the pan in the center of the oven and cook for approximately 45 minutes. Check the "muffins." If the mixture is too liquid, remove the foil and bake until set. Unmold and serve on warmed plates surrounded by watercress.
⋙→ *Serves 12*

S.P.Q.R.
476–1976

Brooklyn's ad hoc committee for the Senate and the Roman People asks your presence at a dinner celebrating the 1,500th anniversary of Romulus Augustulus' abdication in the year 476.
With him ended the Roman Empire in the West.
We shall begin a new half-millennium of the Empire's memory with good food, wine, story, song and dance on October 18, 1976, at 7:00 p.m.
Contributions toward cost will be $15 per person.

Lobster Thermidor

"For our Bastille Day party in 1976," says Father Mitchell, "my friend Ben Citrin of Park Slope and I did an eight-course sit-down dinner for forty people. This was one of the dishes. This party started about 7 p.m. and the desserts were served between 1 and 2 a.m. It was summer, people were relaxed, and it was a fun, fun night.

"This recipe serves two. If you want to serve forty, multiply by twenty!"

2 lobsters, 1½ pounds each
6 tablespoons (¾ stick) unsalted butter
1 green pepper, cored, seeded, and diced
2 minced shallots
8 to 10 mushrooms, sliced
2 tablespoons pimentos, drained and chopped
1 teaspoon paprika
½ cup medium-dry sherry
4 tablespoons brandy
4 to 6 ounces (½ to ¾ cup) heavy cream
2 egg yolks
Salt and pepper to taste
½ cup breadcrumbs
Paprika for sprinkling

❶ Steam or boil the lobsters until cooked, about 20 minutes. Plunge them immediately into cold water. When cool enough to handle, remove the claws and legs. Split the lobsters down the back, but do not cut all the way through; later you will fill the shells. Remove the tail meat. Discard the sand sacs and any matter left in the shells.

❷ Crack the claws and remove the meat. Chop the claw and tail meat into small cubes.

❸ In a large skillet, heat 3 tablespoons of the butter. Add the lobster meat, green pepper, shallots, and mushrooms. Cook over moderately high heat, stirring, for about 3 minutes. Add the pimento pieces, stir again. Add the paprika, sherry, and brandy. Raise the heat and cook until the mixture reduces and thickens slightly.

❹ Have ready the cream beaten with the egg yolks and seasoned with salt and pepper. Over low heat, add it to the mixture in the skillet and stir to combine. Spoon the mixture into the two shells.*

Preheat the broiler to its highest point.

❺ Sprinkle the lobsters evenly with the breadcrumbs, and drizzle with the remaining butter, melted. Sprinkle with paprika. Place under the broiler until the crumbs are browned and the sauce bubbling. ➼ *Serves 2*

*You can prepare the Lobster Thermidor ahead to this point. Reheat in a 325 degree F oven for about 15 minutes, then brown under the broiler.

Arabic Atlantic Avenue. (Clockwise) baker and storefront; Charlie Sahadi and olives; pastry shop storefront.

NEAR EAST
183
BAKERY
MEAT & SPINACH
PIES
WHOLE WHEAT
BREAD
ZATA
SIMS
RINGS & B
PASTR

PASTRY & GROCERY
شركة الحلويات والبقالة الشرقية

MIDDLE EASTERN SPICE IN BROOKLYN

A number of the shops along Atlantic Avenue between Court Street and the East River have been selling Middle Eastern food and goods for almost one hundred years, since large numbers of "Syrians"—many of whom came from what is now Jordan, Iraq, and Lebanon—began their exodus to the United States.

Many still live around here, bolstered by a new wave of arrivals from an unstable part of the world: Palestinians, Yemenites, and others in search of a better life. As well as locals, shoppers at such souks as the Damascus Bakery, the Oriental Pastry Shop, and the Sahadi Importing Company include carloads of Middle Easterners from out of town, who buy hundreds of dollars' worth of foodstuffs to sustain them until the next trip.

Perhaps the chief entrepreneur of the neighborhood is Charlie Sahadi, an owner of the company started in Manhattan by his uncle in 1895. Charlie has modernized. He carries, of course, the fourteen kinds of olives and pickles his customers expect; the four sizes of bulgur wheat, and the pungent sumac, sour tamarind, and heady za'tar spice mixture; but people take a number as they do at any conventional store. Fancy teas and jams line the shelves. Sahadi's is less daunting than other stores on Atlantic Avenue to non-Arabic American shoppers in search of Middle Eastern fare.

"We're not all on Atlantic Avenue," says Lillian Habib. "There have been Arab-American enclaves in Park Slope and especially in Bay Ridge for maybe seventy years. In Bay Ridge we can get anything we want—baked goods, and we have a butcher from the 'other side' who knows exactly how to prepare lamb for kibbee."

Sultan's Delight, Inc., P.O. Box 253, Staten Island, NY 10314, will mail Middle Eastern ingredients anywhere in the United States. For a catalog, send a stamped self-addressed envelope.

Couscous Salad

Christine Sahadi Whelan, Charlie's daughter, runs a thriving take-out and catering business at the family store. "So many Arab-American women are just too busy to cook in the week," she explains. "But they want Arab food for their families." This somewhat cross-cultural salad is her own invention (Arabs rarely eat curry). It's perfect for a picnic and would, in fact, go very nicely with Chicken Salad with Chutney (see page 314).

1 bunch green onions or scallions, white and light green parts only
1 medium red pepper
½ cup raisins
½ cup golden raisins
½ cup canned chickpeas, drained
½ teaspoon salt
½ teaspoon allspice
2½ teaspoons curry powder
½ teaspoon freshly ground black pepper
¼ cup fresh lemon juice
¾ cup olive oil
2 cups couscous prepared according to package directions, cooled

❶ Dice the onions and red pepper. Add raisins and chickpeas.

❷ In a small bowl, whisk together the salt, allspice, curry powder, black pepper, and lemon juice. Gradually add the oil in a thin stream.

❸ Fluff the cooled couscous with a fork, and mix in the raisin mixture. Stir in the dressing, coating all ingredients. Chill before serving. Serve, if you like, on romaine lettuce leaves. ⟫→ *Makes 6 main-dish servings, 8 to 10 side-dish servings*

The Lebanese Family Store

"I've always felt safe here in Park Slope," says Susan Saydah. "My parents had a momma-papa store and I worked there too, as a child. My father's two sisters lived with us, and they did the cooking. My mother worked in the store. In the mornings I'd deliver pita bread and milk to customers before I went to school.

"The women customers used to get dolled up in the afternoon and come to the store, or order by phone. I realize now that Saydah Brothers—my uncle was in the business too—was a gourmet store. Wonderful fruits and vegetables. Dad ground his own lamb—Middle Easterners love lamb—and the store smelled of dried mint, garlic, and allspice. I'd come home from school, have a snack, then go to work in the store.

"On Sunday, we had people in for dinner at about 1:30. Lebanese and Syrians are not like the Italians, who enjoy eating all afternoon—we had our meal, put everything away, then went into the living room and socialized.

"We were great for belly dancing to Arabic music, especially my sister Vicky. Guests with nice voices would sing. This partying went on until the early evening.

"One of the biggies in Lebanese cooking is baked kibbee. On Sunday, we'd have raw-lamb kibbee as an appetizer along with olives and sour pickles and romaine lettuce, then baked kibbee, grape leaves, roast chicken maybe, with browned potatoes and two vegetables. Dessert was homemade ice cream or rice pudding. Dad bought a friend's homemade anisette, and we had wine with dinner. He believed in learning to drink at the table, so we wouldn't be tempted outside. Those Sunday afternoons were merry!"

Susan Saydah (number 1) and friends hanging out, circa 1940.

Kibbee Bissaneeyeh
(Lamb with Wheat, Baked with Stuffing)

"The lamb for kibbee should be completely deveined and defatted," says Susan Saydah. Kibbee is a dish made of lamb ground almost to a paste and mixed with the crushed wheat product called bulgur, or burghul. The stuffing also contains lamb, coarsely ground. This recipe is adapted from Cookin' Good with Sitto, published by St. Ann's Melkite Catholic Church in West Paterson, New Jersey.

Stuffing
2 tablespoons olive oil
1 pound coarsely ground lamb
2 tablespoons pine nuts
1 large onion, finely chopped
Salt to taste
Ground allspice to taste (start with ½ teaspoon)

Kibbee
1½ cups fine bulgur

2 pounds finely ground lamb, preferably from the leg
¼ cup cold water
2 medium onions, grated
2 teaspoons salt
½ teaspoon ground allspice
Pinch freshly grated nutmeg
Pinch cayenne pepper (optional)
3 tablespoons butter, at room temperature

Preheat the oven to 375 degrees F.

❶ Make the stuffing. Heat the oil in a saucepan and add the coarsely ground lamb, the pine nuts, onion, salt, and allspice. Cook, stirring, until browned. Set aside to cool as you make the kibbee base.

❷ Make the kibbee. Soak the bulgur in water to cover for 10 minutes or until softened. Drain well.

❸ Add the finely ground lamb, cold water, and onions and knead the mixture well. Keep moistening your hands so the mixture does not stick to them. Knead in the spices.

❹ Some like a thick kibbee, some a flatter one. About 1½ inches is a good height. Depending on the height you want, butter a round or rectangular baking pan with 1 tablespoon of the butter. (About 10 inches in diameter is fine for 1½-inch-high kibbee.) With wet hands, press half the kibbee mixture into the pan, patting it level.

❺ Spread the stuffing evenly over the base. Cover with the rest of the kibbee mixture and pat with moistened hands. With a knife dipped in cold water, cut a diamond pattern through the layers. Dot with the remaining butter. Bake for 10 minutes, then lower the heat to 325 degrees F. Bake for another 10 to 15 minutes, or until browned and bubbling. Do not overcook. Serve hot with yogurt and salad. ⫸→ *Serves 6 to 8*

Old Ways Are Best

"I'm one of five children born and raised in Bay Ridge," says Lillian Habib. "My parents were Americanized, but maintained a Lebanese household. We ate Arabic food and did not know what a baloney sandwich was till we were in our teens. Our home had Oriental rugs. We wanted to be like other kids, with ham sandwiches and broadloom. But the five of us grew to love our heritage."

Bameh Bilameh
(Lamb and Okra)

Mrs. Habib calls this "an ordinary peasant dish, but a very good one." She has lectured and given demonstrations of Arabic cooking. "Frozen or canned okra is always available," she says, "and though you could use fresh, it becomes so soft that there is little difference in the end result."

1 tablespoon olive oil
1 pound lamb, cut into 1½-inch cubes
4 large garlic cloves
1 large onion, chopped
Salt and pepper to taste
1 28-ounce can crushed tomatoes
2 cups water
2 packages frozen okra or 2 cans, drained and rinsed
Juice of 1 lemon
1 teaspoon sugar

❶ Heat the oil in a large heavy pot. When the oil is hot, put the meat, garlic, onion, salt and pepper in the pot and brown the meat cubes lightly. Add the tomatoes and the water.

❷ Cover the pot, bring to the boil, then lower the heat and simmer for 30 minutes or until the meat is somewhat tender. Add more water if needed. Add the okra, lemon juice, and sugar and simmer for 15 minutes. Serve with *Ruz* (recipe follows). ⟫→ *Serves 4*

Ruz
(Rice for Bameh Bilameh)

¼ pound butter
½ cup vermicelli, crushed to break into small pieces

1 cup converted rice
2 cups water
Salt and pepper to taste

❶ In a saucepan, melt the butter over low heat. Add the vermicelli and cook, stirring, until lightly browned. Add the rice and mix well.

❷ Add the water and bring to the boil, stirring. Add salt and pepper, cover, let simmer approximately 20 minutes, and taste. If the rice is still hard to the bite, add more hot water and cook a little longer. The rice is cooked when it is tender and the water is all absorbed. ➠ *Serves 4*

▲▲▲▲▲▲▲▲▲▲▲▲▲▲▲▲▲▲▲▲▲▲▲▲▲▲▲▲▲▲

La-Him Bil-Furrn
("Meat in the Oven" Vegetable and Beef Casserole)

*E*va Najjar says this dish is a good example of the Middle Eastern approach to healthful eating: a very little beef flavors a lot of vegetables. "The meat cooks very fast, and juices go into the vegetables," she says. The seasoning, da aa, known as "Syrian mixed spices," is a mélange of cardamom, cloves, nutmeg, allspice, black pepper, and cinnamon. If you cannot find da aa, Mrs. Najjar suggests you use 1 teaspoon of allspice.

2 cups eggplant, cut into 2-inch chunks
2 cups white potatoes, cut into ¼-inch slices
2 cups zucchini, cut into ½-inch slices
¾ green bell pepper, cut into 1-inch pieces

1 8-ounce can tomato sauce
2 teaspoons salt
1 to 1½ teaspoons *da aa*
¼ pound ground chuck

Preheat the oven to 400 degrees F.

❶ Mix all ingredients except the meat and place in a 9-inch × 13-inch × 2-inch glass or metal baking dish. Cover tightly with foil. Bake for 45 minutes.

❷ Remove the foil, baste the vegetables with the juices, and arrange marble-size dollops of meat over the vegetables. Return to the oven and bake for 10 minutes; stir gently and bake for 10 minutes more. ➠ *Serves 2 or 3*

Em-Jad-Da-Ra
(Syrian Lentils with Rice)

"This is what was called a 'Friday meal' in my home," says Eva Najjar of Park Slope. "It is a meatless dish for fast days, and in the old days, many fasted for forty days in Lent. We eat it on other days as well. Accompany it with a green salad and homemade yogurt" (see page 298). This dish is traditionally cooked all together in one pot, but if you are worried about both lentils and rice becoming tender at the same time, cook them separately. Rice cooks in about 20 minutes, but lentils can be unpredictable.

1 cup brown lentils
¾ cup long-grain rice
2 teaspoons salt, or to taste

4 cups water
2 large onions
½ cup olive oil

❶ Sort the lentils and wash them under running water. Rinse the rice and set it aside.

❷ Combine the salt and water in a large heavy saucepan. Add the lentils, bring to the boil, then lower the heat so that the liquid simmers. Cook the lentils, partially covered, until they are about three-quarters done—still hard, but softening at the edge. Add the rice. Cook until the rice is tender and the water is absorbed.

❸ Meanwhile, peel and quarter the onions, and cut them into slivers. Heat the oil to the sizzling point in a large heavy skillet. Cook the onions, stirring them frequently, until they are brown and crisp; watch carefully or they may burn.

❹ Transfer the lentils and rice to a heated platter, mounding it attractively. Holding back the onions with a slotted spoon, pour the hot oil over the *em-jad-da-ra*. Garnish with the reserved crisp onions. ⋙➤ *Serves 4*

▲▲▲▲▲▲▲▲▲▲▲▲▲▲▲▲▲▲▲▲▲▲▲▲▲▲▲▲

Stuffed Grape Leaves for One Thousand? No Problem.

Samira Ghorra runs an efficient operation at Samira's International Kitchen in Bay Ridge, the fastest-growing Arabic neighborhood in the city. She came to Brooklyn from Lebanon at the age of fourteen, and learned to cook by watching her mother. Daughters Nadia and Edmonda manage the business. Samira will cater a banquet for one thousand people, and she'll also cook for you on one day's notice. After all, she has prepared exquisite food for Middle Eastern U.N. ambassadors for years, including a weeklong stint during some *very* important negotiations that involved a future president of the United States. "I don't know about the meetings," daughter and helper Nadia gleefully reports, "but all they talked about at dinner was the food!"

"The best of our cooking is simple but subtle," says Samira. "And food that is a day old is old food."

Yab-Ra
(Samira Ghorra's Stuffed Grape Leaves)

Samira, of course, makes stuffed grape leaves in quantity. Her method is to line the bottom of the pot with beef soup bones of the same thickness, and then layer the stuffed grape leaves on top of them. They elevate the little packets so they don't stick, and add richness to the broth. But, she says, "this is purely optional. Otherwise, line the pot with a layer of grape leaves."

A 16-ounce jar grape leaves, preferably Orlando brand
1 pound chopped beef
⅓ cup converted rice
2 teaspoons salt
1 tablespoon black pepper
Cloves from 1 large head of garlic, peeled
½ cup freshly squeezed lemon juice
Water
¼ pound (1 stick) unsalted butter
Juice of 1 lemon

❶ Rinse the grape leaves well in several changes of water to rid them of salt. Put them in a colander until you are ready to roll them. Save a few to line a 10-inch pot.

❷ Make the filling by mixing together the beef, rice, salt and pepper with your hands.

❸ Spread out a grape leaf, dull side up, stem end facing you, on a work surface. Place about 1 teaspoon of the filling on the center of the leaf. (For larger leaves, use a little more.) Start to roll up the leaf. Tuck in the sides to enclose the filling, then continue rolling, making a neat little packet. Continue until all the leaves are filled.

❹ If you are not using the bones (and it is unlikely that you are), line the pot with a few layers of leaves. Place the rolled leaves, seam side down, on top of them. Build layers; you should have about four.

❺ As you work, tuck garlic cloves among the packets. Mix the lemon juice with enough water to barely cover the vine leaves. Cut the stick of butter in small pieces and dot them over the top.

❻ Place a plate, about 1 inch smaller than the diameter of the pot, on top of the grape leaves. Cover the pot and bring it to the boil. Lower the heat and let simmer for about 1 hour. Test a grape leaf; if the leaf is tough and the rice not sufficiently cooked, steam a while longer. Just before the leaves have cooked, squeeze the juice of a lemon over them.

❼ Use tongs to remove the cooked leaves to a platter. Strain the cooking juice and keep it to refresh the leaves if you are serving them later. Serve the garlic cloves with the stuffed grape leaves. ⫸ *Makes about 6 dozen*

▲▲▲▲▲▲▲▲▲▲▲▲▲▲▲▲▲▲▲▲▲▲▲▲▲▲▲▲▲▲

THE AFRICAN HERITAGE

In urban America, only Chicago has a larger black population than Bedford-Stuyvesant, a neighborhood that has had its problems, but one that has, perhaps, the largest and finest stock of nineteenth-century houses in the country. Brooklyn had a very large black population in its early days, too. In 1776, one-third of the population was black.

Bed-Stuy (a name coined by the Brooklyn <u>Daily Eagle</u> in 1931) has a lively arts center in Restoration Plaza on Fulton Street, where the Billie Holiday Theatre plays a full season. Nearby is McDonald's Dining Room. (No, <u>not</u> to be confused with any fast-food chain!) For almost half a century, the restaurant has served as a center to churchgoers and members of the Kiwanis, Lions Club, and business groups. Mrs. Rachel Garet remembers: "My father worked an extra job so that he could take us to McDonald's on Sunday. He wanted us to know what it was like to go to a fine restaurant with tablecloths and be waited on."

The old-fashioned sobriquet for Brooklyn as "Borough of Churches" is still viable in Bedford-Stuyvesant. The churches are the community's strength and its glory. The congregations are large and the spirit vibrant. There is a sense of joy, of pride, and a real under-standing of how to have fun; which, of course, includes eating well.

A 1930s Girlhood in Stuyvesant Heights

Vivian Bennett and Sylvia Edwards, active members of the Bridge Street African Wesleyan Methodist Episcopal Church, recall their Brooklyn youth, mostly spent in Stuyvesant Heights, now called Bedford-Stuyvesant:

Sylvia. "When I was seven years old in 1932, my mother gave me a little stove that worked, and I still have it. When my mama cooked on Sunday, she would give me a little something to put in a tiny pan, and I'd put it on my stove. I always liked to cook; they tell me my grandmother on my mother's side was a fine cook. Fine cooks on my father's side, too.

"When we were growing up in the Depression, my mother and father both had to work, so my sister and I started dinner. It had to be ready when my father got home! And we did not eat until the whole family was there to sit down together.

"My family was from South Carolina; I came to Brooklyn when I was four. We started out in Sheepshead Bay where a colony of relatives had settled, where my great uncle had a big house. Sheepshead Bay was more or less country then. We then moved to a tremendous apartment in Brownsville. That building had everyone in it—Irish, Germans, Italians, Jews. The streets were full of pushcarts. My older sister learned Yiddish along with her friends. Then we moved here, to what is now called Bedford-Stuyvesant. It was called Stuyvesant Heights then. This section is where the elite lived, more than fifty years ago. It was a beautiful area. Trees! It was gorgeous."

Vivian. "It seems that Sylvia followed me around Brooklyn by just a few years. My mother seemed to move us about every two years. I asked her why we moved so often and she said, 'Well, I've just got to keep moving until I find a place I like!'

"My memory goes back to the corner grocery stores. How the grocer ever managed, I don't know. The owner got everything you needed—no walking up and down the aisles like the supermarket. I

Vivian Bennett (right) and her mother, circa 1944.

believe we did shop just about every day, because we had ice. The iceman would come, and if my mother didn't have much money, she'd leave me ten cents and say, 'Just get a ten-penny piece, Vivian,' and I'd be unhappy, knowing the ten-cent piece wouldn't last long. On the weekends, when there might be more money, we'd get the fifty-cent piece. The iceman came every other day, with his horse."

Sylvia. "In winter, we kept our milk and such in window boxes. They were galvanized iron, with a shelf, and they fit tight into the window. The outside air kept them cold. In Brownsville, we'd take a pitcher to the store, and the man would fill it up with milk. We had an icebox too, and if you forgot to empty the drip pan, boy, were you in trouble!

"Every Friday, men came by with wagons of fresh fish. Everybody ate fish on Friday; it was caught in Sheepshead Bay. The vegetable men came by with their wagons, too.

"On Saturday, my sister and I did the marketing, and you know everyone had chicken every Sunday. With our mother, we'd go to the live poultry market. My mother would feel the breasts, and pick out her chicken. They killed and plucked it, and when we came home, she'd singe it.

"Sunday mornings before we went to church, we always had a big breakfast—grits, salt herring

Sylvia Edwards, age sixteen.

soaked and fried, and we always had stewed fruit. Apricots, prunes, and apples.

"Our big meal was in the afternoon, after church, about three o'clock. We could not eat until the table was set with a starched cloth, and my father was sitting down. My mother was a fantastic cook. A typical meal would be chicken; fresh string or lima beans, or peas; baked macaroni and cheese; and of course the rice and biscuits. South Carolinians eat a lot of rice, and my father would not eat store-bought bread. We had biscuits and rice every night. My mother baked such delicious cakes! She made a seven-layer jelly cake, with jelly between the layers and powdered sugar. That was my father's favorite. And coconut pie with coconut throughout the custard. I used to break my fingernails grating coconut for those pies.

"My mother used to get up early, make that big breakfast, take us to Sunday school and church, and then make that big dinner."

Vivian. "Like Sylvia's, my dad came home from work and at 5:30 we'd be seated at the table eating together. No rummaging around. My mother did not succeed in making a domesticated person out of me, but she did teach me to put on the rice before she came home from work. When I look back on those days, I don't feel at all deprived. To me, those were happy days."

Stewed Fruit

Stewed fruit is nice for breakfast, as an accompaniment to roasts or cold meat, or as a dessert. If the dessert is for adults only, you can add a little alcohol to pep it up. For tarter fruit, use the smaller amount of sugar.

An 11-ounce package of dried mixed fruit (prunes, pears, apples, and apricots) or the equivalent in other dried fruit
2½ cups water
½ to 1 cup sugar
Peeled rind of ½ lemon
1-inch piece of cinnamon stick
2 to 3 tablespoons Grand Marnier, Marsala, or port (optional)

❶ If you are using dried fruit that is very hard, you may have to soak it overnight. If so, measure out 2½ cups of soaking water. Put the fruit, water, sugar, lemon rind, and cinnamon stick in a medium saucepan, bring to the boil, and lower the heat. Simmer, uncovered, for 25 minutes, pushing down on the fruit from time to time, if necessary. If you like very soft fruit, let it simmer longer. Drain the fruit, reserving the juice, and remove the cinnamon stick.

❷ Return the juice to the pan and boil it down rapidly until it thickens somewhat. Pour the juice over the fruit. Add the alcohol, if you are using it. Eat the fruit warm, at room temperature, or chilled. ≫→ *Makes 3 cups*

Seven-Layer Cake

This is the sort of cake that Sylvia's mother used to make for Sunday dinner. You must chill the cake for several hours or freeze it for 30 minutes to firm it enough to cut into layers. If you feel that cutting seven layers is too difficult, cut five or even four. The cake will still be delicious.

....

1 tablespoon butter, at room
    temperature
1¼ cups all-purpose flour
½ teaspoon salt
7 egg whites

1¼ cups sugar
7 egg yolks
3 cups spreadable jam, such as
    strawberry
Confectioners' sugar, for dusting

Preheat the oven to 325 degrees F.

❶ Coat the bottom and sides of a 9-inch springform pan with the butter. Sift together the flour and salt.

❷ In a large bowl or in the bowl of a stationary mixer, beat the egg whites until they begin to thicken. Gradually beat in ¾ cup of the sugar, and beat until the mixture stands in firm peaks.

❸ In a separate bowl, beat the egg yolks with the remaining ½ cup of sugar until the mixture is light and thick.

❹ Beat the flour-salt mixture into the egg yolk mixture, about ¼ cup at a time, beating well after each addition. Scoop the beaten egg whites over the batter, and fold it in with a rubber spatula. Pour the batter into the pan. Bake in the center of the oven for 40 minutes. Cool on a rack to room temperature, then chill or freeze the cake to firm it.

❺ Use a long serrated knife to cut the cake into seven (or fewer) layers. Arrange the layers, upside down, in the order in which you cut them. Put the bottom layer on a serving platter and spread it with about ½ cup of the jam. Continue making layers and spreading with jam. Do not spread jam on the top layer; dust it liberally with confectioners' sugar. ⟫→ *Makes 1 9-inch cake*

▲▲▲▲▲▲▲▲▲▲▲▲▲▲▲▲▲▲▲▲▲▲▲▲▲▲

Bridge Street Church

The African Wesleyan Methodist Episcopal Church is the oldest black congregation in Brooklyn, organized on High Street in 1818. In 1854, the church members marched proudly to a new and better building on Bridge Street in downtown Brooklyn, known to all as the Bridge Street AWME Church. As needs changed and the membership moved away from downtown, church leaders decided to follow them. Thus, in 1938, the congregation moved yet again to Stuyvesant Avenue in Bedford-Stuyvesant. As a fond memento of the past, they retained the Bridge Street name.

The church plays a pivotal role in its members' lives, both spiritual and social. The people are joyous and fervent in prayer, and enthusiastic participants in church recreations. Good food, happily, plays a large part in good times. At the monthly meetings of the Women's Day Committee, which is active in community outreach, a collation (actually, a substantial buffet) is prepared by committee members having birthdays in that month. If it's January, expect beans and rice, sweet and sour carrots, fish cakes and sweet potato pie among the offerings. Sylvia Edwards describes a memorable Women's Day breakfast:

"I had a chef friend come in, with his tall white hat and apron. We had pancakes, grits, pork link sausage, scrambled eggs, and chicken livers. It was set up buffet

The Choir of 1918.

style. You were supposed to have eggs and pancakes *or* bacon, *or* grits and eggs—but those hungry people took something of everything! It was pandemonium, but everybody surely had the best breakfast of their lives."

The first service in the church is at 8 a.m.; the choir arrives at 7:30, so when early service is over, the people are hungry—especially the choir, which stays for the 11 o'clock service. Around 10 a.m., breakfast is offered. A typical breakfast might be hominy grits, eggs, bacon, sausage, fried fish, and occasionally fried chicken. Of course there is coffee, tea, juice, and biscuits. Breakfast is three dollars, surely one of the greatest bargains in Brooklyn or anywhere else.

Different clubs serve dinner after the late service. It could be roast beef or short ribs, lemon-baked chicken and ham with all the accompaniments. Part of the charge—four dollars—goes to the church, part to the club.

The congregation of four thousand has an impressive number of first-rate cooks, and the Women's Day Committee has published two cookbooks. The following recipes are all from Bridge Street members, and a number of them have been adapted from the cookbooks.

The Bridge Street Church.

Women's Day collation, prepared for the January meeting by the January and August Birthday Clubs, 1990.

Coconut Kisses

Somewhere between a candy and a cookie, these little confections of stiff meringue should be kept in airtight containers. You may double the recipe, which is adapted from one submitted by Abigail Mason.

· ·

2 large egg whites
Pinch salt
⅛ teaspoon cream of tartar
½ cup confectioners' sugar

1 cup sweetened or unsweetened shredded dried coconut
1 teaspoon grated fresh orange or lemon rind

Preheat the oven to 250 degrees F.

❶ Beat the egg whites in the bowl of an electric mixer. While the eggs are still foamy, add the salt and cream of tartar. As they begin to stiffen, slowly add the sugar. Whip until very stiff.

❷ With a rubber spatula, fold in the coconut and the rind.

❸ Line two baking sheets with parchment paper. Drop the mixture on the paper from the end of a teaspoon. It will not spread.

❹ Bake, rotating the baking sheets after 10 minutes, for 20 minutes or until the kisses are delicately browned. Ease the paper onto a damp surface and let them steam for 1 minute. Loosen with a spatula and remove to racks. Let the kisses dry thoroughly. ⟫→ *Makes 35 to 40 kisses*

Giblet and Barley Soup

Allan C. Ricks of Bridge Street Church gave us this recipe.

· ·

½ pound chicken gizzards or hearts, or a combination
¼ pound chicken livers
3 cups water
Salt to taste
⅓ cup coarsely chopped onion
4 sprigs parsley
½ bay leaf
2 tablespoons butter
2 teaspoons vegetable oil

1 cup finely chopped onion
1 teaspoon minced garlic
½ pound fresh mushrooms, cut into ¼-inch bits
Juice of half lemon
3 cups fresh or canned chicken broth
⅓ cup medium pearl barley, rinsed
Freshly ground pepper to taste
½ cup heavy cream (optional)
Chopped parsley for garnish

❶ Combine the gizzards, hearts, and livers and put them in a large saucepan. Add the water, salt, onion, parsley, and bay leaf. Bring to the boil, reduce the heat and simmer, partially covered, for 15 minutes. Strain the broth and reserve it. Rinse the giblets and reserve separately. Discard the vegetables and bay leaf.

❷ Meanwhile, heat the butter and oil in a large skillet. Sauté the onion and garlic, stirring occasionally, until the onion is translucent, about 1 minute. Toss the mushroom bits with the lemon juice, add them to the skillet, and sauté over moderate heat, stirring often, until the mushroom liquid has evaporated and the mushrooms begin to brown.

❸ When the giblets are cool enough to handle, cut them into small dice. You should have about 1½ cups. Add to the mushroom mixture and stir. Transfer the mixture to a large stockpot. Add the chicken broth and barley. Bring to the boil, reduce the heat and simmer, partially covered, for 1 hour to 1 hour and 15 minutes, or until the barley is cooked and the giblets are tender. Add the pepper. If desired, stir in the heavy cream. Bring to the boil and serve, sprinkled with parsley. ⫸ *Serves 4 to 6*

Okra Fish Cakes

This recipe is based on one by Mrs. Hazel Griffin. Born in Georgia, Mrs. Griffin, a retired beautician, has lived in Brooklyn for 50 years.

She has four great-grandchildren. "These fish cakes are good cold," she notes. "Nice for a picnic."

1 pound salt pollack or cod
1 pound fresh okra, cut in thin slices
1 cup finely chopped onion
¼ teaspoon hot red pepper
¾ cup cornmeal
¾ cup all-purpose flour

1 teaspoon baking powder
1 cup chopped bell pepper
½ teaspoon salt, if necessary
2 large eggs
Vegetable oil for frying

❶ Soak the fish overnight, changing the water 2 or 3 times. When it pulls apart easily, drain the fish and cover it with fresh water. Gently poach it until tender. Drain the fish and discard the water. When the fish has cooled, flake it with a fork. Remove and discard any bones.

❷ Cook the okra slices, in batches if necessary, in a nonstick pan until they have crisped and are no longer oozing liquid. They should be cooked through. Let them cool.

❸ In a large bowl, mix the flaked fish with the okra, onions, red pepper, cornmeal, flour, baking powder, bell pepper, and salt, if needed. (Occasionally all the salt soaks out of the fish.) Beat the eggs and mix them in. With lightly floured hands (the mixture can be sticky), form patties about 3½ inches round × ½ inch high. Place them on a cookie sheet and chill them for at least 1 hour.

❹ In a large skillet, heat ½ inch of oil until it sizzles when flicked with a drop of water. Cook the patties, a few at a time, until golden, turning them once. Drain on paper towels. ≫→ *Makes 16 patties*

Green Salad with Creamy Mustard Vinaigrette

This salad is from Thressa B. King, who serves it for parties.

1 small head Boston lettuce	1 tablespoon water
½ small head soft curly or red-leaf lettuce	1 tablespoon white-wine vinegar
	2 teaspoons Dijon mustard
2 scallions	Salt and pepper to taste
1 large egg yolk	¼ cup extra-virgin olive oil

❶ Wash and dry the lettuces, and tear them into bite-sized pieces. Wrap in towels and chill.

❷ Thinly slice the scallions crosswise, including most of the green part. Combine the chilled lettuce and scallion in a salad bowl and place in the refrigerator until serving time.

❸ In a small stainless steel bowl set over simmering water, combine the egg yolk and water. Stir until foamy and thickened, taking care not to scramble the yolk. Remove from the heat and whisk in the vinegar, mustard, and salt and pepper to taste. Add the oil in a slow stream, whisking constantly, until the dressing has emulsified.

❹ Drizzle the dressing over the salad, toss, and serve. ≫→ *Serves 4*

A Glimpse of Lucky Lindy

"**Y**ou know, I remember the ticker-tape parade for Charles Lindbergh along Flatbush Avenue downtown in 1927," says Eunice Grey, a Bridge Street Church member. "The school kids got the day off. I was home with the measles, but I wanted to go so much my mother bundled me up and took me. I also remember, a few years later, the hands of the Williamsburg clock being carried on a flatbed truck down Atlantic Avenue—they were huge.

"I was born in Brooklyn, on Bergen Street, but my family came from Barbados. My mother came here first, and got a job—she could cook. My father made shoes, and he brought his tools when he came. My mother said the only shoes she could wear were his. What hurt him the most was that he could not get into the shoe trade because he was a black man. He could likely have owned his own business. He couldn't even get a sanitation job; he went to work in a paint-base factory. All of the men in Barbados had a trade.

"After school I went to the Colony House Community Center. The children went for athletics, and art and cooking lessons. Well-to-do people would pick out a few kids and take them to the opera at the Academy of Music. I really enjoyed that. Not all kids like opera, but I did.

"My mother's cooking was bland but tasty. My father had a pressure, so she didn't use salt. We

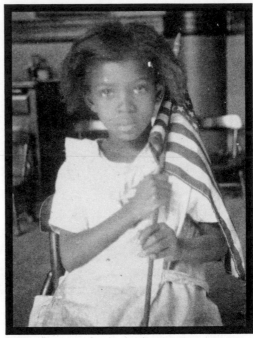

Eunice Grey, age five, in kindergarten.

can attribute our good health to our diet; we had complete vegetable meals, and of course the best beef stew. Friday was always fish day. She'd go to the Belmont Market for fish and fresh-killed chicken. The chicken feet were free; they were the best thing for soup.

"Many Caribbean people worked hard and saved to buy a home. My parents did too; they bought a house and we moved to Bedford-Stuyvesant when I was twelve.

"Mother made codfish cakes and baked on Saturday, until we got Americanized, and then we had franks and beans on Saturday! People make codfish cakes for parties now. I call them cakes, but the Jamaicans call them fritters. Cakes or fritters, they're delicious."

Eunice Grey's Codfish Cakes

"If the cod has any bones, be sure to pull them out," says Mrs. Grey.

½ pound dried boneless codfish
2 eggs, well beaten
½ teaspoon paprika
½ teaspoon onion salt
1 stalk scallion, finely chopped
½ teaspoon black pepper
¼ cup finely chopped onion

¼ cup finely chopped green pepper
¼ cup finely chopped tomato pulp
½ cup flour
1 teaspoon baking powder
½ cup milk
Vegetable oil for deep frying

❶ Soak the codfish for at least 12 hours, changing the water several times. Place in a saucepan with cold water to cover by 3 inches and bring to the boil. Boil for 10 minutes, and taste the fish. If too salty, repeat the boiling. The fish should shred easily. When cool enough to handle, shred it with your fingers and remove any small bones.

❷ In a large bowl, combine the eggs, paprika, onion salt, scallion, black pepper, onion, green pepper, and tomato. Add the flour, baking powder, and milk and mix thoroughly. Add the shredded codfish.

❸ Heat at least 2 inches of oil in a deep skillet until sizzling. Drop tablespoon-sized portions of the fish mixture into the hot oil, about 5 at a time. Fry on both sides for 2 to 3 minutes, until golden brown, and drain on paper towels. ⟫→ *Makes about 40 codfish cakes (or fritters)*

The Ingenious Dietician

Eunice Lewis is a dietician working mostly with diabetics. She has published her own cookbook, *Cooking Without Salt*, to help patients adjust their diets. Eunice created Lewis' Complete Season With-Out-Salt, a blend of garlic and onion powders, paprika, oregano, chili powder, sage, and black pepper, to enliven saltless food. She has won awards for "The Vegetable Parade," a skit that teaches children to eat their veggies, and for "The Measuring Kit," which helps diabetics regulate their diets. "So many of the people I see are from the Caribbean," says Eunice, "and I work with them to adjust the foods that they like."

Eunice recommends the following raw or lightly steamed vegetables for salad: cabbage, carrots, cauliflower, radishes, spinach, tomatoes, broccoli, cucumbers, onions, and tomatoes.

Saltless Garlic Dressing

¼ cup water
3 tablespoons wine vinegar
2 tablespoons vegetable oil
1 clove garlic, peeled

2 teaspoons dried basil
1 teaspoon ground black pepper
¼ teaspoon honey

Combine all ingredients in a jar with a tight-fitting lid. Shake vigorously. Refrigerate and shake again before using. ➤ *Makes about ½ cup*

Eunice Lewis mixing one of her salad dressings.

Saltless Onion Dressing

¼ cup fresh lemon juice
½ cup water
⅓ cup vegetable oil
2 tablespoons grated onion

2 tablespoons chopped chives
2 tablespoons chopped parsley
½ teaspoon dried tarragon
¼ teaspoon pepper

Combine all ingredients in a jar with a tight-fitting lid. Shake vigorously. Refrigerate and shake again before using. ➤ *Makes about 1 cup*

▲▲▲▲▲▲▲▲▲▲▲▲▲▲▲▲▲▲▲▲▲▲▲▲▲▲▲▲▲▲

THE CARIBBEAN CONNECTION

"I think the term 'West Indian' is misleading," says Dee Dee Dailey, a caterer who lives in Sheepshead Bay. "It's much too narrow. I prefer to say 'Caribbean.' The people are a rich mixture. The influences are African, Dutch, English, Danish, Spanish, French, East Indian, and what have you; it makes for a varied, interesting cuisine."

That cuisine has come to Brooklyn. In formerly Jewish Flatbush, shoppers now come for goat meat, cow heel, pig snouts, and coconuts. Jamaican stores sell bottled drinks with stirring names: there is Front End Lifter, Magnum Explosion Combo, and Agony: Peanut Punch Plus.

For the Caribbean community, certain churches are meeting needs for worship, for practical help, and for identity.

"The first Flatbush Reformed Dutch Church was built in 1654," says Irving Choban, former president of the Long Island (now the Brooklyn) Historical Society, and president of the Flatbush Historical Society. "The present church was built in 1798, and its bell has tolled the death of every president since George Washington. The congregation is now perhaps seventy percent black. Many come from former colonies such as Guyana and Curaçao, and the Dutch Reformed religion is their religion. They are made welcome."

Another church that serves the large Caribbean Anglican community is St. John's at Brooklyn, in Park Slope, built on its present site in 1869. Many of its congregation come from such places as Belize, Barbados, and Trinidad, all formerly English.

Members and friends of the Flatbush Reformed Dutch Church have published a small, largely Caribbean cookbook. In the undercroft of St. John's, the women of St. Margaret's Guild hold their annual dinner. The menu is no longer roast beef, mashed potatoes, and vanilla ice cream; it's snapper stew with plantain dumplings, peas and rice, and banana cake. The food has changed, the fellowship remains.

Many Cuisines Make One

"I have roots in both the Spanish- and English-speaking Caribbean," says Dee Dee Dailey, "and my roots are also Southern and Native American." Much of Dee Dee's cooking blends spicy Caribbean and African-American flavors. (She prepares Mediterranean food as well.) "This dish is an adaptation of a recipe my mother, Margaret Lynch Dailey, gave me. Her grandmother was born in Cuba, and the heavy use of garlic and olive oil is part of the African-Hispanic culinary legacy."

Dee Dee Dailey.

Dee Dee Dailey's Pigeon Peas and Rice

½ pound dried pigeon peas (gandules)
3 to 4 tablespoons olive oil
1 large onion, chopped
4 cloves garlic, minced
1 small green bell pepper, chopped
1 teaspoon dried oregano

1 tablespoon dried basil
2 ounces salt pork, cubed (optional)
1 large bay leaf
1 pound long-grain rice
Salt (preferably sea salt) and pepper to
taste

❶ Pick through the pigeon peas, removing any stones or dirt. Cover them with water by 2 inches and let soak overnight.

❷ Heat the oil in a large heavy stewpot and cook the onions, garlic, bell pepper, oregano, basil, and salt pork (if used) for about 2 minutes, stirring. Add the drained pigeon peas and stir in for 1 minute, to blend. Add water (or chicken or vegetable broth) to cover and the bay leaf. Cover, bring to the boil, reduce the heat and simmer for 1 hour, or until the peas are almost tender. Add a little boiling liquid, as needed.

❸ Stir in the rice, and enough liquid to cover. Season with salt and pepper. Simmer the dish for about 20 minutes, or until the rice is cooked and the peas are tender. Let stand for 15 minutes before serving. ⟫➔ *Makes 8 servings*

Dee Dee's Sorrel Beverage

"Sorrel is a popular drink with most Caribbean folk," says Dee Dee. "Packets of sorrel, which is dried hibiscus flowers, can be found in the ethnic markets in Flatbush and in downtown Brooklyn. Mexicans also drink a distillation of hibiscus flowers, which they call Agua de Jamaica. You can find turbinado, a partly refined brown sugar, in Caribbean and health food stores."

2 quarts boiling water
3 ounces dried Jamaican sorrel
   (hibiscus flowers)
Peel of 1 orange
Peel of 1 lime or lemon
1 3-inch cinnamon stick

12 cloves
1 ounce fresh ginger, unpeeled, grated
Honey, sugar, or turbinado sugar to
   taste
15 grains of rice

❶ Pour the boiling water into a large container to which you have added the sorrel, citrus peels, cinnamon, cloves, and ginger. Allow the mixture to steep unrefrigerated for 24 hours.

❷ Strain and discard the solids. Sweeten to taste. Add the rice grains, which will cause the drink to ferment very slightly. Let it stand, unrefrigerated, for another 24 hours. Refrigerate, serve cold. ⟫⁺ *Makes about ¾ gallon*

Sea Trout Salad

Gladys Benn from Guyana enjoys doing handwork at the Older Adult Center at the Flatbush Reformed Dutch Church on Flatbush Avenue. "For this salad, cut the yams into cubes the size of croutons," she says, "and don't cook them too long. They should be firm, not mushy."

1 pound center-cut sea trout
Salt and pepper to taste
1 large lime or lemon
1 pound yams
1 tablespoon minced parsley
6 tablespoons mayonnaise

½ pound cabbage
1 medium cucumber
2 large firm tomatoes
1 head lettuce, leaves separated,
   washed and chilled

❶ Steam the fish in a little water until the flesh turns milky white. Drain it and let it cool. Remove any bones or skin. Flake the flesh, and season it with salt and pepper and the juice of the lime. Cover the fish with plastic wrap and chill overnight.

❷ The following day, peel the yams and cut them into neat cubes. Steam the yam cubes until cooked but still firm. When they are cool, add them to the flaked fish with the parsley and 3 tablespoons of the mayonnaise. Blend carefully with a fork. Do not crush the yam cubes.

❸ Slice the cabbage into fine shreds. Peel the cucumber and cut it into cubes, and cut the tomatoes into neat chunks. Toss the vegetables with the remaining 3 tablespoons of mayonnaise.

❹ Arrange the lettuce leaves on a platter. Heap the fish salad in the center and arrange the tossed vegetables around it. ⟫⟶ *Serves 4*

Callaloo

Mavis George is from Trinidad, and now lives on Eastern Parkway. "We cook callaloo on Sundays," she says. "We serve it as a side dish, with curried chicken or goat, and rice." The kind of pumpkin called calabaza *is sold by the piece in markets catering to Caribbean and Hispanic people, as are the green leaves called* callaloo *or* dasheen.

½ pound fresh okra, cut into ¼-inch
   rounds
1½ cups water
1½ pounds callaloo (dasheen),
   chopped, or 1 package frozen
   chopped spinach, defrosted
1 large onion, sliced
½ pound of pumpkin (calabaza),
   peeled and cut into chunks

1 tablespoon vegetable oil
1 cup unsweetened cream of coconut,
   at room temperature
Salt and pepper to taste
Goya Seasoning Salt
1 hot fresh or dried pepper

❶ Put the okra and water in a large saucepan and bring it to the boil. When the okra seeds turn pink, add the callaloo or spinach, onion, and pumpkin. When the liquid returns to the boil, add the oil. Add the coconut cream, salt and pepper, a dash of Goya seasoning, and the hot pepper. Simmer for ½ hour, or until the vegetables are soft.

❷ Remove the pepper, put the contents into a blender jar or food processor bowl, and purée. ⟫⟶ *Serves 4*

Curried Goat

Evolga Francis.

Both Evolga Francis from the parish of Clarendon in Jamaica and
Lyris George, Mavis's daughter
from Trinidad, contributed to this
recipe. As Lyris says, "Not all, but
much of the food from the Caribbean is cooked in the same way."
Some Americans may balk at goat,
but if it is young, it can be delicious. You may substitute lamb.
    Jamaican curry powder is
flavorful and not powerfully hot.

1½ pounds kid or lamb, cut into small
    serving pieces
1 teaspoon salt
½ teaspoon black pepper
2 to 2½ tablespoons Jamaican or other
    curry powder
1 large onion, chopped
1 large green pepper, cored, seeded,
    and cut into 1-inch pieces

1 teaspoon crumbled dried thyme
1 chili, seeded and diced (optional)
3 tablespoons vegetable oil
2 cups hot water
2 medium potatoes, cut into pieces the
    size of the meat pieces

❶ Rinse the meat pieces and pat them dry. Rub them with the salt, pepper,
and curry powder. Mix in the onion, green pepper, thyme, and optional chili.
Place in a bowl and cover with plastic wrap. Refrigerate for at least 1 hour or
overnight.

❷ Scrape the onion bits and some of the seasonings off the meat pieces.
Heat the oil in a Dutch oven or heavy medium cooking pot with a cover. Brown
the meat pieces, turning them to brown evenly.

❸ Add the rest of the contents of the bowl and cook for a minute or two in
the oil, stirring. Add the water and stir well. Cover the pot and bring to the boil.
Lower the heat and simmer, covered, until the meat is almost tender, 1 hour to 1
hour and 15 minutes. Add the potato pieces and cook until the potatoes are soft
and the gravy has thickened, about 20 minutes. Serve with rice. ⟫→ *Serves 4*

Caribbean Trifle for a Crowd

"The English have had a great influence on many of the islands,"
say Claire Morierce-Shaw, whose
husband is Jamaican. "This dish is
based on English trifle made with
ladyfingers, sherry, raspberry jam,
and custard. In the Caribbean we
use tropical fruits, rum, and coconut. Take out your big, unused
glass punch bowl and assemble
the trifle so everyone can see the
layers."

1 large box of Bird's or Jell-O egg
    custard
3 pounds of pound cake
A 12-ounce jar of pineapple jam or
    guava jelly
3 ripe mangoes

1 bunch (about 8) bananas
½ pint rum or coconut liqueur
2 cups toasted shredded coconut
1 cup heavy cream, whipped
Maraschino cherries (optional)

❶ Make 6 cups of custard, following the recipe on the box. Use less sugar than is called for, or the trifle may be too sweet.

❷ Cut the cake into ½-inch pieces. Spread them with jam or jelly.

❸ Cut up the mangoes and bananas.

❹ Layer the trifle as follows: first the cake, then the rum or liqueur, next the fruit, next the custard, the coconut, the whipped cream, and the cherries, if desired. ➤ *Serves 15 to 20*

Joy in the Street

Every Labor Day, Eastern Parkway is aswirl with people in costumes of fantastic extravagance and dazzling color. For six hours, the street jumps to the beat of calypso and reggae music as floats pass and marchers in towering headdresses, often spanning twenty feet, dance and prance. This is the annual West Indian Day Parade, also called Carnival, attended by half a million happy people.

Carnival is held in Trinidad before Lent, a last splash before the austerities of Lent. But in Brooklyn, and a few other North American cities, Carnival takes place in late summer, so people can celebrate while the weather is fine.

"I came here in 1954," says Carlos Lezama, president and executive director of the association that runs the parade. "What is wonderful is that all the Caribbean islands are represented. There is lots of competition for prizes; teams come up with ideas and themes for costumes, and they work in secret. Many come up from the islands especially to see Carnival.

"Good cooks sell food—rice and peas, curried goat, beef patties, stimulating stuff.

"To live in a country like this is an honor. There is a lot of strength in a community when people come together as one."

Carnival revelers on Eastern Parkway.

Beef Patties, Jamaican Style

These are sold from booths at Carnival. The rest of the year you can buy them at any time in Crown Heights or Flatbush.

Pastry
2 cups all-purpose flour
1 teaspoon salt
¾ cup vegetable shortening
¼ to ⅓ cup ice water

Filling
1 pound ground beef
1 scallion, white part only, chopped
1 teaspoon salt

2 teaspoons black pepper
½ to ¾ teaspoon crumbled dried thyme
About 4 inches of French or Italian bread
1 teaspoon paprika
1 small red pepper, minced, or drops of Caribbean hot sauce, to taste

❶ Make the pastry. Combine the flour and salt in a bowl, and work in the shortening until the dough resembles coarse meal. Add just enough water to make the dough hold together. Wrap the dough in plastic wrap and let it rest in the refrigerator for several hours or overnight.

❷ Make the filling. Combine the beef, scallion, salt, black pepper, and half the thyme. Cook the mixture in a skillet just until the meat loses its pink color but is not browned.

❸ While the meat cooks, soak the bread in water to cover for about 5 minutes. Squeeze the bread but save the water. Grind the bread in a food processor or meat grinder. Put the bread and water in a saucepan with the rest of the thyme and cook until most of the water has evaporated.

❹ Add the bread and the paprika to the meat. Stir in the red pepper or hot sauce and cook over low heat, stirring often, for about 20 minutes.

❺ Roll the dough out about ⅛ inch thick; the dough should not be too thin or it may break when filled. Cut out circles about 6 inches in diameter.

❻ Place a heaping tablespoon of meat in the center of each circle. Using your finger, moisten the edges of the dough with water. Fold the dough over to make a half circle, and crimp the edges with a fork. Repeat until dough and meat are used up.

❼ Place the patties on ungreased baking sheets. Bake about 35 minutes, or until golden brown. ➣ *Makes about 15 patties*

▲▲▲▲▲▲▲▲▲▲▲▲▲▲▲▲▲▲▲▲▲▲▲▲▲▲▲▲▲

Banana Nut Bread

This recipe is based on one in the cookbook of the Belize Hospital Auxiliary, supplied by a member of St. Margaret's Guild of St. John's Church at Brooklyn in Park Slope. Lyle's Golden Syrup, which is actually treacle, is made in England. This delicious syrup can be found in specialty shops. You can also substitute a mixture of half dark, half light corn syrup.

1½ cups self-rising flour
¼ teaspoon salt
4 tablespoons (½ stick) butter or margarine
⅓ cup sugar

½ cup chopped walnuts
1 egg
⅓ cup plus 2 teaspoons Lyle's Golden Syrup
2 very ripe bananas, mashed

❶ Sift the flour and salt into a large bowl. Cut in the butter until the mixture resembles coarse meal. Stir in the sugar and nuts.

❷ Butter a 9-inch × 5-inch × 2-inch loaf pan. Blend the egg and syrup together, and stir in the bananas. Add the flour mixture and stir well.

❸ Pour the mixture into the loaf pan and bake until the loaf is golden, about 45 minutes. ⫸ *Makes 1 loaf*

(From the top) tropical ice store; Los Paisanos butcher shop; dancers in Williamsburg, Feast of Our Lady of Guadalupe.

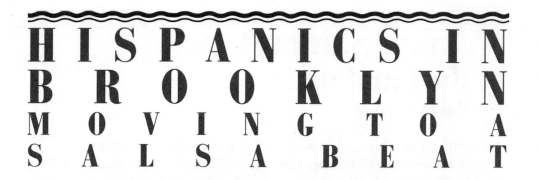

HISPANICS IN BROOKLYN
MOVING TO A SALSA BEAT

Brooklyn's Latinos—nearly twenty percent of the population—add their own distinction to the changing face of the Borough. Along Fifth Avenue in Sunset Park lives a veritable <u>olla podrida,</u> or spicy stew, of Spanish-speaking New World people—Puerto Ricans, Mexicans, Panamanians, and Central and South Americans. The bodegas—small all-purpose grocery stores—carry the foods that Latins crave: pork cracklings, yellow rice, papers for wrapping <u>pasteles,</u> chorizo sausage, adobo seasoning, and cans and solid blocks of coconut milk. Produce stores, increasingly run by Koreans, carry every root and tropical fruit a cook could require. And not just in Sunset Park—Hispanics live all over Brooklyn.

Folkways, customs, and dialects differ, but all Latins give a lot of thought to food. It's important to them, and it's good.

From the Shining Star of the Caribbean
The Puerto Ricans

Puerto Rican merchants settled in Brooklyn as early as 1830, when the Caribbean island was a Spanish colony. However, the American market for sugar and molasses was more important than Spain's, and Brooklyn was the great port of entry. After 1917, Puerto Ricans could come to the United States as citizens. Many chose Brooklyn.

"My uncle owned bodegas along Columbia Avenue in Red Hook," says Tony Velez, a photographer who documented Hispanic communities for the Brooklyn Historical Society. "My family moved here in 1953. I have warm memories of the family getting together before Christmas to make *pasteles*. Every culture has a kind of ravioli, and this is the Puerto Rican kind. There are two basic ingredients, cubed pork that is stewed with raisins, olives, and garbanzo beans, and a wrapping dough called *masa*, made of green bananas, plantains, and a starchy root vegetable like *yautia* or *yuca*. This is a really big deal, a communal effort that takes all day. Someone brings eight or ten pounds of pork, another brings plantains, another makes *sofrito*, the sauce. People drink beer, Pedro Domecq brandy, play records, sing. It's a wonderful coming together of the family. My father Candido was the chef, with my mother Enriqueta assisting.

"You have to make large quantities of *pasteles*—it's the only way. Every family has its own recipe. And people still say, 'Mine is better! I use yuca!' Or 'Nobody's beat mine! This is my father's recipe!'"

Mofongo con Caldo de Pollo
(Luis Loyola's Mofongo with Chicken Broth)

"**I** *have a twin brother," says Luis Loyola, "and our mother put us in a double chair in the kitchen to keep an eye on us as she worked. It must have made an impression, as we both love to cook." Born and raised in Puerto Rico, Professor Loyola teaches anthropology at Manhattan College, specializing in* Mesoamerican, Caribbean, and Latin American cultures. He lives in Sunset Park.

The word mofongo *is of African origin. It is a ball of pork and fried plantain, a fruit that came from Africa with slavery. This is traditional peasant cookery, usually eaten as a main dish for family* occasions. It is also served with pork chops, chicken leg, or fried pieces of pork shoulder. Mofongo is also eaten with broth alone. It must be made shortly before it is eaten, otherwise it gets hard. It must be pounded in a mortar; a food processor does not give satisfactory results.

··

Broth

A 3½ pound chicken, cut into 8 pieces
10 cups water
1 large onion, cut into 4 pieces
3 cloves garlic, crushed
Salt and freshly ground black pepper to taste
1½ teaspoons dried oregano, crumbled

Mofongo

6 green plantains (one for each portion)*
3 to 4 tablespoons vegetable oil
4 large cloves garlic
1½ pounds *chicharrones*, Puerto Rican crackling pork rinds†
Salt and pepper to taste
1 ripe avocado

❶ Make the broth. Put the chicken pieces and water in a soup pot and bring to the boil. Lower the heat and skim off the froth that rises. Add the onion, garlic, salt, pepper, and oregano. Cover and simmer 30 to 45 minutes. Leave the chicken in the broth while you prepare the mofongo.

❷ Make the mofongo. Peel the plantains under running water. Cut the fruit into ¾-inch slices. Heat the oil in a large skillet until it sizzles and fry the plantain slices in batches until soft, approximately 5 minutes on each side, turning once. Plantain must be cooked until very soft. Drain the slices on paper towels. Pound the garlic cloves to a paste with mortar and pestle.

❸ For each portion of mofongo, take 4 ounces of pork rind and the fried slices of one plantain. Pound them, with a little of the garlic paste, in a mortar. Add salt and pepper to taste. The mixture should be somewhat crumbly. Pound again, to mix. As you pound, fat is released from the pork rinds and mixes with the plantain. When a ball is formed, turn the mortar upside down over a soup bowl. Form the mixture into a ball.

❹ Heat the broth and chicken. For each portion, put a piece of chicken, some broth, a mofongo ball, and a slice of avocado in a soup bowl.

≫→ *Makes 6 portions*

*Plantains, which look like large bananas, must be well cooked. They can be found at Hispanic and many other greengrocers.

†Pork rinds are sold at bodegas, Puerto Rican grocery stores. They are bits of fatback rendered in lard. To make them from scratch, cut fatback into small cubes and fry them until the fat is rendered and the remaining bits are crisp. You can then use some of the fat to prepare the mofongo.

Puerto Rican Sofrito

"Sofrito is really the most important element in Puerto Rican cooking," says photographer Tony Velez. "It is what distinguishes our cooking. I use it in such dishes as chicken and rice, bean stews and* pasteles, *the elaborate Puerto Rican tamale served at big parties." Tony's version of sofrito is richer than the traditional one; he uses both oil and tomato paste.*

2 medium onions
½ pound *aji dulces* (tiny green, yellow, orange, and red sweet peppers), minced
3 to 4 cloves garlic
1 to 2 bunches cilantro (fresh coriander)
¼ cup olive oil

3 ounces manzanilla olives and capers with pimentos, preferably Goya brand
Salt and freshly ground pepper to taste
4 ounces tomato paste
8 ounces tomato sauce
4 to 6 drops Tabasco sauce (optional)

❶ Chop the onions very fine and set them aside. Chop the peppers, garlic, and cilantro by hand or in a food processor.

❷ In a heavy skillet, preferably cast iron, heat the olive oil. When it is sizzling add the onion and cook over moderately high heat until onion is wilted. Stir in the pepper mixture and cook for 3 minutes, stirring frequently. Add the olives and capers and salt and pepper to taste. Cook for 3 minutes, then add the tomato paste. Stir well and cook for 2 minutes; add the tomato sauce and optional Tabasco. ⟫→ *Makes about 3½ cups*

Note: Sofrito base can be frozen for several months. Divide it into portions and defrost and use as needed.

Candido, Enriqueta, and Tony Velez.

Bacalao Guisado
(Puerto Rican Codfish Stew)

For years, dried codfish was a staple of poor Puerto Ricans, and indeed of many other people. However, it has become so expensive that guisado is now a costly dish.

This stew is accompanied by a selection of root vegetables found in Hispanic and some Asian markets. Most must be peeled deeply and cut into large chunks, then boiled until tender. The names of these roots can be confusing; depending on country, the same root may go by different names.

Luis Loyola has lightened this dish. In traditional Puerto Rican cookery, a stew also contains tomato sauce, sofrito—a widely used seasoning—olives, capers, and oregano.

2 pounds boneless salt cod
¼ pound salt pork (*tocino*), cut into
　¼-inch pieces
½ large onion, coarsely chopped
1 large green pepper, seeded and
　coarsely chopped
1 large red pepper, seeded and coarsely
　chopped
2 large ripe tomatoes, each cut into 3
　pieces

Vegetable Accompaniments
6 green bananas
Yuca (cassava)
Batata (boniato), also called white
　sweet potato
Yautia (taro)
Name, the true yam
Malanga (yautia blanca)
Platano (plantain)

❶ Soak the codfish in water to cover for at least 4 hours or overnight. Boil it in 3 or 4 changes of water, to soften it and remove the salt. Drain it and break it into pieces.

❷ In a large skillet fry the salt pork pieces until golden brown, turning them often. As you cook the remaining ingredients, stir frequently. Add the onions and fry for 3 to 4 minutes. Add the peppers, fry for 3 to 4 minutes. Add the tomato chunks, fry 2 minutes.

❸ Add the cod pieces to the skillet. Cover, cook over moderately low heat for 15 minutes. Turn the cod pieces, replace the cover, and cook for 15 minutes more.

❹ Meanwhile, in a large pot, boil the root vegetables that are served with the stew. Depending on how many types of vegetables you use, boil at least ½ pound of vegetables for each portion. ⟫→ *Serves 4 to 6*

Arroz Sorpresa
(Surprise Rice)

Herminia Ramos-Donovan wears two hats. There's the official one as Assistant Commissioner for Economic Development in New York City, helping minority businesses to gain city services. The second is a chef's toque, worn as owner of Fina's Restaurant in East New York. This pleasant, reasonable establishment serving the dishes of Commissioner Ramos-Donovan's mother, Fina, is the brightest spot in this troubled neighborhood, and a clear sign of its turnaround. Fina's serves this excellent Surprise Rice.

¼ cup fatback, cut into small pieces
3 cups short-grain rice
6 to 7 cups hot water or chicken stock
2 cups frozen mixed vegetables, defrosted

2 cups Puerto Rican white cheese, *queso del País Indulac*, diced*
Plantain leaves, or substitute parchment paper or foil

❶ Cook the fatback over medium heat in a heavy stockpot, until it has released most of its fat. Stir in the rice, mixing to coat each grain. Add the hot liquid and the vegetables. Cook, uncovered, over moderate heat until the water sinks to the level of the rice. Lower the heat, stir well, cover, and cook for 35 to 40 minutes, until the rice is tender.

Preheat the oven to 400 degrees F.

❷ Mix the rice with the white cheese. Scoop a cup of rice mixture onto a plantain leaf or a 12-inch square of parchment paper or foil. Fold securely into a rectangle and tie with twine. Place the packets of rice in a baking dish. Bake for 10 minutes, unwrap each portion, and serve. ⟫⟶ *Makes 6 servings*

*This Puerto Rican cheese does not melt and its flavor is unique. Using cheddar or Monterey Jack in place of *queso del País Indulac* will change the character of the dish, but it will still be delicious.

Fina's Ensalada de Camarones y Jueyes
(Shrimp and Crabmeat Salad)

1 pound medium shrimp, peeled, deveined, cooked, and diced
1 pound crabmeat, cooked and shredded
1 medium onion, finely chopped
1 green pepper, finely chopped
½ cup manzanilla olives, chopped
⅓ cup white vinegar
⅔ cup light olive oil
3 cloves garlic, crushed
Salt and freshly ground pepper

❶ In a large serving bowl, mix together the shrimps, crabmeat, onion, green pepper, and olives.

❷ In a small bowl mix together the vinegar, olive oil, and crushed garlic. Season with salt and pepper. Let the dressing sit, covered, for at least an hour to infuse it with the garlic flavor. Remove the garlic and pour the dressing over the salad. Toss and serve. ≫→ *Serves 6*

▲▲▲▲▲▲▲▲▲▲▲▲▲▲▲▲▲▲▲▲▲▲▲▲▲▲▲▲

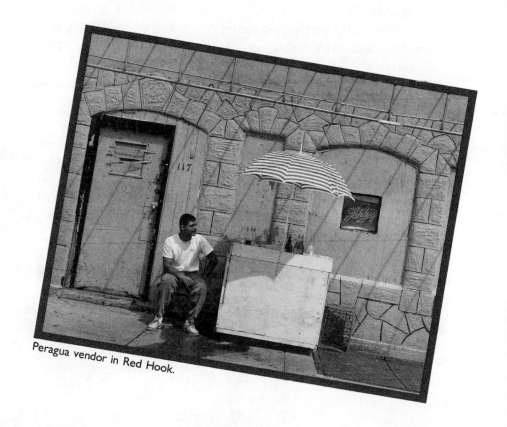

Peragua vendor in Red Hook.

North of the Border
The Mexicans

"**M**exicans have been coming to Brooklyn since the 1970s," says Consuelo de Passos, "especially from the state of Puebla and from Oaxaca, because of hard times at home. Most prefer Brooklyn to Manhattan; Brooklyn has more air." Perhaps because of a housing squeeze, the Mexican community is spread around: in Williamsburg, Sunset Park, and Flatbush.

Consuelo and a number of her friends are active planners of the Feast of Our Lady of Guadalupe, the most important day on the Brooklyn Mexican calendar. The Fiesta de Guadalupe celebrates the patron saint of Mexico.

The center for the fiesta, and for the dispersed Mexicans of the Borough, is All Saints Church in Williamsburg, which has an image of the Virgin of Guadalupe brought from Mexico. In mid-December, the fiesta begins in All Saints with the music of a mariachi band. A procession then carries the image of the Virgin through the streets, children dressed in regional costumes caper alongside, and a group called Los Techuanes performs a masked dance to the music of fife and drum.

"Over a thousand come to this celebration of our culture," says Consuelo, "and people have prepared food that is served in the auditorium. This food has to be simple to feed so many, but when we get together, we can do more elaborate dishes. And some women who are fine cooks prepare food in their spare time to sell to other Mexicans. I am glad to share with you some of my friends' fine dishes. And remember: we Mexicans never pile our plates with three or four foods. You must taste each dish, and enjoy it."

The festive Mexican table. Consuelo de Passos in the embroidered blouse.

Esperanza Fuentes' Pipián Verde
(Chicken with Pumpkin Seeds and Green Tomatoes)

Epazote, *which this dish calls for, is a pungent herb that Mexicans find it hard to do without. Dried epazote can be found at stores selling Mexican products, and a variety of it seems to grow wild in many places, including Brooklyn. Consuelo de Passos picks it, "but only in someone's back yard, not in the park. Too many dogs!"*

A 2½- to 3-pound chicken, cut into pieces
1 small onion, sliced
2 cloves garlic, peeled and crushed
½ teaspoon salt
2 cups water or chicken stock
1¼ cups hulled raw pumpkin seeds (*pepitas de calabaza pelada*)
1¼ cups quartered fresh Mexican green tomatoes in husks (*tomatillos verdes*), or the equivalent amount of drained canned tomatillos (do not use standard tomatoes)
4 fresh jalapeño peppers, slit, with seeds and stems removed, chopped fine
¼ cup oil
3 sprigs of epazote, if available

❶ Put the chicken, onion, garlic, and salt in a heavy saucepan. Add the water, cover, and bring to the boil. Lower the heat and simmer the chicken until tender, about 30 minutes. Drain, set the chicken aside and reserve the broth.

❷ The pumpkin seeds must be pulverized dry, not with a liquid. Put them in a blender jar and blend them to a paste. Set aside. Next, blend the tomatillos to a purée. Set them aside.

❸ Cook the jalapeños in the oil, stirring, for about 2 minutes. Add the pumpkin seeds, the tomatillos, and the sprigs of epazote, if you have them. Cook, stirring, for 3 minutes. Add enough of the chicken broth to make a sauce thicker than heavy cream. Simmer the sauce for 10 minutes. Add the chicken pieces and heat through. Arrange on a platter and serve with hot white rice.

⇒ *Serves 6*

Huachinango a la Veracruzano
(Red Snapper, Veracruz Style)

Dolores Echeverria is from Vera-cruz, on the Gulf of Mexico. This is her version of a famous dish from the region. Many fish in the Veracruzano style are made with green olives; Dolores omits them. She suggests you serve the fish with a salad containing green olives and sliced hard-boiled eggs.

A 4-pound red snapper, cleaned, head and tail on
½ cup fresh lime juice
Salt
½ cup olive oil

1 large onion, finely chopped
8 garlic cloves, minced
6 tablespoons finely chopped parsley
1 cup coarse bread crumbs

Preheat the oven to 400 degrees F.

❶ Wash the fish well. Slash the skin in 3 or 4 places on each side. Place the fish on a platter and pour the lime juice on both sides of the fish and in the cavity. Salt the fish lightly, inside and out. Let the fish marinate in the refrigerator for 1 to 2 hours. Turn it once.

❷ In a saucepan, heat the oil until it sizzles. Cook the onion and garlic, stirring, for 3 minutes. Add 3 tablespoons of the chopped parsley. Pick up the mixture in a slotted spoon, letting most of the oil drain back into the pan. Stuff the fish with this mixture.

❸ Add the bread crumbs and the rest of the parsley to the oil. Stir to mix.

❹ Place the fish on an oiled rack in a pan just large enough to fit it. Pat the bread crumb mixture evenly over it, except for the tail. Place a piece of oiled foil around the tail, and lightly drape a bonnet of oiled foil around the head, but not touching it. This will prevent tail and head from burning. Bake for 40 to 45 minutes, or until the fish is cooked through. ⋙ *Serves 4 to 6*

Arroz a la Mexicana
(Mexican Rice)

Serve this as a separate course, in the same way Italians serve pasta. This dish is what the Mexicans call a sopa seca, or dry soup, which usually follows a real soup. The rice should not be dry.

1 clove garlic
1 small onion, quartered
2½ cups chicken broth
3 large tomatoes, peeled and quartered

3 tablespoons vegetable oil
1 cup long-grain rice
Salt and pepper to taste
2 parsley sprigs

❶ Put the garlic, onion, and ½ cup of the broth in the blender and blend to a purée. Remove it and set it aside. Blend the tomatoes to a purée.

❷ Heat the oil in a skillet and fry the rice, stirring, until golden. Transfer the rice to a saucepan and add the puréed garlic and tomato mixtures. Cook, stirring, for about 5 minutes. Add the remaining broth and salt and pepper to taste. Add the parsley sprigs. Cover, bring to the boil, lower the heat and let simmer for about 20 minutes, or until the water is absorbed. Remove the parsley sprigs before serving. ≫→ *Serves 4*

Helping Our Own
The Panamanians

Brooklyn's Panamanians can be called a bridge between the Hispanic and West Indian communities, as their forebears were recruited from many islands of the Caribbean to work as laborers and artisans on the Panama Canal. As the laborers intermarried with Panamanian women, Spanish replaced English as their primary language. Older members of the Brooklyn group, like Anesta Samuel, are products of both cultures, and want to preserve old ways. Mrs. Samuel's cooking is a case in point: it is Hispanic, with island touches, such as hot pepper sauce.

Anesta Samuel.

"Not too many Panamanians lived in Brooklyn until after the Second World War," says Mrs. Samuel. "That's when my husband Henry and I came. Back then, it was very difficult to get an education in Panama. We encouraged friends to send their children up to stay with us while they studied. I'd hear them talk about their hard times with money. So in 1953, we started a little group to begin a way of helping them. We crocheted, we held bake sales, we managed to raise some funds."

In 1956 the group offered a $500 scholarship to a young Panamanian, Roberto Reid, in his last year of medical school. Today Dr. Reid heads the urology department at Albert Einstein College of Medicine.

The group, called the Dedicators, held its first Debutante Ball in 1964. This cotillion is the major fund-raiser in the effort to provide, in the Dedicators' words, "financial assistance, professional and moral guidance through our scholarship program." In 1982, Panama honored the Dedicators' founder Anesta Samuel with the Order of Vasco Nuñez de Balboa, the highest civilian honor.

"We have raised over $200,000 in scholarships over the years," Mrs. Samuel says with pride. "We have graduates from Columbia, Georgetown, Boston—all over the country. That makes me feel good!"

Arroz con Pollo
(Anesta Samuel's Chicken with Rice)

"I *serve this for parties, PTA meetings, and other large gatherings,"* *says Mrs. Samuel. "I always make this amount, and I* *really don't know how to cut the recipe down. If there is any left over, people are happy to take some home."*

6 2½-pound frying chickens
2 lemons
Salt
1 head celery, chopped
6 large onions, chopped
6 green and red bell peppers, cored, seeded, and diced
10 ounces tomato sauce
10 ounces tomato paste
8 ounces solid unsweetened coconut cream

¾ pound (3 sticks) unsalted butter
12 cups rice
A 6-pack of beer ("least expensive brand")
1 cup soy sauce
1 cup water
1 cup Worcestershire sauce
3 cups stuffed olives
1 small bottle capers, drained
1 small jar pimentos
Dashes tropical pepper sauce

❶ Wash the chickens, cut them into pieces, rub them with cut lemon halves, and sprinkle with salt. Put the chicken pieces to steam in a small amount of water. Cook gently for about 30 minutes, until the chicken is tender enough to take off the bone. Let it cool, and pull the flesh from the bones.

❷ In a very large pot (you may divide the ingredients between two pots) put the chopped vegetables, tomato sauce and paste, coconut milk, and the chicken flesh. Cover tightly and let simmer for about 20 minutes.

❸ Meanwhile, in a large skillet, melt 1 stick of butter. Brown 4 cups of the rice in the butter over moderate heat. This will take about 10 minutes. Brown the remaining rice, 4 cups at a time, in 1 stick of melted butter.

Preheat the oven to 250 degrees F.

❹ Add the rice and beer to the chicken pot. The level of liquid must be 1 inch above the ingredients. If it is not, top it off with boiling water. Cover tightly and allow to steam in the oven for about 1 hour. (You can also cook it at a bare simmer on top of the stove.)

❺ After 1 hour, add the soy sauce, water, Worcestershire sauce, olives, capers, pimentos, and pepper sauce to taste. Reduce the oven temperature to 200 degrees F. Cover the pot (or pots) and return it to the oven for 20 minutes.
➤ *Serves 30*

Henry Samuel's Party-size Banana Fritters

It's nice to have a good recipe to use up over-the-hill bananas. These fritters are Henry Samuel's specialty.

2 over-ripe bananas, cut into chunks
1 cup all-purpose flour
2 eggs
2 tablespoons melted butter
2 drops vanilla
1 teaspoon baking powder
¼ cup milk
½ cup water
¼ teaspoon salt
⅛ teaspoon grated nutmeg
¼ cup sugar
Oil for frying

❶ Put the bananas, flour, eggs, and melted butter in a blender jar or food processor bowl. Blend.

❷ Starting with the vanilla, add the rest of the ingredients (except the oil) slowly, blending as you go.

❸ Heat 2 inches of oil in a skillet until sizzling. Drop a tablespoon of batter in the hot oil for each fritter; cook them in batches and let them drain on brown paper or paper towels. ➳ ***Makes approximately 30 fritters***

P O L I S H
G R E E N P O I N T

At the very top of Brooklyn lies Greenpoint, a great port and shipbuilding center in the 19th century. Wealthy shipowners and builders erected Federal rowhouses and brownstones, many of which still stand. The Union's iron-hulled gunship, the <u>Monitor,</u> was constructed here in 1862. By the mid-1870s, the area had become a bustling industrial belt that included neighboring Williamsburg. Polish, Irish, and Italian immigrants came to work in the factories, and many of their descendants still live in this self-contained working-class community.

Hispanics and artists fleeing Manhattan rents are now joining the ethnic mix in Greenpoint, but the flavor of this section of Brooklyn is largely Polish. And the influx of thousands of new Polish pro-Solidarity immigrants reinforced the image. At least 30,000 of Greenpoint's people are Polish. The Polish-Slavic Federal Credit Union is a model lender of mortgage monies, and the adjacent Community Cafeteria, part of the corporation, will help those who are respectable though hungry.

"We get no money from the city or state," says a director of the Polish-Slavic Corporation, which runs the cafeteria as well as an array of support services for the newly arrived. Anyone can buy a meal, though it may not be easy if you don't speak Polish. Persist, and you get a lot for your money—the price of a large meal is $3.50 with soup, $3 without.

One who returned to the Greenpoint of his youth is Walter Zablocki. After a career in publishing spent elsewhere, he came back to run the family business, the White Eagle Bakery. The bakery once made everything from bagels to wedding cakes, but now the sole product is <u>chruścik,</u> crisp bits of deep-fried dough dusted with confectioners' sugar. (The word <u>chruścik</u> translates as "little fried thing.") "This was originally a leftover product," says Walter.

(Left) Polish-Slavic Federal Credit Union; (below) West Nassau Meat Market; cheerful workers at the Community Cafeteria.

"During the war, we employed a Polish Jewish communist baker who had learned to make intricate pastry birds' nests in Austria before he fled. My mother sold the broken bits by the half pound. The birds' nests are long gone, but people come from far away for chruścik, especially during the holidays. This building was built in 1890 as a bakery, and it still is one. The baking business keeps me out of trouble; I'm up at 3:30 a.m., I work till 4 p.m., then I do paperwork. But it keeps me physically fit."

"Greenpoint is a well-maintained community," says Jolanta Gubernat, a pediatrician who lives in Greenpoint with her family. "We have a variety of butchers making their own kielbasa, head cheese, and liverwurst, and a number of émigré restaurants and 'workers' meal' cafeterias. You'll find a lot of bread and potatoes, dill on everything, Kosciusko mustard only with sausages, and horseradish mixed with cooked, grated beets."

A Polish Home from Home

The Polska Restauracja is a cheerful, spanking-clean, and modest small restaurant on Greenpoint Avenue. Polish newspapers are thoughtfully provided for solitary diners, and the owner, Mrs. Ziemianowicz, speaks no English. But can she cook! Jolanta Gubernat kindly translated her recipes.

Mrs. Ziemianowicz, owner of the Polska Restauracja.

Beef Gulasz

Soaking the meat is a Polish custom that you may not wish to follow. Mrs. Ziemianowicz suggests *you serve the* gulasz *with kasha, noodles, potato pancakes, or potatoes.*

Vegetable Broth

1 carrot
1 parsley root (petrushka) or 6 sprigs parsley
½ stalk celery
½ leek
1 onion
2 cups water
Pinch salt

Gulasz

1 pound stewing beef, in one piece
2 tablespoons vegetable oil
2 large onions, chopped
2 cups Vegetable Broth (above)
3 whole allspice berries
2 to 3 teaspoons imported paprika
Maggi seasoning, to taste
1 tablespoon flour mixed with 3 tablespoons water

❶ Clean and chop the vegetables for the broth. Cover with the water, add salt, and simmer, covered, for 30 minutes. Strain.

❷ Soak the beef in water for 15 minutes, pat it dry, and cut it into cubes.

❸ Heat the oil in a large skillet and brown the meat cubes along with the onions for about 15 minutes. Transfer the meat and onions to a heavy pot with a lid.

❹ Add the vegetable broth, allspice, paprika, and a few dashes of Maggi. Simmer until the meat is tender, about 1 hour. When the meat is almost tender, stir in the flour-water mixture, and cook for 10 minutes more. Adjust the seasoning with more Maggi, if desired. ⟫→ *Serves 4*

Vegetable Soup for Four People

Mrs. Ziemianowicz uses Vegetable Broth to make the soup. Triple the recipe on page 282 to yield 6 cups of broth.

1 carrot, diced
1 parsley root (petrushka), shredded, or ¼ cup chopped parsley
½ stalk celery, chopped fine
½ leek, chopped fine
6 cups Vegetable Broth (see preceding recipe)

1 small cauliflower, cut into florets
¼ pound green beans, chopped, or lima beans
2 small potatoes, cut into cubes
¼ to ½ cup cream
Salt and pepper to taste

❶ Put the carrot, parsley root, celery, and leek in a saucepan and cover with the Vegetable Broth. Simmer for 30 minutes.

❷ Add the cauliflower, green beans, and potato cubes and cook for 15 minutes more. Stir in the cream, season with salt and pepper, and bring to the boil. ⟫→ *Makes 4 servings*

Carp with Gray Sauce

Gray Sauce, Szary Sos, *is served with both carp and tongue, and is usually made with beef stock. For carp, fish stock often replaces beef* stock. *Thanks to Jolanta Gubernat and Shirley King for help with the recipe.*

1 carp, 4 to 6 pounds, cleaned, head and tail left on

Poaching Liquid
Enough water to cover the fish
1 large onion, roughly chopped
2 carrots, roughly chopped
½ cup sliced celery root
1 small parsley root (petrushka)
3 stalks celery with leaves, roughly chopped
Slice of lemon
½ bay leaf
1 tablespoon salt

❶ Place the fish in a container or poacher that fits it comfortably. Cover the fish with water. Take the fish out of the water and refrigerate it until you are ready to cook it.

❷ Put all of the remaining poaching liquid ingredients into the water. Bring it to the boil, cover, lower the heat and let simmer for 25 minutes. Let the water cool a little.

❸ Lower the fish into the barely simmering liquid. (If you do not have a poacher with a grid, wrapping the fish in cheesecloth and tying both ends makes it easy to handle without danger of breaking it when you remove it.) Poach the fish for 35 to 50 minutes, according to size. Drain it well, place it on a warmed platter, and serve it with Gray Sauce (recipe follows).

Gray Sauce

1 tablespoon browned flour
1 tablespoon unsalted butter
1½ cups fish stock or beef stock
4 peppercorns
2 whole cloves
1 small bay leaf
A small piece of honey cake (½ ounce), or ½ teaspoon honey
1 teaspoon sugar
2 chopped pitted prunes
4 teaspoons fresh lemon juice
2 tablespoons finely chopped blanched almonds
½ cup dry red wine
2 tablespoons golden raisins

❶ As the fish poaches, make the Gray Sauce.

First, brown the flour. Place it in a dry nonstick skillet over moderate heat and stir until the flour browns.

In a saucepan, combine the butter and flour and mix until smooth. Add the fish broth, the peppercorns, cloves, bay leaf, honey cake, sugar, chopped prunes, and lemon juice. Bring to the boil, lower the heat, cover, and simmer for 30 minutes.

❷ Meanwhile, in a small saucepan, combine the almonds, wine, and raisins. Simmer for 10 minutes. Add these ingredients to the larger saucepan, remove the peppercorn, cloves, and bay leaf, and serve with the carp.

≫→ *Makes about 2 cups*

Leniwe Pierogi
(Lazy Pierogi)

Called "lazy" because these are all-in-one dumplings, rather than ones made from skin and filling.

The dough is very soft and tender, so work quickly. You need a farmers' cheese that is firm and *somewhat dry. If they should fall apart in boiling water—not likely, but it can happen—just drain them well, divide them into portions, and serve. Non-Poles will never know the difference.*

2 ounces farmers' cheese	¾ cup all-purpose flour
3 large eggs, separated	3 tablespoons unsalted butter
½ teaspoon salt	¾ cup coarse breadcrumbs
½ teaspoon sugar	

❶ Combine and beat the cheese, egg yolks, salt, and sugar together to form a smooth paste. This is best done in a food processor equipped with the metal blade. Transfer mixture to a wide mixing bowl.

❷ Beat the egg whites with a pinch of salt until stiff. Fold the egg whites and flour, alternately, into the cheese mixture. Chill the dough for 30 minutes or longer; it will be easier to work.

❸ Transfer half of the dough to a well-floured board. (You will need to move the board.) With floured hands, pat and shape it into a roll about 1½ inches thick × 8 inches long. Do the same with the rest of the dough. Flour a sharp knife and cut the dough, on the diagonal, into 24 pieces.

Preheat the oven to 200 degrees F.

❹ Have ready a large wide pot of lightly salted boiling water. Take the board to the stove and tip in about 8 pierogi. Boil them, uncovered, for 5 minutes. Transfer them with a slotted spoon to a warm platter and place it in the oven as you cook the next 2 batches.

❺ Melt the butter over moderate heat in a small skillet. Stir in the breadcrumbs and cook, stirring, until they are crisp and brown, about 5 minutes. Blot or drain any water from the serving platter and sprinkle the pierogi with breadcrumbs. ≫→ *Makes 4 to 6 appetizer servings*

ECHOES OF LITTLE GERMANY

Between 1840 and 1860, a time of heavy German immigration to the United States, Brooklyn developed a large Little Germany in what came to be the Eastern District. This district was formed when the city of Brooklyn annexed the formerly independent towns of Bushwick and Williamsburg, as well as North Brooklyn. Bushwick, especially, was so German that as early as 1835 it was called "Dutchtown."

The year 1840 was an important one for Brooklyn's Germans; that year a Bavarian brewer named John Wagner introduced lager beer, the foundation of Brooklyn's great brewing enterprises.

By the 1950s, with much middle-class movement to the suburbs, definite German sections of Brooklyn had ceased to exist. Just a few echoes remain, such as the Peter Luger Steak House in Williamsburg (page 378). This bastion of beef and beer is about all that reminds us of the German presence here.

The German Deli

William Jannen, a lawyer, "was raised in a German deli." His family had a deli (called The Deli) in East New York from 1949 to 1960. He tells the story:

"East New York was very Irish then, but my family figured that everybody would like deli food, and they were right. The meat was pricey, but it was the best around. We carried groceries, but made no serious attempt to compete with the supermarket. Our advantage was that we were open seven days a week, and we gave credit.

"Our competition was the Jewish deli, but we carried different meats. Besides the usual—baloney, salami, ham, Swiss and American cheeses—a German deli always had roast pork. We also had head cheese, smelly Limburger cheese, and Virginia ham, and German and American potato salads. Each

Friday, we sold clam chowder; my father made it with a beef stock base, but did he tell? That was a very Catholic neighborhood, so there was no meat on Friday, but he wasn't about to change his recipe. I guess he figured that if they didn't know, they didn't sin.

"For my parents, there was no division between working life and social life. They knew all their provisioners well, and were related to a number of them. And they liked dealing with the public—they thrived on it. My father thought nothing of having six or seven different items cooking on the stove or in the oven, waiting on customers and telling my brother and me what to do, all at the same time.

"Every Christmas, we made hundreds of pounds of marinated herring and herring salad. Here are the versions we used at home."

Marinated Herring

"Making this was always a seat-of-the-pants operation," says Bill Jannen. "We call this a 'big piece' dish, unlike herring salad, which is diced." Jannen recommends that you serve it as a first course, with black bread.

1 quart herring chunks
2 sour or half-sour pickles
2 green apples, such as Granny Smith

1 to 2 large onions, sliced
1 pint sour cream

❶ Skin and bone the herring chunks. (You can buy the prepared tidbits, but they are expensive and often too sweet.) Cut the chunks into ¼- to ½-inch pieces.

❷ Slice the pickles lengthwise, then cut them into small chunks. Peel, core, and cut the apples into ¼-inch slices. Cut the slices into thirds. Peel the onions and cut them into thin slices, then cut the slices in half.

❸ Mix the herring, pickles, apples, and onions with the sour cream. Refrigerate the dish overnight, covered. Taste it the next day; you may wish to make adjustments, such as adding more onion, pickle, or sour cream.

⫸ *Makes 6 cups*

Herring Salad, German Deli Style

Y*ou must use tart apples, or the salad will be too sweet. Use just a touch of mayonnaise — don't overwhelm the herring taste. You need only a touch of sugar if the pickles and apples are too sour. This is a fine holiday buffet dish.*

8 large matjes herring fillets in wine sauce, drained and rinsed
2 16-ounce cans beets, drained
2 pounds boiled new potatoes, peeled
2 dill pickles
2 sour pickles
3 green apples, such as Granny Smith
1 large onion, peeled
1 3½-ounce jar capers, drained
Mayonnaise to taste
Sugar to taste

Chop the herring, beets, potatoes, pickles, apples, and onion into small dice. Combine them well with the capers, and add enough mayonnaise just to combine. Cover and refrigerate overnight to let the flavors blend. Taste, and add a bit of sugar, if necessary. ⫸ *Makes about 10 cups*

German Potato Salad

*"**H**ere's how we made it in the deli,"* *home." There is no mayonnaise in*
says Bill Jannen. "If you wanted *German potato salad. The potatoes*
bacon, you added it at *marinate in the warm dressing.*

3 pounds boiling potatoes
⅓ teaspoon freshly ground pepper
1 medium onion, grated
⅔ cup water
⅓ cup cider vinegar

1 teaspoon salt
1 tablespoon sugar
1 tablespoon salad oil
6 slices crisp bacon, crumbled
   (optional)

❶ Boil the potatoes in lightly salted water. When they are cool enough to handle, peel them and slice them into a bowl. Add the pepper and grated onion.

❷ Put the water, vinegar, salt, sugar, and oil in a small pan and bring it to the boil. Pour over the potatoes and mix well. Let sit 10 minutes, then mix again. Cover the bowl and chill the salad. Before you serve it, pour off any liquid that has accumulated in the bottom of the bowl and top with crumbled bacon, if you are using it. ⟫➔ *Makes about 5 cups*

▲▲▲▲▲▲▲▲▲▲▲▲▲▲▲▲▲▲▲▲▲▲▲▲▲▲▲▲▲

A Pail of Beer and Sauerbraten

"When I was a girl, we spent Sundays and special holidays at my Aunt Ella Bodenlos' house in Bushwick," recalls Katherine Bohlinger. "Bushwick was very German then. All of the family would gather round the dining room table. Before our afternoon dinner Uncle John, Aunt Ella's husband, and Daddy would set off for the local brewery, each with his beer pail, and come back laughing, pails filled to the brim with cold frothy beer. Dinner was almost always wonderful sauerbraten with all the trimmings—red cabbage, light and fluffy potato dumplings, and homemade applesauce, fragrant with cinnamon."

Sauerbraten

The Bodenlos' sauerbraten was quite traditional, but this one is not. Brooklynite Bunny Pollack's stepfather, Leo Nald, was born in Baden Baden, Germany, and brought the recipe to Brooklyn. The results are most delicious. "For a big party, I make two batches," says Bunny.

4 cups water
2 cups cider vinegar
½ teaspoon freshly ground white pepper
2 teaspoons salt
1 large bay leaf
3-inch cinnamon stick
1 tablespoon whole mustard seeds
1 tablespoon whole allspice
½ cup golden raisins
1 large onion, sliced
1 cup sugar
5- to 6-pound pot roast, shoulder or rump
2 tablespoons vegetable oil
2 tablespoons butter
2 tablespoons flour

❶ Put the water, vinegar, and all seasoning ingredients, including raisins, onions, and sugar, into a nonreactive stockpot and bring them to the boil. Stir well and boil for 3 minutes.

❷ Put the roast in a large bowl and pour the mixture over it. Ideally, the liquid should cover the roast. If it does not, place a double layer of cheesecloth over the meat; the cheesecloth will "wick up" the liquid, keeping the meat moist. When the liquid is cool, place the bowl in the refrigerator. Leave the meat in the refrigerator for five to six days, turning it daily.

❸ When you are ready to cook the sauerbraten, take it from the liquid and wipe it dry. Strain the liquid and discard the solids.

Preheat the oven to 325 degrees F.

❹ In a large heavy skillet, heat the oil and brown the sauerbraten on all sides, turning it with wooden spoons. When it is nicely browned put it in a heavy pot with a lid. Add 2 cups of the strained liquid and reserve the rest, as some will be needed for the gravy. Bring the liquid to the boil on top of the stove, then place the roast in the oven. Cook for 3 to 4 hours, until very tender. Check the sauerbraten from time to time, and turn it. If it seems to be cooking too fast, lower the heat.

❺ Let the sauerbraten rest on a warm platter before you slice it.

❻ Make the gravy: melt the butter in a large skillet or saucepan and stir in the flour. Let cook for 2 minutes, stirring. Pour in the degreased juices from the sauerbraten pan, and add enough of the reserved marinating liquid to make 2 cups of gravy. Cook, stirring, for several minutes until the gravy is thickened. Slice the meat, pour a little gravy over the slices, and serve the rest in a sauceboat. Accompany with potato dumplings and braised red cabbage.

➤➤ *Serves 6 to 8*

"Barnacle Bill" Bohlinger wets his whistle before lunch.

Subway Savvy, Sixty-Odd Years Ago

Helen A. Kraus is a 1925 graduate of Erasmus Hall High School. "Although I lived in the Bushwick section," she says, "I was able to attend Erasmus Hall High School, in the Flatbush section, provided my attendance was regular and on time. It cost me five cents to get there via the BMT to Atlantic Avenue, where I transferred to the Franklin Avenue line to get to school. Other lines were more direct, but they cost ten cents. My five-dollar weekly allowance was for transportation and lunches (forty cents at the sweet shop for a sandwich and coffee). When I discovered the five-cent route, my father rewarded me by not deducting the fifty cents saved from my allowance."

George Kraus's first birthday cake, Bushwick Avenue, 1939.

Amarita
(German-Style French Toast)

"Cooking for one can be dull, but this is a quick and nourishing little dish," says Helen Kraus.

1 egg
½ cup milk
Pinch salt
2 slices slightly stale bread

1 tablespoon vegetable oil
Sugar (or artificial sweetener)
Lemon wedges

❶ Beat the egg, milk, and salt together. Trim the crusts from the bread and dip them in the mixture.

❷ Heat the oil in a skillet and fry the slices on both sides until browned. Serve with a sprinkling of sugar and a squeeze of lemon juice. ⇛ *Serves 1*

THE GREEKS

"The Greek community of Brooklyn numbers around 150,000," says an official of Saints Constantine and Helen Cathedral, "and half of them live in Bay Ridge. Most run their own businesses. They are churchgoers, and they send their children to Greek parochial schools. We want our children to know our language and culture, and to revere the family unit."

Holy Day procession (left); Orpheus Society fashion show at Prospect Hall, May 1988 (below and bottom).

Vine Leaves in Bay Ridge

Catherine Durakis (right) with best friend Stella, Greek school play, 1939.

"**I**mmigrants came from every part of Greece in the first ten years of this century," says Catherine Durakis. "My father came from Crete as a boy in 1909, and my mother came from Smyrna, in Turkey, which was largely Greek then. Many Greeks settled in downtown Brooklyn. I was born there in 1923.

"My sister and I went to after-school classes given by the Greek Orthodox church of Saints Constantine and Helen on Schermerhorn Street. We learned folkways and dances, and they taught us to read and write Greek. Of course we spoke it at home.

"My father, like so many Greeks, went into the restaurant business. He was a waiter at the old St. George Hotel. The St. George was the best hotel in Brooklyn.

"Our parents had to struggle, but they wanted us to be educated. My sister was an artist, and I played the piano and sang. I was a high school music teacher for thirty-three years, and a supervisor of music in elementary schools. I had wanted to perform, but unfortunately my mother thought only bad girls went on the stage. I was also assistant choir director for twenty-five years, for the All-City High School Chorus.

"People think of Bay Ridge as Scandinavian, but it has become very Greek in recent years. Greeks started moving here in the late 1950s, and lots more came in the '60s.

"We can see the water from our second story; we bought this house because it was big enough for my piano. I'm Vice President of the Garden Club of Bay Ridge, and I grow tomatoes and herbs on my terrace.

"What I'm known for, though, are my preserved vine leaves. We have a grape arbor, and I pick the leaves in June, when they are at theirmost tender, to use for the stuffed vine leaves called *dolmades*. Here is what you do: you pick a goodly batch of perfect leaves, and rinse them. Boil two quarts of water with half a cup of olive oil and blanch the leaves, a handful at a time, for just a few seconds. Drain them in a colander, then pack them in foil, in the amounts you think you'll want for a batch of dolmades, and freeze them until you need them. Blanching them with the oil makes them pliable. I recently defrosted a batch that I'd frozen three years ago, and they were good as new."

Galato Boureko
(Custard Filling in Filo Dough)

"This is my mother's recipe," says
Catherine Durakis.

Custard
2 cups milk
1 cup sugar
2 tablespoons cornstarch
½ cup cool water
6 eggs
½ teaspoon vanilla

10 sheets filo dough
1 cup melted unsalted butter
Syrup
2 cups water
2¼ cups sugar
Rind of 1 lemon
1 teaspoon lemon juice

❶ Bring the milk to just below the boil and add the sugar. Stir until the sugar melts. Set aside.

❷ Dissolve the cornstarch in the water. Beat the eggs in a large bowl for 5 minutes. Add the cornstarch mixture and beat for 1 minute more.

❸ Put the milk-sugar mixture over low heat and slowly add the egg mixture. Keep stirring until it is thickened. Stir in the vanilla. Let the custard cool, stirring from time to time so that a crust does not form.

Preheat the oven to 350 degrees F.

❹ Butter a 9-inch × 13-inch × 2-inch pan. Lay on a sheet of filo dough and brush it thoroughly with melted butter. Lay on 4 more sheets, brushing each with butter. Do not trim the filo overhang. Pour in the custard filling, and fold the filo dough over the custard to partially cover it.

❺ Top the custard with 5 more sheets of filo dough, trimmed to fit the pan. Butter each layer of filo. Score the pastry into diamonds, cutting only through the top layers of filo dough. Pour on the remaining melted butter evenly. Dip your hands in cold water and shake them over the pastry. Bake for 30 minutes, or until the filo dough is flaky and brown.

❻ Meanwhile, make the syrup. Put the water, sugar, and lemon rind into a saucepan and bring to the boil. Boil, uncovered, for exactly 5 minutes. Remove the rind and add the lemon juice. Let the syrup cool slightly.

❼ As soon as the custard pastry is cooked, place it on a rack and pour the syrup slowly and evenly over it. Let it cool. Serve at room temperature or chilled. ≫+ *Serves 6 to 10*

▲▲▲▲▲▲▲▲▲▲▲▲▲▲▲▲▲▲▲▲▲▲▲▲▲▲▲

THE NEWCOMERS

Populations shift. People move, singly or in groups, and new arrivals take their places. Where once the immigrants to Brooklyn came mostly from Europe and the rural South, now they come from Central America, Asia, and the Caribbean. Flatbush alone took in 17,706 between 1983 and 1987, the largest group being Haitians. Africa is represented, too: a small number of Nigerians have moved to Flatbush. Says the pastor of Our Lady of Refuge Church: "This is a beautiful neighborhood—we're a real United Nations. Whites, blacks, Hispanics, some Koreans. Every single West Indian and Caribbean island. Christians, Jews, Moslems. It's quite a neighborhood." It's a fragrant one, too. Cookshops, bakeries, and restaurants scent the air with heady Indian and Asian spices. This is no neighborhood for dieters. It's almost impossible to stroll the streets and not be tempted by Indian <u>buryani</u> or the West Indian soft bread called <u>roti.</u>

Traditionally immigrants come to improve their lives, and to learn skills and trades that can help them. Some, like Sesha Ganesh of Park Slope, come highly educated. And though John Gillespie's people are hardly new arrivals—they came in the 1920s—the Newfound-landers represent the groups who moved to Brooklyn as hopeful foreigners and stayed to become Brooklynites, and Americans . . . as the new arrivals who take their places will surely do.

The Indians
Seeing the World

Sesha Ganesh, a mathematics teacher, and her husband came from India in 1973, basically "to see the world." They liked what they saw of Park Slope so much that they stayed.

Sesha is a Brahman Hindu, and as such is a strict vegetarian who also eschews such vegetables as onion and garlic, forbidden to Brahmans. She finds almost everything she needs for Indian cooking at the Park Slope Cooperative, of which she is a member.

Butternut Squash with Tofu

This delicious dish is a nice example of adaptive cooking; as a vegetarian, Sesha took readily to tofu and sour cream when she found them available. The asafetida gives, she says, "a characteristic oniony scent."

1½ pounds butternut squash
2 cakes firm tofu (bean curd)
2 tablespoons vegetable oil
½ teaspoon black mustard seeds
¼ teaspoon turmeric

Pinch asafetida (methi powder), optional
1 small red chili pod
1 teaspoon salt
¾ cup sour cream

❶ Peel the squash deeply, down to the orange flesh, and cut it crosswise into 1-inch slices. Remove the seeds, using a melon baller, spoon, or small knife, and cut the slices into pieces about 1½ × 1 inch.

❷ Cut the tofu into 1½-inch cubes and pat it dry with paper towels. In a 10-inch skillet, preferably nonstick, heat 1 tablespoon of the oil. Fry the cubes, turning them from time to time, until they are lightly browned.

❸ In a wok or skillet that has a lid, heat the remaining tablespoon of oil. Add the mustard seeds. When they have popped, add the tofu cubes, squash cubes, turmeric, asafetida, chili pod, salt, and sour cream. Combine well with a metal spatula or wooden spoon. Cover and cook over moderate heat, about 15 minutes, or until the squash is tender. ⇒ *Serves 4 to 6*

Yogurt

Sesha Ganesh finds making yogurt both easy and economical. "We eat yogurt with every meal," she says, "at least two or three cups each day." Not only Indians like Sesha eat a lot of yogurt; so do Syrians and Lebanese. Sesha has used skim milk too, but feels that whole milk makes better yogurt. You can double the recipe.

1 quart whole milk   ¼ to ½ cup commercial plain yogurt*

Bring the milk to the boil in a large saucepan and boil it hard for 10 minutes; take care it does not stick. Pour the milk into a glass container and let it become tepid—just slightly warm. Stir in the commercial yogurt, cover with plastic wrap, and set it in a warm place to set, about 6 hours. Refrigerate.

➤ *Makes 4 cups*

*You will need the commercial yogurt as a starter only for the first batch. Use some of your own yogurt for each subsequent batch.

▲▲▲▲▲▲▲▲▲▲▲▲▲▲▲▲▲▲▲▲▲▲▲▲▲▲▲▲▲▲

From the North Atlantic to Brooklyn

"In the late 1920s, Newfoundland had a depression," says John Gillespie, a printer, "and a sizeable number, including my family, moved to Brooklyn. Newfoundland is a land of seafarers, and the men came to get work on the waterfront. There was a heavy concentration in Park Slope at 9th Street, and in the '40s and '50s many moved to Sunset Park. There were enough men to form a branch of the Veterans of the First Newfoundland Regiment of the First World War. They met at Prospect Hall; the last man died just last year, at the age of 93."

Newfoundland Pea Soup

John says, "Serve as is, or make it a main dish by pouring the soup over boiled potatoes."

1 pound yellow split peas

1 ham bone, with some meat left on (the more the better)

3 quarts water

3 large onions, finely chopped

3 large carrots, finely chopped

1 tablespoon salt

❶ Wash the peas, cover them with water, and bring to the boil in a heavy soup pot. Boil for 2 minutes; drain the peas.

❷ Return the peas to the pot along with the rest of the ingredients. Simmer, partially covered, for 2 hours. ⫸⤳ *Serves 6 to 8*

▲▲▲▲▲▲▲▲▲▲▲▲▲▲▲▲▲▲▲▲▲▲▲▲▲▲▲▲

Toward a New Life
Not a Melting Pot but a Cooking Pot

CAMBA, standing for the Church Avenue Merchants Block Association, organized in 1979 to promote business in North Flatbush. It soon merged with an educational program working with newly arrived refugees. "Cambodians, Laotians, and Vietnamese were disoriented and badly in need of support," says Mila Santos, who runs the refugee program. "The merchants saw that if the new people in the neighborhood are stabilized and integrated, everyone prospers." CAMBA aids five thousand people each year from all five boroughs, and myriad national groups.

Good food plays a part in helping to create an environment where students can learn. "I came to CAMBA to teach English as a second language and help people to find jobs," says Debra Rice. "Classes run in three-month cycles, and during that time we have a number of parties where people bring food, and also prepare food here at CAMBA. It's a communal effort, students cooking together. We'll always have at least three Haitians, for example, and they'll cook a dish. Other groups, such as Rumanians or Laotians, will also make food together. Everyone contributes. It's very informal, and a great way to get everyone to relax and practice vocabulary. No one stays silent over food. People sit on the floor, cutting up vegetables—there are always a lot of vegetables, especially for the Asian dishes. There is music and dancing. We had a great party at the Cambodian New Year!

"Students also set up a sort of restaurant, and prepare and sell food to the CAMBA staff. As many as a hundred people can be fed. They'll do this several times during a class cycle. It's great to see people from very different cultures learning to appreciate each other's cooking."

CAMBA students contributed the following recipes.

Laotian Salad

Three young sisters, Bounhang, Savannallay, and Khaysa Phrasavath, created this salad, a substantial one. They have been in Brooklyn for four years. With CAMBA's help, their English has progressed and they now attend regular schools.

12 eggs
1 cup peanuts
½ head garlic
2½ bunches scallions
3 bunches cilantro
3 small heads romaine lettuce
4 ripe but firm tomatoes
5 cucumbers

¼ cup water
3 tablespoons sugar
½ teaspoon plus 3½ tablespoons
   corn oil
1 pound beef
2 teaspoons fish sauce (*nuoc mam*)
½ cup fresh lemon juice

❶ Hard-boil the eggs and let them cool. Crush the peanuts with a mortar and pestle or chop them in the bowl of a food processor.

❷ Mince the garlic cloves. Trim the scallions and cut each crosswise into 5 pieces. Slice the pieces into thin strips.

❸ Cut off most of the cilantro stems, then break each sprig into 3 pieces.

❹ Break the romaine leaves in half. (If they are large, break them again.)

❺ Slice the tomatoes. Peel and slice the cucumbers into rounds.

❻ Boil the water and add the sugar; stir to dissolve. Add ½ teaspoon of the oil. Set aside.

❼ Heat 1 tablespoon of the oil in a large skillet and cook the garlic, stirring, until it becomes lightly golden. Remove and set aside.

❽ Cut the meat into small cubes. In the same skillet heat the remaining corn oil and add the meat cubes and fish sauce. Cook for 5 to 7 minutes, stirring. Remove from the heat.

❾ Cut the eggs into small chunks.

❿ Place all the ingredients except the eggs in a large serving bowl. Mix gently with your hands. Add the eggs and mix. Add the lemon juice and mix again. ➺ *Serves 12 or more as part of a buffet*

Rice and Chickpeas with Raita

"I came from Pakistan in 1989," says S. Hussain. "I am a mother and a housewife. I'm a student at CAMBA and now I can speak English. I'm looking for a job. I'm happy here but sometimes I miss my country and my culture."

....

1 cup basmati rice

1 small onion

2 tablespoons vegetable oil

¼ teaspoon cumin seeds

3 cloves

1 3-inch cinnamon stick

5 black peppercorns

1 black cardamom pod

Pinch salt

2¼ cups water

1 cup long-grain rice

½ cup canned chickpeas, rinsed

❶ Soak the rice in water for 20 minutes.

❷ Slice the onion lengthwise into slivers. In a large saucepan heat the oil and brown the onion, stirring. Add the spices and cook for 1 minute. Add the 2¼ cups water and the salt and bring to the boil. Drain the rice and add it and the chickpeas. Stir. Bring to the boil again, partially cover, and lower the heat.

❸ When the rice is almost done, cover the pan tightly. Cook 5 minutes longer. Remove from the heat but leave the lid on.

❹ As the rice cooks, make the Raita. Use commercial yogurt, or make your own (see page 298).

1 cup plain yogurt

2 tablespoons water

1 medium onion, finely chopped

1 medium tomato, chopped into small
pieces

½ teaspoon hot red pepper

½ teaspoon cumin seeds, crushed

Salt to taste

Beat the yogurt and water together. Add the onion, tomato, and spices.

≫→ *Serves 4*

Rosemode Jean Pierre's Haitian Rice with Mushrooms

CAMBA *has taught Rosemode enough English to prepare her for a nursing education. She enjoys cooking for her two children, and looks with hope to the future.*

Haitian black mushrooms richly color this dish, more so than dried European mushrooms, which have much the same flavor. In Brooklyn as in Haiti, Rosemode discards the mushrooms after she has soaked them. "I want only the color and the flavor," she says. However, the mushrooms are tasty in themselves.

1 ounce (about 1 cup) dried
    mushrooms, such as Polish
    mushrooms
3 cups warm water
3 tablespoons vegetable oil
2 cloves garlic, finely chopped
2 scallions, finely chopped, including
    green part

1½ cups long-grain rice, rinsed in cold
    water
Salt and freshly ground pepper to taste
½ teaspoon crumbled dried thyme, or
    1 tablespoon chopped fresh thyme
1 small hot red or green pepper
1 package frozen peas, defrosted
1 tablespoon unsalted butter

❶ Break up the mushrooms and soak them in the warm water until softened, 15 to 30 minutes. Set the mushrooms aside and strain the liquid. Reserve it.

❷ In a large skillet heat the oil until sizzling; add the garlic, scallions, and rice. Cook, stirring, until the oil is absorbed and the garlic and scallions are soft. Add the mushroom pieces and the reserved mushroom water, plus another cup of water. Season to taste with salt and pepper. Stir in the thyme and the hot pepper. Bring the mixture to the boil, cover, and turn the heat as low as you can. Cook until the liquid is absorbed, 20 to 25 minutes. Before the last 10 minutes of cooking, stir in the peas and the butter. If at any point the dish seems dry, add a little boiling water.

❸ Before serving, remove the hot pepper. ⟫➔ *Serves 4 to 6*

Sarmale
(Maria Drindiri's Rumanian Stuffed Cabbage)

Maria, her husband, and son have lived in Sunset Park for almost a decade. She misses her Rumanian family acutely, but appreciates the freedoms she has here. Maria, who is a student at CAMBA, loves to cook. "If the cabbage rolls are small and neat," she says, "it signifies that the cook is a delicate woman."

1 large head cabbage
3 to 4 tablespoons salt
¼ cup peppercorns
2½ pounds ground pork
½ pound ground bacon
2 medium onions
3 tablespoons raw rice

¼ cup vegetable oil
2 ounces tomato paste or 1 cup
 chopped fresh tomato pulp
Salt and pepper to taste
1 teaspoon crumbled dried oregano
1 teaspoon imported paprika

❶ Put the cabbage into a crock or nonreactive pot that just fits it. Cover with water to which you have added the salt and soak the cabbage for 5 days. Shake the pot each day. Soaking will soften the leaves and give a slightly sour taste to the cabbage. Reserve the water.

❷ Separate the leaves. Save the tough outer leaves for lining the pot.

❸ Mix the pepper, pork, bacon, onion, rice, and oil well. Form balls of the mixture as wide as a half-dollar piece. Put a ball on a corner of a cabbage leaf and roll it, tucking in the sides. Repeat with the rest of the leaves.

❹ Shred the tough outer leaves and use them to line a heavy soup pot. Cover them with a layer of cabbage rolls, seam side down, placed close together. Top them with a row of rolls at right angles to the bottom row. End with a third row, at right angles to the second row. (It may help to weight the rolls with a plate, to keep them from bobbing as they cook.)

❺ Cover the rolls with water by 1 inch, using half fresh water and half reserved soaking water. Add the tomato paste or pulp. Season with salt and pepper (it is unlikely that you will want much salt). Add the oregano and paprika.

❻ Cover the pot and bring the mixture to the boil. Reduce the heat, partially cover, and simmer the cabbage rolls for about 2 hours. Shake the pan gently now and then. If the water seems to be evaporating fast, add a little boiling water. At the end of cooking, however, the water should be no higher than three fingers (about 2½ inches). ⟫➜ *Serves 8*

Pun Reach's Cambodian Chicken Curry

Well into his middle years, Pun Reach knows very little English. "Cooking is a form of communication for him," says his teacher, Debra Rice.

....

2 tablespoons minced garlic
2 tablespoons minced fresh ginger
¼ cup mashed and minced fresh lemon grass
3 tablespoons crushed peppercorns
3 tablespoons vegetable oil
2 pounds chicken, cut into 2-inch cubes

1 onion, sliced
½ pound potatoes, peeled and cut into 2-inch pieces
¼ pound halved green beans
3 cups unsweetened coconut milk
Soy sauce to taste
Oriental shrimp or fish sauce to taste

❶ Mix together the garlic, ginger, lemon grass, and crushed pepper.

❷ Heat the oil in a large skillet or heavy pot. Cook the chicken cubes over moderate heat, turning frequently, until they are lightly browned. Set aside. Cook the onion, stirring, for about 3 minutes, until slightly softened.

❸ Return the chicken to the pot and add the garlic mixture, potatoes, and beans. Add the coconut milk and bring to the boil. Lower the heat and cook, partially covered, for 30 minutes or until tender. Season with soy and shrimp sauces. Serve with fluffy rice.

➤➤ *Serves 4*

▲▲▲▲▲▲▲▲▲▲▲▲▲▲▲▲▲▲▲▲▲▲▲▲▲▲▲▲▲

4

Cornerstones of the Borough

INSTITUTIONS: The Botanic Garden, Prospect Park, the Brooklyn Museum, the Central Library, the Historical Society, Brooklyn Union Gas, "The Honeymooners." And the Dodgers.

"In the latter part of the last century," says Everett Ortner, "people came from all over to study what was called 'The Brooklyn Experience.' Other communities perceived that Brooklyn was exceptionally well governed, that business throve, and that the citizens mostly got their fair share of services. They wanted to know the secret of Brooklyn's success."

Things may never again appear as rosy as they did in America's cocksure age, but in fact much of the solid foundation that underlay the Borough's optimism and prosperity then remains in place now. The great cultural institutions are expanding or adapting as they serve a changing public. "The Brooklyn Botanic Garden has the largest membership of any botanic garden in the world," says Donald Moore, President Emeritus of the Garden, "because of the depth and extent of our publications. Our membership is worldwide."

And Brooklyn itself is an institution, one embedded deep in the national psyche. Sure, the mention of the name may get a laugh, but usually an affectionate one. The Honeymooners, those two struggling, ever-hopeful blue-collar couples from Bensonhurst, belong to us all. As for the national pastime, there is only one field of dreams, alive forever in the memories of those who love baseball, and that is Ebbets Field.

THE BROOKLYN
BOTANIC GARDEN

The Brooklyn Botanic Garden, adjacent to Prospect Park and situated on 52 acres behind the Brooklyn Museum, was founded in 1910 on a city waste dump. Today its herb garden, recognized as one of the finest in the country, features among its many plants thirty that are used as foodstuffs, and sixty that are used as condiments. Elizabeth Remsen Van Brunt (1893–1986) was for many years honorary curator of culinary herbs at the Garden, and a fine cook who understood the fillip a judicious use of herbs can give to a dish. She was born in Brooklyn to a descendant of Rutgert Joeston Van Brunt, who settled in New Utrecht, one of the original six Dutch towns of what would become Brooklyn, in 1657. There is a Van Brunt Street, and also a Van Brunt Post Office. Her mother was Anna Remsen, for whose family Remsen Street was named.

"I remember her herb courses, especially herbs in cooking," says Betty Scholtz, Director Emeritus of the Garden. "We loved her herb stories: the hospitalized soldiers she taught during World War II, relating their X-rated rosemary-induced dreams; and her sister, who criticized Elizabeth's housekeeping, being mollified by having basil, the happy herb, slipped into her food."

(From the top) map of the Herb Garden; the Administration Building, with magnolias in bloom; children with vegetable crop, 1931.

Elizabeth Van Brunt's Herbed Tomato Juice

1 quart tomato juice
Juice and grated rind of 1 lemon
Juice and grated rind of 1 orange
The following fresh herbs:
    2 sprigs basil
    1 sprig rosemary
    6 chive leaves
    2 sprigs marjoram
    1 sprig spearmint, if desired
Or the following dried herbs:
    1 teaspoon basil
    ½ teaspoon marjoram
    ¼ teaspoon rosemary
Salt and pepper, if desired
Sprinkling of fresh chives

Elizabeth Remsen Van Brunt crushing rosemary.

Steep the citrus rinds and the fresh herbs, tied together with a string and lightly bruised with a wooden spoon, in the juice for 1 to 2 hours before serving. If you use dried herbs, tie them in a muslin bag. Before serving, squeeze and remove the herbs. Just before serving, sprinkle on the chives. ⋙→ *Serves 6*

Elizabeth Van Brunt's Potpourri

Potpourri is not to eat, but to delicately scent a room or the drawers of a bureau. Place potpourri in a bowl or sew handfuls into little bags. The delightful scent lasts a long time.

2 quarts rose petals, gathered on sunny
    days when the dew is off

Dry the leaves to crispness on screening or paper. Store in airtight containers until time to mix the potpourri in late summer or fall.

❶ Cut strips of orange peel about 2 inches × ½ inch; scrape the white pith off. Stick with a few cloves and dry. Add to the petals.

❷ To blend the potpourri, add the following dried ingredients:

2 tablespoons cardamom seeds

2 tablespoons anise seeds

1 tablespoon powdered orris root (a fixative)

1 cup lavender

1 cup lemon verbena leaves

½ cup rose geranium leaves

❸ Combine thoroughly, then add:

¼ cup rose oil

¼ cup brandy

Sprinkles of ground cloves and cinnamon, if desired

❹ Blend well, and store tightly to ripen for 2 weeks. Fill potpourri jars but keep them covered except on occasion. After a length of time, add more oil or brandy to enhance fragrance.

Note: Any fragrant leaves or blossoms, such as violet, mock orange, mint, syringa, or ambrosia, may be added, if well dried.

Elizabeth Van Brunt's Seed Cookies

½ cup vegetable shortening

½ cup sugar

1 egg, beaten

¾ cup all-purpose flour

½ teaspoon salt

½ teaspoon vanilla

Sesame seeds, aniseeds, or caraway seeds

❶ In a large bowl, blend the shortening and sugar together with a wooden spoon, then stir in the egg.

❷ Blend in the flour, salt, and vanilla. Chill the mixture for ½ hour.

Preheat the oven to 350 degrees F.

❸ Roll marble-sized balls and place them 2 inches apart on lightly greased baking sheets. Gently press a few seeds on each ball. (If you use aniseeds, crush them first.) Dip the tines of a fork in water and flatten each ball.

❹ Bake for 10 minutes, rotating the pans after 5 minutes, or until the edges just begin to brown. Remove the baking sheets and let the cookies harden for 2 minutes; use a spatula to place them on racks. ⋙➜ *Makes 48 cookies*

Brooklyn Botanic Garden Herb Bread

M iss Van Brunt also developed this recipe.

1 package yeast
1 teaspoon sugar
¼ cup lukewarm water
3 cups bread flour
1 teaspoon salt
1 teaspoon freshly grated nutmeg
1 teaspoon rubbed dried sage or ½
   teaspoon chopped fresh sage

4 teaspoons caraway seeds, bruised
¾ cup milk
2 tablespoons vegetable shortening
1 egg, beaten
1 egg, for egg wash
Sesame seeds, for sprinkling

❶ Combine the yeast, sugar, and water in a small bowl and set it aside until bubbling.

❷ Sift together the flour, salt, and nutmeg. Stir in the sage and caraway seeds.

❸ Heat the milk until it is almost boiling; add the vegetable shortening. Stir to melt, set aside until lukewarm. Whisk in the egg.

❹ Add the milk mixture to the yeast mixture, combining well with a rubber spatula. When blended, gradually add the flour mixture.

❺ Turn the dough out onto a floured surface, and knead until it is smooth and elastic, about 7 minutes. Add more flour by the tablespoon, if necessary. Place the dough in a large oiled bowl, turn it, and cover it with oiled plastic wrap. Let it rise in a warm place until it is doubled.

❻ Punch the dough down, knead it again, and shape it into a loaf. Place the dough in an oiled 9 × 5-inch bread pan. Cover with the same plastic wrap; let it rise until doubled.

Preheat the oven to 375 degrees F.

❼ Paint the top of the loaf with egg beaten with a little water and sprinkle with sesame seeds. Bake for 40 to 45 minutes, until browned. ≫→ *Makes 1 loaf*

Tilling the Soil

The Children's Garden at the Botanic Garden began in 1914, and since then some 215,000 young people, aged 9 to 17, have cultivated the same patch of land. In an average year, the 250 participants in the gardening program bring in a weighty harvest: one and one-half tons of tomatoes, a ton of kohlrabi, a half ton of beans, over 17,000 radishes, and thousands of beets, carrots, scallions, squash, eggplants, cucumbers, and ears of corn.

This program is educational, and one of the skills learned is cooking. Under close supervision, youngsters chop vegetables into strips and stir-fry them in a wok. They are delighted to know that you can eat flowers, too—Deep-Fried Squash Blossoms are a great favorite.

Children's Garden Stir-Fry

2 tablespoons vegetable oil
1½ cups mixed vegetables, cut in fine
    strips (such as zucchini, carrots,
    string beans, kohlrabi, green
    peppers, and onions)

2 tablespoons tamari or low-sodium
    soy sauce

❶ Over high heat, heat the oil in a wok until it sizzles. Carefully add the vegetables and stir-fry for 2 minutes, tossing and turning the strips with two long-handled metal spoons.

❷ Add half the tamari and stir-fry for 1 minute more, or until the vegetables are tender but still crisp.

❸ Tip the vegetables onto a plate and add the remaining tamari.

⟫→ *Serves 2*

PROSPECT PARK

"Though every Prospect pleases,
and only man is vile."—old hymn

Frederick Law Olmsted and Calvert Vaux, the greatest of nineteenth-century park designers, considered Prospect Park their finest achievement, better than Central Park, better than their great parks in Buffalo, Washington, and Toronto.

The architects deliberately designed the 526-acre park as an oasis from urban life, a place where gentry and weary workers alike could rusticate, relax, and picnic. Picnic they still do, especially in the Long Meadow, the longest continuous open sweep in any American city park.

Vignettes of various views, 1889.

Barbara McTiernan's Picnic for a Concert

Barbara McTiernan, a Park employee, is a picnic enthusiast. Here are her suggestions for a satisfying spread when the Metropolitan Opera and the New York Philharmonic visit the Park each summer: slices of mozzarella marinated in red-wine vinegar, olive oil, and a touch of Dijon mustard, and sprinkled with chopped fresh dill, parsley, and basil; Chicken Salad with Chutney; and Prospect Park Brownies.

Chicken Salad with Chutney, Served with Cantaloupe

6 cups cooked chicken or turkey, cut into cubes
2 cups chopped celery
1 or more teaspoons curry powder
2 cups mayonnaise
¾ cup mango chutney, chopped
2 ripe cantaloupes

Combine all ingredients except the melon and chill. Cut the melon into slices and take off the rind. Garnish each plate with a few melon slices.

≫→ *Serves 6 to 8*

A & S Kite Day, Prospect Park, June 1984.

Prospect Park Brownies

Sheep in the Long Meadow, 1903.

Brownies

4 1-ounce squares unsweetened
    chocolate
½ cup (1 stick) unsalted butter
3 eggs
¼ teaspoon salt
1 cup sugar
1 teaspoon vanilla
½ cup all-purpose flour
1 cup nuts, coarsely chopped

Frosting*

1½ 1-ounce squares unsweetened
    chocolate
2 tablespoons butter
¼ cup heavy cream

⅓ cup firmly packed brown sugar
Pinch salt
½ teaspoon vanilla
½ teaspoon sherry or rum extract
    (optional)
1½ cups confectioners' sugar

Preheat the oven to 350 degrees F.

❶ Butter an 8-inch-square baking pan.

❷ Melt the chocolate and butter together. Let the mixture cool, or the brownies will be heavy.

❸ Beat the eggs with the salt until foamy. Gradually add the sugar and vanilla, beating until the mixture is creamy. Quickly stir in the chocolate mixture, then the flour, and fold in the nuts.

❹ Bake for 20 minutes and cool on a rack.

❺ To make the frosting, combine the chocolate, butter, cream, brown sugar, and salt in a small saucepan. Bring to the boil and cook, stirring constantly, until the chocolate is melted and the mixture is smooth. Remove from the heat, add the flavorings, and stir in the confectioners' sugar.

❻ Frost the cooled pan of brownies and let the frosting harden before cutting brownies into bars or squares. ➠ *Makes 1 8-inch pan of brownies*

*The recipe makes enough frosting for 2 pans of brownies. Refrigerate or freeze extra frosting.

▲▲▲▲▲▲▲▲▲▲▲▲▲▲▲▲▲▲▲▲▲▲▲▲▲▲▲▲

Prospect Park's Great Friend

Poet Marianne Moore, who lived for thirty years in Fort Greene, was a lover and defender of the Park. In 1964, she appealed to City Hall to save the decaying Boathouse and to fund the Park adequately. Enthusiasts formed the Friends of Prospect Park, choosing as their symbol of restoration the Camperdown Elm, planted in 1872 and in imminent danger of collapse. Miss Moore's poem about the tree brought both renown and funds to save it. Miss Moore died in 1972. She had requested that, in lieu of flowers, mourners send contributions to the Camperdown Fund.

Oatmeal Cookies

__M__arianne Moore kept a series of what she called "reading diaries," in which she commented on things that she had read. (She also kept conversation diaries.) Although according to her nieces she was not a cook, she jotted down a cookie recipe that must have appealed to her. It is from a diary she kept between 1930 and 1943.

This recipe, just as Miss Moore wrote it, is not difficult to follow. Bear in mind that "soda" is baking soda, and that a moderate oven is 350 degrees F.

....

¾ cupful shortening
1 cup brown sugar
1 or 2 eggs well beaten
½ cup sour milk or buttermilk
2 tablespoons molasses

2 cupfuls flour
1 teaspoon soda
1 teaspoon cinnamon
4½ cups rolled oats
1 cup raisins

Cream shortening add the sugar gradually & beat till light. Add egg, sour milk and molasses.

Mix and sift flour, soda and cinnamon. Add the oats and raisins and mix thoroughly.

Drop from teaspoon on greased baking tins & bake in oven about 10 minutes.

Bears in the Picnic House

The 1927 Picnic House is no architectural gem—the official Prospect Park Handbook scorns it as a building that "resembles a rural schoolhouse of the roaring twenties, an awkward, prosaic, cubic pile, which the graceful sweep of Long Meadow could very well do without." No matter, the Picnic House has been the site of many jolly events, such as this 1932 presentation of "The Three Bears."

That roistering writer Henry Miller (1891–1980) wrote a version of "The Three Bears," called "Goldilocks," which appeared in his book *Plexus.* Miller proudly said of himself, "I am a patriot—of the 14th Ward Brooklyn, where I was raised. The rest of the United States doesn't exist for me, except as idea, or history, or literature." The 14th Ward was Williamsburg.

Miller was supposedly telling a bedtime story to two children. They must have been delighted with the bears' diet:

"O.K. . . . *Once upon a time . . .* there were three bears: a polar bear, a grizzly bear, and a Teddy bear . . .

"The polar bear ate nothing but ice, ice cold ice, fresh from the ice house. The grizzly bear thrived on artichokes, because artichokes are full of burrs and nettles . . .

"As for the Teddy bear, why he drank only skimmed milk. He was a grower, you see, and didn't need vitamins."

And as for Goldilocks: "Suddenly little Goldilocks entered the forest. She had a lunch basket with her and it was filled with all sorts of good things, including a bottle of Blue Label Ketchup."

Children from the Bay Parkway Playground, 1932.

▲▲▲▲▲▲▲▲▲▲▲▲▲▲▲▲▲▲▲▲▲▲▲▲▲▲▲▲

Hungry Birders

"**B**rooklyn has a fantastic array of bird habitats," says John Yrizarry, president of the Brooklyn Bird Club. "Almost four hundred bird types pass through in a year. Some insectivorous birds have come ten thousand miles. We see geese, cormorants, herons—they pour out of the sky on a good flight evening, and they're found all through Prospect Park. They'll stay as long as they need to regain energy; some stay a week, others just a few hours."

The Bird Club began in 1903, and since 1927 members have participated in the Christmas Bird Count sponsored by the Audubon Society. In the old days, hunters went out before Christmas, seeing how many species they could bag for the pot. The Audubon Society thought to use the occasion for counting, not shooting, and half a million people throughout the country now take the annual bird census. In Brooklyn, the event takes place in the third week of December.

"When John became president, we started inviting the birders back here for dinner after the count," says Mary Yrizarry. "The teams go out at dawn, all over Brooklyn. I stay home and prepare food for the cold and hungry crews. As the light fades and the teams begin to trickle in, the first of many pans of lasagna goes into the oven. Over mulled wine or hot cider, they discuss the day's adventures. The teams compile the final list and there's a certain rivalry to see who spotted 'best bird of the day.'

"I designed the menu so that it could be prepared ahead of time, be presented hot over a two- to three-hour period, and could be eaten with just one fork. We have lasagna, garlic bread, salad, and cake. I make a meatless lasagna, because so many birders are vegetarians."

"In 1989, we sighted one hundred and twenty-five species," says John, "including a bald eagle, very rare in winter here. You know, there is no official Brooklyn bird. I nominate the bluejay; it's sassy, and it's just a little lighter than Dodger blue."

Vegetarian Lasagna

Note that the dish is assembled with uncooked pasta. "It really works!" says Mary Yrizarry.

1 large fennel bulb
1 large onion
4 garlic cloves
2 tablespoons olive oil
1 large jar mushroom spaghetti sauce
   (about 30 ounces)
1 pound lasagna noodles

1 bag frozen broccoli pieces
1 large green pepper, cored, seeded,
   and chopped
1 quart ricotta cheese
¾ cup grated Parmesan cheese
1 large package skim-milk mozzarella,
   sliced

❶ Chop the fennel, onion, and garlic. Heat the oil in a large skillet and cook the vegetables until they just begin to brown. Add the spaghetti sauce and simmer, uncovered, for about 30 minutes. Add ½ cup or more water after 15 minutes to keep the sauce liquid.

❷ Cover the bottom of a 9-inch × 13-inch baking pan with some of the sauce. Layer with half the uncooked lasagna noodles. Scatter on the broccoli and green pepper, dot on the ricotta, and sprinkle with half the Parmesan cheese. Cover with the remaining noodles and sauce. Cover with the sliced mozzarella and the rest of the Parmesan. May be prepared ahead of time to this point.

Preheat the oven to 350 degrees F.

❸ Cover the pan with foil. Bake for 30 minutes, uncover the pan, and bake for 15 minutes more. ⮞ *Serves 8 to 10*

Mulled Wine

½ gallon red jug wine
½ to 1 cup sugar
3 cinnamon sticks
1 tablespoon whole cloves

½ teaspoon cardamom seeds
½ orange, sliced thin
½ cup white raisins

Combine all the ingredients in a large nonreactive saucepan and heat to just below the boil. Stir occasionally to blend flavors. Pour into a punch bowl and ladle into cups. ⮞ *Makes ½ gallon*

THE BROOKLYN MUSEUM

This great structure on Eastern Parkway is ranked among the world's leading museums, with the finest Egyptian collection outside of Cairo or London, and twenty-eight important period rooms, including the Jan Martense Schenck house, built in Flatlands in 1675 and moved to the museum in 1952. Extensive expansion is under way, and in a few years the Brooklyn Museum will be able to display most of its two million objects.

Flanking the entrance are two monumental statues, heroic women representing Manhattan and Brooklyn. John Muir, an urban geologist and founder of the Brooklyn Center for Urban Environment, has noted that these ladies are very much in character: "Manhattan is imperious and regal; gathered around her are the symbols of wealth and power, and her foot rests on a money box. Brooklyn, however, is maternal. Children dangle from her lap, and surrounding her are the symbols of home and church."

Marce-Pain

This recipe for the confection called marzipan, hand written in Dutch, was found in the Brooklyn Museum's library collection.

Take one pound bitter almonds very finely pounded, sprinkled with rose water, and one pound sifted sugar. Put this in a pan and let come to a boil, until it becomes sticky. Then roll out as a dough, on board well sprinkled with powdered sugar, with rolling pin roll mass to inch thickness.

Cut figures and lay these on clean sheet of paper. Bake slowly in moderate oven. Before they are quite done, paint them over with a solution of white of egg—use rose water and powdered sugar and finish baking.

Do not take them from the paper before cooled, or they will break.

Marzipan

Marguerite Lavin, Coordinator of Rights and Reproductions at the Brooklyn Museum, is an enthusiastic and skilled confectioner. She has worked out a modern version of the old recipe. "The egg white isn't necessary," she says, "and instead of painting the confections, I knead pastry colorant into the dough. The colorant comes in eight or more colors, and you can find it in specialty shops. It is very intense; just a little on the tip of a toothpick will color a piece of dough the size of an egg. And you can mix your own range of colors. I've made tiny cabbages, insects, peaches, and bunches of grapes, among other things. I use them on family birthday cakes."

1 cup prepared almond paste, such as Odense brand, at room temperature

1 cup confectioners' sugar, sifted

1½ teaspoons rosewater

❶ Combine the almond paste, sugar, and rosewater, and mix them well. Put the mixture on a cool work surface and knead it for 10 to 20 minutes, until it is very pliable. (Wrapped in plastic wrap, it will keep for weeks in the refrigerator.)

❷ Pull off as much of the dough as you want to fashion a figure. Knead food colorant into it. Shape your figure.

Preheat the oven to 250 degrees F.

Marzipan (continued)

❸ The figures need to cure, but not bake. The oven must never rise above 250 degrees F or the figures will melt. Cover baking sheets with parchment paper, arrange the figures on them, and let them cure in the oven for about 1 hour. Cool completely on a rack before removing the figures from the paper.

≫→ *Makes about 40 ¾-inch figures*

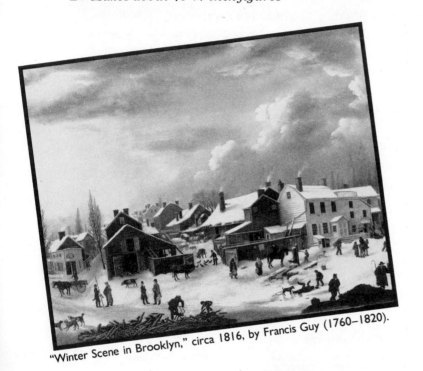

"Winter Scene in Brooklyn," circa 1816, by Francis Guy (1760–1820).

View of Brooklyn Bridge, by Samuel Halpert (1884–1930).

Caviar Mousse

The museum relies greatly on its volunteers, such as Evelyn Ortner of Park Slope, former president of the Committee of the Brooklyn Museum. The very civic-minded Mrs. Ortner is on the board of trustees of the Brooklyn Academy of Music (BAM); she is chairman of the board of St. Ann's Center for Restoration and the Arts and is founder and former president of the Friends of BAM. She also finds time to cook, and very well.

4 ounces (1 stick) unsalted butter, melted

2 7-ounce cans tuna, packed in water, drained

1 teaspoon finely chopped green scallion tips

6-ounce jar herring tidbits in wine

4 ounces black caviar, or lumpfish caviar

¼ teaspoon garlic powder

½ teaspoon sugar

4-ounce jar red caviar, or salmon or whitefish roe

❶ Put the melted butter in a blender or food processor bowl. Add ⅓ of the tuna, blend or process for several seconds; add the rest of the tuna in two batches. Blend until smooth, scraping down the bowl from time to time.

❷ Add the scallion tips, herring, 1 heaping tablespoon of the black caviar, the garlic powder, and sugar. (Do not use garlic salt, as it gives an unpleasant taste.) Blend the mixture until it is smooth and the consistency of whipped cream.

❸ Pack the mixture into a buttered 2-cup mold and cover with foil or plastic wrap. Refrigerate the mold for 6 hours or overnight, or freeze it.

❹ Unmold the refrigerated mousse about an hour before serving, or 2 hours if the mousse is frozen. (To unmold, run a sharp knife around the edge of the dish, dip it for several seconds in hot water, and invert it on a serving dish.) If the mousse cracks or breaks, don't worry—just shape it back together with a butter knife.

❺ Drain the jar of red caviar for 5 minutes to remove liquid. Spread the sides of the mousse with remaining black caviar, and the top with the red caviar. Serve with rounds of pumpernickel or rye bread. ⇢ *Serves 12*

From the Library's picture collection. (From the top) reading the *Eagle,* 1946; Treat potato chip factory, 1954; Miss Ovenkrust, 1954. (Opposite) packing olives with pimentos, 1953.

THE CENTRAL LIBRARY

Nineteenth-century Brooklyn established a library system in keeping with its ambitions as a great, autonomous city. The library system is still independent of New York City. The archives of the Central Library on Grand Army Plaza contain a wealth of culinary material from Brooklyn's past, including the morgue, or reference library, of the Brooklyn <u>Daily Eagle</u> from 1904 to 1954. The <u>Eagle</u> is also on microfilm.

"We have special book collections of Brooklyn authors, too," says Elizabeth White, chief librarian of the Brooklyn Collection, a mass of information pertaining to the borough. "Walt Whitman, Henry Miller, and Marianne Moore are all represented."

Chicken Breast with Madeira and Shallots

Entrance to the Library.

Harriet Rosen, a librarian at the Central Library who contributed this recipe, has a particular interest in the American cookbook collection of the Central Library. "Use inexpensive Madeira," she says.

1 skinless, boneless chicken breast,
    sliced into thin cutlets
Salt
6 shallots, peeled and sliced into
    4 lengthwise pieces
2 tablespoons unsalted butter

¾ cup Madeira
1 tablespoon golden raisins
2 tablespoons chicken stock (optional)
2 teaspoons vegetable oil
2 tablespoons dry white wine or
    vermouth

❶ Lightly salt the chicken cutlets, and refrigerate them until ready to cook.

❷ In a small heavy saucepan with a lid, sauté the quartered shallots in 1 tablespoon of the butter until they just begin to brown, about 5 minutes. Add the Madeira, raisins, and optional chicken stock. Lower the heat and let the mixture simmer for about 30 minutes, covered, until the shallots are soft and the liquid has reduced to about 2 syrupy tablespoons.

❸ Put the remaining tablespoon of butter and the oil in a large skillet, preferably nonstick. Cook the cutlets over moderately high heat, turning once, until lightly speckled and cooked through. This is a matter of minutes. Remove the cutlets to a heated platter.

❹ Discard any fat remaining in the skillet. Pour in the white wine and scrape up any bits of meat. Boil until only a spoonful remains, and pour this over the cutlets. Cover them with the shallot mixture, and serve. ⟫→ *Serves 2*

THE BROOKLYN HISTORICAL SOCIETY

Founded in 1863 as the Long Island Historical Society, a repository for genealogical and other material, the Brooklyn Historical Society is housed in a redbrick and terra-cotta landmark built by the Society in 1881. It houses a vast collection of books, manuscripts, photographs, and artifacts, all relating to the borough and its diverse people.

The permanent exhibit on the first floor presents Brooklyn's history: the themes include the Dutch, the Brooklyn Bridge, the Navy Yard, Coney Island, the Dodgers, Brooklynites, and a changing series of ethnic themes. Approach with reverence the kitchen set from "The Honeymooners"; there's the icebox that Norton raided almost nightly, cadging snacks and enraging Ralph Kramden with requests: "Hey, Ralph! Got any chow chow? Got any piccalilli?" Those are evidently old Brooklyn favorites. It happens that the Society can supply recipes, from its copy of The Echo Cook Book of 1886:

The Long Island Historical Society (now the Brooklyn Historical Society), architectural rendering, circa 1880.

Chow Chow

Two quarts each of onions, cauliflower, and small pickles, one dozen small peppers; put all in a weak brine for thirty-six hours; make a dressing of three quarts vinegar, one half pound of mustard, one-half pound brown sugar, one ounce ginger, one ounce turmeric, two ounces curry powder, one pint salad oil; boil the dressing ten minutes and pour on while hot.

Note: To make the brine, add 6 tablespoons of salt to each quart of water used. If necessary, heat the water to dissolve the salt, but let it cool before use. Make enough brine to cover the vegetables. Process the Chow Chow in jars immersed in a boiling water bath.

Picalily [sic]

One peck green tomatoes chopped, four tablespoons of salt, let stand overnight; one cabbage chopped; boil in vinegar half an hour: add twelve green peppers, one pint grated horseradish, one pint of molasses, one tablespoon of cinnamon and cloves.

Note: You will probably need at least 2 gallons of cider vinegar.

Cutouts of Ralph Kramden and Ed Norton in the Kramdens' run-down kitchen. Original set from the "Honeymooners" television series.

BROOKLYN UNION GAS

The ancestor of the very community-minded Brooklyn Union Gas Company was incorporated in 1825, with the purpose of lighting the city's streets. Unfortunately, no one cared, and stockholders' money was refunded.

By 1847, Brooklyn, with 100,000 people one of the largest cities in the country, was ready to illuminate its thoroughfares. Lots of companies were eager both to fill the need and to clobber the opposition; crews of thugs, known as "gas-house gangs," battled it out, seizing customers and territory until it became plain that everyone was losing the war. In 1895, the seven largest companies consolidated to form The Brooklyn Union Gas Company.

The main reason for capitulation was the threat of electricity; gas had lost the lighting business, and from now on its real purpose was heat, most specifically cooking heat. Gas-industry people weren't caught unawares; in 1890, Brooklyn Gas Light, one of the consolidating companies, had presented a series of lectures on the revolutionary idea of "cooking with gas." In 1908, Brooklyn Union Gas established a Home Service Department, presenting lectures and classes throughout the Borough. A company bulletin from 1927 reports that "at a demonstration at the Academy of Music, angel food cake and marshmallow frosting were prepared." An Elks Club demonstration in 1929 "was the scene of unusual feminine activity." Subjects were budget planning, child feeding, and fuel saving. The Home Service Department and its test kitchen continued until the late '60s.

By that time, however, Brooklyn was in decline. A gas company cannot just pick up its pipelines and move. It works, or it fails. In a brilliant publicity move, Brooklyn Union Gas decided to renovate a grand brownstone in the failing Victorian neighborhood of Park Slope, in hopes of attracting families back to Brooklyn's beautiful urban neighborhoods. The Cinderella Program, as it was called, was sensationally successful in its aims of enabling financing, cutting red tape, and revitalizing neighborhoods. Brooklyn's renaissance owes a lot to its gas company.

Lillian Beckford, manager of consumer affairs for Brooklyn Union Gas and a super-volunteer for any number of projects, including "Meals on Heels," which carries food to the homebound elderly, produced these recipes. Lillian says: "The most interesting thing about Brooklyn is its diversity. I come from a Southern background, where you were either white or black. So living on a block in Boerum Hill that has every race and religion is very stimulating. We work together, and we try to accommodate one another."

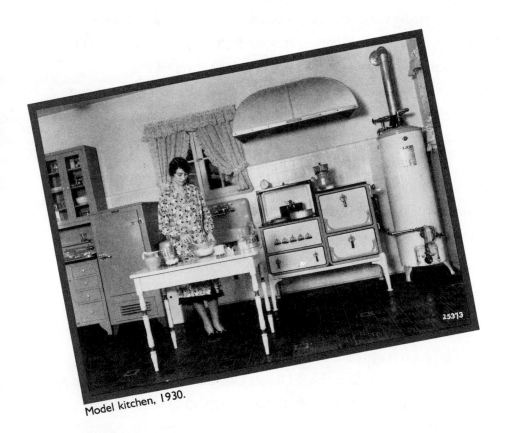

Model kitchen, 1930.

Chicken Country Captain

"This Georgia recipe was originally made with a bottle of ketchup," says Lillian Beckford.

"Southerners like things sweet. Now we make it with stewed tomatoes and just a little ketchup."

A 3⅓-pound frying chicken, cut in 6 pieces, or 6 breast pieces
½ cup all-purpose flour
1 teaspoon salt
¼ teaspoon freshly ground pepper
¼ cup vegetable oil
1 cup chopped onion
1 cup chopped green pepper

1 garlic clove, minced
1½ cups water
2 cups stewed tomatoes
3 tablespoons ketchup
2 teaspoons curry powder
½ teaspoon thyme
½ cup currants
½ cup sautéed slivered almonds

❶ Remove the chicken skin and discard it. Put the flour, salt and pepper in a paper bag, twist the top shut, and shake to mix. Put the pieces in the bag, one by one, and shake to coat.

❷ Heat the oil to sizzling in a large skillet. Brown the chicken pieces, turning them once. Do not crowd the pan or the pieces will steam, not brown. Remove them to a platter.

❸ Add the onion, green pepper, and garlic to the oil. Cook, stirring, until lightly browned. Add the water, tomatoes, ketchup, curry powder, and thyme. Mix well.

❹ Return the chicken to the skillet, cover, and bring the sauce to the boil over high heat. Immediately reduce the heat and simmer for 30 minutes.

❺ Arrange the chicken on a platter, surrounded by mounds of rice. Stir the currants into the sauce and pour it over the chicken. Sprinkle with the almonds.

≫→ *Serves 4 to 6*

Prune Cake with Buttermilk Glaze

Lillian Beckford says she gets raves when she serves this cake.

....

Cake

2½ cups sifted all-purpose flour

1 teaspoon baking soda

1 teaspoon cinnamon

1 teaspoon freshly ground nutmeg

1 teaspoon allspice

1 teaspoon salt

1 cup vegetable oil

1⅓ cups sugar

3 eggs

1 cup buttermilk

1 cup cooked prunes, pitted

1 cup chopped pecans

1 teaspoon vanilla

Glaze

1 cup sugar

½ cup buttermilk

½ teaspoon baking soda

1 tablespoon white corn syrup

½ cup butter

½ teaspoon vanilla

Preheat the oven to 300 degrees F.

❶ Grease and flour a 9-inch × 12-inch × 2-inch baking pan.

❷ Sift the flour, baking soda, cinnamon, nutmeg, allspice, and salt together.

❸ Combine the oil, sugar, and eggs in a large bowl, mixing well. Stir in the flour mixture and buttermilk alternately. Fold in the prunes, pecans, and vanilla.

❹ Pour the mixture into the pan and bake in the center of the oven for 1 hour.

❺ While it is baking, make the glaze. Combine all the ingredients and boil for 2 minutes. Place the pan on a rack and pour the hot glaze over the hot cake. Leave in the pan until cool. ⤞ *Makes 1 cake*

Gas refrigerator signs on Flatbush Avenue, 1931.

DEM BUMS, GONE FOREVER

The team, 1952.

In these days when even mediocre players are millionaires, it is nice to remember a time when the players—including the stars—were real, down-to-earth guys. Heroes, sure, but guys who lived in Brooklyn neighborhoods, watered the lawn, maybe even had to have a job in the winter to make ends meet.

The Dodgers of the late 1940s and '50s were the best-loved team in the history of the game. They were perceived as underdogs who often won, but never lost the human touch. Everybody felt at home, rooting and munching hot dogs in Ebbets Field, a situation that led to its downfall—it was just too small.

"Ebbets Field let you feel that you were in the structure and feeling a part of the action; something that's missing, I think, nowadays," says Joseph Stevens, Jr. "My dad was born in Brooklyn in 1906," Ken Vought says. "He was a lawyer, and the price of box seats wasn't an issue. But he insisted on sitting in the bleachers. 'These guys here really know about baseball and care about the Bums,' he'd say." Love

of the Bums was truly for everyone; Pulitzer Prize—winning poet
Marianne Moore praised the team in her "Hometown Piece for
Messrs. Alston and Reese," written the year the Dodgers won the
Series.

Fans had the Sym-phony, Gladys Gooding at the organ, and the
famed Hilda Chester who swung her cowbell when a Dodger
homered. Haberdasher (later Borough President) Abe Stark
promised a new suit to any batter who managed to hit his
advertising sign. Right fielder Carl Furillo's mighty arm kept the
danger to Stark at a low, and legend has it that Stark gave Furillo a
suit, now and then, in gratitude.

The Dodgers took the Yankees in the World Series in 1955, and in
1956 they won a pennant. Then, in 1957, club owner O'Malley
moved the franchise to California. It was all over.

"We maintain and preserve the spirit and memory of the Dodgers,"
says Marty Adler, President of the Dodgers Hall of Fame. "We've
accumulated shirts, scorecards, and other memorabilia over the
years, and it's on loan to the Brooklyn Historical Society. Former
Dodgers miss the adulation they need—and each year we lose a
couple of guys."

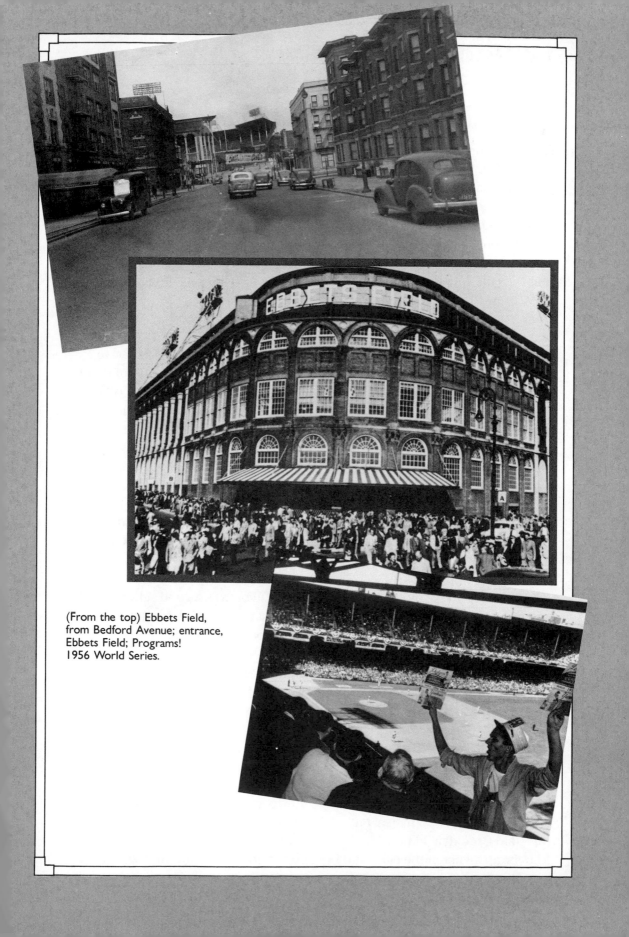

(From the top) Ebbets Field, from Bedford Avenue; entrance, Ebbets Field; Programs! 1956 World Series.

Feeding the Fans

Soda vendor at Ebbets Field.

Harry M. Stevens, who emigrated from England in 1882, gave us the stirring phrase "You can't tell the players without a scorecard!" From hawking scorecards, Stevens went on to found a great stadium concession business, starting with peanuts and soft drinks. Reasoning that fans missed the action when they threw their heads back to swig soda from a bottle, he was the first to give straws with drinks so everyone could keep eyes on the ball.

Harry's grandson, Joseph B. Stevens, Jr., chairman of the board of the company, sold scorecards and peanuts at Ebbets Field in his student years: "Peanuts came in huge burlap sacks, and they had to be warmed. The vendors scooped them from the heating bin and put them into paper sacks. The quantity had to be just right, so they could toss a sack twenty rows away.

"Our hot dogs, highly spiced with a garlic flavor, came from Stahlmeyer. And the mustard was always Gulden's. In fact, in 1941, Harry's granddaughter Alice married a Gulden. The newspapers said, 'Hot dog married the mustard!'"

George Whitfield, a Stevens vendor, "had almost as many fans as the players," a Stevens executive says. George recalls those days:

"I was born in Jamaica, but raised in Brooklyn. I knew Mr. Ebbets, an owner of the club, and I got a job with Stevens. You had to boil the franks; you put fifty of them in a net, then fished them out of a vat. The vendors had an insulated metal container that held the dogs, and a compartment on each side of the container held twenty-five rolls. You'd go out and sell, come back and pick up another load. This went on till the seventh or eighth inning. We'd yell, 'Hot franks, a frank and a roll.'

"With beer, you'd yell 'Cold beer.' If you was a good seller, from the first to the eighth inning, you were good for maybe twenty trays of twenty-four cans. You worked strictly on commission. With a weekend doubleheader, you could make fourteen dollars. That was a big day!

"I remember that Casey Stengel wouldn't let the players eat or drink coffee before the game. And Babe Ruth, when he came over to the Dodgers, always had a big mug of coffee and a greasy ham sandwich. Never hot dogs, ham sandwiches."

The Brooklyn Sym-phony

They dressed like bums with dented top hats, played cacophony—not music—on their instruments, made an awful racket, and Dodger fans loved them. And why not? The Symphony loved the Dodgers. Leader of the band was Jack "Shorty" Laurice, a feisty little dynamo. The group was stationed in Section 8 of the ballpark. The band got together in 1937.

"In Ebbets Field, Section 8 was like family—the season-ticket holders called it the Section 8 Club," recalls Joe Laurice, Shorty's brother and a member of the band. "Once a stranger, in his cups, came in and started cursing. Shorty said, 'Hey, Mack, calm down—there are women and children here.' The guy said, 'The hell with it!' So Shorty took off his wristwatch. He was so short he had to stand on his seat, but he hit the guy and knocked him out! The cops threw the man out. There was no foul language in Ebbets Field.

"The band used to play 'Three Blind Mice' when the umpires came out. The Dodgers took us on road trips. In Philadelphia, the City of Brotherly Love, they'd throw peanuts and empty beer cans at the Sym-phony. Shorty would say, 'The fans have better pitching arms than the Phillies!'

"Shorty's wife used to have the ballplayers to her house to eat. She used to make meatballs for Jackie Robinson and the rest. The size of a baseball!"

The Sym-phony in action, 1951.

Theresa Laurice's White Clam Sauce

Joe's wife Theresa laughs when she remembers Shorty's theme song: "I come from Brooklyn, and Brooklyn is out of this world. I come from Brooklyn—almost everyone there is hard berled."

"Shorty liked my clam sauce," *she says.*

½ pound spaghetti or linguine
¼ cup olive oil
1 clove garlic, minced
2 tablespoons white wine or water
½ teaspoon salt
½ teaspoon freshly ground pepper
½ teaspoon crumbled dried oregano
1 tablespoon minced parsley
An 8-ounce can whole or minced clams with juice

❶ Bring a large pot of lightly salted water to the boil and cook the pasta.

❷ While the pasta cooks, heat the oil in a large skillet and lightly brown the garlic, stirring. Add the wine or water, salt, pepper, oregano, and parsley. Add the clams and cook until they are heated through. Toss with the pasta and serve. ⟫→ *Serves 2 or 3*

▲▲▲▲▲▲▲▲▲▲▲▲▲▲▲▲▲▲▲▲▲▲▲▲▲▲▲▲▲

Ebbets Field.

What the Dodgers Taught Me,
by Holly Redell

"**S**ocial skills came with having a home team in Brooklyn. On my first date, I went to Ebbets Field with a kid named Howard. Sitting high in the stands I learned how to behave at a ball game—raucously. Howard didn't last. Maybe my enthusiasm put him off.

"Not long ago, I was telling a friend about a fund-raising campaign I've started for Prospect Park, where I work. The idea is to get one dollar from everyone who has a connection with Brooklyn.

One in every seven Americans—the actual statistic—yields the number of 40 million. My friend at once pressed five dollars on me, and tried hard to make me promise we would cover over the Prospect Park lake and reconstruct Ebbets Field on top. Though there's no chance of that happening, I don't know a single Brooklyn Dodger fan who doesn't believe that somehow, someday, the Bums will come home where they belong."

Food to Take to the Ball Game

Holly Redell has great spirit for the sport, and feels that taking along good eats adds to the enjoyment.

Croustades

Cut a long French baguette or Italian loaf into two or three sections. Cut off the pointy ends. With a long, sharp knife remove as much of the inside as possible, being careful not to pierce the crust. Stuff with any of the following fillings (or one of your own devising), wrap in foil, and freeze. When ready to serve, partially thaw and slice. By the time you get to the stadium, the croustade rounds will be ready to eat.

Fillings

Cream cheese flavored with sardines, chives, olives, or what you like.

"Pâté": In a food processor or grinder, put about 2 cups of leftover cooked meat which you have cubed. Add a small onion cut in quarters, a large clove of garlic, the juice of half a lemon, lots of pepper, and about 1 stick of butter. When this mixture looks like pâté, it is ready. You may want to adjust the seasonings. Hint: Leftover pork tends to be bland and will need much seasoning.

The "Off-the-Record" Dinners

Meyer Robinson is the former president of the Monarch Wine Company, maker of Manischewitz kosher wine. An ardent fan, he got the idea to invite the players over to the winery following an afternoon game when the next scheduled game was at night. "Plenty of interval between games," says Mr. Robinson. "These dinners were off the record, only the players, no press. It was a time to let their hair down.

"Monarch Wine was in the Bush Terminal, and Ebbets Field was only 15, 20 minutes away. We were great fans. I remember that the players walked through to the dressing room on a runway that separated them from the fans by a grill. The fans got really close. As a matter of fact, that's how Gil Hodges met his wife. She was a fan, they got acquainted, and eventually married.

"I knew the ballplayers well.

Leo Burati, the man in charge of our trucking, just loved to cook. We had a lot of big spaghetti dinners.

"The players would come about 5:30, and the building was pretty secluded there on 2nd Avenue. But sometimes the kids around the neighborhood found out about the dinner, and there'd be a mob waiting for autographs. We'd wind up about 9:30, 10 o'clock.

"These were male-only affairs. Ah, the food, the wine, the levity! Years later, I'd meet some of the men at the Baseball Writers' Dinner and they'd say, 'Those were great dinners you had at your winery.' Years later, Duke Snider, Pee Wee, all of them, they said; 'We still think about those spaghetti dinners.'"

For a scaled-down version of an Off-the-Record Dodger dinner, see Podres Spaghetti Sauce (page 342).

The players with Meyer Robinson (right).

Feeding the Players

Besides the Off-the-Record dinners, the Dodgers ate quite well both as guests and at home. Carl Erskine recalls some great food: "Dr. Morris Steiner and his wife Martha often hosted the Reeses, Sniders, Walkers, and Erskines—leg of lamb was a favorite.

"Our butcher near Fort Hamilton was Joe Rossi. He'd invite us for four-hour Italian feasts, and when we were stuffed beyond belief he'd bring out a steamboat round of roast beef. That was before the fresh-fruit dessert.

"After I retired and occasionally came back to New York on business, I'd call Joe and have him meet me at the airport with fifteen pounds of veal cutlet. It is impossible to get veal trimmed 'the Brooklyn way' anywhere else in the world."

Home cooking was pretty tasty in Dodger homes, as the recipes given us by Dodger wives show. No wonder those fellas could pitch, hit, field, and run!

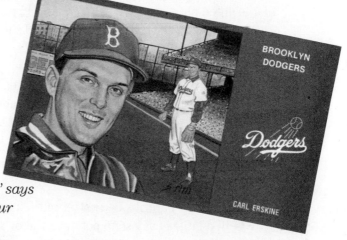

Betty Erskine's Three-Corn Casserole

"Eat this with some great veal," says Carl Erskine. "This is one of our favorites."

8 tablespoons butter, softened
1 cup sour cream
1 egg
1 16-ounce can whole-kernel corn, drained

1 16-ounce can cream-style corn
1 9-ounce package corn-muffin mix
1 cup grated cheddar cheese (optional)

Preheat the oven to 375 degrees F.

Mix the butter, sour cream, and egg well in a large bowl. Stir in the cans of corn and the muffin mix. Spoon it into a buttered 2-quart casserole. Bake for 1 hour. If you decide to use the cheese, add it after 45 minutes, and stir well. The dish is cooked when it is slightly puffed. ⟫→ *Serves 4 to 6*

Podres Spaghetti Sauce

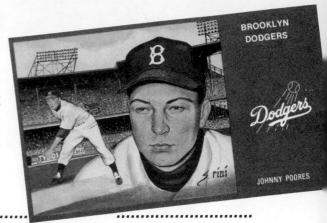

BROOKLYN DODGERS

Dodgers

JOHNNY POORES

"All the Dodgers were big spaghetti fans," says Joni Podres, wife of the winning pitcher in the final game of the '55 Series. "This is Johnny's favorite. A little garlic bread and mixed salad, and you are all set."*

Sauce

4 pork spareribs, separated, about ½ pound

½ cup vegetable or olive oil

2 medium onions, chopped

1 large green pepper, chopped

2 garlic cloves, minced

2 28-ounce cans Hunt's blended tomatoes

2 6-ounce cans tomato paste

1 teaspoon crushed dried oregano

1 teaspoon crushed dried basil

2 teaspoons chopped parsley

⅛ teaspoon black pepper

Pinch crushed hot pepper flakes

Pinch sugar

Salt to taste

2 8-ounce cans tomato sauce

Meatballs

1½ pounds ground chuck

½ pound ground pork

3 slices bread, soaked in water

2 small garlic cloves, minced

1 egg

1 teaspoon ketchup

1 tablespoon ground Parmesan cheese

Salt to taste

1 to 1½ pounds spaghetti or other pasta

❶ Fry the spareribs in a skillet until browned. Set them aside.

❷ In a large heavy soup pot, heat the oil and cook the onions and green pepper, stirring often, until soft. Add the garlic, canned tomatoes, and spareribs. Stir in the tomato paste and add 2 cans of water. Add the oregano, basil, parsley, black pepper, hot pepper, and sugar. Add a little salt, if you wish. Cover, bring to the boil, lower the heat and simmer for 1 hour.

❸ Meanwhile, make the meatballs. Combine the ingredients with your hands, or use a wooden spoon. The mixture should be well blended. Shape 1½-inch meatballs; you should be able to make 14 or 15. Brown them lightly.

❹ After an hour add the meatballs to the soup pot with the tomato sauce and spareribs. Cook for 1 hour more. Cook the pasta according to package directions.

❺ Put the pasta in a large bowl and pour the sauce over it.

⟫→ *Serves 4 to 6*

Kapoosta
(Pork and Cabbage Soup)

"My husband is of Lithuanian descent," says Mrs. Johnny Podres, "and this recipe was handed down through his family. We enjoy it throughout the winter."

2 pounds spareribs, cut in several
   pieces
1½ quarts water
1 teaspoon salt
Pepper to taste
1 large onion, chopped

1 bay leaf
1½ pounds cabbage, shredded
¼ cup wine vinegar
1 28-ounce can tomatoes, drained
1 medium onion, minced

❶ Put the spareribs in a large soup pot, and cover the spareribs with the water. Add the salt, pepper, chopped onion, and bay leaf. Bring to the boil, lower the heat and let simmer for 1½ hours, until the meat is tender and falling off the bone. Remove the meat from the bones, chop it, and set it aside.

❷ Add the shredded cabbage to the broth and boil for 5 minutes. Add the vinegar, tomatoes, and minced onion. Simmer for 20 minutes, then add the chopped pork to the pot. Correct the seasoning and let the pork heat through.
➤ *Serves 6*

Cassata Siciliana

Cookie Lavagetto's pinch-hitting in the '47 Series was one of the great moments in baseball history. "This dessert was a favorite of Cookie's," says his widow Mary.

A 9-inch × 5-inch pound cake
2 cups ricotta cheese
4 1-ounce squares semisweet chocolate
1 ounce orange liqueur, such as
   Cointreau

1½ cups raspberry jam
2 cups chocolate frosting or whipped
   cream
Toasted whole unsalted almonds for
   garnish (optional)

❶ Buy or bake a pound cake. Chill the cake for 1½ hours. Trim the edges and uneven places so that the cake is level on all sides. Slice the cake lengthwise into 3 or 4 slices. Place the base slice on a serving platter.

❷ Force the ricotta cheese through a sieve into a bowl and beat it until it is smooth.

❸ Chop the chocolate into fine bits in a blender or food processor. Mix the chocolate bits with the liqueur and jam. Spread the base slice with a portion of the ricotta cheese and spread on a portion of the chocolate-liqueur-raspberry jam. Repeat, building layers, ending with a top layer of plain cake.

❹ Gently press down the filled cake. Use a spatula to even up the sides. Cover the cake with plastic wrap and refrigerate it for 24 hours.

❺ Before serving, frost the cake with a favorite chocolate frosting or with whipped cream. Garnish it, if you like, with almonds. ≫→ *Serves 12*

Roast Leg of Lamb

"One of my sons is a Christian Brother," says Mary Lavagetto. "Not long ago he phoned me and asked me for this old family recipe. He called back to say that all the brothers really loved it. The recipe sounds rather complicated, but after you prepare it once, it is amazingly simple to do.

"Serving suggestions: Garnish the platter with watercress or parsley and accompany with baby red potatoes, green beans, or asparagus. Serve with a good red wine."

A 6- to 7½-pound leg of lamb
½ cup Grey Poupon Dijon mustard
2 cloves garlic, minced
1 teaspoon crushed dried thyme

⅓ cup olive oil
⅓ cup soy sauce
½ cup white wine or dry vermouth
½ cup beef or chicken stock

❶ Shave off all but a ¹⁄₁₆-inch layer of fat around the leg. Mix the mustard, garlic, and thyme together. Whip the mixture as you slowly add the oil, then add the soy sauce. The mixture should be as thick as mayonnaise. Slather the mixture over and around the leg. Let it sit for 2 hours at room temperature.

Preheat the oven to 450 degrees F.

❷ Arrange the leg on a rack in a roasting pan. Roast for 15 minutes, then lower the heat to 350 degrees F.

❸ It will take approximately 1¼ to 1½ hours for the roast to reach a meat-thermometer reading of 125 to 130 degrees. If you prick the meat and the juices run light pink, the meat will be medium rare. Cook longer if you like your meat well done.

❹ Remove the lamb to a platter. Skim off the fat in the roasting pan and deglaze the pan by pouring in the white wine. Bring it to the boil, scraping up all the bits adhering to the pan.

❺ Pour the juices into a saucepan, add the stock, and let simmer for 10 to 15 minutes. Strain into a warmed gravy boat.

❻ The meat will have rested 20 minutes and is ready to slice. There will be enough gravy to moisten each slice. ➤➤ *Serves 8 to 10*

My Grandmother's Chicken,
Mrs. Clem Labine

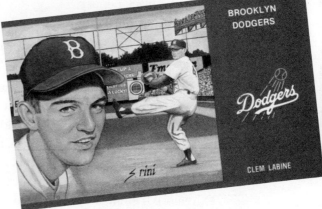

Mrs. Clem Labine, wife of the Dodgers' great relief pitcher, contributes a recipe and a memory:

"My grandmother had 13 children, and I was the first-born grandchild. 'Nona,' as I called her, kept me busy in her kitchen or on the porch, which she called the *piazza*. It was my job to separate the tender inner leaves of wild dandelions for salad, and to strip the outer leaves for her to boil and then fry in olive oil with garlic. In late summer, we would go into the garden, Nona with her salt shaker in her apron pocket. She'd pick a large ripe tomato, wash it under the hose, sprinkle it with salt, and we'd share it, still warm and sweet from the sun.

"On Sunday she went to early mass, so she could spend the morning cooking. Our Sunday dinner was always the same: antipasti, soup with escarole and tiny meatballs, macaroni with meatballs and braciole, and my favorite — her roast chicken. My mother, father, and I went to 11 o'clock mass. Nona said the chicken was best when the priest gave a long sermon; she liked to cook it until it practically fell off the bone. She never trussed chickens; she felt they browned better untrussed. When you make the dish, please use *red* wine, and a blue enamel roasting pan; Nona said those two were essential."

You can cook two small chickens, as Nona did, or one large roaster. Nona used ten garlic cloves, but a head of garlic is not excessive. The garlic becomes sweet and mild as it cooks in the pan juices.

Edvigia Spino's Roast Chicken

A 6½- to 7-pound chicken, or 2 3½-
   pound chickens
2 tablespoons olive oil
1 teaspoon salt, or to taste
Freshly ground black pepper
2 teaspoons dried oregano

1 teaspoon dried rosemary, crumbled,
   or 2 sprigs fresh rosemary
10 unpeeled garlic cloves, or 1 head
   garlic, separated
1½ cups red wine, preferably Chianti

Preheat the oven to 350 degrees F.

❶ Rinse the chicken(s) and pat dry with paper towels. Rub the chicken, and the bottom of a roasting pan, with the oil. Salt and pepper the bird and rub it, inside and out, with oregano and rosemary.

❷ Place the chicken in the pan. Fold the wings under, but do not truss it. Scatter the garlic cloves around the bird. Roast for 1½ to 2 hours, or until the skin is brown and crisp and the internal temperature measures 165 to 170 degrees F. Baste often with the pan juices.

❸ Remove the chicken to a heated serving platter. Skim off as much fat as possible from the pan juices. Over high heat, add the wine to the pan. Scrape any browned bits clinging to the pan into the sauce and press the garlic cloves with the back of a wooden spoon. The garlic will be completely soft, and will dissolve in the sauce. Cook until the sauce is reduced by one half and is thickened. Strain the sauce into a warmed gravy boat, pressing down on the garlic cloves again. There will be about 1 tablespoon of dark-red sauce to moisten each portion. ⟫→ *Serves 6 to 10*

▲▲▲▲▲▲▲▲▲▲▲▲▲▲▲▲▲▲▲▲▲▲▲▲▲▲▲▲

Mrs. Carl Furillo's Buttermilk Cake

BROOKLYN DODGERS

Dodgers

CARL FURILLO

"Don't ice this cake," says Fern Furillo, "you'll ruin it. I like to use more vanilla than I've called for here, but tastes differ. A lot of vanilla or a little, you'll be proud to serve this cake."*

2 cups sugar

1 cup vegetable shortening

¼ teaspoon salt

4 eggs

½ teaspoon baking soda

1 cup buttermilk

3 cups Softasilk cake flour

3 tablespoons imitation vanilla or 1 tablespoon pure vanilla

1 cup chopped pecans

6 whole pecans

Preheat the oven to 350 degrees F.

❶ In the bowl of a stationary mixer or in a large bowl with a hand mixer, cream the sugar, vegetable shortening, and salt. Add the eggs, one at a time, beating until blended.

❷ Add the baking soda and buttermilk and beat well.

❸ Add the flour and vanilla, beat well. Fold in the chopped pecans.

❹ Spray a 10-inch-wide × 4-inch-high tube pan with vegetable spray. Pour in the batter and smooth the top. Arrange the 6 pecans on the surface. Bake for 1 hour, or until a toothpick inserted in the center of the cake comes out clean. Cool on a rack. ≫→ *Makes 1 cake*

Scooter's Savory Snack

Holy cow! How does the son of a Brooklyn trolley-car driver and a pieceworker wind up a *Yankee?* Isn't that, uh, *treason?* Not really. As the man who's been called the greatest shortstop and bunter in baseball says, "Everybody but the Yankees turned me down. Brook-lyn can be proud of her own, and anyway, we're talking American League, not National."

Scooter Rizzuto says, "This is a food I grew up with back in Brooklyn. So, I figured that it was more than appropriate for *The Brooklyn Cookbook*. Here it is.

Phil Rizzuto's Sausage Rolls

NEW YORK YANKEES

Srini

PHIL RIZZUTO DAY

"To *make this recipe very easy, you can use frozen dough. However, it is more true to the recipe if you make your own."*

Dough

1 package active dry yeast
2 cups warm water
4 cups all-purpose flour
1 tablespoon salt
3 tablespoons olive oil

Filling

3 pounds Italian sausage
1 large white onion
Cayenne pepper, if desired

❶ In a small bowl, place the yeast and water. Stir together until the yeast dissolves (approximately 1 to 2 minutes).

❷ Put the flour in a large bowl. Add the salt, olive oil, and the yeast-and-water mixture. Stir until all ingredients are blended together. Continue to stir the contents of the bowl until the dough is of a consistency easy to handle. (You may have to add a small amount of flour if the dough is rough handling.)

❸ Cover the bowl with plastic wrap, then place a small towel over the plastic wrap. Let this mixture rise for about 4 hours.

❹ While the dough is rising, prepare your sausage mixture. Take 3 pounds of sausage out of the casings and put into a bowl. Grate one large white onion into the sausage, then mix thoroughly together. (Cayenne pepper may be added to the sausage if it is desired hot.)

❺ After the dough has risen, roll a small portion out until it is a thin sheet. (Be sure not to roll the dough too thin. This is to ensure that the dough will not rip.)

Preheat the oven to 350 degrees F.

❻ Take the sausage mixture and spread it on the dough. Wrap the dough over the sausage mixture so that it looks like a tube. Cut slices of the dough and sausage as you would a jelly roll.

❼ Place each slice on a cookie sheet and bake for approximately 20 minutes, or until the dough is light brown. Repeat procedure until all dough and sausage mixture is gone. ➽ *Makes about 30 small servings*

▲▲▲▲▲▲▲▲▲▲▲▲▲▲▲▲▲▲▲▲▲▲▲▲▲▲▲▲▲

The Honeymooners
RALPH and Neapolitan Knockwurst

Who's the Greatest? Alice, of course, to her husband Ralph and to all of us who think "The Honeymooners" are among the immortals and never mind staying up late for reruns.

In the 1950s television series, Jackie Gleason played Ralph Kramden, a bus driver from Brooklyn with a big appetite for life and for food. Upstairs from the Kramdens' stark apartment lived their friends Ed and Trixie Norton.

"Food figured prominently in 'The Honeymooners,'" says Peter Crescenti, co-president and founder of RALPH—that's the Royal Association for the Longevity and Preservation of the Honeymooners, a thriving fan club. "Because of Gleason's size, it was an ongoing joke. And skinny little Norton ate much more than Ralph and never gained a pound. Norton had a *weird* appetite; every Wednesday night he'd have chow mein and potato pancakes.

"In an episode called 'The Worrywart,' Ralph gets a letter from the IRS; he immediately envisions himself in jail. Norton invites himself to dinner and wolfs down the spaghetti and meatballs that Ralph is too upset to eat. Norton constantly demands, 'Got any ketchup? Got any piccalilli? Any chow chow?' Ralph explodes: 'When I get through with you, there's gonna be piccalilli all over Bensonhurst!' That became one of the great catch phrases for Honeymooners fans.

"RALPH bought the original Bensonhurst kitchen set used on the series. It had turned up in the mid-'80s at a toy show. We paid $1,500 for it, and it's on loan to the Brooklyn Historical Society, the famous icebox with its drip pan, Alice's rickety stove, and all.

"When the Raccoon Lodge that

RALPH fan club members do the "Chef of the Future" routine from the "Honeymooners" episode "Better Living Through TV."

Ralph and Ed belonged to won a bowling tournament, they threw a victory feast. The spread was three different kinds of pizza, pigs' knuckles, and sauerkraut, and Ralph Kramden's favorite food in the world—Neapolitan knockwurst. At our first convention in 1984, we drew twenty-three hundred people, and we served all of these foods. People just went crazy; even those who weren't hungry ate it just to say, 'I had Neapolitan knockwurst at the convention.'

"Poor Ralph's big plans always failed, but in a way he was a visionary. On one episode this big dreamer and schemer tried to start a no-cal pizzeria. He was ahead of his time."

Neapolitan Knockwurst

This dish probably existed only in the fertile mind of a scriptwriter, but Donna McCrohan, a staunch member of RALPH, came up with a tasty version to satisfy loyalists (and Royalists).

2 hero sandwich rolls
1 pound knockwurst
2 large green bell peppers
2 large red bell peppers
2 medium onions
4 medium tomatoes
1 tablespoon olive oil
½ cup jarred spaghetti sauce

❶ Slice the rolls in half, pull out and discard some of the soft center.

❷ Slice the knockwurst into ½-inch-thick slices. Core and seed the peppers and cut them into ½-inch-thick slices. Slice the onions. Cut the tomatoes into 1-inch chunks.

❸ In a large skillet, cook the knockwurst until it is lightly browned. Add the oil, and cook the peppers and onions with the knockwurst, stirring, until the onions are translucent and soft. Add the tomato chunks and cook just long enough to warm them; you want something that stands up to your teeth when you bite into them.

❹ Divide the filling between the rolls. Heat the sauce in the pan and spoon it over the filling; you want just enough to add flavor. Press the top halves onto the sandwiches and eat. Wear a napkin around your neck. ⟫⊸ *Serves 2*

Prospect Hall

Built in the 1890s as a German opera house, used as a convention center, a gathering place for Park Slope society, and now a private catering establishment, the elaborate, four-story Prospect Hall claims several firsts: it was the first building in the city of Brooklyn to be electrified, and the first to install an Otis elevator. In the 1940s, the team that became the Boston Celtics played basketball here.

When banks and other institutions need to serve dinner to huge numbers of people, they turn to Prospect Hall. The ballroom can hold 3,000 people. Weddings, small and large, are a specialty. (Brides love sweeping down the staircase.) Do you remember the wedding scene in *Prizzi's Honor*? The vast room, the laden tables of food? It was shot here.

FIRST CLASS CATERING

The Grand Prospect Hall

263 PROSPE
BROOKLY

(718)

The Grand Victorian Ballroom.

The Montauk Club

"In opulent late-nineteenth-century Brooklyn, clubs—both men's and women's—sprang to life by the dozen," says Everett Ortner. "Clubs were necessary to show wealth and status. The Venetian Gothic Montauk Club, with its terra-cotta frieze of Montauk Indians, opened as a men's club in 1889.

"All United States presidents from McKinley through Johnson came here," says Mr. Ortner, who is the Montauk's historian. "Our membership is now open to everyone."

Elaborate testimonial dinners were a specialty; the menu here is for one of the many annual banquets honoring Senator and orator Chauncey Depew.

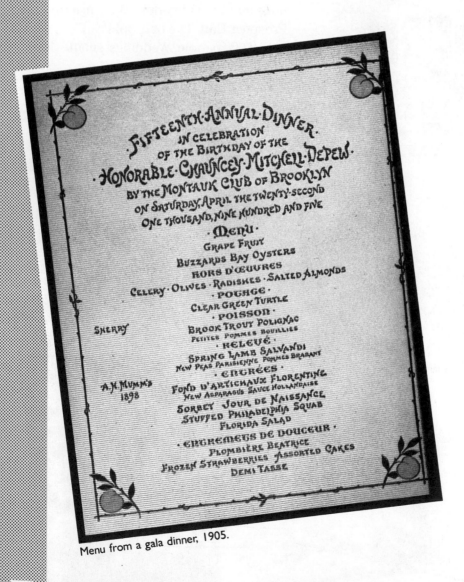

Menu from a gala dinner, 1905.

5

Brewed, Made, Sold, and Served in Brooklyn

COMMERCIAL CLASSICS: The Elixirs (from Brooklyn Beer to Fox's U-Bet syrup), the Comestibles (from Ba-Tampte Pickles to Gold's Horseradish), the Food Purveyors, and the Eating Establishments

Of course not all family businesses are still thriving after a half-century or longer, but an impressive number of those that do are Brooklyn's own. Perhaps it's because the generations trust and respect each other. As Meyer Silberstein of Ba-Tampte Pickle Products says, "I did my best. Now it's my sons' turn."

Of the establishments selling food, Waldbaum's has grown from a dairy store to a very large chain of supermarkets by adhering to a simple but effective principle: respect your customers, and treat them as you would your family. The Park Slope Food Co-op, one of the largest in the country, goes even further—it *is* family, in that all members must share in the work of running this complex food operation.

Restaurants come and go (mostly go), but the time-honored quartet here have all been in business for over half a century. Is it because Brooklynites are loyal? Only in part. You keep them happy, they'll be loyal. These restaurants are doing the job.

The Brooklyn Brewery is new, but its product—beer—was once a mainstay of Brooklyn's prosperity. The last of the old-time breweries closed in the '70s. But now great beer is back in Brooklyn, and that's heady news for us all.

THE ELIXIRS

Brooklyn Beer

Between 1850 and 1880, eleven breweries flourished in a small section of Bushwick. Among them were John Liebmann (founder of the Rheingold Breweries) and Edelbrew. Most of the breweries in this German neighborhood had adjacent beer gardens, also known as "summer gardens," with thumping oompah bands. By 1898, Brooklyn boasted over forty-five beer plants, including Piels and Trommer's; it was one of the great brewing centers of the world. As the Brooklyn *Daily Eagle* pointed out in October 1907, enough was produced to provide every man, woman, and child in the Borough with two barrels of beer or ale a year.

Then came Prohibition. Only a handful of breweries survived. But the great brewing tradition, sparked by Bavarian immigrants in the 19th century, continued, and in 1960 Brooklyn was the major producer of beer in America. However, rising costs forced Piels, Schaefer, and finally Rheingold to close their plants, and by 1973 Brooklyn was beerless. But good news! Brooklyn has suds again. Entrepreneurs Stephen Hindy, formerly a journalist, and Tom Potter, formerly a banker,

Miss Rheingold, 1955.

founded Brooklyn Brewery to make "pre-Prohibition" Brooklyn Lager, a premium, naturally carbonated, nutty brew. If the logo reminds you of the old Dodgers, that is strictly intentional. Hindy and Potter are doing their bit to even the trade gap; they're exporting Brooklyn Beer to Japan. "The name 'Brooklyn' has a strong image to the Japanese," says Hindy. "It conjures up images of a downtown, hip lifestyle."

Brooklyn Beer Cheese

Full-bodied hoppiness makes Brooklyn Lager an excellent cooking beer. Ellen Foote, who is married to Steve Hindy, contributes this recipe for beer cheese, an appetizer.

2 cloves garlic, finely chopped
4 teaspoons Worcestershire sauce
1 teaspoon hot pepper sauce
1 teaspoon dry mustard
½ teaspoon salt
1 cup Brooklyn Lager
4 cups (1 pound) freshly grated sharp
    cheddar cheese

❶ In a deep bowl, crush the garlic with the back of a spoon. Beat in the Worcestershire and hot pepper sauces, mustard, and salt. Stirring constantly, pour in the beer in a slow stream. Beat in the cheese, 1 cup at a time, until the mixture is smooth. (The Beer Cheese can also be made in a food processor.)

❷ Pack the cheese into a 2-cup mold or crock. Cover it with plastic wrap and refrigerate for 24 to 48 hours before serving. Serve with crisp crackers and more Brooklyn Lager. ⫸ *Serves 6 to 8*

Brooklyn Brown Ale Bread

Brown Ale is the latest addition to the Brooklyn Brewery line. Gail Flanery, a painter and printmaker, says it's the quality of the ale that makes this bread so good. Of course, she's married to Tom Potter, one of the owners of the Brooklyn Beer company. You can make the bread with lager, too, but dark ale is best. This recipe makes a dense, flavorful round loaf.

1¼ cups rye flour
2¼ to 2¾ cups all-purpose white flour
2 packages active dry yeast
½ cup warm water
⅔ cup Brooklyn Brown Dark Ale

1 tablespoon honey
1 tablespoon butter
1 teaspoon caraway seeds
1 teaspoon salt
½ teaspoon garlic powder

❶ Mix the rye flour and 1½ cups of the white flour.

❷ In a large warm bowl, combine the yeast and ½ cup of warm water. Set aside.

❸ Gently heat the beer, honey, and butter just until the butter melts. Pour it into the yeast mixture. Stir in the caraway seeds, salt, and garlic powder. Add 1½ cups of the flour mixture and stir until smooth. Add ¾ cup of the remaining flour; turn out on a floured work surface and knead until smooth, adding the rest of the flour as needed to make a soft dough. Knead until smooth, about 4 minutes.

❹ Have ready a greased round 8- or 9-inch cake pan or shallow casserole. Shape the dough into a ball, place it in the pan, and pat it flat. Turn it over and flatten it to fit the pan. Cover it with oiled plastic wrap and let it rise in a draft-free place for 45 minutes.

Preheat the oven to 375 degrees F.

❺ Bake the bread for 35 to 40 minutes, or until a toothpick inserted in the center comes out clean. Let it cool in the pan for 10 minutes, then cool it on a rack. ⫸ *Makes 1 round loaf*

▲▲▲▲▲▲▲▲▲▲▲▲▲▲▲▲▲▲▲▲▲▲▲▲▲▲▲▲▲

Fox's U-Bet Chocolate Syrup

What's a classic? You're asking what's a classic? Fox's U-Bet Chocolate Flavor Syrup is a *classic*. You absolutely cannot make an egg cream without Fox's U-Bet. David Fox is the third-generation Fox to make Brooklyn's elixir. The firm, founded sometime between 1910 and 1920 ("Honest to God, I don't know when this thing started exactly"), began in a Brownsville basement. It's still in Brownsville, but in an 18,000 square foot location. The recipe for U-Bet remains the same: Brooklyn water, sugar, corn sweeteners, cocoa, and some "secret things."

The name "U-Bet" dates from the late '20s, when Fox's grandfather got wildcatting fever and headed to Texas to drill for oil. "You bet" was a friendly term the oilmen used. His oil venture a failure, he returned to the old firm, changing Fox's Chocolate Syrup to Fox's U-Bet. He said, "I came back broke, but with a good name for the syrup," his grandson relates.

Fox has fan letters from Mel Brooks, Don Rickles, Jerry Lewis, and a slew of just plain U-Betaholics. To quote Mel Brooks: "You got to get Fox's U-Bet syrup. If you use any other syrup, the egg cream will be too bitter or too mild." Nowadays U-Bet is sold in every state, "except maybe Utah."

You shouldn't have to ask, but there is no egg or cream in an egg cream. Just milk, seltzer, and U-Bet.

Egg Cream for One

A little milk (maybe 3 ounces)
A lot of seltzer (8 ounces)

More Fox's U-Bet than you would think (2 ounces at least)

Pour milk into a regular-sized glass. Spritz seltzer in until white foamy head reaches top of glass. Spoon in syrup and mix with a little wrist action.
➤ *Makes 1 egg cream*

There's only one way to make an egg cream, right? Hey, this is Brooklyn! Ron Schweiger, a high school math teacher, has the *correct* way:

Schweiger Egg Cream

"**M**y grandparents and uncle bought a candy store on East 8th Street and Avenue S in the early 1940s, and all through the '50s it was the place to hang out and watch the ball game, on the black and white TV in the back. They made frappes, and of course the best egg creams.

"First, you use Fox's U-Bet. Take a tall Coke-type glass, from the 1950s. Put in ¾ inch of syrup, then milk up to one-third of the glass. Then you add seltzer from a spritz bottle, the heavy kind with seltzer under pressure. You tilt the glass; if it's tilted, the force of the seltzer squirted under the milk and syrup pushes foam up on the other side. Fill the rest of the glass with more seltzer, stirring as you spritz. The foam should be white, and at least ½ inch thick. The greatest!"

▲▲▲▲▲▲▲▲▲▲▲▲▲▲▲▲▲▲▲▲▲▲▲▲▲▲▲▲

Manhattan Special Coffee Soda

Enrico Caruso loved it. Company-sponsored pool sharks, tank fighters, and baseball farm teams sported the company name. "Gimme a bottle of Manhattan Special!" demanded Dodgers Sal Maglie, Carl Erskine, Ralph Branca, Clem Labine, and Gene Hermanski in an old TV commercial. Manhattan Special Coffee Soda (named not for the island but for the plant's site on Manhattan Avenue in Greenpoint) is the quintessential Italian soft drink, and has been since 1895, when Michael Garavuso began sifting sugar by hand into espresso brewed in small batches and stopping the heavy bottles with corks.

"This is a family business," says

THE ORIGINAL FOR OVER 80 YEARS

PASSARO'S FAMOUS

Manhattan Special®

The World's Most Delicious Pure Coffee Soda

SIX 10 OZ BOTTLES (60 FL OZS)

company president Aurora Passaro. "My great-grandmother, a chiropractor, invented the original formula. My grandfather Lewis began working on a cart in 1908 at the age of nine; he became the distributor. And my father, Al Passaro, bought the business from Michael's daughter.

"When my father was a young man with a route," says Aurora Passaro, "he'd do his quota, then stop off with the other guys for a capocollo, pepper, and provolone hero, and a Manhattan Special. And you absolutely cannot eat a pizza in Brooklyn without one of our sodas!" Apparently you wouldn't want to eat roasted lamb in Saudi Arabia without a Manhattan Special either; the company ships an impressive number of cases there.

Aurora Passaro recommends a scoop of vanilla ice cream in a Manhattan Special: "The perfect float. Nice with a little vodka too," she adds.

Steve Barrison's Super Coffee Milkshake

"I *started making shakes as a teen-ager," says Steve Barrison, "and I was looking for an alternative to chocolate. I wanted coffee, like Mom and Dad. Each time I found a coffee product, I tried it. Manhattan Special adds the right touch. I made shakes daily from the age of thirteen right through college, where I had a refrigerator and a blender in my room. In law school, my study group all drank Steve's Super Shake. Now when I visit friends I make shakes for their teenagers." How does Steve keep lean and keen? "Abdominal exercises. At least seven minutes a day. Guaranteed to work."*

7 ounces milk
2 ounces Manhattan Special Coffee Soda
2 ounces freshly brewed coffee, or 2 teaspoons instant coffee

4 to 5 scoops coffee ice cream
1 to 2 shots Kahlua*
3 ice cubes (more in summer)

Place everything in a blender. Hold the lid and begin blending at the lowest setting, increasing the speed to the highest setting. Blend for at least 2 minutes. ⟫→ *Makes 2 full 8-ounce glasses*

*The addition of alcohol is, of course, only for adults.

▲▲▲▲▲▲▲▲▲▲▲▲▲▲▲▲▲▲▲▲▲▲▲▲▲▲▲

THE COMESTIBLES

▲▲▲▲▲▲▲▲▲▲▲▲▲▲▲▲▲▲▲▲▲▲▲▲▲▲▲▲▲

Ba-Tampte Pickles

What's a pastrami sandwich without a pickle? Don't ask. But be fussy. Get the best, made the old-fashioned way, and packed in good, pure Brooklyn water.

Ba-Tampte Pickle Products, in the Brooklyn Terminal Market in Canarsie, is now seeing its fourth generation of Silbersteins. "My mother's father came to New York in 1908, and sold pickles from a pushcart," says Meyer Silberstein. "My father came from Galicia, in Poland, some years later. He had no trade, so he helped on the pushcart. He married the boss's daughter. By 1914 he opened his own pickle stand, and I was born in that year." The Lower East Side was then the heart of pickle country—the move to Brooklyn would come later, when Mr. Silberstein changed his pickling operation from retail to wholesale.

"At the age of fourteen," he continues, "I told my father I wasn't school material. I helped him, and I opened my own stand. In the old days, we'd make a beautiful display with the pickles, and say, 'Don't touch! No hands!' Invariably, a customer would grab. 'No hands!' I'd yell in Yiddish. 'You should have no feet!' she'd yell back. There was a certain type of busy short woman— you'd think she was catching a train—who pushed her way to the front, grabbed a pickle, and demanded the price, waving it under your nose. Big ones could be a nickel, little ones a penny. No matter how big, she'd insist the pickle was tiny.

"The company was called the Edible Pickle Works, but when we moved to Brooklyn in 1955 we changed the name. A dear friend suggested 'Ba-tampte,' which means 'tasty' in Jewish. Our pickle recipe is the same as every housewife knew—just cucumbers, spices, salt, water, garlic, and dill. That's it. No chemicals. Many pickle factories use dehydrated or liquid garlic, but not us. We use as much as a ton of garlic a week, regardless of price."

"Making pickles is a lot of work," interjects Howard, one of Meyer's sons. "You have to have the right cucumbers, the right water. Some you cure one way, some another. It's a crap shoot; if you guess right, you got a good pickle."

Ba-Tampte makes half-sour and garlic dill pickles, prepared horseradish, mustard, pickled peppers, and sauerkraut. Products are shipped to twenty states, with a large volume of business done in Florida. Meyer's grandson Scott works during summers at Ba-Tampte and is studying business administration in college.

"In my day, the average person ate a pickle that was fully fermented. Now Americans go for half-sours," says Meyer. (The bright green half-sours aren't really pickled; cucumbers are sprinkled with garlic, and flavored with herbs and spices such as mustard seeds, cloves, bay leaves, and coriander. Pickle makers, Ba-Tampte included, keep their spice mixtures a secret. Two days or so in a brine solution, and they are ready for sale.) "If you want them fully sour, don't refrigerate a new jar of pickles. Leave them on the counter for a few days till they get a little cloudy—that means they are fermenting. Open the cap and let the gas escape. Recap and refrigerate. I want it understood that our pickles are not cooked for long shelf life, and we do not use vinegar. I like my pickles yellow, you may like yours green. Pickles can satisfy everybody."

"The Pickle Polka," by Irving Fields.

Gold's Horseradish

The largest root cellar in the world is on McDonald Avenue in Coney Island. There, horseradish root from around the globe is kept at a steady 40 degrees F, waiting to be processed into Gold's Horseradish. Back in 1932, Tillie Gold ground horseradish near an open window to let the fumes escape, added salt and vinegar, spooned the mixture into jars, and pasted on labels by hand. Her husband hawked it from a pushcart. Sons Morris and Herbert took the business much further, and today grandsons Marc, Steven, Neil, and Howard run the business. Gold's makes most of the bottled horseradish in the world. Each little bottle contains only horseradish, salt, and water; grated beets are added to make red horseradish. The company revs up to a double shift before the Jewish holidays of Rosh Hashanah and Passover. The Golds supplied the recipe.

Apple Matzo Kugel with Horseradish

4 matzos
3 eggs, well beaten
Salt to taste
½ cup honey
¼ cup vegetable oil
1 teaspoon ground cinnamon

1 tablespoon horseradish
½ cup chopped walnuts
2 Granny Smith apples, peeled and
   chopped
½ cup white raisins

Preheat the oven to 350 degrees F.

❶ Break the matzos into pieces, soak in water, and drain well.

❷ Combine the eggs, salt, honey, oil, cinnamon, and horseradish. Add to the matzo, mixing well. Stir in the nuts, apples, and raisins.

❸ Place the mixture in a greased 8-inch-square pan and bake for 45 minutes. ⇒ *Serves 6*

Goya

Back in 1936 Don Prudencio Unanue and his wife, Doña Carolina Casal, reasoned that the growing numbers of Puerto Ricans in New York were eager for the familiar foods of their island. Their Goya Foods company began distributing olives, olive oil, and canned fish through the mom-and-pop stores called bodegas that serve New York's Latino neighborhoods. Beginning modestly in downtown Manhattan, Goya Foods soon moved to Brooklyn.

The large Unanue family lived comfortably in the Prospect Park neighborhood. As New York's huge Caribbean population grew, so did Goya, becoming the nation's largest family-owned Hispanic company. It was expected that the kids would work in the plant during school vacations, the boys in the warehouse and the girls in the office. "Unless you were in the hospital or on your deathbed, you were there,"

says Joey, who is now known as Joseph F. Unanue, Executive Vice-President of Goya Foods. It really did not occur to them that the family was rich.

During the 1960s, the huge red and blue Goya sign was a landmark along the Brooklyn–Queens Expressway; "Just past the Goya sign" or "This side of the Goya sign" were familiar directions for motorists. One afternoon four of the young heirs—Joey, Bobby, Tommy, and Carly—were working at the plant. Teenage talk led to a challenge: "Let's climb the sign." An hour later came a call to the front desk: "Four vandals are scaling that fifty-foot-high sign."

The "vandals" are now executives at Goya, still a family concern despite its size. It has moved its headquarters to New Jersey. Eighteen members of the third generation work for Goya, too.

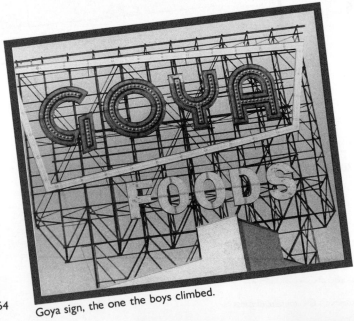

Goya sign, the one the boys climbed.

Five-Bean Salad

Accompany a barbecue with this salad, or serve it as part of any buffet.

⅓ cup red-wine vinegar
2 tablespoons freshly squeezed lime juice
1 teaspoon dry mustard
1 cup or more fruity olive oil, to taste
1 clove garlic, slightly crushed
Salt and freshly ground black pepper to taste

1 16-ounce can each: pink beans, white beans, chickpeas, black beans, cut green beans, preferably Goya, all drained and rinsed
2 small red onions, sliced thin
1 cup cherry tomatoes (optional)
½ cup pitted green olives (optional)

❶ Whisk together the vinegar, lime juice, and mustard. Add the oil, garlic clove, salt and pepper. Let the dressing marinate for 30 minutes.

❷ Remove the garlic clove and toss the beans with the dressing. You may serve the tossed bean salad in a large bowl, or you can toss each variety of bean individually with some of the dressing and layer them separately in a high-sided glass bowl for visual effect.

❸ Garnish the salad with the onion rings and optional tomatoes and olives, and chill for at least 1 hour before serving. ⫸ *Serves 10 or more*

▲▲▲▲▲▲▲▲▲▲▲▲▲▲▲▲▲▲▲▲▲▲▲▲▲▲▲▲

Boar's Head

The snappy rig shown in the picture delivered Mr. Brunckhorst's ham, sausage, and other delicatessen products to mom-and-pop stores, under the brand name Boar's Head.

The company began in 1905, and in 1933 the first plant was built in Brooklyn. The company, in its third generation, now ships all over the United States.

Boar's Head All-American Hero

¼ pound Boar's Head Branded Deluxe Ham
¼ pound Boar's Head Gold Turkey
¼ pound salami
¼ pound Swiss cheese

A loaf of Italian bread, 1 foot long
Mustard
1 or 2 tomatoes, sliced
Lettuce

❶ For fullest flavor, slice the cold cuts and cheese thin. Cut the loaf in half lengthwise. Pull out some of the soft interior from the top half to make a cavity.

❷ Lightly spread the bottom half with mustard. Layer the meats onto the sandwich. Top with cheese, sliced tomatoes, and lettuce. Press the halves together and cut into serving pieces. ⟫→ *Serves 2*

The Boar's Head team and wagon, early twentieth century.

Joyva

Halvah is a Turkish confection made with crushed sesame seeds and honey—crumbly and delicious. Hawked by Middle Eastern vendors at the turn of the century, halvah soon became a favorite with Jewish immigrants, and was sold in delicatessens.

Nathan Radutzky, a Russian immigrant, began making halvah in Brooklyn in 1906. Nathan's sons, Alex, Harry, Max, and Milton, now run the largest halvah operation in the world. They also produce tahini, a paste made of lightly roasted, crushed sesame seeds that is a staple in Middle Eastern dishes.

Yogurt Tahini Dressing

Use this dressing with salad greens or on cooked or raw vegetables.

½ cup tahini paste
½ cup plain yogurt
2 to 3 garlic cloves, minced

½ cup lemon juice
Salt to taste

It is easiest to make this dressing in a blender. Put in all the ingredients and whirl until smooth. For lighter consistency, add a little water.

➤ *Makes 1 cup of dressing*

THE FOOD PURVEYORS

Waldbaum's
Loose Milk and Romance

Today Waldbaum's is a mighty chain of 103 supermarkets, but not so very many years ago the Waldbaum brothers had only a few small dairy stores, carrying milk, eggs, butter, cheese, and canned and smoked fish. To save money, people bought milk "loose," rather than by the bottle. To save her parents a trip, Julia Leffel used to bring an empty pitcher to the store on De Kalb Avenue, leave it, promenade with her girlfriends after supper, and hasten to pick up her pitcher, filled with "loose milk" before ten o'clock when the store closed. "When business was slow, Izzy Waldbaum would come out and sit on the milk-can repository in front of the store. He'd say 'Good night.' Later on, he'd walk me home, carrying the pitcher of milk. See what God does? One never knows," says Julia Waldbaum.

"After Izzy and I were married, I'd put the kids in the car and go help

The store where Julia met Izzy.

368

out when I was needed. But I really stayed home to raise my children," Julia says. The number of stores grew, but "There was personal involvement, and a real family feeling," she continues. "In the back of the store, coffee was going at all times and the employees had lunch there, helping themselves to anything they liked."

"It was after World War II that the chain really began," says Randie Malinsky, Julia's granddaughter. "People wanted to drive to a place that had everything under one roof, instead of going to individual butchers and bakers. And technology—refrigeration and transport—made it possible.

"It was always a family business," says Randie. "Julia's sister Sylvia was the bookkeeper, and her brother Bunny was vice president of frozen foods. Uncle Irving and nephews Joe and Jerry and son-in-law David were part of it. Julia and Izzy's son, Ira, is president and built the chain. So many of us! Even those not directly related were like family. The business grew, relying on these people, from neighborhood mom-and-pop stores to a big chain.

"We celebrated everyone's holidays, the employees' and the customers', too. As time went on, Julia became the good-will ambassador, going to stores and talking to everyone.

"The family part of Julia really

Julia and Izzy in the back yard, Avenue K.

is the essence of her. We're a very large, very close family, and everyone gets together for holidays. We don't go to one 'side' or the other. If we invite our cousins, their in-laws come too. It's what is called *ganz mespuchah* in Yiddish, 'the whole family.' I don't think it's that usual today. And Julia is the center.

"My grandma Julia really is the best cook in the family. She used to come to our house and make *kreplachs* for my mother, and she brought them to family gatherings," says Randie. "I learned everything from my mother," says Julia Waldbaum. "She was the most wonderful woman in the world."

Kreplachs

Kreplachs have been called "Jewish wontons." They are triangular bits of dough with a rich meat filling. "These are kreplachs like my mother made," says Julia Waldbaum. "You want to chop the meat by hand in a wooden bowl, with a curved knife. That's important. It should have a stringy texture, not a ground one. You put them into homemade chicken soup, or you can eat them plain."

Dough
5 eggs
1¼ teaspoons salt
4 tablespoons water
4 cups all-purpose flour

Filling
2½ pounds chuck or leftover pot roast
1 large or 2 small onions
½ cup rendered chicken fat
2 eggs
Salt and pepper to taste

❶ To make the dough, beat the egg slightly, add the salt, water, and 3 cups of the flour. Add as much more flour as is necessary to make a dough that is easy to handle. Knead it by hand for 10 minutes or use a food processor or a heavy-duty mixer equipped with a dough hook. Cover it with plastic wrap or a towel and let it stand for 15 minutes.

❷ Boil the beef (unless you are using leftovers) in lightly salted water until tender. When it is cool enough to handle, chop it well (see above), leaving some texture.

❸ Chop the onion fine and cook it in the chicken fat until soft but not brown. In a bowl, combine the meat and onion and stir in the eggs. Add lots of salt and pepper.

❹ Divide the dough into manageable pieces and roll it out thin. Cut the rolled dough into 2-inch squares. Place about 1 teaspoon of filling on each square, and fold the dough in half diagonally to make a triangle. Pinch the edges together to seal, then fold the corners over and pinch again. (Kreplach can be placed on a baking sheet and frozen at this point.) Let the kreplach rest to dry slightly before boiling.

❺ Have ready a large pot of lightly salted boiling water. Drop in the kreplach in batches, and boil for 20 to 25 minutes.

⋙→ *Makes 100 or more kreplach*

Park Slope Food Co-op

The late 1960s and early 1970s saw the beginning of what the media dubbed Park Slope's "gentrification." This somewhat disparaging term rightly annoyed those people who saw themselves as urban pioneers, reclaiming a once-fine neighborhood that had run drastically to seed. In the late 19th century, Park Slope, an area of some four thousand fine brownstone rowhouses, imposing clubs, and mansions, was the most affluent community in all of the United States. After World War II, when many buildings had become rooming houses for workers in the Brooklyn Navy Yard, young and old joined the rush to suburban Long Island. Park Slope's decline began.

The "gentrifiers" saw themselves not as gentry at all, just young families in search of a real neighborhood and homes to be proud of. Most of them did daunting amounts of work themselves. That meant that Joe and Mary, who'd left their shoebox apartment in Manhattan and spent all they had for a four-story brownstone in the Slope, had, along with potentially elegant space, a change of lifestyle. Both now commuted back to Manhattan by subway, worked all day, came home, changed into jeans, and plunged into plastering, painting, plumbing, and eating take-out pizza and Chinese. For years. And years.

One of the Borough's earliest co-ops: Gertzog's in Sheepshead Bay, 1947.

Out of that do-it-yourself spirit the Park Slope Co-Op was born—people who work jointly, as volunteers, to supply most of their needs at impressive savings. The little buying group begun in 1973 is now the city's largest co-op, with 2,600 members and sales in the millions. No fish, meat, or poultry, but sixty kinds of cheeses, four to six varieties of tomatoes in season, dried Formosa mushrooms, four varieties of rice, rose hips, and paper products.

Each member, and you must be a member to shop, works three hours every four weeks at bagging, office work, and other chores. "You'll save fifty percent off health food prices, and thirty percent off supermarket prices," says produce buyer Joe Holtz, one of only seven paid staff members.

Karen Karp, a restaurant consultant, writes the recipes that appear in the Co-op newsletter. "Sometimes when I'm waiting on line to pay," she says, "and I look around me at the diversity of people, I think that this is what Brooklyn must have been like early in the century. To feel a part of the ethnic mix of the city is my favorite thing about the Co-op."

Pumpkin and Potato Soup with Kale,
Karen Karp

2 tablespoons olive oil
1 medium onion, chopped
3 to 4 cloves garlic, minced
3 tablespoons miso paste*
3 quarts water
1 pound organic new potatoes
1 small organic pumpkin, about 1¾ pounds, to yield 1 pound when peeled and cubed

½ bunch kale, leaves only, washed and torn into bite-sized pieces
3 tablespoons minced parsley
Red-wine vinegar, to taste
Salt and freshly ground pepper, to taste
Hot ground red pepper, to taste
Grated Parmesan cheese to pass at table

❶ Heat the olive oil in a heavy soup pot. Add the onion, reduce the heat to moderate, and cook until the onion is just wilted. Add the garlic and miso; stir until the miso dissolves and colors the onion and garlic.

❷ Add the water. With the pot covered, bring liquid to just below the boil. Reduce the heat and simmer.

❸ Meanwhile, scrub the potatoes and cut them into ½-inch cubes. Peel and cut the pumpkin into ½-inch cubes. Add them to the pot. Simmer for about 20 minutes, or until the potato has cooked. The pumpkin will break up and thicken the soup.

❹ Just before serving, add the kale, the parsley, and the seasonings. Cook just long enough to wilt the kale, less than 1 minute. Pass the cheese at table.

⫸ *Serves 8*

Note: If you plan to serve the soup over several days, just add a little kale with each reheating.

*Miso paste, a flavorful soy product, can be found in Japanese and health food stores.

Fresh Tomato Tart

Because pastry dough freezes so well, make enough for two tarts with one use of the processor. Make this tart only when tomatoes are at their best.

Pastry
1¾ cups all-purpose flour
½ teaspoon salt
1 tablespoon sugar
12 tablespoons (1¼ sticks) cold
    unsalted butter, cut into bits
4 tablespoons ice water

Filling
5 medium ripe tomatoes, thinly sliced

¼ cup Dijon mustard
¾ pound mozzarella cheese, thinly
    sliced
1 tablespoon chopped garlic
2 teaspoons crumbled dried oregano
Kosher salt and freshly ground pepper
    to taste
2 tablespoons fruity olive oil

❶ Put the flour, salt, and sugar in the bowl of a food processor equipped with the metal blade. Pulse several times to sift. Add the butter and pulse until the mixture resembles coarse meal. With the motor running, pour the ice water through the feed tube and process only until a ball begins to form. Remove the dough and cut it in half. Wrap half the dough in plastic wrap and refrigerate it for 30 minutes. Wrap the other half well and freeze it; it will last up to 2 months.

Preheat the oven to 400 degrees F.

❷ Have ready a 10-inch tart pan with a removable bottom. Place the chilled dough on a floured work surface. Roll it out to a 10-inch circle ⅛ inch thick. Gently lift it onto the tart pan bottom. (At this point you can cover it with plastic wrap and chill or freeze it until needed.)

Fresh Tomato Tart (continued)

❸ Slice the tomatoes very thin. Spread the mustard over the dough, and arrange the mozzarella slices to cover the dough completely. Starting at the outside of the tart, begin overlapping tomato slices, working your way to the center. Sprinkle the garlic and oregano over the tart, season with salt and pepper, and drizzle with the olive oil. Place the tart on a baking sheet and bake for 40 minutes. Serve the tart at room temperature. ⋙→ *Serves 4 to 6*

▲▲▲▲▲▲▲▲▲▲▲▲▲▲▲▲▲▲▲▲▲▲▲▲▲▲▲▲▲▲▲

THE EATING ESTABLISHMENTS

▲▲▲▲▲▲▲▲▲▲▲▲▲▲▲▲▲▲▲▲▲▲▲▲▲▲▲▲▲▲▲▲▲▲

Junior's Most Fabulous Restaurant Cafe Bar

Any place that's been in business since 1929, uses 7,500 pounds of cream cheese each week, and ships 2,000 cheesecakes by parcel post each month must be baking something right. Junior's on Flatbush Avenue, the self-styled "Heart and Pulse of Downtown Brooklyn," is part coffee shop, part deli, part restaurant. All the food, from five kinds of muffins at breakfast to the daily ton of brisket and pastrami served 365 days a year, is made on the premises.

"Our decision to stay in Brooklyn after we were almost destroyed by the 1981 fire was important for this area," says Sherry Rosen, granddaughter of founder Harry Rosen. "We are a landmark, and we are the anchor for this neighborhood."

"Why Junior's?" is a question often heard in Brooklyn. The place was originally called Enduro's, but the owner changed it, naming the place after his son, called Junior. Simple.

It's true that the neighborhood has changed since the days when Junior's catered to patrons of downtown Brooklyn's picture palaces like the Paramount across the street, when headliners such as Frank Sinatra and disc jockey Alan Freed sustained the inner man on Junior's smoked lake sturgeon and crispy corned beef. And the Albee and Fox theaters have given way to shopping malls and office buildings. Now Junior's has become what owner Marvin Rosen, son of the founder, calls a "destination" restaurant, not just a convenient drop-in spot, for those who think Junior's is the best there is.

As one loyalist put it: "On chill winter nights or crisp fall evenings, the sight of burgers on the grill in Junior's window was like watching a yule log. In spring and summer, a fabulous ice cream dish made one feel part of Brooklyn's answer to Rome's Via Veneto . . . and where else could one get such cheesecake?"

Junior's Cheesecake

"Body, richness, and a seductively smooth texture" are Marvin Rosen's criteria for his famed cheesecake, developed by baker Eigel Peterson in 1950. Winner of any number of Best Cheesecake contests, the cake was described by one critic as "creamy, rather sweet, with a light texture." Below is Junior's own recipe.

2 tablespoons unsalted butter
Graham crackers
⅞ cup sugar
3 tablespoons sifted cornstarch
30 ounces cream cheese, at room
    temperature

1 extra-large egg
½ cup heavy cream
¾ teaspoon vanilla

❶ Liberally grease the side and bottom of an 8-inch springform pan with the butter. Crush to powder enough graham crackers to lightly coat the bottom. Coat the bottom with the cracker crumbs and refrigerate the pan until ready to use.

❷ Mix the sugar with the cornstarch. Add the cream cheese and stir to blend well; stir in the egg and blend again. Add the heavy cream, a little at a time, and mix. Stir in the vanilla. Spoon batter into prepared pan.

Preheat the oven to 450 degrees F.

❸ Bake for approximately 40 to 45 minutes, until the top is golden brown. Transfer the cheesecake to a rack and let it cool for 3 hours. ⫸→ *Makes 1 8-inch cheesecake*

Abraham & Straus Department Stores

In 1865, Abraham Abraham opened a small dry-goods store on Fulton Street, selling supplies to women who made their own clothes. This small store grew into Brooklyn's finest department store, which Mr. Abraham ran with his partner, Mr. Straus.

In the mid-1920s, says Bud Gilbert, Food Service Director for all fifteen A&S stores, "a certain clientele arrived in chauffeured limousines, specifically to eat in the Garden Room restaurant. It was called the 'white glove' trade. Prime rib was $1.35 and a full turkey dinner, 80 cents. The most expensive item on the menu was lobster; a dinner was $2.35. Actually, the elegant Garden Room was fairly expensive for the time."

Cream of Garlic Soup

A resident of Bay Ridge, Bud Gilbert cooks at home, "all the time." This recipe is a favorite. "I prefer elephant garlic," he says, "because though it's larger, it's milder than regular garlic."

1 loaf stale French bread
3 large sweet onions, coarsely chopped
1 whole head of elephant garlic, peeled and sliced, or 1 whole head regular garlic
4 ounces (1 stick) unsalted butter
1 quart chicken stock, homemade or best quality canned
1 to 2 cups heavy cream
Salt to taste, if needed
2 tablespoons chopped chives, for garnish

❶ Cut the loaf of bread into cubes or thick slices. Put the onions and garlic in a heavy soup pot with the butter. Over low to moderate heat, cook until the onions are translucent and soft. Stir often, taking care that the onions and garlic do not burn.

❷ Add the chicken stock and bring to the boil. Reduce the heat, partially cover, and simmer for 30 minutes.

❸ Off the heat, add the bread to the soup. Let sit, covered, for about 15 minutes, until the bread is thoroughly softened.

❹ Transfer the soup, in batches, to a food processor or blender. Blend to a smooth purée.

❺ Return the soup to the pot. Depending on the thickness desired, add 1 or 2 cups of cream. Reheat gently. Garnish with chopped chives to serve.

≫→ *Serves 6 to 8*

The Peter Luger Steak House

▲▲▲▲▲▲▲▲▲▲▲▲▲▲▲▲▲▲▲▲▲▲▲▲▲▲▲▲▲▲▲▲▲

Just under the Brooklyn side of the Williamsburg Bridge, in a dingy, deserted section of old warehouses and junk-filled lots, stands what many call the finest steak house in America: the Peter Luger Steak House. It's been there since 1887, and the owners see no reason to move. Why should they? Diners by the drove are eager to make the trip.

What they'll find is a serious eating establishment in the ponderous old Germanic style — dark wood walls, bentwood chairs, bare wooden tables, and huge ornate tankards and brass salvers by way of decoration. You want chichi, go somewhere else. People come here for meat and potatoes.

And what meat! The finest short loins and shells are dry-aged in Luger's own lockers, cut into T-bones and shell steaks, then blasted under ferocious gas-flame broilers. This perfect meat needs no hint of charcoal. You get steak thickly sliced, and share it family style.

Meat this good needs great potatoes. Peter Luger's has them.

Luger's German Fried Potatoes

When you work with hot oil you need tranquility, which you are not likely to find in a rush before a dinner party. Therefore it's a good idea to do the first frying early in the day, or even the day before. Strain the oil and save it; it will be good for one more fry.

··

5 large Idaho potatoes
Vegetable oil for frying
1½ cups chopped onions
½ teaspoon paprika
¼ teaspoon salt

6 tablespoons (¾ stick) unsalted
  butter
1 teaspoon salt, or to taste
Freshly ground white pepper, to taste

❶ Peel the potatoes and cut them into ½-inch strips (like French fries). Place the potato strips in a large bowl of cold water as they are cut.

❷ Dry the potato strips well in towels. Pour about ¾ inch of oil into a wide pan like a Dutch oven, or use an electric deep-fryer. Heat the oil to the boiling point. Fry the potatoes in 3 batches until lightly browned; each batch should take about 10 minutes. Turn them from time to time to prevent sticking. Drain on paper. Between batches, let the oil cook for about 3 minutes to evaporate any water from the potatoes; water retards browning. When they are cool, cut the potato strips into ¼-inch cubes.

❸ When the potatoes have cooled, heat 2 tablespoons of the frying oil in a heavy skillet. When it is sizzling, add the onion, paprika, and ¼ teaspoon salt. Cook, stirring, until the onions are soft and lightly browned. Set aside. (The potato dish can be done ahead to this point.)

Preheat the oven to 400 degrees F.

❹ When you are ready to do the final cooking of the potatoes, heat a large heavy iron skillet or other ovenproof pan. Melt the butter and add the potatoes and onion. Mix them together. Cook, stirring occasionally, until the mixture is browned. Season with salt and pepper.

❺ Crisp the potatoes in the oven 5 to 10 minutes. ⟫→ *Makes 6 servings*

▲▲▲▲▲▲▲▲▲▲▲▲▲▲▲▲▲▲▲▲▲▲▲▲▲▲▲▲▲▲▲▲▲▲▲

Gage & Tollner

In 1879 Charles Gage opened an eating house on Fulton Street. Eugene Tollner became his partner a year later, and in 1892 Gage & Tollner moved to its present site, 372 Fulton Street. The restaurant is landmarked, which means that virtually nothing of its interior may be changed: heavy mahogany tables still line both sides of the deep, narrow room, and the mirrored walls reflect the glow of overhead gaslights. Shellfish and chops were always the featured dishes of this venerable house, but its new chef, Edna Lewis—an author whose books celebrate full-flavored, well-seasoned Southern cooking—has brought new verve to Gage & Tollner. The restaurant features her Charleston She-Crab Soup and Spareribs with Red Rice, but she is also happy to cook old favorites that have been on the menu for a century, such as Seasoned Clam Bellies. "I am told that at one time the restaurant served clam bellies in fifty different ways," says Mrs. Lewis. "Today the list is down to sixteen, but clam bellies remain as popular as ever. My favorite is Seasoned Fry."

Mrs. Lewis says that clam bellies are sold, ready to cook, in large cartons. "You needn't add salt, because the cracker crumbs are salty," she notes. "Sometimes the clam bellies are a bit sandy. You have to expect that."

Soft Clam Bellies Seasoned Fry

3 cups cracker crumbs
½ teaspoon black pepper
1 tablespoon paprika

1½ pounds ready-to-cook soft clam bellies
Vegetable oil for deep-frying

❶ Place the cracker crumbs in a large mixing bowl. Add the black pepper and paprika and mix well.

❷ Dip the clam bellies in the crumb mixture and shake off the excess.

❸ In a deep-fryer or other deep pan slowly heat at least 3 inches of vegetable oil until it reaches 375 degrees F on a deep-frying thermometer. Fry the clam bellies for 2 minutes, or until nicely browned. Drain on paper towels. (Fry them in batches so they do not crowd the pan.) Divide the clam bellies among 4 warmed plates. ⟫→ *Serves 4*

Edna Lewis at Gage & Tollner.

▲▲▲▲▲▲▲▲▲▲▲▲▲▲▲▲▲▲▲▲▲▲▲▲▲▲▲▲▲▲▲

The Legendary Bakery
Elegy for Ebinger's

"**A**bandoned and deprived" is how Leonard S. Elman described himself and his fellow Brooklynites when Ebinger's chain of bakeries closed its doors in 1972. Perhaps only the loss of the Dodgers was more lamented.

In 1898, Arthur Ebinger, a German immigrant, opened a store on Flatbush Avenue. He baked specialties of the old country, and his wife waited on the customers. Soon several stores were opened, with a horse-drawn wagon delivering goods baked at the central bakery to the newer stores. Rigorous attention to quality, purity, and taste were the marks of an Ebinger product, and that never changed no matter how many outlets appeared. Only the freshest butter and eggs, the finest chocolate and coconut, were used.

"The only time I ever saw an entire boxcar filled with butter was at Ebinger's," an old-time baker recalls with awe. Ebinger's main glory was its cakes, but customers swore by their pies (pumpkin was a favorite) and their rye, White Mountain, and braided challah breads.

Sons Arthur, George, and Walter began sweeping the floors in the bakery, in the hoary apprentice tradition of learning the business from the ground up. It was Arthur who expanded the business to retail stores throughout the Borough; alas, overexpansion into Long Island sent the company into bankruptcy. At the time of closing there were at least fifty-eight stores.

Brooklynites remember: **Leonard S. Elman.** "You bought only cake at Ebinger's. And you went willingly, enthusiastically to buy it,

Ebinger's, closed.

even if that meant accompanying your mother or sister. Three Ebinger's cakes stir the fondest recollections of my contemporaries, regardless of gender: chocolate hard-icing cake, buttercream cake, and finally, of course, Chocolate Blackout Cake, with its layers of moist chocolate cake, soft chocolate cream separating the layers, soft creamy chocolate icing, sprinkled over with crumbs of the chocolate cake itself.

"Brooklynites are united in the belief that their lives were impoverished when Ebinger's closed its doors for the last time, the victim of supermarkets and calorie counting. (We kept an Ebinger's hard-icing cake in our freezer for a year after the last Ebinger's store closed. We finally ate it, feeling as if we were drinking our last bottle of 1929 Lafite.)"

Elizabeth White. "I learned about Ebinger's the day after I came to work in the Brooklyn Collection of the Public Library. When I got to my new job, I heard my fellow workers talking about going to buy a cake at Ebinger's. From the way they were talking, in a mixture of awe and greed, I knew this was not just a cake—it was almost like Percival describing the Holy Grail with overtones of, in more modern terms, Indiana Jones contemplating a vision of the Lost Ark. Later, when I had my first taste of Blackout Cake, I understood."

Nancy Sandack Fried. "I remember eating the Napoleon, a dark, chocolate-covered 'egg,' with butter-cream in the center. When we had company, Mother always bought the Boston cream pie, and often the lemon meringue, too. My favorite of all was the buttercream layer cake, with just the right amount of sugar. And the French crumb cake, and their white bread, called, I think, White Mountain loaf. Our Ebinger's was on Flatbush Avenue, just steps from the Albemarle Theatre. It's still there, in my memory."

Harriet Rosen. "The women who worked at Ebinger's were of a mold. Very clean, very sterile looking, and they had to be careful of their appearance. They wore white uniforms, and little hairnets. God forbid a strand should blow loose. Nothing was touched by their hands, even though they were spotless; they always took a piece of wax paper to pick up food.

"At first, the women who worked at Ebinger's were all white, but as Ebinger's stores opened in black neighborhoods, they hired black women. And they were exactly like the others; same hairnets, same super-clean uniforms."

Chocolate Blackout Cake

Ebinger's large bakery did not, of course, make Blackout Cakes one at a time. At Ebinger's plant the bakers could concoct vats of batter, pudding filling, and frosting, and no doubt those thrifty Germans noticed that crumbs were going to waste when the layers of chocolate cake were sliced. It must have been a pleasing solution to use them up by sprinkling them over the cakes.

This is a fussy cake to make, but if you want Ebinger's, this is the only place you'll get it. Ceri E. Hadda, a professional food writer and baker, developed the recipe. Ceri says, "The recipe is an approximation of the classic cake. It's three layers of a rich, one-bowl chocolate cake sandwiched between a deep, dark chocolate pudding, then covered with buttercream and cake crumbs. If you want to skip the pudding, the recipe makes enough frosting to ice all three layers."

Cake

¾ cup unsweetened cocoa powder
1 cup milk
4 ounces (1 stick) unsalted butter, at room temperature
¼ cup vegetable shortening
2 cups sugar
3 eggs
2 teaspoons pure vanilla
2¼ cups cake flour
1 teaspoon baking powder
1 teaspoon baking soda
½ teaspoon salt

Pudding Filling

⅔ cup sugar
2 tablespoons cornstarch
¼ teaspoon salt
1½ cups milk
3 1-ounce squares unsweetened chocolate, chopped
1 teaspoon vanilla

Frosting

4 1-ounce squares unsweetened chocolate
4 ounces (1 stick) unsalted butter
1½ teaspoons vanilla
3 eggs
3 cups confectioners' sugar

Preheat the oven to 350 degrees F.

❶ Make the cake. Butter two 9-inch cake pans; dust them with flour and tap out the excess. Set aside.

❷ Stir the cocoa with some of the milk to form a paste. Stir in the rest of the milk, and beat with a whisk until the mixture is smooth. Set aside.

❸ In the bowl of an electric mixer combine the butter, shortening, sugar, eggs, and vanilla; beat for 1 minute, or until the mixture is fluffy.

❹ Sift together the flour, baking powder, baking soda, and salt. Add the mixture, alternately with the cocoa mixture, to the contents of the bowl, beating between additions. Begin and end with the flour mixture, and beat only until the dry ingredients are absorbed. Divide the batter between the cake pans and smooth the tops with a spatula to even them.

❺ Bake for 35 to 40 minutes, or until the layers shrink from the sides of the pans and the tops spring back when gently pressed with a fingertip. The cake is dense and moist, so be careful not to overbake it. Cool the layers on wire racks for 10 minutes, then carefully invert them onto the racks. Turn right side up and let cool completely.

❻ Make the pudding. Combine the sugar, cornstarch, and salt in a small heavy saucepan. Gradually add the milk, mixing thoroughly with a wire whisk. Add the chocolate. Place over moderate heat and cook, stirring constantly, until the mixture thickens and bubbles for 3 minutes. Remove from the heat and stir in the vanilla. Pour into a small bowl and put plastic wrap or wax paper directly on the surface to prevent a skin from forming.

❼ Make the frosting. Melt the chocolate in the top of a double boiler. Remove it from the heat and cool slightly. In a medium bowl, beat the butter, vanilla, and eggs until well mixed. The mixture will not blend completely—do not worry. Gradually beat in the sugar, about 2 tablespoons at a time, beating well after each addition. Beat in the melted chocolate. Chill the frosting while assembling the rest of the cake, about 15 minutes.

❽ Cut each cake layer in half horizontally, using a serrated knife. You now have 4 layers, 3 for the cake assembly and 1 for the outside crumbs. Place one of the layers in the food processor bowl and pulse-chop to make crumbs; set aside. (Or break it up with your hands.)

❾ Sandwich the remaining 3 layers with the chocolate pudding filling, assembling the cake on a cardboard circle or the bottom of a springform pan, if possible. Frost the side and top of the cake with the chocolate frosting. Working over a baking sheet lined with aluminum foil or wax paper, hold the cake in the palm of your hand. With the other hand, gently press the cake crumbs all over the top and sides of the cake, pressing them to adhere. Pick up any crumbs that drop and press them back on. ⟫⟶ *Makes 1 cake*

▲▲▲▲▲▲▲▲▲▲▲▲▲▲▲▲▲▲▲▲▲▲▲▲▲▲▲▲

Mickeys

Mickeys were cheap street food—roasted potatoes sold by vendors during the first half of this century. They were also do-it-yourself kid food, unimaginably delicious to the young chefs. Mickeys were not indigenous to Brooklyn—probably every urban area had them—but they were a part of the passing spring and fall scene:

"We used to build bonfires on the street in Flatbush out of old crates we collected," recalls Rod Kennedy, Sr. "I was an active mickey cook from around 1925 till a few years later. We lived on one side of the street and my aunt on the other, and I'd run up and beg a potato from my mother or my aunt—whoever'd give me one. We stuck the potatoes right in the coals. Our parents never seemed to worry about the fires, even though the kids were under eight years old. We were rugged! You left the potato in the fire until you could poke a hole through it with a stick. The outside of the potato was charred to a cinder. Of course we ate the whole thing."

Dolly De Simone remembers: "When the coal trucks came by, we used to hook some coals. There was a stable near us in South Brooklyn, where they parked the vegetable-wagon horses. We'd go in there and build a fire and roast potatoes. If you had a piece of butter in the house, you'd go in without your mother knowing, and take a little butter for your potato."

Mimi Sheraton's mickey variation was more refined: "Most of the houses were heated with coal in the '30s," she says. "The boys would go to the basement and get lumps of coal, and the girls would bring the potatoes. We'd take them to a vacant lot, along with large-size empty grapefruit juice or one-pound coffee cans. We would put burning coals in the bottom of the can, then a few little potatoes, and then more hot coals. I recall the mickeys cooking in about 20 or 30 minutes. The outsides were very charred, and we didn't eat that part."

Ms. Sheraton also remembers the sweet potatoes that vendors sold on street corners, cooked on charcoal braziers, cracked open, and served on newspaper with a lump of butter. "I loved the mingled smells of charcoal and roasting sweet potatoes," she says.

Bygone Street Food

The classic French dessert called *charlotte russe* is an elegant mold of ladyfingers, filled with flavored Bavarian cream. But to old-time Brooklynites, a charlotte russe was a round of sponge cake topped with sweetened whipped cream, chocolate sprinkles, and sometimes a maraschino cherry, surrounded by a frilled cardboard holder with a round of cardboard on the bottom. As the cream went down, you pushed the cardboard up from the bottom, so you could eat the cake. Charlotte russe, charley roose, charlotte roosh (pronunciations varied), these were Brooklyn ambrosia.

Linda Romanelli Leahy. "When I was a kid in the '50s, it was a big treat to walk up to 86th Street, starting at 23rd Avenue and going up to about 17th Street. They called it 'under the el.' It was a mix, Jewish and Italian. There were lots of pushcarts. The charlotte russe carts had blue-glass enclosures at the top. We called them 'charley rooses.' They were fresh and wonderful! They went fast."

Andrew Ramer. "That cream was so dense! We bought them on 86th Street. Funny, I thought 'chararusse' was a Jewish word."

Everett Ortner. "Back in the Depression, we lived on Flatbush, off Coney Island Avenue. My memory is that every third store was empty. Unemployed men used to rent a storefront for a short time and set up a little business, and there was a charlotte russe seller in every block. They cost 3 cents. Good, but more cardboard than cake."

Mimi Sheraton. "We had them only in winter, I recall, because refrigeration back in the '30s wasn't so good. If you pushed too hard on the cardboard bottom, the whole thing flopped on the pavement, so you had to be careful."

Roderick Kennedy, Sr. "In 1925, we lived off Flatbush Avenue, on East 2nd Street. After school we'd pass a little store that had the charlotte rooshes in the window. You'd go by and just melt, you wanted one so much. The paper cup was filled with whipped cream. Way up high!"

Brooklyn's taste for charlotte russe goes back a long way. The

Rod Kennedy, Sr., working up an appetite for mickeys and charlotte russe, late 1920s.

McKinley Cook Book, by the Ladies of the Williams Avenue Methodist Church (published in 1897), contains a recipe by Mrs. C. E. Hubbell for Charlotte Russe Cake: *Four eggs, and one cup sugar, beat together twenty minutes. Add four table-spoonfuls cold water, one cup of flour, one tea-spoonful Cleveland's Superior Baking Powder, and small quantity of salt thoroughly sifted together, one tea-spoon of extract. Bake in one loaf. Filling—Whip one-half pint rich cream, add sugar and flavoring to taste.*

Evidently the Methodist ladies expected you to know the proper oven temperature, and what "extract" is. They must have been strong, or had strong hired girls, to beat eggs for twenty minutes. As was common at the time, the book had a commercial sponsor, Cleveland's Baking Powder. The recipe actually does work; use an electric mixer, vanilla extract, and bake in a 9-inch by 13-inch pan for forty minutes at 350 degrees F. It produces a rather coarse sponge loaf with excellent keeping qualities.

The charlotte russes of memory were made with baker's topping, a commercial product sold to bakers. For the home version, use whipped heavy cream sweetened with confectioners' sugar and flavored with a drop of vanilla extract.

Charlotte Russe

This recipe was developed by Linda Romanelli Leahy of Park Slope.

··

Sponge
½ cup all-purpose flour
½ teaspoon baking powder
¼ teaspoon salt
4 eggs, separated
1 tablespoon cold water
½ cup plus ⅓ cup sugar

½ teaspoon vanilla extract
⅓ cup confectioners' sugar
Topping
Whipped cream
Chocolate sprinkles
Maraschino cherries

Preheat the oven to 350 degrees F.

❶ Butter and flour a 15½-inch × 10½-inch jelly-roll pan. Sift together the flour, baking powder, and salt. Set aside.

❷ In a mixer bowl, beat the egg whites and water together; gradually add the ½ cup sugar. Beat on high until glossy. Set aside.

❸ In a mixer bowl, beat the egg yolks until thickened, about 2 minutes. Add the ⅓ cup sugar gradually; then add the vanilla. Beat for 2 minutes more. Fold the yolks into the whites, then fold in the dry ingredients; don't overmix.

❹ Spread the batter evenly in the pan. Bake for 12 to 15 minutes, until lightly browned and springy to the touch.

❺ Meanwhile, sprinkle a clean towel with the confectioners' sugar. Turn the cake out onto the towel and place it on a rack to cool. Cut out rounds of cake with a 2½-inch cookie cutter. (Makes 15 or 16 rounds.) Top each round with whipped cream, sprinkles, and a maraschino cherry. (If you'd like more cake, use 2 rounds to a serving.) ➤ *Makes 15 or 16 charlotte russes*

▲▲▲▲▲▲▲▲▲▲▲▲▲▲▲▲▲▲▲▲▲▲▲▲▲▲▲▲▲▲▲▲▲▲▲

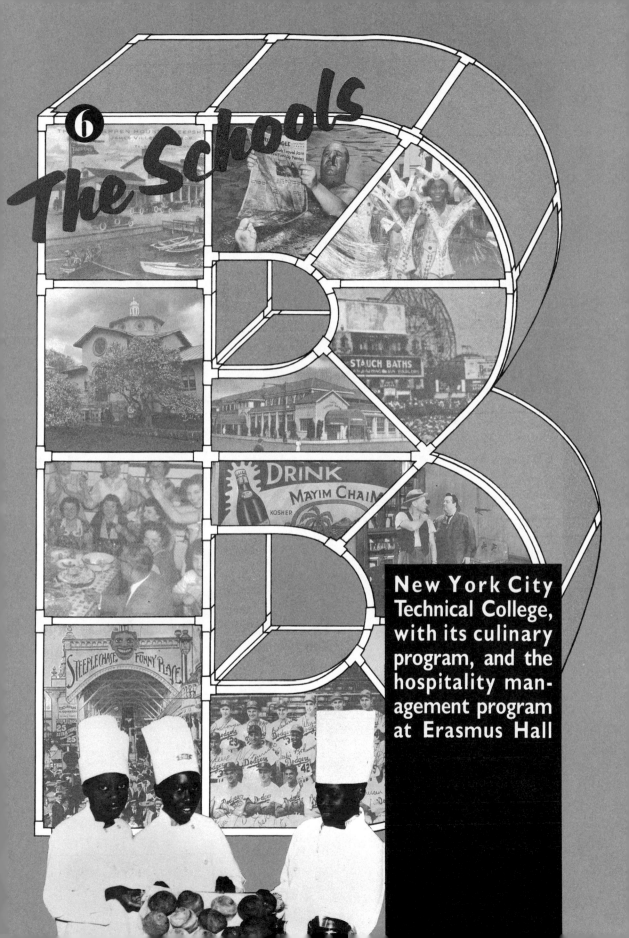

6

The Schools

New York City Technical College, with its culinary program, and the hospitality management program at Erasmus Hall

Brooklyn students can get a firm start in the culinary arts, thanks to a new college and a very old school. The college was founded after World War II. The school, opened in 1787, is only ten days younger than the Constitution of the United States.

NEW YORK CITY TECHNICAL COLLEGE

It has no campus, no fancy buildings, no football team. But it does have a first-rate school of hotel and restaurant management that charges only a modest tuition for excellent culinary grounding. The only technical college in the city, New York City Technical College was founded in 1947 to educate and train students to take active places in the postwar world.

Tech offers both two- and four-year degrees, and it has the oldest culinary program of its kind in New York City. Motivation is needed: most students attend classes by day and work in restaurants at night, but those who stay the course go on to rewarding professional careers. "This is very practical training," says Professor Julia V. Jordan. "You learn to produce." Sixty-five percent of Tech's students are the first generation in their families to go to college, and eighty-three percent are minority students. As to future employment, Gerald Griffen, chairman of the program, says, "I only wish we had enough graduates to meet the demand."

The following four recipes are adapted from The City Tech Cookbook, 1988. Others are contributed by two Brooklyn caterers and a chef, all Tech graduates.

Spiced Pecans

Steven Mengel, class of 1973, devised the recipe. He is now Executive Sous-Chef at the Green-briar in White Sulphur Springs, West Virginia.

½ cup unsalted butter
1½ cups brown sugar
1 tablespoon ground cumin

1½ teaspoons cayenne pepper
¾ teaspoon dry mustard
5 cups pecan meats

Preheat the oven to 375 degrees F.

❶ In a large skillet, melt the butter over moderate heat. Add the brown sugar, cumin, cayenne, and mustard. Cook until the sugar is melted and the ingredients are well combined. Toss the pecans in the mixture until well coated.

❷ Arrange the pecans on baking sheets and toast in the oven for 5 to 10 minutes, until the pecans are lightly browned. ⟫→ *Makes 5 cups*

Cold Snapper Salad

This salad is from Stanley I. Kramer, class of 1960, and executive chef of the Oyster Bar in New York's Plaza Hotel. Radicchio is red-leafed chicory, crisp and slightly bitter in taste.

Fish
A 1-pound red snapper fillet
2 large shallots, sliced
White pepper
½ cup dry white wine
1 sprig fresh tarragon
Butter for brushing foil

Vinaigrette
2 teaspoons finely chopped shallots
1 tablespoon red-wine vinegar
2 teaspoons tarragon vinegar
4 tablespoons extra-virgin delicate
  olive oil
1 teaspoon chopped fresh tarragon
Salt and white pepper to taste
Radicchio, torn into bite-sized pieces
Lamb's or Bibb lettuce
Frisée (curly endive), white part only

Preheat the oven to 325 degrees F.

❶ Measure the fillet at its thickest point. Grease a small baking dish and sprinkle in the shallots. Place the fillet over them and season with pepper. Add the wine and tarragon sprig.

❷ Brush the dull side of a piece of foil with butter and cover the dish tightly with the foil, buttered side down. Cook for 10 minutes per inch of the fillet's thickness; that is, if the fillet is ½ inch thick, cook for 5 minutes. The fish is done when the interior is snowy white. Let it cool to room temperature or chill. For serving, cut it into strips.

❸ Make the vinaigrette. Place the shallots and the vinegars in a small bowl. Slowly whisk in the oil. Add the tarragon and season to taste with salt and pepper.

❹ In all, you will need 3 to 4 cups of salad greens. Place them in a bowl and toss with the vinaigrette. Mound the greens in the center of 2 serving plates and surround with strips of snapper. ➤➤ *Serves 2*

Eggplant Crepes

*T*hese *"crepes," a spin on standard eggplant parmigiana, show what a talented young cook can devise. George Abel won the Class of 1986 award for them. The dish can be prepared ahead of time and baked when the crowd arrives.*

··

2 medium eggplants	1 tablespoon salt
4 pounds fresh spinach	⅛ teaspoon fresh ground white pepper
2 cups all-purpose flour	⅛ teaspoon freshly ground nutmeg
6 eggs, lightly beaten	2 quarts tomato sauce
1 cup olive oil	1 pound Monterey Jack cheese, cut into
2 pounds ricotta cheese	24 thin slices
4 egg yolks	Ripe olives and minced parsley, for
2 cups sliced pitted jumbo ripe olives	garnish

❶ Peel the eggplants and cut them lengthwise into 24 slices ¼ inch thick. Salt them lightly and let them stand for 30 minutes. Trim the spinach, wash it well, and steam it until cooked. Chop the spinach and squeeze out as much water as you can. Set it aside.

❷ Pat the eggplant slices dry with paper towels. Put the flour and eggs in shallow bowls. Heat the oil in a large skillet and fry the eggplant slices in batches, first dipping each slice into flour and then into beaten egg. (Hold the slice over the bowl with eggs for a moment to let excess drip off.) Brown the slices for 1 minute on each side. Set them on paper towels to drain.

Preheat the oven to 375 degrees F.

❸ Combine the ricotta and egg yolks. Stir in the spinach, olives, and seasonings, blending them thoroughly.

❹ Spread 2 cups of the tomato sauce in a 21-inch × 13-inch × 3-inch baking pan. Place about ½ cup of ricotta mixture on each eggplant slice. Roll it lengthwise and place it in the baking pan. Spoon the remaining tomato sauce over the "crepes," and top each with a slice of cheese. Bake them for 20 minutes, or until they are hot and bubbling. Serve 2 crepes per portion, garnished with ripe olives and sprinkled with parsley. ⟫→ *Makes 12 servings*

Rum Ribs

Technical College graduate John O. Phillips doesn't cook professionally, though he could; he is an architect in New York's Department of City Planning.

....

2 2-pound racks pork spareribs
4 quarts boiling water
1 teaspoon salt
1½ teaspoons ground cloves
5 cloves garlic, peeled and crushed
2 teaspoons ground ginger

1 teaspoon freshly ground black pepper
2 bay leaves, crushed
1 cup dark rum
½ cup packed brown sugar
⅓ cup freshly squeezed lime juice

Preheat the oven to 350 degrees F.

❶ Cook the racks in the boiling water for 10 minutes with salt, ½ teaspoon of the cloves, and 1 clove of garlic. Drain the ribs and pat them dry.

❷ Combine the remaining cloves and garlic, the ginger, pepper, and bay leaves. Rub the mixture into the meaty side of each rack. Place the ribs, meaty side up, in two roasting pans. Bake them for 30 minutes.

❸ Pour off any rendered fat and reduce the heat to 325 degrees F. In a small bowl, combine the rum, brown sugar, and lime juice. Continue baking the ribs for 60 minutes, basting them with the rum mixture every 10 minutes. After 30 minutes, turn the ribs.

❹ When the meat is cooked, the sauce will be syrupy and will stick to the ribs. Remove them to a carving board and cut between ribs into serving sections. ⟫→ *Makes 4 servings*

Confetti Chicken Salad,
Charles Stamps

Charles Stamps of Stamps Wesley Caterers says his cuisine is "a continental mixture"—of several continents. "Southern with French, German with Italian, and sometimes a touch of Africa or the Orient." Stamps, a graduate of New York City Technical College, has cooked all his life. "Both my father and grandfather were chefs," he says. "And my grandfather invented a very efficient potato-chip cutter." He spends his spare time working with kids in Bedford-Stuyvesant, "giving something back to the community."

4 large chicken breasts with bones and skin (about 3½ pounds)
4 cups chicken broth, homemade or canned
½ cup dry white wine
1 teaspoon celery seeds
½ cup mayonnaise
5 tablespoons bottled Russian dressing
2 bunches scallions, sliced thin, the white and most of the green parts
½ teaspoon onion powder
½ teaspoon garlic powder
1 teaspoon freshly ground white pepper
⅓ cup each finely diced red, green, and yellow bell peppers
Chilled cucumber slices or endive leaves, for serving

❶ Cover the chicken breasts with the broth and wine, add the celery seeds, bring to the boil, reduce the heat and simmer, uncovered, for 5 to 8 minutes. The breasts should be cooked through but firm. Let them cool in the broth to intensify flavor.

❷ Remove the skin and bones and cut the chicken into small pieces. In a large mixing bowl, combine the chicken, mayonnaise, Russian dressing, scallions, onion and garlic powders, white pepper, and the diced peppers. Chill for several hours or overnight. Serve mounded on a platter, arranged on chilled cucumber slices, or placed in the tip of an endive leaf. ⟫→ *16 appetizer servings, or main course for 6 to 8*

Cream of White Onion Soup for Ten

Richard F. Malaga, chef and caterer, is a graduate of New York Tech and now is an instructor there. He also apprenticed in France. "For vegetarians and those watching calories, use water instead of stock and eliminate the cream," Richard says.

6 ounces (1½ sticks) unsalted butter

1 tablespoon flour

8 cups finely chopped onions (about 10 medium onions)

5 shallots, finely chopped

2 leeks (white part only), trimmed, split, thoroughly washed, and finely chopped

6 garlic cloves, finely chopped

1 medium potato, peeled and diced small

12 cups chicken stock

1 cup heavy cream

Salt, white pepper, and crumbled dried thyme to taste

Finely chopped parsley, for garnish

❶ In a heavy stockpot or kettle, melt the butter, stir in the flour, and add the vegetables. Cook over low heat, stirring, to "sweat" the vegetables until they are limp, about 8 minutes.

❷ Add the stock, bring to the boil, lower the heat, and partially cover the pot. Cook, stirring occasionally, until the vegetables are tender. Purée the soup, in batches, in a food processor, or leave as is.

❸ Return the puréed soup to the pot. Add the cream and seasonings and bring the soup to just below the boil. Garnish with the parsley and serve.

≫→ *Serves 10*

Melicia's Hot Fruit Fritters with Vanilla Ice Cream

Chef Melicia Phillips, a 1984 graduate of New York City Technical College, was formerly sous-chef at Manhattan's Chanterelle. "Most restaurant cooking isn't really practical for home kitchens," she says, "but these recipes are exceptions."

. . . .

Beer Batter

2½ cups all-purpose flour

½ cup flat beer

1 egg, lightly beaten

1 tablespoon vegetable oil

¼ teaspoon salt

2 egg whites

Fritters

Vegetable oil for frying

6 pieces of pineapple, 2 inches × ½ inch × ½ inch

1 apple, peeled, cored, and cut into 6 wedges

4 strawberries

1 teaspoon cinnamon and ½ cup sugar mixed together, for dusting

2 scoops vanilla ice cream

❶ Sift the flour into a mixing bowl. Add the beer, egg, oil, and salt and whisk.

❷ In another bowl, whisk the whites until they form stiff peaks. Fold the whites into the flour mixture with a rubber spatula, using an under-and-over motion.

❸ To make the fritters, heat 2 inches of oil in a deep fat fryer, deep skillet, or wok. Dip pieces of fruit into the batter and fry, a few at a time, until golden brown. Drain on paper towels.

❹ Toss the fruit pieces in the cinnamon-sugar mixture. Arrange the fruit around the rim of two serving plates and place a scoop of ice cream in the center. ➠➔ *Serves 2*

Trout with Pecans and Lemon

Here is another of Melicia Phillips's recipes.

....

3 tablespoons olive oil
½ cup milk, for dredging
½ cup all-purpose flour, for dredging
2 butterflied trout, 12 ounces each
2 tablespoons minced parsley

4 tablespoons unsalted butter
1 tablespoon fresh lemon juice
½ cup pecan pieces
½ teaspoon salt
¼ teaspoon freshly ground pepper

❶ Heat the olive oil to sizzling in a large heavy skillet. Have the milk and flour in shallow bowls. Dip each trout in the milk, let it drip off excess, then dip it in the flour. Sauté until golden brown, turning once. Remove to a warmed serving platter or two plates while you make the sauce. Sprinkle generously with parsley.

❷ Wipe out the pan and melt the butter in it. When the butter just begins to brown, add the lemon juice, pecans, salt and pepper. Pour immediately over the trout and serve. ➠➔ *Serves 2*

THE HOSPITALITY MANAGEMENT PROGRAM AT ERASMUS HALL

Erasmus Hall High School, "the Eton of Brooklyn," opened in 1786 as Erasmus Hall Academy, built by the townspeople of Flatbush to educate future ministers and teachers. The school was named for the Dutch humanist and scholar Desiderius Erasmus (1466–1536). Girls were admitted in 1801, and in 1896 the school became part of the public system, changing its name to Erasmus Hall High School. Times change and needs change, and now Erasmus has followed the lead of the much newer New York City Technical College, establishing a hospitality program that includes cooking and hotel and restaurant management. The 140 students who participate in the program operate their own restaurant, where twice a week they serve three-course meals, on china, in a well-appointed mustard-colored dining room. The fourteen- to eighteen-year-old students, divided into groups of ten, alternate jobs. They wear wait-staff uniforms in the dining room, and chef's garb, including the high

Erasmus Hall, the eighteenth-century building.

<u>toque blanche,</u> in the kitchen. They also serve as tour guides in the original 1786 building, which has become a museum of education where visiting schoolchildren enjoy writing with quill pens and jumping on the kind of feather beds used by the original boarders. Given the difference in the students' ages, the programs at Erasmus and Tech are not so very different. That's because Thomas Lenihan, the assistant principal who runs the program, is a Tech graduate.

"Bear in mind that this course is also exploratory," he explains. "A young person may find that she dislikes working with food, or he is not comfortable serving the public. But they've learned skills, and how to deal pleasantly with people." Enthusiastic participants are urged toward Tech or the Culinary Institute of America, which offers many minority scholarships.

Erasmus Hall bilingual students selling muffins made in the culinary program.

Cranberry-Orange Relish Cups

Jamie Gigantiello, a cooking teacher at Erasmus Hall High School, developed this recipe for students learning the culinary arts. The filled shells make a fine garnish for a buffet table where turkey is served.

24 oranges
5 cups sugar

5 cups orange juice
5 packages (15 cups) cranberries

❶ Cut a small slice from each end of 15 oranges so that they can sit flat. Cut these oranges in half, cutting to form sawtooth edges. Scoop out the pulp and reserve; place the shells in the refrigerator to chill.

❷ Peel the remaining oranges with a potato peeler. Cut the peel (no white must be on it) in extremely fine julienne strips. Place the julienne strips in a large pot of water and bring to the boil. Drain the strips immediately and discard the water.

❸ Make a syrup with the sugar, reserved pulp, and 5 cups of juice extracted from the peeled oranges. Bring the mixture to the boil and boil for exactly 5 minutes, uncovered.

❹ Place the peels and the cranberries in the orange syrup and cook just until the cranberries pop open. Remove from the heat. Spread the relish on baking sheets or jelly-roll pans and chill.

❺ Fifteen minutes before serving, fill the orange shells with the cranberry relish. ⟫→ *Makes 30 cups*

BIBLIOGRAPHY

Anderson, Will. *The Breweries of Brooklyn.* Anderson, 1976.

Bennett, Gertrude Ryder. *Living in a Landmark.* Marshall Jones Company, 1980.

Brooklyn Fact and Trivia Book. The Fund for the Borough of Brooklyn, Inc., 1986.

The Brooklyn Neighborhood Book. The Fund for the Borough of Brooklyn, Inc., 1985.

Handwerker, G. Murray. *Nathan's Famous Hot Dog Cookbook.* Gramercy Publishing Company, 1983.

McCullough, David W., and Jim Kalett. *Brooklyn . . . and How It Got That Way.* The Dial Press, 1983.

Miller, Rita Seiden, ed. *Brooklyn, U.S.A.* Brooklyn College Press, 1979.

Rudd, Irving. *Ebbets Field—A Memoir.* SportsFan Promotions, 1984.

Snow, Richard. *Coney Island: A Postcard Journey to the City of Fire.* Brightwaters Press, 1984.

Willensky, Elliot. *When Brooklyn Was the World—1920–1957.* Harmony Books, 1986.

I N D E X

sandwiches (*cont.*)
  at Football Weddings,
    77–9
  hockfleisch, 52, 53
  Santa Rosalia Regina Pacis,
    90–1
Santos, Mila, 299
sarmale (Maria Drindiri's
  Rumanian stuffed
  cabbage), 303
Satmar Shmura Matzoh
  Bakery, 198
sauce
  blueberry, for blintzes,
    spirited, 154
  cinnamon hot apple, for
    blintzes, 154
  crabmeat, Grandpa's
    spinach fettucine
    with, 151
  cream, flounder or fluke
    in, 60
  Genoese, with pot roast,
    92
  gray, carp with, 284
  marinara, very quick,
    137
  sofrito, Puerto Rican,
    268
  spaghetti, Podres, 342
  white clam, Theresa
    Laurice's, 338
  zucchini, linguine with,
    Lena Gaimaro's, 109
sauerbraten, 290
sausage(s)
  and cabbage, baked,
    Debbie Chechilo's,
    102
  knockwurst, Neapolitan,
    350
  and peppers, 124
  rolls, Phil Rizzuto's, 348
Savarese, Andre, 89
Savarese, Jackie, 89
Savarese, John, 89
Save the Kings, 187
Saydah, Susan, 233, 234
Saydah Brothers, 233
scallops, Jackie Savarese's,
  89
Scandinavians, 205–17
Scholtz, Betty, 307
Schwartz, Arthur, 139–40,
  183
Schwartz, Bertha, 171

Schwartz, Leo, 174–5
Schweiger, Ron, 258–9
Sciallo, Rosalie, 127
Sciallo, Sal, 126
Scicolone, Michele, 88, 95,
  96, 104
seafood
  calamari, Philomena's
    (Celia's mother's),
    82
  see also fish; shellfish
Seagate, 35
sea trout salad, 256
sea urchins, 110
seed cookies, Elizabeth Van
  Brunt's, 310
Sensible Cook, The, 9
Sephardic Jews, 201–4
sesame seed(s)
  cookies, Elizabeth Van
    Brunt's, 310
  tofu, pan-fried, 164
shallots, chicken breast
  with Madeira and,
  326
Sheedy, Mary Harrigan,
  224
Sheepshead Bay, 54–6, 58–
  66, 68, 241
Sheepshead Bay Fishing
  Fleet Association, 58
Sheepshead Bay Racetrack,
  55, 56
shellfish
  crab(meat), 132–3
  and mac, Aunt Jean's,
    133
  sauce, Grandpa's
    spinach fettucine
    with, 151
  and shrimp salad
    (Fina's ensalada de
    camarones y jueyes),
    271
  Lobster Thermidor, 229
  scallops, Jackie
    Savarese's, 89
  shrimp
    and crabmeat salad
      (Fina's ensalada de
      camarones y jueyes),
      271
    grilled, Bamonte's, 112
Sheraton, Mimi, 66, 385
Shields, Gerry, 172
Shmura matzo, 198–9

Shrem, Adele, 182
shrimp
  and crabmeat salad,
    (Fina's ensalada de
    camarones y jueyes),
    271
  grilled, Bamonte's, 112
Silberstein, Meyer, 354,
  361–2
Sills, Beverly, 160
Simmons, Marie, 122
Sineno, John, 32–4
Singer, Lee, 53
Singer, Lou, 52, 145–6
Singer, Pat, 49
Smith, Betty, 19
snapper salad, cold, 392
Society for the
  Preservation of
  Weeksville and
  Bedford-Stuyvesant
  History, 12
soda bread
  about, 222
  Irish, 223
  Nell Moogan's, 223
sofrito, Puerto Rican, 268
sole with artichoke hearts
  from Monte's
  Venetian Room, 86
Somers, Barbara, 177
soup
  barley and giblet, 247
  borscht, Anna
    Sternstein's, 51
  chicken
    about, 178, 181
    with dill, Mother's, 182
    matzo balls for, 180
    Nana's Christmas, 122
    Phyllis Schweiger's,
      "just like my
      grandma's," 179
    rich chicken broth for,
      178
  escarole, with tiny
    meatballs, 108
  garlic, cream of, 377
  lentil and pasta minestra,
    121
  Manhattan clam chowder,
    Lundy's, 66
  pea, Newfoundland, 298
  pumpkin and potato,
    with kale, Karen
    Karp's, 372

PHOTOGRAPHIC ACKNOWLEDGMENTS

The photographs and other illustrative material reproduced in this book were provided with the permission and courtesy of the following:

Endpaper map adapted from a map designed by Keith Godard of Studio Works, copyright © The Fund for the Borough of Brooklyn; The Brooklyn Historical Society, 3, 4, 11, 15, 26 (third from top), 54 (top), 56; Pieter Claesen Wyckoff House, 6; Modern Images, 8 (top); John Gallagher, 8 (bottom); The Brooklyn Public Library, 12, 18, 326; The Weeksville Society, 13; George T. Guzzio, 20, 26 (top), 40 (top), 161; Kraft General Foods, 21; Richard Snow, 26 (bottom); collection Rod Kennedy, Jr., 26 (second from top, bottom), 30 (top), 37 (both); Coney Island USA, Inc., 27; Sam Henriques, 28; Philip's Candy Store, 30 (bottom); Nathan's, 31; Hilton Flores, 32, 33, 35; The New York Aquarium, 36; Sharyn Felder, 40 (bottom four photos), 43, 45, 46, 48, 49, 174, 175; Jerry Sternstein, 50; Brooklyn Remembered, Ron Schweiger, 54 (middle and bottom), 64 (both), 65; Don Brown, 57; Anne O' Driscoll, 59; Steve Barrison, 62; Dolly De Simone, 72, 74, 78; Linda Romanelli Leahy, 79, 113; Celia Cacace, 81; the Montemarano family, 85; Carla Gahr, 87, 129 (top), 230 (second and third from top), 280 (all), 282, 283; the Savarese family, 89; Regina Pacis, 90; Michele Scicolone, 92; Mary Hirschel, 97; Warren J. Fuchs, Jr., 99; Our Lady of Mount Carmel church, 104; Jimmy Venezia, 106; Anthony Bamonte, 111; Gioia Timpanelli, 120; Jack Clemente, 125; Sal Sciallo, 127; the Barbati family, 129 (bottom); Philip Juliano, 132; Father Ronald Marino, 135; Arthur Schwartz, 139; Ilene Kristen, 142; the Felder family, 143; Lou Singer, 145; Al Lewis, 150; Alvin Cooperman, 156; Andrew Ramer, 158 (both); Barbara Gregory, 170; Joan Garvin, 171; Marion D. Meyerson, 173; Marcia Bricker, 183, 190 (top); Bruce Friedman, 187; *The Arch*, Erasmus Hall yearbook, 189; Irving I. Herzberg, 190 (bottom three photographs), 192, 198, 381; Flarecorp, 194; Con Edison, 200; Rae Dayan, 202; Norwegian Singing Society, 205; Norma Andreasen, 206; Mrs. Ivan Johnson, 210; Imatra, 212 (all), 213; Mabelle Lundahl, 215, 217; Al O'Hagen, 218; the Brooklyn Chamber of Commerce, 221; the Moogan family, 222; the Walsh family, 225; Father Walter Mitchell, 228; Jim Kalett, 230 (top and bottom); Susan Saydah, 233; Vivian Bennett, 241; Sylvia Edwards, 242; Bridge Street AWME Church, 245, 246 (both); Eunice Grey, 250; Eunice Lewis, 252; Dee Dee Dailey, 255; Evolga Francis, 258; Kenneth Brown, 260, 261 (all); Tony Velez, 264 (all), 271, 272; Barbara Zerman, 268; S. Anesta Samuel, 276; White Eagle Bakery, 281; Beverly Hegmann, 291; Helen Kraus, 292; Church of the Three Hierarchs, 293 (top); Grecian Heritage Foundation, "Orpheus," Inc., 293 (right and bottom); Catherine Durakis, 294; *Brooklyn Botanic Garden Record*, 1943, 308 (top); John Calabrese Photography, 308 (middle); Louis Buhle for the Brooklyn Botanic Garden, 308 (bottom); Trader Publications, 309; The New York Historical Society, 313; Ray Wiggers, Prospect Park Administrator's Office, 314; Prospect Park Administration, 315, 317; The Rosenbach Museum & Library, Philadelphia, 316; The Brooklyn Museum, 320, 322 (both); The Brooklyn Public Library, Brooklyn Collection, *Eagle* Collection, 324 (all), 325, 335 (middle), 371; The Brooklyn Historical Society, 327, 328, 355 (right); Brooklyn Union Gas, 330, 332; Meyer Robinson, 333, 340; Harry M. Stevens, Inc., 335 (top and bottom), 336; Joe Laurice, 337; Baseball Hall of Fame, 338; Historic Limited Editions, John Zaso, 341, 342, 343, 345, 347, 348; RALPH, care of Peter Crescenti, 349; Prospect Hall, 351 (both); Everett Ortner, 352; the Brooklyn Brewery, 355 (left); H. Fox & Co., 358; Manhattan Special, 359; Irving Fields, 362; Gold's Horseradish, 363; Goya Foods, Inc., 364; Boar's Head Provisions, Inc., 366; Waldbaum's, 368; Julia Waldbaum, 369; Junior's Most Fabulous Restaurant Cafe Bar, 375; Gage & Tollner, 380; the Kennedy family, 386; Erasmus Hall High School, 398; Erasmus Hall High School Hospitality Program, 399.

A NOTE ABOUT THE AUTHORS

Lyn Stallworth

Lyn Stallworth has been a Brooklyn brownstoner for fourteen years; before that she lived in France, Greece, and Manhattan. Her Park Slope house was built in 1880. She is the author of several cookbooks and numerous magazine articles, and was senior editor of the magazine The Pleasures of Cooking. *Ms. Stallworth researched and wrote for the Time-Life Books series Foods of the World, and wrote and edited books for the Beard/Glaser/Wolf Great Cooks series. She attended cooking schools in France, Mexico, and New York, and currently teaches cooking in the Culinary Arts program at New York's New School.*

Rod Kennedy, Jr.

Despite the fact that his great-great-grandfather was trampled to death at the opening of the Brooklyn Bridge, Roderick Kennedy, Jr., still loves the borough of his antecedents. A collaborator on books about Atlantic City and British country homes, he also founded Toltec Press, a publisher of conceptual art books. His recent work includes posters for the Smithsonian and the Brooklyn Dodgers, and he is the president of Stadia Tins, Ltd., which produces replicas of major sports stadia, including Ebbets Field.

A NOTE ON THE TYPE

The text of this book was set in an ITC version of Century, a type family originally designed in 1894 by Linn Boyd Benton (1844–1932). Benton cut Century in response to a request by Theodore L. De Vinne for an attractive, easy-to-read typeface to fit the narrow columns of his Century Magazine. *Early in the 1900s Benton's son, Morris Fuller Benton, updated and improved Century in several versions for his father's American Type Founders Company. Century is the only American typeface cut before 1910 that is still widely used today.*

Composed by The Sarabande Press, New York, New York

Printed and bound by Courier Book Companies, Westford, Massachusetts

Designed by Stephanie Tevonian